GCSE
History

OK, so the new Grade 9-1 History GCSEs are pretty tricky... but with this brilliant CGP book by your side, they won't seem so tough.

It's packed with everything you need to get your head around the subject, including clear study notes, sample answers and plenty of exam-style practice questions.

We've even included a full set of practice exam papers at the end of the book, plus fantastic advice to help you score top marks.

How to access your free Online Edition

This book includes a free Online Edition to read on your PC, Mac or tablet. You'll just need to go to **cgpbooks.co.uk/extras** and enter this code:

1910 2279 9227 7339

By the way, this code only works for one person. If somebody else has used this book before you, they might have already claimed the Online Edition.

Complete
Revision & Practice
<u>Everything</u> you need to pass the exams!

Contents

Germany, 1890-1945

Superpower Relations and the Cold War, 1941-1991

Exam Skills

Practice Papers

Published by CGP

Editors:
Chloe Anderson, Izzy Bowen, Emma Cleasby, Alex Fairer, Catherine Heygate, Louise McEvoy, Jack Perry.

Contributors:
Peter Callaghan, Rene Cochlin

With thanks to Rebecca Tate for the proofreading.

With thanks to Ana Pungartnik for the copyright research.

Coordinated by Paddy Gannon.

Acknowledgements:
With thanks to The Art Archive / Palazzo Barberini Rome / Collection Dagli Orti for permission to use the image on page 1.
With thanks to © iStock.com for permission to use the images on pages 3, 17 and 24.
With thanks to Photo Researchers / Mary Evans Picture Library for permission to use the images on pages 4, 34, 54 and 86.
With thanks to Mary Evans Picture Library for permission to use the images on pages 7, 14, 20, 26, 27, 35, 98, 110, 119, 122, 132, 137 and 207.
With thanks to Historic England / Mary Evans for permission to use the image on page 9.
With thanks to INTERFOTO / Bildarchiv Hansmann / Mary Evans for permission to use the image on page 12.
With thanks to Mary Evans / Everett Collection for permission to use the images on pages 16, 66, 152 and 173.
With thanks to The Art Archive / Granger Collection for permission to use the images on pages 30, 73, 77, 78, 83, 105 (Dudley miniature) and 108.
With thanks to Illustrated London News Ltd/Mary Evans for permission to use the images on pages 32, 65 and 135.
Statistics about attitudes towards the NHS on page 40. From King's Fund analysis of NatCen Social Research's British Social Attitudes survey data.
http://www.kingsfund.org.uk/projects/public-satisfaction-nhs/bsa-survey-2015.
With thanks to Mary Evans/Interfoto for permission to use the image on page 53.
With thanks to Mary Evans/Classic Stock/C.P. Cushing for permission to use the image on page 57.
Extract from transcript of an interview with White Eagle, Chief of the Ponca Tribe on page 80. Author: Lorrie Montiero. © American Native Press Archives and Sequoyah Research Center.
With thanks to Mary Evans / Iberfoto for permission to use the images on pages 99 and 186.
With thanks to National Museums NI / MARY EVANS for permission to use the image on page 100.
With thanks to Look and Learn for permission to use the image on page 101.
Image of Burghley House on page 105. Image copyright Anthony Masi. This file is licensed under the Creative Commons Attribution 2.0 Generic license.
https://creativecommons.org/licenses/by/2.0/deed.en
Second extract on page 112. Copyright © 2014, 2009, 2002. From A History of England, Volume 1: Prehistory to 1714 by Clayton Roberts.
Reproduced by permission of Taylor and Francis Group, LLC, a division of Informa plc.
With thanks to Mary Evans Picture Library/DOUGLAS MCCARTHY for permission to use the image on page 114.
With thanks to Antiquarian Images/Mary Evans for permission to use the image on page 126.
With thanks to Thaliastock / Mary Evans for permission to use the image on page 146.
With thanks to Mary Evans Picture Library / WEIMAR ARCHIVE for permission to use the image on page 149.
With thanks to Mary Evans / Sueddeutsche Zeitung Photo for permission to use the images on pages 151, 153, 165, 193 and 210.
With thanks to Mary Evans / SZ Photo / Scherl for permission to use the image on page 156.
Extract on page 157. From School for Barbarians: Education Under the Nazis (Dover Books on History, Political and Social Science). Dover Publications Inc.; Reprint edition (28 Mar. 2014).
First extract on page 159. Copyright © 2006 Eric A Johnson and Karl-Heinz Reuband, What we Knew: Terror, Mass Murder and Everyday Life in Nazi Germany. Reprinted by permission of Basic Books, a member of the Perseus Books Group.
Second extract on page 159. Abridged extract from Democracy and Nazism: Germany, 1917-1945. A/AS Level History for AQA Student Book by Nick Pinfield. © Cambridge University Press 2015.
With thanks to Mary Evans / Imagno for permission to use the images on pages 169, 181 and 191.
Extract on page 211. From Account Rendered: A Dossier on my Former Self by Melita Maschmann, plunkettlakepress.com/ar.
First extract on page 212. An abridged extract from "A Child of Hitler: Germany in the Days When God Wore a Swastika" by Alfons Heck.
Original copyright 1985, Renaissance House Publishers, Phoenix, Arizona USA.

Every effort has been made to locate copyright holders and obtain permission to reproduce sources.
For those sources where it has been difficult to trace the copyright holder of the work, we would be grateful
for information. If any copyright holder would like us to make an amendment to the acknowledgements,
please notify us and we will gladly update the book at the next reprint. Thank you.

ISBN: 978 1 78294 609 0
Printed by Bell & Bain Ltd, Glasgow.
Clipart from Corel®

Based on the classic CGP style created by Richard Parsons.

How History Works

Historians have such an <u>easy life</u>. They <u>read</u> old documents and <u>rewrite</u> them... right? Actually, they do <u>a bit more</u> than that. For GCSE History, <u>you</u> have to <u>become</u> a historian, so you'd best be sure what they <u>really do</u>.

Historians use **Sources** to **Find Out** about the **Past**

1) <u>Sources</u> are things that historians use to <u>find out about</u> and <u>make sense of</u> the past.

2) They can be <u>written</u> (e.g. newspapers, government reports) or <u>visual</u> (e.g. photographs, maps, films).

3) Sources can be categorised as either <u>primary</u> or <u>secondary</u>:

Primary Sources

<u>Primary sources</u> are evidence <u>from the period</u> you're studying. For example, a <u>newspaper report</u> on the First World War from 4th September 1914, or a <u>picture</u> of Henry VIII that was painted during his reign.

Secondary Sources

<u>Secondary sources</u> are evidence <u>about</u> (but not from) the period you're studying. For example, a <u>1989 book</u> called 'Origins of the First World War', or a <u>website</u> that details all the <u>portraits</u> ever painted of Henry VIII.

Historians have to **Interrogate** and **Interpret** every source

© The Art Archive / Palazzo Barberini Rome / Collection Dagli Orti

King Henry VIII, 1540

1) Historians have to be <u>very careful</u> with sources. To make sure they're using sources <u>accurately</u>, historians <u>interrogate</u> every source they use. This means they ask themselves a series of <u>questions</u> about the source's <u>background</u>.

- **What** is this source?
  E.g. It is a painting of King Henry VIII.
- **Who** made this source?
  E.g. It was produced by the King's official painter, Hans Holbein.
- **Why** did they make the source?
  E.g. He was asked to paint it by the King.
- **Where** and **when** was it made?
  E.g. It was made in the Palace of Whitehall in 1540.

2) Historians use their answers to work out <u>how useful</u> and <u>how reliable</u> a source is. For example:

- This is a <u>professional</u> painting made <u>during</u> Henry's reign (meaning the painter could have <u>met</u> Henry). So this should be a <u>useful</u> source for finding out what Henry looked like.

- BUT perhaps the painter would have been <u>punished</u> if he didn't show Henry looking good, so it may not be entirely <u>reliable</u>.

> A source that presents a one-sided view is <u>biased</u>.

3) After they've interrogated a source, historians need to <u>interpret</u> it.

> This means deciding <u>what it tells them</u> about the topic they're studying.

> Henry was the <u>king</u> — people would have <u>done</u> what he <u>told</u> them to.

4) For example, Henry was probably quite a <u>large man</u> with <u>fair hair</u> and a <u>beard</u>. But the painter may have been told to make the picture to <u>Henry's liking</u> — so based on just this picture, you can't really say for sure <u>how big</u> he really was.

5) Historians look at <u>lots of</u> sources, and <u>compare</u> them against each other. If sources <u>contradict</u> one another, they'll try to work out <u>why</u>, and what this tells them about the past.

> For example, another painting might show Henry as very <u>unattractive</u>. But a historian might <u>interpret</u> it <u>differently</u>, depending on whether Henry had <u>seen</u> and <u>approved of</u> the painting, or whether it had been made by one of Henry's <u>enemies</u> and was perhaps <u>biased against</u> him.

Learning how to interpret sources is really important

When you're studying GCSE History, you need to interrogate and interpret every source you see. Don't always assume what you see or read is an exact description of life way back when.

How History Works

Historians can use the information in <u>various sources</u> to get a better understanding of a particular period. This involves <u>linking</u> events together, and working out <u>why</u> things happened the way they did.

Historians study **Change** and **Continuity**

1) One way to get an idea of what happened in the past is to look at <u>changes</u> and <u>continuities</u> over time.

2) <u>Change</u> is when something happens to make things <u>different</u>.

   • Changes can be <u>quick</u> — e.g. a law <u>making</u> secondary education free.

   • Or they can be <u>slow</u> — e.g. a <u>gradual change</u> in a society's literacy levels.

3) <u>Continuity</u> is the <u>opposite</u> of change — it's when things stay the <u>same</u>
   — e.g. people believed for hundreds of years that <u>disease</u> was God's punishment for <u>sin</u>.

4) These ideas are opposites — think of <u>continuity</u> as a <u>flat line</u> going along
   until there is a sudden <u>change</u> and the line becomes a <u>zigzag</u>:

The <u>most important</u> changes in history are called <u>turning points</u>. After a turning point, life might never be the same again.

5) Change and continuity can happen <u>at the same time</u> in different parts of society.

   • For example, when the <u>Normans</u> conquered England in 1066, many of the
     richest people in English society lost their <u>jobs</u> and <u>status</u> (= change).

   • But life didn't actually change very much for <u>peasant farmers</u> (= continuity).

6) There are <u>all sorts</u> of things that a historian might look at for change or continuity.
   Some things might be <u>obvious</u> (e.g. a new king or queen would be an obvious change).
   But historians are also very interested in whether <u>more everyday</u> aspects of society are showing
   change or continuity — e.g. <u>attitudes</u>, <u>lifestyles</u>, <u>beliefs</u>, <u>fashions</u>, <u>diets</u>... the list is endless.

Historians think about **Causes** and **Consequences**

1) <u>Cause</u> means the <u>reason</u> something happened — e.g. the causes of the First World War.

2) <u>Consequence</u> means what happened <u>because</u> of an
   action — it's the <u>result</u> of an event, e.g. a consequence of
   the First World War was that a lot of young men were killed.

Any time you have an event in history, think about <u>what caused it</u> and <u>the effect it had</u> — it's a really good way to show the examiner how different historical events are <u>linked</u> to each other.

3) Causes and consequences can be either <u>short-term</u> or <u>long-term</u>.

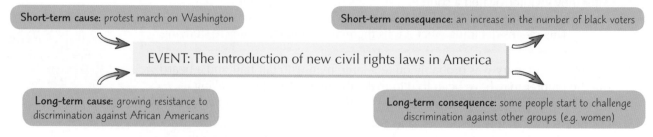

Short-term cause: protest march on Washington

Short-term consequence: an increase in the number of black voters

EVENT: The introduction of new civil rights laws in America

Long-term cause: growing resistance to discrimination against African Americans

Long-term consequence: some people start to challenge discrimination against other groups (e.g. women)

4) Historians also think about how different causes and consequences <u>interact</u>. For
   example, there might be a <u>chain</u> of causes that lead to an event, or one consequence
   of an event might be <u>more important</u> than all the rest.

You can think of these as the Four Cs of history

As you use this book, make sure you think about 'the Four Cs' on each page. When you identify causes, consequences, changes and continuities, add them to your revision notes and learn them.

Health and Medicine in Britain, c.1000-present

Timeline of Important Dates

Here's a timeline showing the order of key events in the history of British health and medicine since around 1000.

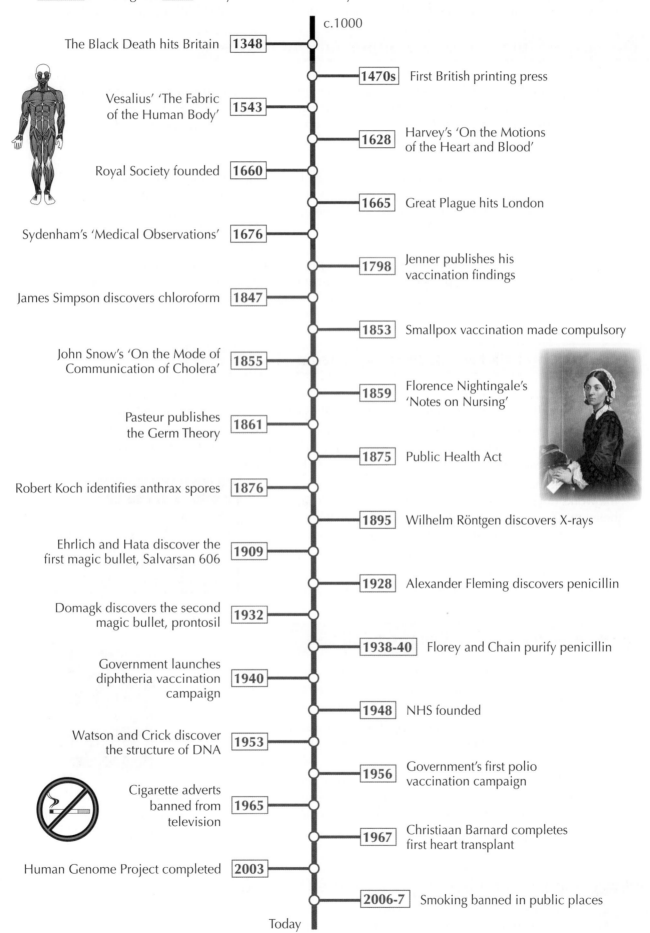

c.1000

The Black Death hits Britain — **1348**

1470s First British printing press

Vesalius' 'The Fabric of the Human Body' — **1543**

1628 Harvey's 'On the Motions of the Heart and Blood'

Royal Society founded — **1660**

1665 Great Plague hits London

Sydenham's 'Medical Observations' — **1676**

1798 Jenner publishes his vaccination findings

James Simpson discovers chloroform — **1847**

1853 Smallpox vaccination made compulsory

John Snow's 'On the Mode of Communication of Cholera' — **1855**

1859 Florence Nightingale's 'Notes on Nursing'

Pasteur publishes the Germ Theory — **1861**

1875 Public Health Act

Robert Koch identifies anthrax spores — **1876**

1895 Wilhelm Röntgen discovers X-rays

Ehrlich and Hata discover the first magic bullet, Salvarsan 606 — **1909**

1928 Alexander Fleming discovers penicillin

Domagk discovers the second magic bullet, prontosil — **1932**

1938-40 Florey and Chain purify penicillin

Government launches diphtheria vaccination campaign — **1940**

1948 NHS founded

Watson and Crick discover the structure of DNA — **1953**

1956 Government's first polio vaccination campaign

Cigarette adverts banned from television — **1965**

1967 Christiaan Barnard completes first heart transplant

Human Genome Project completed — **2003**

2006-7 Smoking banned in public places

Today

Disease and the Supernatural

In medieval England, treatment of disease was <u>poor</u>. The key problem was a <u>lack of understanding</u> of the <u>causes</u> of disease. Many people believed that disease was caused by evil spirits or <u>supernatural</u> beings.

Disease was thought to have Supernatural Causes

1)   Many people believed that disease was a <u>punishment from God</u> for people's <u>sins</u>. They thought that disease existed to show them the error of their ways and to make them become better people. Therefore, they thought that the way to cure disease was through <u>prayer</u> and <u>repentance</u>.

2)   Disease was also thought to be caused by evil supernatural beings, like <u>demons</u> or <u>witches</u>. Witches were believed to be behind outbreaks of disease — many people were tried as witches and executed.

3)   People believed that some diseases could be caused by <u>evil spirits</u> living inside someone. Members of the Church performed <u>exorcisms</u>, using chants to remove the spirit from the person's body.

The Church had a big Influence on medieval medicine

1)   The <u>Roman Catholic Church</u> was an extremely powerful organisation in medieval Europe. It dominated the way people studied and thought about a range of topics, including medicine.

2)   The Church encouraged people to believe that disease was a <u>punishment from God</u>, rather than having a natural cause. This <u>prevented</u> people from trying to <u>find cures</u> for disease — if disease was a punishment from God, all you could do was pray and repent.

3)   The Church made sure that scholars of medicine learned the works of <u>Galen</u> (see p.5) as his ideas fit the Christian belief that God <u>created</u> human bodies and made them to be <u>perfect</u>. It also stopped anyone from <u>disagreeing</u> with Galen.

4)   The Church outlawed <u>dissection</u>. This meant that medieval doctors <u>couldn't</u> discover ideas about human <u>anatomy</u> for themselves — they instead had to learn Galen's <u>incorrect</u> ideas.

Comment and Analysis

The Church's influence over medieval medicine meant that there was <u>very little change</u> in ideas about the cause of disease until the Renaissance — the Church and its messages were so influential that people were <u>unable to question them</u>.

Astrology was used to Diagnose disease

1)   <u>Astrology</u> is the idea that the <u>movements</u> of the <u>planets</u> and <u>stars</u> have an effect on the Earth and on people. Astrologers in medieval England believed that these movements could cause <u>disease</u>.

2)   Astrology was a <u>new way</u> of diagnosing disease. It was developed in <u>Arabic</u> medicine and brought to Europe between <u>1100</u> and <u>1300</u>.

3)   Medieval doctors owned a type of calendar (called an <u>almanac</u>) which included information about where particular planets and stars were at any given time. The doctor then used this information to <u>predict</u> how patients' health could be affected.

4)   Different <u>star signs</u> were thought to affect different parts of the body.

A woodcut from 1490 showing two astrologers looking at the positions of the Sun and Moon.

REVISION TASK

Supernatural beliefs prevented effective treatment

Look at the woodcut of the astrologers above. Scribble down a few sentences explaining how useful you think it would be to a historian studying medieval beliefs about the causes of disease.

Natural Explanations

Some treatments in medieval Britain were based on <u>natural theories</u> and <u>observation</u> of the physical world.

Medicine was dominated by the Four Humours Theory

After the fall of the <u>Roman Empire</u>, much Ancient <u>Greek</u> and <u>Roman</u> medical knowledge was <u>lost</u> in the West. The <u>Theory of the Four Humours</u> was eventually brought back to western Europe via the <u>Islamic world</u> (see p.6). Many medieval doctors based their <u>diagnosis</u> and <u>treatment</u> on this theory.

The Theory of the <u>Four Humours</u> was created by the Ancient Greek doctor <u>Hippocrates</u> (c.460-c.377 BC). Hippocrates believed that the body was made up of <u>four fluids</u> (or <u>humours</u>) — <u>blood</u>, <u>phlegm</u>, <u>yellow bile</u> and <u>black bile</u>. These were linked to the <u>four seasons</u> and the <u>four elements</u>. They needed to be in <u>balance</u> for good health.

E.g. in <u>winter</u> we get <u>colds</u>. So Hippocrates thought that in winter the body created an excess of <u>phlegm</u>. Sadly, Hippocrates failed to see that a bunged up nose, fevers, etc. are <u>symptoms</u> of the disease — he thought they were the <u>cause</u>.

E.g. someone with a <u>cold</u> (too much cold, wet <u>phlegm</u>) could be given chicken, pepper or wine (all considered <u>hot</u> and <u>dry</u>) to correct the <u>imbalance</u>.

The Theory of the Four Humours was developed further by another Greek doctor, <u>Galen</u>, who was born in AD 129 and worked for much of his career in <u>Rome</u>. Galen believed that diseases could be treated using <u>opposites</u>. He thought that different foods, drinks, herbs and spices had a <u>humour</u>, which could <u>balance</u> the excessive humour that was causing the disease.

The Miasma Theory blamed Bad Air for causing disease

1) The <u>miasma</u> theory is the idea that <u>bad air</u> (or miasma) causes disease when someone breathes it in. This bad air may come from human <u>waste</u> or <u>dead bodies</u> — anything that creates a <u>bad smell</u>.

2) The miasma theory originated in Ancient <u>Greece</u> and <u>Rome</u>, and was incorporated by <u>Galen</u> into the Theory of the Four Humours. The idea became extremely popular in medieval Britain.

3) The miasma theory was so influential that it lasted until the <u>1860s</u>, when it was replaced by the <u>Germ Theory</u> (see p.21). Miasma often prompted people to do <u>hygienic</u> things, like cleaning the streets, which sometimes helped to stop the spread of disease (but for the wrong reasons).

Comment and Analysis

The Four Humours and miasma were both <u>incorrect</u> theories. But they assumed disease had a <u>natural</u> cause, rather than a supernatural one. This was important, as it suggested that people weren't <u>powerless</u> against disease — they could <u>investigate</u> and <u>take action</u> against it.

Hippocrates and Galen were very Influential

The work of <u>Hippocrates</u> and <u>Galen</u> was extremely influential in medical diagnosis and treatment.

- Hippocrates and Galen wrote down their beliefs about medicine. These were <u>translated</u> into Latin books, which were considered important texts by the <u>Roman Catholic Church</u>. Like the Bible, Hippocrates' and Galen's ideas were considered the <u>absolute truth</u>.

- Many of their ideas were taught for <u>centuries</u> after their deaths, including the <u>incorrect</u> ones. For example, Galen only ever dissected <u>animals</u> — animal and human bodies are very different, so some of his ideas about <u>anatomy</u> were <u>wrong</u>. Medieval doctors were <u>not allowed</u> to perform their own dissections, so they continued to learn Galen's incorrect ideas.

- Some of Hippocrates' and Galen's ideas were so influential that they continue to be used <u>today</u>. The <u>Hippocratic Oath</u> is the <u>promise</u> made by doctors to obey rules of behaviour in their professional lives — a version of it is still in use today. Hippocrates and Galen also believed that doctors should <u>observe</u> their patients as they treat them.

Galen's teachings remained undisputed for centuries

For answers where you need to write and explain multiple points, it's worth making a rough plan before you begin to write. This will make sure you answer the question and don't veer off the topic.

Islamic Medicine

In the medieval period, Islamic medicine was miles ahead of European medicine. Arabic ideas eventually made their way to Europe — including knowledge of the all-important Galen and Hippocrates.

Arab doctors kept Classical Knowledge alive

1) While a lot of medical knowledge was lost in the West after the fall of the Roman Empire, medical ideas like the Four Humours and treatment by opposites (see p.5) were kept alive by Islamic scholars.

2) In the 9th century, Hunain ibn Ishaq (also known by his Latin name Johannitius) travelled from Baghdad to Byzantium to collect Greek medical texts. He translated these into Arabic.

3) This classical knowledge was eventually brought to Europe by Avicenna (or Ibn Sina), a Persian who lived from around AD 980-1037. Avicenna wrote the 'Canon of Medicine', which brought together the ideas of Galen and Hippocrates, and was the most important way that classical ideas got back into Western Europe.

4) This work and other Islamic texts were translated into Latin in Spain (which was partly Christian and partly Islamic) or Italy. The Crusades also made Europeans aware of the scientific knowledge of Islamic doctors.

> **Comment and Analysis**
>
> Islamic medicine was generally more rational and evidence-based than European medicine, partly due to their knowledge of classical (Ancient Greek and Roman) medical texts.

> The Crusades were a series of wars fought by Christian Europeans against Muslims. They were an ultimately unsuccessful attempt to retake Jerusalem and the surrounding areas associated with the early history of Christianity.

Islamic doctors made several New Discoveries

1) Albucasis (or Abu al-Qasim, born c.AD 936) wrote a well thought-out book describing amputations, the removal of bladder stones and dental surgery — as well as methods for handling fractures, dislocations and the stitching of wounds.

2) In the 12th century, Avenzoar (or Ibn Zuhr) described the parasite that causes scabies and began to question the reliability of Galen.

3) Ibn al-Nafis, who lived in the 13th century, also questioned Galen's ideas. He suggested (correctly) that blood flows from one side of the heart to the other via the lungs — and doesn't cross the septum (the dividing wall between the left and right sides of the heart). Ibn al-Nafis' work wasn't recognised in the West until the 20th century.

> **Comment and Analysis**
>
> In the Islamic world, as in Western Europe, religion strongly influenced the development of medicine. For example, Islam, like Christianity, prohibited dissection.

The autobiography of Usama ibn Munqidh, a 12th century Muslim doctor, suggests the difference between Islamic and European medicine. Usama describes how he treated a knight with a sore on his leg by using a poultice, and a woman who was 'feeble-minded' by advising a new diet. Then a French doctor arrived and claimed Usama knew nothing. He cut off the knight's leg with an axe, and cut the woman's head with a razor and rubbed the skull with salt. Both patients died.

Alchemy helped to develop New Drugs

1) Alchemy was the attempt to turn base (ordinary) metals into gold and to discover the elixir of eternal life.

2) Alchemy traces its origins back to the Egyptians and it was preserved in the Islamic world.

3) Unlike modern chemistry, much superstition was included — an unsuccessful experiment was as likely to be blamed on the position of the stars or the spiritual purity of the alchemist as anything else.

4) Even so, Arabic alchemists invented useful techniques such as distillation and sublimation, and prepared drugs such as laudanum, benzoin and camphor.

Islamic medicine was more advanced than British medicine

Imagine that you've been tasked with 'selling' Islamic medicine to Europe. Write an advert for Islamic medicine, including a list of the ways it was more advanced than European medicine.

Treating Disease

As the Middle Ages went on, medical treatments continued to be based on ideas we'd nowadays consider very <u>unscientific</u>. <u>Treatments</u> were <u>ambitious</u> though, and <u>theories</u> quite <u>sophisticated</u> in their <u>own ways</u>.

Prayer and Repentance were major treatments

1) Disease was believed to be a punishment from God, so sick people were encouraged to <u>pray</u>. The sick often prayed to <u>saints</u>, in the hope they would intervene and stop the illness. Medieval people also believed that <u>pilgrimages</u> to <u>holy shrines</u> (e.g. sites containing the remains of saints) could cure <u>illnesses</u>.

2) Others took their <u>repentance</u> one step further. <u>Flagellants</u> were people who whipped themselves in public in order to show God that they were sorry for their past actions. They were particularly common during <u>epidemics</u>, such as the Black Death (see p.10).

3) Many <u>doctors</u> had <u>superstitious beliefs</u> — e.g. some used <u>astrology</u> to diagnose and treat illness (see p.4), or believed that saying <u>certain words</u> while giving a treatment could make that treatment more effective.

Bloodletting and Purging aimed to make the Humours balanced

1) <u>Bloodletting</u> and <u>purging</u> were popular treatments because they fitted in with the <u>Four Humours Theory</u> (see p.5).

2) If someone apparently had too much blood inside them, the doctor would take blood out of their body through <u>bloodletting</u> — they might make a small <u>cut</u> to remove the blood or use blood-sucking <u>leeches</u>.

3) Some people were accidentally <u>killed</u> because too much blood was taken.

4) <u>Purging</u> is the act of getting rid of other fluids from the body by <u>excreting</u> — doctors gave their patients <u>laxatives</u> to help the purging process.

Comment and Analysis

<u>Bloodletting</u> caused more deaths than it prevented, but it remained a popular treatment. This shows the strength of medieval people's <u>beliefs</u> in the face of <u>observational evidence</u>.

Purifying the Air was thought to Prevent Disease

1) The <u>miasma</u> theory (see p.5) led people to believe in the power of <u>purifying</u> or <u>cleaning</u> the air to prevent sickness and improve health.

2) Physicians carried <u>posies</u> or <u>oranges</u> around with them when visiting patients to protect themselves from catching a disease.

3) During the <u>Black Death</u> (see p.10), <u>juniper</u>, <u>myrrh</u> and <u>incense</u> were burned so the <u>smoke</u> or <u>scent</u> would <u>fill the room</u> and stop bad air from bringing disease <u>inside</u>.

Purifying the air was also seen as important for helping with <u>other health conditions</u>. In the case of <u>fainting</u>, people <u>burned feathers</u> and made the patient <u>breathe in their smoke</u>.

Remedies were Early Natural Medicines

1) Remedies bought from an <u>apothecary</u>, local <u>wise woman</u> or made at <u>home</u> were all popular in medieval Britain and contained <u>herbs</u>, <u>spices</u>, <u>animal parts</u> and <u>minerals</u>.

2) These remedies were either <u>passed down</u> or <u>written</u> in books explaining how to mix them together. Some of these books were called '<u>Herbals</u>'.

3) Other remedies were based on <u>superstition</u>, like <u>lucky charms</u> containing 'powdered unicorn's horn'.

This medieval print shows a doctor and an apothecary. The plants in the middle show the importance of herbal remedies.

Medieval medical treatments were extremely varied

Choose any three treatments from this page. For each one, write a sentence explaining why people in medieval England believed it would be effective against disease.

8

Treating Disease

In the Middle Ages, people were extremely fortunate if they were treated by a doctor. Most had to go to an apothecary, a public hospital or a barber-surgeon if they needed treatment for something.

People used lots of Different Healers

1) Physicians were male doctors who had trained at university for at least seven years. They read ancient texts as well as writings from the Islamic world (see p.6) but their training involved little practical experience. They used handbooks (vademecums) and clinical observation to check patients' conditions. But there were fewer than 100 physicians in England in 1300, and they were very expensive.

2) Most people saw an apothecary, who prepared and sold remedies (see p.7), and gave advice on how best to use them. Apothecaries were the most common form of treatment in Britain as they were the most accessible for those who could not afford a physician.

3) Apothecaries were trained through apprenticeships. Most apothecaries were men, but there were also many so-called 'wise women', who sold herbal remedies.

There were Few Public Hospitals

1) Most public hospitals were set up and run by the Church. There were relatively few such hospitals, but they were very popular and highly regarded.

2) The main purpose of hospitals was not to treat disease, but to care for the sick and elderly. The hospital provided its patients with food, water and a warm place to stay. Most hospitals were also more hygienic than elsewhere, because they had developed water and sewerage systems.

3) Some monasteries also cared for the sick, the elderly or the poor (see p.9).

4) Most sick people were treated at home by members of their family.

> Famous hospitals like St. Bartholomew's and St. Thomas' in London started life as church establishments. The monastery at Canterbury Cathedral already had a complex water and sanitation system by 1250.

Surgery — work for Barbers, not doctors

1) Medieval surgery was very dangerous — there was no way to prevent blood loss, infection or pain. It was therefore only attempted rarely and for very minor procedures, e.g. treating hernias or cataracts.

2) There were a few university-trained, highly paid surgeons, but surgery as a whole was not a respected profession in medieval times — most operations were carried out by barber-surgeons (who also cut hair).

Some Progress was made in Surgery

1) Hugh of Lucca and his son Theodoric worked as surgeons in Italy in the early 13th century. They recognised the importance of practical experience and observation, and questioned some of Galen's ideas — their thoughts appear in Theodoric's textbooks.

2) They began dressing wounds with bandages soaked in wine, because they noticed that the wine helped to keep wounds clean and prevent infection. They made this discovery by chance.

3) They also realised that pus was not a healthy sign, unlike other doctors at the time who might try to cause wounds to pus because they believed it would release toxins from the body.

4) Some surgeons tried to find ways to reduce pain during operations. For example, John of Arderne created a recipe for an anaesthetic in 1376 which included hemlock, opium and henbane (a relative of deadly nightshade). In carefully controlled doses this may have worked — but was very likely to kill.

Comment and Analysis

Hugh and Theodoric's approach was unusual in the Middles Ages. It wasn't until the Renaissance that people started to question widely-held beliefs about the causes of disease, and to carry out experiments to find more effective methods of treatment and prevention.

There were few trained doctors in medieval England
Some of the marks in the exam are for using specialist terminology — so make sure you know it.

Health in Towns and Monasteries

In the medieval period, how <u>healthy</u> people were had a lot do with the area <u>where they lived</u>.

Living Conditions in Towns were pretty Poor

1) Most towns were <u>small</u>, especially after the <u>Black Death</u> when a lot of people died (p.10). Houses were usually made of <u>wood</u> and were <u>crammed together</u> — <u>overcrowding</u> and <u>fires</u> were common problems.

2) A lot of <u>towns</u> didn't have <u>clean water supplies</u> or <u>sewerage systems</u> — waste was chucked into the <u>street</u> or into <u>rivers</u> to be washed away. Sewage from <u>latrines</u> (pits with wooden seats) leaked into the <u>ground</u> and got into <u>wells</u>.

3) Businesses and homes <u>weren't separated</u> — butchers, tanners and dyers threw <u>toxic waste</u> into rivers and residential streets. People had to get their <u>drinking water</u> from rivers and wells that were <u>contaminated</u>.

4) In the <u>13th century</u>, a <u>water channel</u> called the <u>Great Conduit</u> was built to bring <u>clean water</u> into London, as the Thames was getting <u>too toxic</u>.

5) In <u>1388</u>, the <u>government</u> ordered <u>town authorities</u> to keep the streets <u>free of waste</u>. Towns introduced <u>public health measures</u> to tackle waste, sewage and pollution and to create a <u>clean water supply</u>.

> York and London both <u>banned</u> people from <u>dumping waste</u> in the street. These cities also built <u>latrines</u> over <u>rivers</u> so that sewage could be <u>carried away</u>.

> London eventually banned <u>any waste</u> from being thrown into the Thames — <u>carters</u> were hired to <u>collect waste</u> and take it <u>out</u> of the city.

> Many towns, like York, ordered <u>toxic businesses</u> like butchers, tanners, fishmongers and dyers to move <u>outside</u> the city walls.

Comment and Analysis

> People <u>broke these rules</u> and officials struggled to <u>enforce</u> them. People knew that <u>dirty water</u> and <u>bad health</u> were <u>linked</u>, but <u>they didn't</u> really <u>understand</u> the <u>risks</u>. Town authorities didn't have enough <u>money</u> or <u>knowledge</u> to <u>properly</u> fix these public health issues.

Monasteries were Healthier than Towns

Monasteries had <u>cleaner water</u> than towns and had good systems for getting rid of <u>waste</u> and <u>sewage</u>. Monks also had access to <u>books</u> on healing and they <u>knew</u> how to <u>grow herbs</u> and make <u>herbal remedies</u>.

> This is what historians think <u>Fountains Abbey</u> in Yorkshire might have been like.

> <u>Sick monks</u> were cared for in <u>infirmaries</u>. These <u>infirmaries</u> normally had their own <u>kitchen</u> that served <u>good meals</u> and <u>meat</u> to help sick monks to <u>recover</u>.

> Monasteries <u>separated</u> clean and dirty <u>water</u>. They had one water supply for <u>cooking</u> and <u>drinking</u> and one for <u>drainage</u> and <u>washing</u>, so people didn't have to drink <u>dirty water</u> like they did in towns.

> Some monasteries had <u>hospitals</u> that <u>cared</u> for <u>poor people</u> from the <u>local community</u> when they were sick and gave shelter to <u>travellers</u>. <u>Benedictine</u> monks believed <u>caring</u> for the sick was the <u>most important</u> Christian duty.

> Most monasteries were built near <u>rivers</u>. If there was no river, <u>man-made waterways</u> were built to supply <u>clean water</u>.

> <u>Latrines</u> were put in <u>separate buildings</u>, which were often built over streams of <u>running water</u> that <u>carried sewage away</u>.

Infirmary

Kitchen

Guest Houses

It was <u>easier</u> to create <u>healthy living conditions</u> in <u>monasteries</u> than it was in towns.

1) Monasteries were <u>wealthy</u>, so they could <u>afford</u> to build <u>infrastructure</u> like latrine buildings and waterways to keep their water <u>clean</u>. Towns had to rely on <u>wealthy individuals</u> to <u>fund</u> these kinds of projects.

2) Monastery <u>populations</u> were <u>small</u> and had <u>one leader</u> (the Abbot) — he had the <u>power</u> to <u>enforce</u> rules about cleanliness and waste disposal. Getting <u>hundreds</u> of <u>townspeople</u> to adopt cleaner habits was <u>trickier</u> — towns didn't have one person <u>in charge</u> who could easily <u>enforce</u> public health measures.

Poor living conditions led to poor public health

Draw two boxes — one with the heading 'Towns' and the other with the heading 'Monasteries'. Fill in the boxes with bullet points about health and living conditions in each location.

The Black Death in Britain

The <u>Black Death</u> first struck in the <u>14th century</u>. People tried to limit its <u>spread</u>, but couldn't <u>stop</u> the disease.

The **Black Death** was a devastating **Epidemic**

1) The <u>Black Death</u> was a series of <u>plagues</u> that swept Europe in the <u>14th century</u>. It was really two illnesses:

- **Bubonic plague**, spread by the bites of fleas from rats carried on <u>ships</u>. This caused <u>headaches</u> and a <u>high temperature</u>, followed by pus-filled <u>swellings</u> on the skin.
- **Pneumonic plague** was <u>airborne</u> — it was spread by coughs and sneezes. It attacked the <u>lungs</u>, making it <u>painful to breathe</u> and causing victims to cough up <u>blood</u>.

2) The disease first arrived in Britain in <u>1348</u>. Some historians think at least a <u>third</u> of the British population died as a result of the Black Death in 1348-50. There were <u>further outbreaks</u> of the Black Death throughout the Middle Ages.

People **Didn't Know** what **Caused** the Black Death

No-one at the time knew what had <u>caused</u> the plague.

1) Some people believed that the Black Death was a <u>judgement from God</u>. They thought the cause of the disease was <u>sin</u>, so they tried to <u>prevent</u> the spread of the disease through <u>prayer</u> and <u>fasting</u>.

2) Some blamed <u>humour</u> imbalances (see p.5), so tried to get rid of the Black Death through <u>bloodletting</u> and <u>purging</u>. Those who thought that the disease was caused by <u>miasma</u> carried strong smelling <u>herbs</u> or lit <u>fires</u> to <u>purify</u> the air.

3) Some people also carried <u>charms</u> or used 'magic' <u>potions</u> containing <u>arsenic</u>.

> **Comment and Analysis**
>
> One of the main reasons why the Black Death killed so many was because people <u>didn't know</u> what caused the disease. Their ideas about the cause of disease were <u>wrong</u>, so their attempts at prevention and treatment were mostly <u>ineffective</u>.

Local Governments tried to **Prevent** the spread of the disease

1) Some people in Winchester thought that you could catch the plague from being <u>close</u> to the <u>bodies of dead victims</u>. When the town's cemetery became <u>too full</u> to take any more plague victims, the townspeople refused to let the bishop extend the cemetery in the town centre. Instead, they insisted that <u>new cemeteries</u> be built outside of the town, away from the houses.

2) The town of Gloucester tried to <u>shut itself off</u> from the outside world after hearing the Black Death had reached Bristol. This suggests that they thought the plague was spread by <u>human contact</u>. Their attempt at prevention was <u>unsuccessful</u> — many people in the town <u>died</u> of the Black Death.

3) In November 1348, the disease reached London. In January 1349, King Edward III <u>closed Parliament</u>.

The Black Death caused **Social Change**

1) After the Black Death, there were <u>far fewer workers</u> around. This meant that they could demand <u>higher wages</u> from their employers, and <u>move around</u> to find better work. The <u>cost of land</u> also <u>decreased</u>, allowing some peasants to buy land for the first time.

2) These changes threatened the power of the elites. The government created <u>laws</u>, such as the <u>1349 Ordinance of Labourers</u>, to try and stop peasants moving around the country.

3) Some people think the Black Death helped cause the <u>Peasants' Revolt</u> in 1381, and, eventually, the collapse of the <u>feudal system</u> in Britain.

EXAM TIP

People were unable to prevent or treat the Black Death

In the exam, remember to check the number of marks each question is worth. If a question's worth double the marks of another question, then you'll need to give it double the time to answer it properly.

Exam-Style Questions

Q1
> Write a summary examining medieval beliefs about the causes of disease.
> Use examples to support your answer.   [9 marks]

Q2
> Why did the responses to the Black Death in the Middle Ages have a limited
> effect on the spread of the disease? Explain your answer.   [10 marks]

Q3
> 'Medicine did not advance very much in Britain in the Middle Ages (c.1000-c.1500).'
>
> Explain how far you agree with this statement.   [16 marks]

c.1500-c.1700: The Medical Renaissance in Britain

Continuity and Change

The Renaissance was a time of <u>new ideas</u> and fresh <u>thinking</u>. People began to <u>challenge</u> old beliefs, and there were many <u>new developments</u> in doctors' <u>knowledge</u> and <u>skills</u>.

The **Renaissance** was a time of **Continuity** and **Change**

1) In the Renaissance there was a <u>rediscovery</u> of knowledge from classical <u>Greek</u> and <u>Roman</u> times. Western doctors gained access to the original writings of <u>Hippocrates</u>, <u>Galen</u> and <u>Avicenna</u> (a Persian physician who lived between 980 and 1037 AD). These <u>hadn't been available</u> in the medieval period. They led to <u>greater interest</u> in the <u>Four Humours</u> Theory and <u>treatment by opposites</u> (see p.5).

2) But the Renaissance also saw the emergence of <u>science</u> as we know it from the <u>magic</u> and <u>mysticism</u> of medieval medicine. People thought about how the human body worked based on <u>direct observation</u> and <u>experimentation</u>.

3) This was partly because many of the new books that had been found said that <u>anatomy</u> and <u>dissections</u> were very important. This encouraged people to <u>examine</u> the body themselves, and to come to their <u>own conclusions</u> about the causes of disease.

4) People began to <u>question</u> Galen's thinking and that of other ancient doctors. However, his writings <u>continued to be studied</u>.

> <u>Protestant Christianity</u> spread across Europe during the <u>Reformation</u>, reducing the influence of the <u>Catholic Church</u>. Although <u>religion</u> was still <u>important</u>, the Church no longer had so much control over medical teaching.

This woodcut shows physicians debating over a medicine book.

The **Medical Knowledge** of doctors **Improved**

1) Many doctors in the Renaissance trained at the <u>College of Physicians</u>, which had been set up in <u>1518</u>. Here they read books by <u>Galen</u>, but also studied <u>recent</u> medical developments. <u>Dissections</u> — showing how the body actually worked — also became a <u>key part</u> of medical training.

2) The College of Physicians encouraged the <u>licensing</u> of doctors to stop the influence of <u>quacks</u>, who sold <u>fake medicines</u> (see p.14). Some of the college's physicians (such as <u>Harvey</u> — see p.16) made <u>important discoveries</u> about disease and the human body.

3) New <u>weapons</u> like <u>cannons</u> and <u>guns</u> were being used in <u>war</u>. This meant that doctors and surgeons had to treat injuries they <u>hadn't seen before</u>, forcing them to quickly find <u>new treatments</u>.

> There were some <u>technological</u> developments too. <u>Peter Chamberlen</u> invented the <u>forceps</u> (probably at some point in the 1600s), which are still used today to help with <u>childbirth</u>.

4) <u>Explorations</u> abroad brought <u>new ingredients</u> for drugs back to Britain, including <u>guaiacum</u> — believed to cure syphilis — and <u>quinine</u>, a drug for <u>malaria</u> from the bark of the <u>Cinchona</u> tree.

5) In the <u>1530s</u>, Henry VIII closed down most of Britain's <u>monasteries</u> (this was called the '<u>dissolution of the monasteries</u>'). Since most hospitals had been set up and run by monasteries (see p.9), this also led to the <u>closure</u> of a large number of <u>hospitals</u>. The sudden <u>loss</u> of so many hospitals was <u>bad</u> for people's <u>health</u>.

6) The monastic hospitals were gradually <u>replaced</u> by some <u>free hospitals</u>, which were paid for by <u>charitable donations</u> (see p.23). Unlike the monastic hospitals, which had been run by monks, these new hospitals were run by trained <u>physicians</u>, who focused more on <u>getting better</u> from <u>illness</u>.

Physicians started to question ancient medical ideas

It really helps to add some facts to support your answer — a useful date, for example. But make sure it's relevant to what you're trying to say — the details should be used to support your argument.

Continuity and Change

Change was pretty rapid during the Renaissance — <u>new technology</u> sped things up by allowing ideas to be circulated more easily. Despite this, some doctors still treated new ideas with <u>suspicion</u>.

The **Spread** of **New Ideas** accelerated **Change**

The invention of printing

- Printing meant that books could be <u>copied</u> more <u>easily</u> — in the past, new ideas had to be <u>widely accepted</u> before anyone would bother copying them by hand. <u>Students</u> in <u>universities</u> could have their own <u>textbooks</u> for the first time, letting them study in detail.
- People could also question <u>existing</u> ideas and have scientific <u>debates</u>. At least <u>600</u> different editions of <u>Galen's</u> books were printed between 1473 and 1599. Lots of people <u>knew</u> his theories, but with so many different versions around, it was <u>unclear</u> what Galen had originally written — this made his writings seem <u>less reliable</u> and easier to <u>question</u>.

The first British <u>printing press</u> was set up in the <u>1470s</u>.

Comment and Analysis

Huge <u>progress</u> was made in the Renaissance — and the <u>printing press</u> and the <u>Royal Society</u> helped spread the <u>new ideas</u>. But most people <u>couldn't read</u>, so new ideas only had an impact on a <u>small part</u> of society. <u>Most</u> people in the Renaissance were using the <u>same treatments</u> as people in the <u>Middle Ages</u> (see p.7-8).

The Royal Society

- The <u>Royal Society</u> was founded in <u>1660</u>. Its motto was '<u>Nullius in verba</u>', which means '<u>take no-one's word for it</u>' — the society wanted to encourage people to be <u>sceptical</u> and to <u>question</u> scientific ideas.
- The Royal Society helped to spread <u>new scientific theories</u> and got people to <u>trust new technology</u>. Its scientific journal '<u>Philosophical Transactions</u>' allowed more people to read about new inventions and discoveries.

Paré improved **Surgical Techniques**

1) <u>Ambroise Paré</u> was a French barber-surgeon born in <u>1510</u>. Surgery was still a <u>low status</u> profession. Paré worked for a <u>public hospital</u>, then became an <u>army surgeon</u>.

Paré also designed quite sophisticated <u>artificial limbs</u>.

2) As an army surgeon, Paré treated many <u>serious injuries</u> caused by <u>war</u>. His experience treating these wounds led him to develop some <u>improved surgical techniques</u>:

- At this time, <u>gunshot wounds</u> often became <u>infected</u>. Doctors didn't understand <u>why</u> this happened or how to <u>treat</u> it. The usual treatment was to <u>burn</u> the wound with a <u>red hot iron</u>, or to pour <u>boiling oil</u> onto it. This may have worked in some cases, but it often did more harm than good.

A <u>cool salve</u> is a type of ointment.

- During one battle, Paré <u>ran out</u> of oil and resorted, by chance, to a simple <u>cool salve</u> instead. To his surprise the patients treated in this way did <u>better</u> than the ones scalded with oil.
- Paré also improved the treatment of <u>amputations</u>. Before Paré, the severed <u>blood vessels</u> left by amputation were sealed by burning their ends with a <u>red hot iron</u> (cauterisation). Paré invented a method of tying off the vessels with <u>threads</u> (ligatures). This was <u>less painful</u> than cauterisation, so it reduced the chances of the patient dying of <u>shock</u>. However, it did increase the risk of <u>infection</u>.

3) Paré <u>published</u> his ideas to enable other doctors to read about them — <u>British surgeons</u> used the methods of Paré and took inspiration from his work. Over time, his ideas helped <u>improve</u> surgical techniques.

4) Paré's ideas were <u>resisted</u> by doctors who felt that a <u>lowly surgeon</u> shouldn't be listened to. He eventually became surgeon to the <u>King of France</u>, and it was only with the <u>King's support</u> that his ideas started to be accepted.

New ideas didn't really affect the majority of the population

When answering a question about change or continuity, think about all of the different areas of health and medicine. Change in one area didn't necessarily mean change in another.

Continuity and Change

Although ideas spread rapidly, there was still <u>continuity</u> in many aspects of medical care.

Lots of **Old Treatments** were still used

A woodcut from c.1670 showing a quack selling his 'miraculous' cures.

1) Many doctors were reluctant to accept that <u>Galen</u> was <u>wrong</u>. This meant that they continued to use similar treatments to the Middle Ages, like <u>bloodletting</u> and <u>purging</u> (see p.7).

2) Doctors were still very <u>expensive</u>. As a result, most people used <u>other healers</u> (e.g. apothecaries and barber-surgeons — see p.8), like in the <u>medieval period</u>. Some people turned to <u>quack doctors</u> who sold <u>medicines</u> and <u>treatments</u> in the street. Their cures were often <u>fake</u>, though some may have worked.

3) <u>Superstition</u> and <u>religion</u> were still important. People thought the <u>King's touch</u> could cure <u>scrofula</u> (a skin disease known as the 'King's Evil'). <u>Thousands</u> of people with scrofula are thought to have visited King Charles I (1600-1649) in the hope of being cured.

<u>Wise women</u>, who were skilled in <u>herbal remedies</u>, carried on providing medical attention in the community. <u>Wealthy ladies</u> sometimes took this role — they would care for <u>local families</u>.

> Lady Grace Mildmay (1552-1620) was a wise woman who was <u>highly educated</u> and read lots of medical books. She used her knowledge to <u>help patients</u>. She also kept <u>detailed records</u> of her treatments.

Poor living conditions had a **Bad Effect** on people's **Health**

1) Living conditions in Renaissance towns were <u>terrible</u> — they were <u>less healthy</u> than medieval ones.

2) <u>Overcrowding</u> was a big problem and there was a lack of <u>light</u> and <u>fresh air</u> in houses. <u>Streets</u> were <u>unclean</u> — there weren't any <u>sewerage systems</u> or any sort of <u>rubbish collection</u>. Finding <u>clean water</u> could be quite hard.

3) <u>Local authorities</u> began to <u>improve</u> conditions. They used <u>Acts of Parliament</u> to get <u>power</u> to do things like <u>keep roads clean</u>. <u>Housing improved</u> and some <u>towns</u> were planned with living conditions in mind.

> Poor living conditions meant <u>disease</u> spread <u>quickly</u> around towns. Since towns were becoming more <u>closely connected</u> through trade, disease also began to spread <u>easily</u> around the <u>country</u>.

Hospitals were still **Fairly Basic**

1) Most Renaissance hospitals were for the <u>sick</u> and the '<u>deserving</u>' poor — those who led hardworking, respectable lives. People might have to <u>work</u> in hospital, not just be treated. Those with <u>incurable</u> or <u>infectious</u> diseases like smallpox were often not allowed in.

2) <u>St Mary of Bethlehem's</u> hospital (or '<u>Bedlam</u>') was Britain's first '<u>lunatic</u>' institution. Many of its inmates actually had <u>learning disabilities</u> or <u>epilepsy</u>, or were just <u>poor</u>. People even <u>visited</u> the hospital to watch the patients for <u>entertainment</u>.

3) Other hospitals like <u>St Bartholomew's</u> in London became centres of <u>innovation</u> and <u>new research</u>.

Comment and Analysis

<u>Hospital care</u> was still in its <u>early stages</u> in the Renaissance. Many hospitals mainly focused on <u>moral</u> or <u>spiritual</u> education. But health and sickness were becoming more of a <u>priority</u>.

REVISION TASK

Renaissance treatments were similar to those of the Middle Ages

Make two lists of the key features of medieval and Renaissance medicine — how much had changed? Think about the experience of the average person, as well as new scientific discoveries.

Vesalius and Sydenham

Vesalius and Sydenham believed that direct observation was the best way to learn about the body. They encouraged people to gain practical experience, and to use dissection to understand anatomy.

Vesalius wrote Anatomy books with Accurate Diagrams

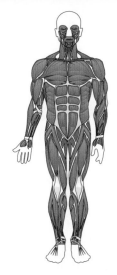

1) Vesalius was born in 1514 and was a medical professor in Padua, Italy. He believed that successful surgery would only be possible if doctors had a proper understanding of human anatomy.

2) Vesalius was able to perform dissections on criminals who had been executed. This let him study the human anatomy more closely.

3) He wrote books based on his observations using accurate diagrams to illustrate his work. The most important were 'Six Anatomical Pictures' (1538) and 'The Fabric of the Human Body' (1543).

4) His works were printed and copied (see the printing press, p.13), allowing lots of people to read about his ideas.

> Vesalius' work helped point out some of Galen's mistakes. For example, in the second edition of 'The Fabric', Vesalius showed that there were no holes in the septum of the heart.

5) Vesalius's findings encouraged others to question Galen. Doctors also realised there was more to discover about the body because of Vesalius' questioning attitude.

6) Vesalius showed that dissecting bodies was important, to find out exactly how the human body was structured. Dissection was used more and more in medical training for this reason.

Comment and Analysis

The work of Vesalius didn't have an immediate impact on the diagnosis or treatment of disease. However, by producing a realistic description of the human anatomy and encouraging dissection, Vesalius provided an essential first step to improving them.

Thomas Sydenham used Practical Experience

1) Thomas Sydenham (1624-1689) was a Renaissance physician who worked in London. He was the son of a country squire, and fought in the English Civil War before becoming a doctor. He has been called the 'English Hippocrates' because of the big impact of his medical achievements.

2) Sydenham didn't believe in the value of theoretical knowledge. Instead he thought that it was more important to gain practical experience in treating patients. As a doctor, he made detailed observations of his patients and kept accurate records of their symptoms.

3) Sydenham thought that diseases could be classified like animals or plants — the different types of disease could be discovered using patients' symptoms.

4) Sydenham is known for showing that scarlet fever was different to measles, and for introducing laudanum to relieve pain. He was also one of the first doctors to use iron to treat anaemia, and quinine for malaria (see p.12).

5) Sydenham wrote a book called 'Medical Observations' (published in 1676), which was used as a textbook by doctors for 200 years. His descriptions of medical conditions like gout helped other doctors to diagnose their patients more easily.

Comment and Analysis

Sydenham's work on classifying diseases helped make diagnosis a more important part of doctors' work. Before, the emphasis had been on prognosis — predicting what the disease would do next.

Vesalius and Sydenham believed in direct observation

Scribble down the main achievements of both Vesalius and Sydenham. Then note down the impact of their ideas — did they change things? Think about short-term and long-term effects.

William Harvey

William Harvey is a key person in the history of Renaissance medicine. He made hugely important discoveries about how blood circulates around the body and his work helped to advance people's knowledge of anatomy.

Harvey discovered the Circulation of the Blood

1) William Harvey was born in 1578 and worked in London at the Royal College of Physicians, before becoming Royal Physician to James I and Charles I.

2) Harvey studied both animals and humans for his work. He realised that he could observe living animal hearts in action, and that his findings would also apply to humans.

3) A new type of water pump was invented at around the time of Harvey's birth. This new technology gave Harvey a comparison and inspiration for how the heart worked.

4) Before Harvey, people thought that there were two kinds of blood, and that they flowed through two completely separate systems of blood vessels. It was thought that:

- Purple 'nutrition-carrying' blood was produced in the liver and then flowed through veins to the rest of the body, where it was consumed (used up).
- Bright red 'life-giving' blood was produced in the lungs and flowed through arteries to the body, where it was also consumed.
- This may show the continuing influence of Galen, who had suggested this kind of system about 1400 years earlier.

> Harvey was one of many British doctors who studied medicine at a university in Italy or France. During the Renaissance, major new discoveries were being made at these European universities — the discoveries of Vesalius (see p.15) were made at Padua University. British doctors who studied in Europe learnt the latest ideas in medicine and brought them back to Britain.

5) Harvey realised this theory was wrong. From experiments, he knew that too much blood was being pumped out of the heart for it to be continually formed and consumed. Instead he thought that blood must circulate — it must go round and round the body.

Harvey's research was a Major Breakthrough in Anatomy

1) Harvey's ideas changed how people understood anatomy.

2) His discoveries gave doctors a new map showing how the body worked. Without this map, blood transfusions or complex surgery couldn't be attempted.

3) Harvey also showed that Vesalius had been right about how important dissection was.

4) However, Harvey's work had a limited impact on diagnosis and treatment of disease:

> Although people knew more about the body's anatomy because of Harvey, medical treatments and surgical techniques were still very basic.

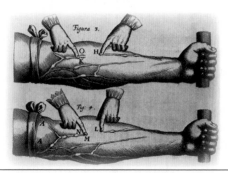

A diagram from Harvey's book 'On the Motions of the Heart and Blood' (1628), showing blood circulation in the arm.

- Not everyone believed Harvey's theories — it took a long time before doctors used them in their treatments.
- When people did attempt blood transfusions, they were rarely successful — because of blood loss, shock, and because the wrong blood types were used.
- Bloodletting, which was supposed to keep the Four Humours in balance (see p.7), also continued to be performed, even though Harvey had shown the reasoning behind it to be wrong.

EXAM TIP

Harvey used diagrams to show his findings

In the exam, be sure to present a balanced argument. Don't just write what you think without showing you understand the other side — you will likely lose marks.

The Great Plague

The Great Plague struck London in 1665 and had a devastating impact. From prayers to bloodletting, people's responses to the Great Plague were eerily similar to the reaction to the Black Death (see p.10).

The **Great Plague** hit London in **1665**

1) In 1665, London was struck by the Great Plague. This was a rare but deadly recurrence of the medieval Black Death.

2) London's death toll was about 100,000 — this was around 20% of the city's population. Many people fled the city, but only richer people had this option.

3) Doctors and priests were often most affected because the sick went to them for help.

Like the Black Death, the Great Plague was spread by the bites of fleas from rats. The people at the time didn't know this, though.

Superstition still dominated **Treatment**

Just like responses to the Black Death 300 years before (see p.10), most treatments for the Great Plague were based on magic, religion and superstition.

1) This included wearing lucky charms or amulets, saying prayers and fasting. Special remedies were made using ingredients like dried toad.

2) Bloodletting was still used, even though this probably made the plague worse — it created wounds which could become infected.

3) Other people thought that miasma caused the disease (see p.5). They carried around posies of herbs or flowers to improve the air.

4) Perhaps the most extreme treatment was strapping a live chicken to the swellings — people thought the disease could be transferred from the plague victim to the chicken.

Comment and Analysis

Living conditions were very poor in Renaissance England, so it isn't a surprise that the plague came back. Death records show that the poorest, most crowded areas of London were worst hit.

People tried to **Prevent** the plague from **Spreading**

Local councils took measures to try to stop the spread of the plague. They were largely ineffective because they didn't know the cause of the disease.

1) Councils tried to quarantine plague victims to prevent them passing on the disease to others. The victim's house was locked and a red cross was painted on their door, along with the words "Lord have mercy upon us".

2) Areas where people crowded together such as theatres were closed.

3) People tried not to touch other people. E.g. if someone had to give money in a shop, the coins might be placed in a jar of vinegar.

4) The dead bodies of plague victims were buried in mass graves away from houses. Carts organised by the authorities roamed the city to the infamous cry of "bring out your dead!", collecting corpses for burial.

5) Local councils paid for lots of cats and dogs to be killed, because they thought they carried the plague.

Comment and Analysis

The responses to the plague came from local councils — they did more to try to combat the Great Plague than they had done for the Black Death 300 years previously. But there were no national government attempts at prevention.

The plague gradually began to disappear. Many people think the Great Fire of London in 1666 helped wipe it out, by effectively sterilising large parts of London — it burned down the old, crowded houses, killing the plague bacteria.

Responses to the Plague and to the Black Death were similar

Split your page in two. On one side, list all of the ways the Great Plague was similar to the Black Death (see p.10). On the other side, list the ways in which it was different.

Worked Exam-Style Question

This sample answer will give you an idea of how to compare two historical periods. It's worth spending time thinking about how the answer has been structured — the comments will help you with this.

Q1 Explain the similarities between surgery at the time of Ambroise Paré and surgery in the period 1700-1900. [8 marks]

One similarity was the <u>impact of war on surgical methods</u> in both periods. In the 1500s, when Paré was working, surgeons had to react to the injuries caused by new military technology like cannons. The demands of war led to the development of new surgical methods, such as <u>Paré's ligatures, which he used to tie the ends of severed blood vessels during amputations</u>. Equally, in the 1700s John Hunter invented a new approach to treating gunshot wounds. <u>Like Paré, Hunter's new technique was inspired by his work as an army surgeon</u>, highlighting the importance of war to the development of surgery in both periods.

This gives more <u>specific</u> information.

This is an important feature of <u>both</u> periods.

Comparing the two periods in <u>every point you make</u> shows your answer is <u>focused</u> on the question.

<u>Another similarity</u> is that new surgical ideas could take a long time to make an impact. Even though Paré published his work, many doctors refused to take his innovations seriously — it was only once he became the French king's surgeon that his ideas gained recognition. <u>Similarly</u>, in the period 1700-1900, surgeons were slow to adopt anaesthetics. As early as 1799, Humphry Davy identified nitrous oxide as a possible anaesthetic, but his findings were ignored. Anaesthetics only began to be widely used in surgery over fifty years later, after <u>Queen Victoria gave birth to her eighth child using chloroform in 1853</u>.

To get a high mark, you need to give <u>more than one</u> similarity.

Use words like 'similarly' to show that you are <u>comparing</u>.

At the time of Paré, surgeons' lack of understanding about the importance of good hygiene while operating meant that many patients died of infection. Paré's ligatures eased pain but increased the chance of infection. Lack of understanding about hygiene was also a problem for much of the period 1700-1900. Surgeons were still working in dirty clothes and unhygienic conditions in the 1860s — they were reluctant to wash their hands with chloride of lime between operations, as they found it too unpleasant. <u>It was only in the years after the publication of Pasteur's Germ Theory in 1861 that surgeons began to understand the importance of good hygiene</u>. The introduction of Joseph Lister's carbolic spray in the 1860s reduced infection, and hygiene improved even further with the development of aseptic surgical methods from the late 19th century.

Make sure you include plenty of <u>specific, relevant information</u>.

Use <u>wider knowledge</u> of the period to support your argument.

Exam-Style Questions

Q1   Explain how the work of William Harvey (1578-1657) was important for the development of medicine.   [8 marks]

Q2   Explain why ideas about the human body changed significantly in Britain during the Renaissance period (c.1500-c.1700).

You could talk about the printing press and the work of Vesalius in your answer.   [12 marks]

Q3   'Beliefs about medicine were transformed during the Renaissance period (c.1500-c.1700).'

Explain how far you agree with this statement.   [16 marks]

Vaccination

Until the 1700s, people had <u>few</u> effective ways to <u>prevent</u> the spread of <u>disease</u>. <u>Edward Jenner's</u> discovery of the <u>smallpox vaccine</u> was a <u>landmark</u> in the development of <u>preventive medicine</u>.

Before Jenner the only way to prevent **Smallpox** was **Inoculation**

1) In the 1700s, <u>smallpox</u> was one of the most <u>deadly</u> diseases — in 1751, over 3500 people died of smallpox in London alone.

2) At the time, the only way to prevent smallpox was through <u>inoculation</u>. This was introduced into Britain from Turkey by Lady Mary Wortley Montagu in 1718.

3) Inoculation involved making a <u>cut</u> in a patient's arm and soaking it in pus taken from the swelling of somebody who already had a <u>mild form</u> of smallpox.

> Inoculation was successful in preventing the disease, but it meant patients had to <u>experience smallpox</u> before they could become immune — some <u>died</u> as a result.

Jenner discovered a link between **Smallpox** and **Cowpox**

1) <u>Edward Jenner</u> (born in 1749) was a country doctor in <u>Gloucestershire</u>. He heard that <u>milkmaids</u> didn't get smallpox, but they did catch the much milder <u>cowpox</u>.

2) Using careful <u>scientific methods</u> Jenner investigated and discovered that it was true that people who had had <u>cowpox</u> didn't get <u>smallpox</u>.

3) In 1796, Jenner <u>tested</u> his theory. He injected a small boy, <u>James Phipps</u>, with pus from the sores of <u>Sarah Nelmes</u>, a milkmaid with cowpox. Jenner then infected him with smallpox. James <u>didn't catch</u> the disease.

4) Jenner <u>published</u> his findings in <u>1798</u>. He coined the term <u>vaccination</u> using the Latin word for cow, <u>vacca</u>.

> **Comment and Analysis**
>
> Jenner was important because he used an <u>experiment</u> to test his theory. Although experiments had been used during the Renaissance, it was still <u>unusual</u> for doctors to <u>test</u> their theories.

Jenner's vaccination was **Successful** despite **Opposition**

1) Some people <u>resisted</u> vaccination. Some <u>doctors</u> who gave the older type of inoculation saw it as a <u>threat</u> to their livelihood, and many people were <u>worried</u> about giving themselves a disease from <u>cows</u>.

2) But Jenner's discovery soon got the approval of <u>Parliament</u>, which gave Jenner <u>£10,000</u> in 1802 to open a vaccination clinic. It gave Jenner a further <u>£20,000</u> a few years later.

3) In 1840 vaccination against smallpox was made <u>free</u> for infants. In 1853, it was made <u>compulsory</u> for infants.

4) The vaccine was a <u>success</u> — it contributed to a big fall in the number of smallpox cases in Britain.

> **Comment and Analysis**
>
> The government's attempts to get people vaccinated against smallpox were <u>surprising</u> given attitudes at the time. People believed in a <u>laissez-faire</u> style of government — they thought that government <u>shouldn't get involved</u> in people's lives. The vaccination policy <u>went against</u> this general attitude.

A cartoon from 1802 by James Gillray, with cows bursting out of vaccinated patients' sores. Vaccination was met with a lot of <u>opposition</u> — some groups in Britain published pamphlets against vaccination.

> Jenner didn't know why his vaccine worked. This <u>lack of understanding</u> meant Jenner <u>couldn't</u> develop any other vaccines. This was only possible after the Germ Theory was published (see p.21), when <u>Pasteur</u> and others worked to discover vaccines against other diseases, like chicken cholera and anthrax.

Jenner couldn't replicate his methods to develop other vaccines

Split your page in half. On one half, write a list of facts about Jenner's discovery of the smallpox vaccine. On the other half, write a short paragraph explaining why some people opposed it.

The Germ Theory

Although people's understanding of <u>anatomy</u> had improved greatly during the Renaissance, there was still plenty to learn. The <u>causes of disease</u> was an area that still needed proper explanation.

Pasteur was the first to suggest that Germs cause disease

Germs and other <u>micro-organisms</u> were discovered as early as the 17th century. Scientists thought that these microbes were <u>created</u> by <u>decaying matter</u>, like rotting food or human waste — this theory was known as <u>spontaneous generation</u>. It led people to believe that <u>disease caused germs</u>.

1) The French chemist <u>Louis Pasteur</u> was employed in <u>1857</u> to find the explanation for the <u>souring</u> of sugar beet used in fermenting industrial <u>alcohol</u>. His answer was to blame <u>germs</u>.

2) Pasteur proved there were germs in the air — he showed that sterilised water in a closed flask <u>stayed sterile</u>, while sterilised water in an open flask <u>bred germs</u>.

> Pasteur's discovery was partly due to Antonie <u>van Leeuwenhoek's</u> invention of the <u>microscope</u> in the 17th century. <u>More advanced microscopes</u> were developed during the 1800s. They allowed scientists to see much <u>clearer images</u> with a lot <u>less light distortion</u>.

3) In <u>1861</u>, Pasteur published his <u>Germ Theory</u>. In it he argued that <u>microbes</u> in the air <u>caused decay</u>, not the other way round. He also suggested that some <u>germs caused disease</u>.

4) In 1867, Pasteur published evidence <u>proving</u> there was a link between germs and disease, demonstrating that germs caused a disease in <u>silkworms</u>.

The Germ Theory was met with scepticism at first...

People <u>couldn't believe</u> tiny microbes caused disease. It didn't help that the germ responsible for each disease had to be identified <u>individually</u>, as this meant it was <u>several years</u> before the theory became useful.

...but it eventually gained popularity in Britain

- The theory helped inspire <u>Joseph Lister</u> to develop <u>antiseptics</u> (see p.26).
- The theory confirmed <u>John Snow's</u> findings about <u>cholera</u> (see p.28).
- The theory linked disease to poor living conditions (like contaminated water). This put pressure on the government to pass the <u>1875 Public Health Act</u> (see p.29).

Robert Koch used dyes to identify microbes

1) The German scientist <u>Robert Koch</u> built on Pasteur's work by linking specific diseases to the particular <u>microbe</u> that caused them. This technique was called '<u>microbe hunting</u>'.

2) Koch identified <u>anthrax</u> bacteria (<u>1876</u>) and the bacteria that cause <u>septicaemia</u> (<u>1878</u>), <u>tuberculosis</u> (<u>1882</u>) and <u>cholera</u> (<u>1883</u>).

3) Koch used revolutionary <u>scientific methods</u>:

- He used <u>agar jelly</u> to create solid <u>cultures</u>, allowing him to breed lots of bacteria.
- He used <u>dyes</u> to <u>stain</u> the bacteria so they were more visible under the microscope.
- He employed the newly-invented <u>photography</u> to record his findings.

4) Koch's techniques were important as they allowed other <u>microbe hunters</u> to find the specific bacteria which cause other diseases (see p.22).

The Germ Theory was a tremendous breakthrough

Split your page into three sections, with the headings: individuals, technology and changing attitudes. Under each heading, list the ways in which that factor contributed to the Germ Theory.

The Fight against Germs

Pasteur and Koch <u>weren't friends</u> — in 1871 Germany beat France in the <u>Franco-Prussian War</u>, so there was a great <u>national</u> and <u>personal rivalry</u> between the two scientists. This <u>competition</u> fuelled their next discoveries.

Pasteur developed **Vaccines** for **Anthrax** and **Rabies**

1) In <u>1877</u>, hearing of <u>Koch's</u> discovery of the anthrax bacteria (see p.21), <u>Pasteur</u> started to compete in the race to find and combat <u>new microbes</u>.

2) Pasteur's assistant, <u>Charles Chamberland</u>, injected some chickens with a cholera culture that had been <u>weakened</u> by being accidentally left out on the desk while he was on holiday. The chickens <u>survived</u>. The team tried again with some <u>newly cultured</u> cholera, but the chickens still survived.

3) They worked out that the weakened (<u>attenuated</u>) cholera had made the chickens <u>immune</u>. Chamberland's error had produced a <u>chance</u> discovery.

4) The team produced an <u>attenuated</u> version of the <u>anthrax</u> bacteria to make <u>sheep</u> immune. They showed this in a public experiment in <u>1881</u>. They used a similar method to find a vaccine for <u>rabies</u>.

Koch's Methods helped other **Microbe Hunters**

Other scientists used Koch's methods (see p.21) to find and combat the <u>bacteria</u> that caused other diseases.

1) The <u>diphtheria</u> germ was discovered by <u>Edwin Klebs</u> in 1883.

2) <u>Friedrich Loeffler</u> cultured the diphtheria germ and thought that its effect on people was due to a <u>toxin</u> (poison) it produced. <u>Emile Roux</u> proved Loeffler right.

3) In 1891, <u>Emil von Behring</u> produced an <u>antitoxin</u> (a substance that cancels out the toxins produced by germs) from the blood of animals that had just recovered from diphtheria. This could be used to <u>reduce</u> the effect of the disease.

4) <u>Ronald Ross</u> received the Nobel Prize in 1902 for his discovery of how <u>malaria</u> is transmitted. Ross' Nobel Prize was disputed by <u>Giovanni Battista Grassi</u>, who also discovered how malaria is transmitted. However, <u>Koch</u> supported Ross' claim and so he retained the prize.

Paul Ehrlich discovered the first **Magic Bullet** — **Salvarsan 606**

<u>Antibodies</u> were identified as a <u>natural defence mechanism</u> of the body against <u>germs</u>. It was known that antibodies only attacked <u>specific microbes</u> — so they were nicknamed <u>magic bullets</u>. In 1889, <u>Paul Ehrlich</u> set out to find <u>chemicals</u> that could act as <u>synthetic antibodies</u>.

1) First, Ehrlich discovered <u>dyes</u> that could kill the <u>malaria</u> and <u>sleeping sickness</u> germs.

2) In 1905, the bacteria that causes the sexually transmitted disease <u>syphilis</u> was identified.

3) Ehrlich and his team decided to search for an <u>arsenic compound</u> that was a <u>magic bullet</u> for syphilis. They hoped it would target the bacteria <u>without</u> poisoning the rest of the body. Over <u>600</u> compounds were tried, but none seemed to work.

4) In 1909, <u>Sahachiro Hata</u> joined the team. He rechecked the results and saw that compound <u>number 606</u> actually appeared to work. It was first used on a human in 1911 under the trade name <u>Salvarsan 606</u>.

After Ehrlich and Hata's discovery, more <u>magic bullets</u> were discovered. The second magic bullet, <u>prontosil</u>, was discovered by <u>Gerhard Domagk</u> in 1932. Prontosil was used to combat <u>streptococcus</u>, a type of bacteria that can cause blood poisoning.

After the Germ Theory, there were huge improvements in medicine

If you're asked to explain why discoveries like these are important, think about how they are linked to improvements in medicine. This will help you to explain their impact on the development of medicine.

Surgery and Hospitals

Over time, surgeons became <u>more important</u> and developed their approach to surgery. From the 18th century, hospitals also focused more on <u>treating</u> patients (rather than just <u>caring</u> for them) as well as <u>teaching</u>.

Surgeons became more Important

In the Middle Ages, surgeons <u>weren't respected</u> compared to doctors (see p.8). In the 1700s and 1800s, surgeons began to gain the same status as doctors. In 1800, the <u>London College of Surgeons</u> (later the Royal College of Surgeons) was created, which <u>set training standards</u> for surgeons for the first time.

John Hunter was a well-known Surgeon and Scientist

1) Hunter (1728-93) joined his brother William, a doctor, at his <u>anatomy school</u> in London where they <u>dissected human corpses</u>. Over 12 years, Hunter developed an <u>unrivalled knowledge</u> of the human body.

2) Hunter became an <u>army surgeon</u> and a popular <u>teacher</u>. He made several important <u>medical discoveries</u>. He learned more about <u>venereal disease</u> (sexually transmitted infection), a major cause of illness at the time, and introduced a new approach to the treatment of <u>gunshot wounds</u>.

3) In <u>1785</u>, Hunter introduced a <u>new</u> way to treat an <u>aneurysm</u> (a bulge in a blood vessel) in a man's thigh. He <u>tied off</u> the blood vessel to encourage blood to flow through <u>other vessels</u> in the leg, stopping it from having to be <u>amputated</u>.

4) Hunter encouraged <u>better approaches</u> to surgery. This included <u>good scientific habits</u> like <u>learning</u> about the <u>body</u> to understand illness, <u>experimenting</u> to find better ways to treat disease, and <u>testing</u> treatments (e.g. on <u>animals</u>) before using them on people.

Hunter's <u>pupils</u> included doctors like <u>Edward Jenner</u> (see p.20), so his methods and ideas were <u>passed on</u>. This improved the way people conducted <u>scientific research</u>.

Hospitals focused more on Treatment and Learning

1) From the early 18th century, several <u>charity hospitals</u> opened, including The London Hospital and Guy's Hospital. They were funded by the <u>rich</u>, and offered <u>largely free</u> treatment to the poor. Some <u>specialised</u> in treating certain illnesses, or provided somewhere for mothers to <u>give birth</u>.

2) Only those who were likely to <u>recover quickly</u> were admitted. This was because of a <u>lack of space</u> and the risk of illnesses <u>spreading</u>. The '<u>deserving</u>' poor (those who led hardworking, respectable lives) had more chance of being admitted.

3) <u>Dispensaries</u> provided <u>free non-residential care</u> to poor people. <u>Medicines</u> and <u>non-surgical</u> services from people like <u>dentists</u> and <u>midwives</u> were given without charge.

4) Most poor people were treated in <u>workhouses</u> — large buildings that people went to if they couldn't look after themselves (e.g. because of unemployment, illness or old age). <u>Conditions</u> were <u>poor</u>, but from the 1850s a partially successful movement began to <u>improve conditions</u> in <u>workhouse infirmaries</u>.

5) In the 19th century, some hospitals were founded alongside <u>universities</u> or <u>medical schools</u>, including Charing Cross Hospital, University College Hospital and King's College Hospital. These hospitals were used as <u>training schools</u> for doctors, and for conducting <u>scientific research</u>.

6) <u>Cottage hospitals</u>, run by <u>GPs</u>, opened from the 1860s. They provided care for people in <u>rural</u> areas.

Comment and Analysis

Before the 18th century, many hospitals focused only on <u>caring</u> for people. In the 18th and 19th centuries, <u>treating</u> diseases became more important.

Surgery and hospitals continued to improve

Make some notes comparing surgery between 1700 and 1900 with surgery in medieval times. Keep adding to your notes as you read on — things advanced quite a lot in the 20th century.

Developments in Nursing

Before the 1800s, hospitals were often <u>dirty</u> places that people associated with <u>death</u> and <u>infection</u>. <u>Florence Nightingale</u> helped change that — by improving <u>hospital hygiene</u> and raising <u>nursing standards</u>.

Florence Nightingale improved army hospitals

1) <u>Florence Nightingale</u> (1820-1910) brought a new <u>discipline</u> and <u>professionalism</u> to a job that had a very <u>bad reputation</u> at the time. Despite <u>opposition</u> from her family, she studied to become a nurse in <u>1849</u>.

2) When the <u>Crimean War</u> broke out in 1853-54, <u>horror stories</u> emerged about the <u>Barrack Hospital</u> in <u>Scutari</u>, where the British wounded were treated.

3) <u>Sidney Herbert</u>, who was both the <u>Secretary of War</u> and a friend of her family, asked for Nightingale to go to Scutari and sort out the hospital's <u>nursing care</u>.

4) The military <u>opposed</u> women nurses, as they were considered a distraction and inferior to male nurses. Nightingale went anyway, with <u>38 hand-picked nurses</u>.

5) Using methods she had learned from her training in Europe, Nightingale made sure that all the wards were <u>clean</u> and <u>hygienic</u>, that water supplies were adequate and that patients were fed properly.

6) Nightingale improved the hospital a lot. Before she arrived, the <u>death rate</u> in the hospital stood at <u>42%</u>. Two years later it had fallen to just <u>2%</u>.

Mary Seacole (1805-1881) also Nursed in the Crimea

- Mary Seacole learnt nursing from her mother, who ran a boarding house for soldiers in <u>Jamaica</u>.

- In 1854, Seacole came to England to <u>volunteer</u> as a nurse in the Crimean War. She was rejected (possibly on <u>racist</u> grounds) but went anyway, paying for her <u>own</u> passage.

- Financing herself by <u>selling goods</u> to the soldiers and travellers, she nursed soldiers on the <u>battlefields</u> and built the <u>British Hotel</u> — a small group of makeshift buildings that served as a hospital, shop and canteen for the soldiers.

- Seacole couldn't find work as a <u>nurse</u> in England after the war and went <u>bankrupt</u> — though she did receive support due to the press interest in her story.

Nightingale used her fame to Change Nursing

1) In 1859, Nightingale published a book, '<u>Notes on Nursing</u>'. This explained her methods — it emphasised the need for hygiene and a professional attitude. It was the standard <u>textbook</u> for generations of nurses.

2) The public raised £44,000 to help her <u>train nurses</u>, and she set up the <u>Nightingale School of Nursing</u> in <u>St. Thomas' Hospital</u>, London. Nurses were given three years of training before they could qualify. Discipline and attention to detail were important.

3) By <u>1900</u> there were <u>64,000</u> trained nurses in Britain from colleges across the country.

4) In <u>1919</u> (after Nightingale's death) the <u>Nurses Registration Act</u> was passed. This made training <u>compulsory</u> for all nurses.

> As well as improving hospital care, Florence Nightingale is credited with helping turn nursing into a <u>respectable profession</u>, particularly for <u>women</u>. This was formalised in 1916, when <u>The Royal College of Nursing</u> was founded. It began to admit <u>men</u> in 1960.

> The 1800s also saw a massive increase in <u>hospital building</u>. Hospitals became <u>cleaner</u> and <u>more specialist</u>, catering for rich patients as well as the poor.

Comment and Analysis

The Germ Theory wasn't published until 1861, so initially Florence Nightingale <u>didn't know</u> what the cause of disease was — she believed in the <u>miasma theory</u>. But her teachings suggested that good <u>hygiene</u> could prevent the spread of disease.

Nightingale became a champion for better hospitals and nursing

REVISION TASK Make a list of all of Florence Nightingale's achievements. At the end of your list, write a sentence explaining what you think her most important achievement was.

Anaesthetics

Improving the hygiene and sanitation of hospitals helped to prevent many unnecessary deaths. But the two problems of pain and infection were yet to be solved. The answer to the first of those was anaesthetics.

Anaesthetics solved the problem of Pain

Pain was a problem for surgeons, especially because their patients could die from the trauma of extreme pain. Natural drugs like alcohol, opium and mandrake had long been used, but effective anaesthetics that didn't make the patient very ill were more difficult to produce.

- Nitrous oxide (laughing gas) was identified as a possible anaesthetic by British chemist Humphry Davy in 1799 — but he was ignored by surgeons at the time.
- The gas had been dismissed as a fairground novelty before American dentist Horace Wells suggested its use in his area of work. He did a public demonstration in 1845, but had the bad luck to pick a patient unaffected by nitrous oxide — it was again ignored.

- In 1842, American doctor Crawford Long discovered the anaesthetic qualities of ether, but didn't publish his work. The first public demonstration of ether as an anaesthetic was carried out in 1846 by American dental surgeon William Morton.
- Ether is an irritant and is also fairly explosive, so using it in this way was risky.

- James Simpson was a Professor of Midwifery at Edinburgh University. Looking for a safe alternative to ether that women could take during childbirth, he began to experiment on himself. In 1847, he discovered the effects of chloroform.
- After Queen Victoria gave birth to her eighth child while using chloroform in 1853, it became widely used in operating theatres and to reduce pain during childbirth.
- Chloroform sometimes affected the heart, causing patients to die suddenly.

1) General anaesthesia (complete unconsciousness) is risky, so local anaesthesia (numbing of the part being treated) is better for many operations.
2) In 1884, William Halsted investigated the use of cocaine as a local anaesthetic. His self-experimentation led to a severe cocaine addiction.

Early Anaesthetics actually led to a Rise in death rates

1) Anaesthetics led to longer and more complex operations. This was because surgeons found that unconscious patients were easier to operate on, meaning they could take longer over their work.
2) Longer operating times led to higher death rates from infection, because surgeons didn't know that poor hygiene spread disease. Surgeons used very unhygienic methods.

- Surgeons didn't know that having clean clothes could save lives. Often they wore the same coats for years, which were covered in dried blood and pus from previous operations.
- Operations were often carried out in unhygienic conditions, including at the patient's house.
- Operating instruments also caused infections because they were usually unwashed and dirty.

Comment and Analysis

Anaesthetics helped solve the problem of pain, but patients were still dying from infection. This meant the attempts at more complicated surgery actually led to increased death rates amongst patients. The period between 1846 and 1870 is sometimes known as the 'Black Period' of surgery for this reason.

The impact of anaesthetics wasn't completely positive

In the exam, remember to be specific about the information you use. For example, rather than writing about anaesthetics in general terms, try to use specific types to explain your answer.

Antiseptics

Anaesthetics had solved the problem of <u>pain</u>, but surgeons were still faced with a high death rate from operations due to the amount of <u>infection</u>. <u>Antiseptics</u> and later <u>asepsis</u> helped prevent this by killing germs.

Antisepsis and Asepsis reduce infection

There are two main approaches to <u>reducing infection</u> during an operation:

- **Antiseptic** methods are used to <u>kill germs</u> that get near surgical wounds.
- **Aseptic** surgical methods aim to <u>stop any germs</u> getting near the wound.

Joseph Lister pioneered the use of Antiseptics

1) <u>Ignaz Semmelweis</u> showed that doctors could reduce the spread of infection by washing their hands with <u>chloride of lime</u> solution between patients. However, it was very <u>unpleasant</u>, so wasn't widely used.

2) <u>Joseph Lister</u> had seen <u>carbolic acid</u> sprays used in <u>sewage works</u> to keep down the smell. He tried this in the operating theatre in the early 1860s and saw reduced infection rates.

3) Lister heard about the <u>Germ Theory</u> in 1865 — he realised that germs could be in the air, on surgical instruments and on people's hands. He started using carbolic acid on <u>instruments</u> and <u>bandages</u>.

4) The use of <u>antiseptics</u> immediately <u>reduced death rates</u> from as high as 50% in 1864-66 to around 15% in 1867-70.

5) Antiseptics allowed surgeons to operate with less fear of patients dying from infection. The <u>number of operations</u> increased tenfold between 1867 and 1912 as a result.

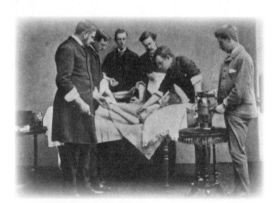

A photograph of a surgical operation taken in the late 1800s. You can see Lister's carbolic spray on the table on the right. The operating theatre isn't aseptic though — the surgeons aren't wearing sterile gowns or surgical gloves.

Comment and Analysis

Antiseptics (and later asepsis) solved the problem of <u>infection</u>. This, combined with the use of <u>anaesthetics</u> (see p.25) to stop pain, improved British surgery — many deaths were prevented as a result of antiseptics and anaesthetics.

Asepsis reduced the need for Nasty Chemicals

Since the late 1800s, surgeons have changed their approach from <u>killing germs</u> to making a <u>germ-free</u> (aseptic) environment.

1) Instruments are carefully <u>sterilised</u> before use, usually with high temperature steam (<u>120 °C</u>).

2) Theatre staff <u>sterilise their hands</u> before entering — and wear sterile gowns, masks, gloves and hats. Surgical <u>gloves</u> were invented by <u>William Halsted</u> in <u>1889</u>.

3) The theatres themselves are kept <u>scrupulously clean</u> and fed with <u>sterile air</u>. Special tents can be placed around the operating table to maintain an area of even stricter hygiene in <u>high risk</u> cases.

4) Aseptic surgery <u>reduced</u> the need for a carbolic spray, which is <u>unpleasant</u> to get on your skin or breathe in — many doctors and nurses didn't like to use it.

REVISION TASK

Anaesthetics and antiseptics prevented surgical deaths

Write a paragraph summarising whether you think anaesthetics (see p.25) or antiseptics were a greater breakthrough for 19th century surgery. Think about how each one helped to improve surgery.

Public Health

The <u>industrial revolution</u> began in the 18th century. Lots of people moved into <u>cities</u> like London to work in factories. The places they lived were <u>cramped</u>, <u>dirty</u> and great for spreading <u>diseases</u> like cholera.

Overcrowding in Towns led to Poor Living Conditions

Houses in Yorkshire in the late 1800s.

1) During the 18th and 19th centuries, lots of people <u>moved</u> from the countryside to <u>towns</u> to work in factories. The towns grew so <u>quickly</u> that good housing couldn't be built fast enough — instead, houses were built as <u>close together</u> as possible, with <u>little outside space</u> and <u>poor ventilation</u>.

2) <u>Overcrowding</u> was a big problem. Workers had little money, so tried to live in the <u>smallest possible space</u> — families with four or more children often lived in a <u>single room</u>. The poorest lived in <u>cellars</u>.

3) People <u>didn't understand</u> the need for clean water or good sewerage systems. Most houses had <u>no bathroom</u> — they instead shared an outside toilet, called a <u>privy</u>.

4) Each privy was built above a <u>cesspit</u>. Cesspit and household waste was collected by <u>nightmen</u>, who threw the waste into rivers or piled it up for the rain to wash away.

5) Water companies set up <u>water pumps</u> in the streets, which were <u>shared</u> between many houses. The pumps' water supply was often <u>contaminated</u> by waste from the cesspits or rivers.

Cholera epidemics Killed Thousands of people

1) <u>Cholera</u> reached Britain in 1831. By 1832 it was an <u>epidemic</u> — over 21,000 people in Britain died of cholera that year.

2) Cholera spreads when <u>infected sewage</u> gets into drinking water. It causes extreme <u>diarrhoea</u> — sufferers often die from <u>loss of water</u> and <u>minerals</u>. Both <u>rich</u> and <u>poor</u> people caught the disease.

> Cholera epidemics <u>recurred</u> in 1848, 1853-54 and 1865-66.

3) At the time, people <u>didn't know</u> what caused cholera — the best theory was <u>miasma</u> (see p.5). The government started regulating the burial of the dead, but this did little to halt the spread of cholera. The 1832 epidemic declined and interest was lost.

Chadwick's Report led to the 1848 Public Health Act

1) In 1842, the social reformer <u>Edwin Chadwick</u> published a report on poverty and health. The report showed that <u>living conditions</u> in <u>towns</u> were <u>worse</u> for people's health than conditions in the <u>countryside</u>.

2) Chadwick's report <u>suggested</u> that the government should <u>pass laws</u> for proper <u>drainage</u> and <u>sewerage</u> systems, funded by <u>local taxes</u>.

3) Chadwick's report and another <u>cholera epidemic</u> in <u>1848</u> (which killed 53,000 people) put <u>pressure</u> on Parliament to pass a <u>Public Health Act</u>.

4) The 1848 Act set up a central <u>Board of Health</u> (which included Chadwick as a member) and allowed any <u>town</u> to set up its own <u>local board of health</u> as long as the town's <u>taxpayers</u> agreed.

Comment and Analysis

The impact of the 1848 Act was <u>limited</u> — towns <u>could</u> set up health boards but <u>very few chose to</u>, and those that did often <u>refused</u> to spend any money to improve conditions. Chadwick <u>annoyed</u> a lot of people, and was forced to retire in 1854. The central Board of Health was <u>dismantled</u> in 1858.

EXAM TIP

Overcrowded towns helped to spread cholera

To gain some of the higher marks, you might need to incorporate wider knowledge of particular periods. For example, you should know the impact of the industrial revolution on people's health.

Health and Medicine in Britain, c.1000-present

Public Health

Despite the work of Chadwick (see p.27) and John Snow, cholera returned to Britain in 1865. However, the eventual acceptance of Snow's findings and the 'Great Stink' of 1858 did prompt key changes in public health.

Snow linked Cholera to Contaminated Water

John Snow was a London doctor who showed that there was a connection between contaminated water and cholera. For a long time he had suspected that the disease was waterborne, but had very little proof.

1) When cholera broke out in the Broad Street area of London in 1854, Snow set out to test his theory. He interviewed people living in Broad Street and made a map of the area showing where cases of the disease had been.

2) Snow's investigations showed that all victims used the same water pump on Broad Street. He convinced the local council to remove the handle from the pump. This brought the cholera outbreak to an end.

> Snow published his findings in 1855, in a report entitled 'On the Mode of Communication of Cholera'.

3) It was later discovered that a nearby cesspit had a split lining — its waste had leaked into the pump's water supply.

Comment and Analysis

Snow's findings took a while to make an impact — it was not until the Germ Theory (see p.21) was published that his theory became widely accepted. But eventually Snow's findings helped lead to a change in attitudes — people realised that waterborne diseases like cholera needed a government response in order to clean up the streets and waterways. This contributed to the 1875 Public Health Act (see p.29). Like Jenner (see p.20), Snow was also important for using observation and evidence to support his theory.

The 'Great Stink' struck London in 1858

1) Industrial cities had poor sewerage systems (see p.27). In London, the introduction of flush toilets made this problem worse — they increased the volume of waste entering cesspits. A lot of the waste overflowed and drained into the Thames.

2) In the summer of 1858, hot weather caused the river's water level to drop and bacteria to grow in the waste. This produced a smell that was so bad it affected large parts of London and stopped Parliament from meeting.

3) The situation pushed the authorities in London to agree to build a new, expensive sewer system.

Bazalgette Cleaned up London with New Sewers

- The government knew that the sewerage system needed improving, but the 'Great Stink' persuaded them to act sooner than planned.
- Joseph Bazalgette was the chief engineer of the Metropolitan Board of Works, which was responsible for public works in London.
- To reduce the stink, Bazalgette was appointed in 1859 to build a new London sewer system. The sewers transported waste that was normally dumped into the Thames away from heavily populated areas to the Thames Estuary. About 1300 miles of sewers were built.
- The sewer system was officially opened in 1865.

Comment and Analysis

When Bazalgette started work on his sewers, people still didn't understand how diseases like cholera spread. They were trying to get rid of the bad smells coming from the Thames. The fact they stopped cholera by cleaning the drinking water was unintended.

Unfortunately, Snow's work was ignored for a long time

Go back through this section and write down the name of every key individual. Next to their name, write down what they did, when they did it and why it was important to health and medicine.

Public Health

Mounting evidence of the need to <u>clean up towns</u> and a breakdown in <u>laissez-faire beliefs</u> caused the government to <u>take action</u> on public health. This eventually resulted in another <u>Public Health Act</u> being passed in <u>1875</u>.

Public Opinion began to Change

For most of the 19th century, people believed in a <u>laissez-faire</u> style of government — they thought the government <u>shouldn't intervene</u> in public health. But then things began to <u>change</u>.

- Evidence from Chadwick and Snow (see p.27-28), and Pasteur's <u>Germ Theory</u> (see p.21), showed that cleaning towns could <u>stop</u> the spread of disease.
- In 1867, the <u>Second Reform Act</u> was passed giving nearly <u>1 million more men</u> the vote, most of whom were industrial <u>workers</u>.
- Several <u>reformers</u> helped <u>change attitudes</u> towards health. <u>William Farr</u> was a statistician who recorded <u>causes of death</u>. He used his statistics to press for reforms in areas where death rates were <u>high</u>.

> Now they had the vote, <u>workers</u> could put <u>pressure</u> on the government to listen to concerns about health. For the first time, politicians had to address <u>workers' concerns</u> in order to <u>stay in power</u>.

The 1875 Act improved Public Health

In the 1870s the <u>government</u> finally took action to improve public health.

1) In 1871-72, the government followed the Royal Sanitary Commission's proposal to form the <u>Local Government Board</u> and divide Britain into '<u>sanitary areas</u>' administered by officers for public health.

2) In 1875, <u>Benjamin Disraeli's</u> government passed another <u>Public Health Act</u>. It forced councils to appoint <u>health inspectors</u> and <u>sanitary inspectors</u> to make sure that laws on things like <u>water supplies</u> and <u>hygiene</u> were followed. It also made councils maintain <u>sewerage systems</u> and keep their towns' <u>streets clean</u>.

3) The 1875 Public Health Act was <u>more effective</u> than the one passed in 1848 because it was <u>compulsory</u>.

Chamberlain Cleared Birmingham's Slums

1) Disraeli also brought in the <u>Artisans' Dwellings Act</u> in 1875.
2) This let local councils <u>buy slums</u> with poor living conditions and <u>rebuild them</u> in a way that fit new government-backed housing standards.
3) However, few councillors used the Act. An exception was <u>Joseph Chamberlain</u>, who became Mayor of <u>Birmingham</u> in 1873.
4) Chamberlain persuaded the city authorities to buy the local <u>gas</u> and <u>water</u> companies to make sure people had <u>good supplies</u> of both.
5) In <u>1875</u>, Chamberlain cleared an area of the city's <u>slums</u> and built a <u>new street</u> in their place. He also <u>improved</u> some of the slum housing.

Comment and Analysis

There were several changes to public health during the industrial revolution, and the <u>1875 Public Health Act</u> was the biggest. The work of the <u>government</u> and <u>individuals</u> like Chadwick, Snow and Farr were key to these changes. <u>Technology</u> (like Bazalgette's sewers), the <u>1867 Reform Act</u> and the <u>cholera epidemics</u> were other factors that prompted improvement.

The 1875 Act involved major government intervention in health

Using information on p.27-29, write a list of the factors which led to the 1875 Public Health Act. For each factor, write a sentence explaining how that factor helped cause the Act.

Worked Exam-Style Question

This sample answer will help you to assess the usefulness of a source. Have a look at the comments to get a good idea of how best to use the source and your own knowledge to write your answer.

Source A — an English cartoon by John Leech, published in 1858. It was published with a caption that said, 'Father Thames Introducing his Offspring to the Fair City of London'. It shows figures representing diphtheria, scrofula and cholera rising from the river.

© The Art Archive / Granger Collection

Q1 Look at Source A. Using the source and your own knowledge, explain how useful Source A would be to a historian studying cholera. [8 marks]

Make sure you <u>directly address</u> the question in each paragraph.

Cholera first reached Britain in 1831 and grew into an epidemic by 1832. <u>Source A is useful because it shows that cholera was still a problem in Britain more than two decades later in 1858</u>. Indeed, the source suggests that London was largely powerless against cholera, as <u>the woman representing the city has her shield down by her side, unable to stop the diseases</u>. This sense of powerlessness may reflect the government's consistent failure to take effective action against cholera, <u>despite repeated epidemics between 1832 and 1858</u>. As a result, Source A is useful because it shows how ineffective the government's response to cholera was in the first few decades after the disease reached Britain.

Use details from the source to <u>back up</u> your points.

Using your <u>own knowledge</u> shows you have a good understanding of the subject.

This <u>refers back</u> to evidence from the source.

Source A is also useful because it shows the fear surrounding cholera in Britain in 1858. <u>The corpse-like figures rising out of the water suggest that cholera symbolised death</u>, and that Londoners were under attack from the disease. This idea may be linked to the high death rate from cholera — <u>an epidemic in 1848 killed 53,000 people</u>. The source therefore gives historians an idea of people's views of cholera at the time.

This answer uses <u>broad knowledge</u> of the period to support each point.

Use your knowledge about the <u>source</u> itself (<u>who</u> created it, <u>when</u> it was created and <u>why</u> it was created) to support your answer.

Source A also offers an insight into how people in 1858 thought cholera spread. The figure of cholera is rising from the river, which is clearly polluted — dead animals have been washed ashore. The link the cartoonist makes between pollution and cholera suggests people's continued belief in the '<u>miasma theory</u>' — the idea that inhaling bad smells caused disease. This suggests that even though John Snow had shown cholera was waterborne in 1854, <u>his ideas were still not widely accepted in 1858, when this cartoon was published</u>. Source A is therefore useful because it shows that John Snow's ideas took time to be accepted and that miasma was still believed to cause diseases like cholera in 1858.

Exam-Style Questions

Chadwick concluded that 'the various forms of epidemic... and other disease caused... chiefly amongst the labouring classes by atmospheric impurities produced by decomposing animal and vegetable substances, by damp and filth, and close and overcrowded dwellings prevail amongst the population in every part of the kingdom...

As to the means by which the present sanitary condition of the labouring classes may be improved:— The primary and most important measures, and at the same time the most practicable... are drainage, the removal of all refuse of habitations, streets, and roads, and the improvement of the supplies of water.'

Source B — an extract from 'An Inquiry into the Sanitary Condition of the Labouring Population of Great Britain,' by Edwin Chadwick, which was presented to Parliament in 1842. Chadwick was secretary of the Poor Law commissioners.

Q1

Look at Source B. Using the source and your own knowledge, explain how useful Source B would be to a historian investigating public health in the 19th century. [8 marks]

Q2

'Pasteur's Germ Theory was an important breakthrough in the improvement of people's health in 19th century Britain.'

Explain how far you agree with this statement. [16 marks]

The Impact of the First World War

The First World War (1914-1918) caused devastation in Europe. But the soldiers' injuries gave surgeons opportunities to find new techniques for diagnosis and for carrying out more complex operations.

The First World War made X-rays more Reliable and Mobile

Wilhelm Röntgen discovered X-rays in 1895. X-rays pass easily through soft flesh, but less well through bone. X-ray images could therefore be produced by directing X-rays at a body part in front of a photographic plate.

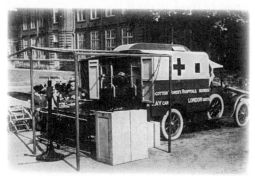

A photograph from 1915, showing a First World War hospital car equipped with mobile X-ray equipment.

1) X-rays were used from the start of the First World War to find broken bones, but the equipment included glass tubes that were unreliable and often stopped working. Also, it was often located in hospitals miles away from the battlefields.

2) The American scientist William Coolidge had invented a more reliable X-ray tube in 1913. The 'Coolidge tube' became widely used by the end of the war, and is still used today.

3) In 1914, the Polish scientist Marie Curie developed mobile X-ray units (ambulances equipped with X-ray machines) which allowed doctors to transport X-ray equipment.

The war also increased the number of radiologists — people who know how to operate X-ray equipment. Curie and French scientist Antoine Béclère set up training schools to teach doctors how to use X-ray equipment.

The problem of Blood Loss was overcome as a result of the war

The idea of blood transfusions was known from the 17th century, but they were rarely successful because the blood of the recipient often clotted. Blood also clotted if it was stored outside the body.

1) In 1900, Karl Landsteiner discovered blood groups. Certain blood groups couldn't be mixed together as the blood would clot, blocking the blood vessels. Landsteiner's discovery meant doctors could perform more successful blood transfusions, as long as the donor's blood group was the same as the patient's.

2) During World War I the seriousness of wounds from gunshots and explosive shells meant that many soldiers died of blood loss. This made being able to store blood very important.

3) In 1914, doctors found that sodium citrate stopped blood clotting so it could be stored. In 1917, this discovery allowed the first ever blood depot to be set up at the Battle of Cambrai.

4) In 1946, the British National Blood Transfusion Service was established.

Patients always suffer some blood loss during surgery. If a lot of blood is lost, this can be fatal. Blood transfusions helped to prevent this cause of death by enabling surgeons to replace any blood lost during surgery.

War sped up the development of Plastic Surgery

1) Doctors in France and Germany had been working on skin graft techniques since before the First World War. Their work helped pave the way for Harold Gillies, who set up a plastic surgery unit for the British Army during the war.

2) Gillies was interested in reconstructing facial injuries so that patients could have a normal appearance. He developed the use of pedicle tubes, and kept detailed records of his achievements.

A pedicle tube is a skin graft technique where skin is partially cut from a healthy part of a patient's body, grown and then attached to the damaged area of the patient to cover any scarring.

3) Gillies' work was continued during the Second World War by his assistant, Archibald McIndoe. A lot of McIndoe's patients were pilots who had been trapped inside burning aircraft.

EXAM TIP — The First World War prompted changes in surgery

In the exam, you could be asked about factors that caused change. One of the most important of these was war, which improved both modern surgery and modern public health (see p.39).

Modern Ideas about the Causes of Disease

The Germ Theory (see p.21) was a major breakthrough in identifying the causes of disease, but identifying bacteria couldn't explain every disease. Viruses, genetics and lifestyle were all found to impact on health.

Viruses were discovered at the turn of the century

Despite their successes with bacteria, Pasteur and Koch (see p.21) were unable to find the cause of some diseases, as they were caused by microbes called viruses which were too small to see under a microscope.

1) In 1892 the Russian microbiologist Dmitry Ivanovsky investigated mosaic, a disease that was killing tobacco plants. He found that the cause was an extremely small microbe that remained in water even after bacteria were removed. In 1898, the Dutch scientist Martinus Beijernick found that these microbes had different properties to bacteria — he labelled these microbes viruses.

2) The discovery of viruses led to their successful treatment. Unlike bacteria, viruses aren't destroyed by antibiotics (see p.35). Instead, doctors can prescribe antiviral drugs, but they only prevent a viral infection from growing — only the body's immune system can destroy a virus for good.

DNA has given an insight into Genetic Conditions

1) Genes are the chemical 'instructions' that plan out human characteristics, like sex and hair colour. They are stored in cells as DNA. Your DNA is a mix of your parents' DNA.

The structure of DNA is a double helix.

2) The structure of DNA, a double helix (a kind of spiral) that can reproduce itself by splitting, was first described in 1953 by Francis Crick and James Watson.

3) Watson and Crick's discovery allowed other scientists to find the genes that cause genetic conditions — diseases that are passed on from one generation to another. These include cystic fibrosis, haemophilia and sickle-cell anaemia.

4) Knowledge of genetic conditions has improved diagnosis and treatment of them. Scientists can now produce a synthetic protein to replicate the work of a faulty gene and treat inherited conditions using techniques like gene therapy.

5) One of the biggest breakthroughs in genetic research was made in 2003 with the completion of the Human Genome Project — this identified all the genes in human DNA.

Lifestyle Factors can increase the Risk of some Diseases

A healthy diet, exercise and other lifestyle factors have long been suggested as ways to prevent illness, but it was only in the 20th century that lifestyle choices were linked to particular health conditions:

1) Smoking has been shown to cause lung cancer (see p.42).
2) Obesity increases the chance of getting heart disease or diabetes.
3) Drinking too much alcohol has been shown to cause liver disease.
4) Overexposure to ultraviolet radiation (e.g. from sunlight) can cause skin cancer.

Comment and Analysis

The advances in science and technology since 1900 have shown that there is not just one cause of disease. In addition to bacteria, we now know that disease can be caused by viral infections, genetic mutations and our lifestyle choices. This makes their treatment and prevention even more complex — with so many different causes, treatment needs to be more targeted to the specific disease.

REVISION TASK

Doctors now have a much better idea of what causes disease

Use this page to make a list of the causes of illness that people didn't know about in 1875, but did know about in 2000. For each one, write the name of a disease it is associated with.

Developments in Diagnosis

New causes of disease demanded new ways of diagnosing them. These new methods were introduced <u>rapidly</u> in the 20th century, due to innovations in <u>science and technology</u>, from computers to X-rays.

Blood Tests allow doctors to Diagnose more illnesses

Blood tests were first introduced to test <u>blood groups</u> before blood transfusions (see p.32). Since then, blood tests have been used to test for a <u>range of diseases</u>.

1) Blood tests can be used to check a patient's <u>cholesterol level</u>. This can help diagnose their chance of suffering a <u>heart attack</u> or <u>stroke</u>.

2) Blood tests can be used to check a patient's <u>DNA</u> (see p.33). This can help diagnose a <u>genetic condition</u>, like haemophilia or cystic fibrosis.

3) Some blood tests can be used to show whether a patient has a certain type of <u>cancer</u>, including ovarian cancer, prostate cancer and breast cancer.

Blood tests make diagnosis more <u>accurate</u>, providing doctors with clearer information of what is wrong. This means they can be more <u>confident</u> when deciding how best to treat their patients.

Symptoms Can Be Monitored More Easily

Devices have been introduced to allow doctors and patients to <u>monitor symptoms</u>.

- <u>Blood pressure</u> monitors were invented and developed in the 1880s and 1890s. They let doctors and patients see whether disease, lifestyle factors or medicines are causing high blood pressure, which can cause damage to the <u>heart</u>.

- <u>Blood sugar</u> monitors were introduced in the mid 20th century. They allow those with <u>diabetes</u> to make sure their blood sugar is at the right level.

An important change in the 20th century is the use of monitoring devices by people in their <u>own homes</u> — this has allowed individuals <u>greater control</u> over their own health.

Doctors can see more of the body with Medical Scans

1) The use of <u>medical scans</u> began in 1895 when Wilhelm Röntgen discovered <u>X-rays</u>. X-ray images improved with the invention of the 'Coolidge tube' in 1913 (see p.32).

An X-ray image of a hand from 1904. Early medical scans used <u>dyes</u> so that blood vessels and organs showed up on the X-ray images. These were <u>swallowed</u> or <u>injected</u> into the patient.

2) Advances in <u>computers</u> allowed doctors to use <u>ultrasound</u> scanning — this uses high frequency <u>sound waves</u>, which bounce off the patient's organs and other tissues to create an image of them on the computer.

3) Computed Tomography (<u>CT</u> or CAT) scans were invented in 1972 by Godfrey Hounsfield. They use X-rays and a <u>computer</u> to make detailed images of parts of the patient's body.

4) Magnetic Resonance Imaging (<u>MRI</u>) scans were initially invented in 1970s but became widely used in the 1980s. These use extremely powerful <u>radio waves</u> and magnetic fields to construct images.

Comment and Analysis

Improvements in <u>technology</u>, like medical scans, have given doctors a much more <u>detailed</u> picture of what's going on inside their patient's body. This has enabled them to <u>intervene</u> much <u>earlier</u>, before the disease has become too advanced. <u>Early treatment</u> is generally more <u>effective</u> and has a higher chance of <u>success</u>.

EXAM TIP Blood tests and medical scans improved modern methods of diagnosis
In the exam, you only have a limited amount of time to answer each question. If you're spending too long on one question, write a conclusion then move on to the next question.

Penicillin

In the 1800s, Pasteur discovered that <u>bacteria</u> cause disease. But it wasn't until the 1900s that doctors were able to <u>treat</u> bacterial diseases. This was partly due to the discovery of <u>penicillin</u>, the first <u>antibiotic</u>.

Fleming discovered Penicillin — the first Antibiotic

1) <u>Alexander Fleming</u> saw many soldiers die of septic wounds caused by <u>staphylococcal</u> bacteria when he was working in an army hospital during the <u>First World War</u>.

2) Searching for a cure, he identified the <u>antiseptic</u> substance in tears, <u>lysozyme</u>, in 1922 — but this only worked on <u>some</u> germs.

3) One day in 1928, he came to clean up some old <u>culture dishes</u> on which he had been growing <u>staphylococci</u> for his experiments. By chance, a <u>fungal spore</u> had landed and grown on one of the dishes.

4) What caught Fleming's eye was that the <u>colonies</u> of staphylococci around the <u>mould</u> had stopped growing. The <u>fungus</u> was identified as <u>Penicillium notatum</u>. It produced a substance that <u>killed</u> bacteria. This substance was given the name <u>penicillin</u>.

5) Fleming <u>published</u> his findings between 1929 and 1931. However, <u>nobody</u> would <u>fund</u> further research, so he <u>couldn't</u> take his work further. The industrial production of penicillin still needed to be developed.

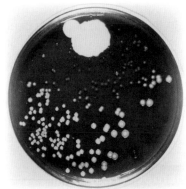

The original plate on which Fleming first observed the growth of Penicillium notatum.

Florey and Chain found a way to Purify Penicillin

1) Since it is a natural product, penicillin needs to be <u>purified</u>. A breakthrough was made by <u>Howard Florey's</u> team in Oxford between 1938 and 1940. <u>Ernst Chain</u>, a member of the team, devised the <u>freeze-drying</u> technique which was an important part of the purification process.

2) At first, Florey and Chain <u>didn't</u> have the <u>resources</u> to produce penicillin in large amounts. They made penicillin for their first <u>clinical trial</u> by growing <u>Penicillium notatum</u> in every container they could find in their lab. Their patient began to recover, only to die when the penicillin <u>ran out</u>.

Florey took penicillin to America for Mass Production

Florey knew that <u>penicillin</u> could be vital in treating the <u>wounds</u> of soldiers fighting in World War II. British <u>chemical firms</u> were too busy making <u>explosives</u> to start mass production — so he went to <u>America</u>.

1) US firms were also not keen to help — until America <u>joined the war</u> in 1941. In December 1941, the US government began to give <u>grants</u> to businesses that <u>manufactured</u> penicillin.

2) By 1943, British businesses had also started <u>mass-producing</u> penicillin. Mass production was sufficient for the needs of the <u>military medics</u> by 1944.

3) After the war, the <u>cost</u> of penicillin fell, making it more accessible for <u>general use</u>. Fleming, Florey and Chain were awarded the <u>Nobel Prize</u> in 1945.

4) Today, penicillin is used to treat a <u>range</u> of <u>bacterial</u> infections. Other <u>antibiotics</u> were discovered after 1945, including treatments for lung infections, acne and bacterial meningitis.

Fleming discovered penicillin, but Florey and Chain purified it

A key event may have several causes. While individuals (like Florey, Chain and Fleming) were key in the discovery of penicillin, it was large institutions like governments that funded its mass production.

Modern Treatments

Penicillin became one of the first mass-produced drugs, helping to build the modern pharmaceutical industry. However, the overuse of antibiotics like penicillin has led to the emergence of antibiotic resistance.

The **Pharmaceutical Industry** has really taken off

For new treatments like magic bullets (see p.22) and antibiotics (like penicillin — see p.35) to make an impact, they needed to be made available to lots of people. This meant they had to be manufactured on a large scale.

1) In the late 19th and 20th centuries, the booming chemical industries in Britain, Germany, Switzerland and the United States were best placed to mass-produce these new drugs and medicines.

2) The success of their mass-produced drugs in the 1940s (particularly penicillin) helped the modern pharmaceutical industry take off.

3) Pharmaceutical companies have played an important role in researching and developing new medicines. They also mass produce these drugs to sell worldwide. These companies have been important in helping to cure new diseases and researching new forms of treatment.

Chemotherapy

Chemotherapy is the treatment of cancer using drugs. It began to be developed during World War II when doctors found that nitrogen mustard (a chemical in mustard gas) could be used to reduce cancer tumours. Other drugs were later discovered, including a compound in folic acid that blocks the growth of cancer cells. Pharmaceutical companies have been producing cancer drugs since the 1960s.

Antibiotic Resistance makes drugs **Less Effective**

1) Antibiotic resistance is when a type of bacteria adapts so it isn't affected by antibiotics anymore. This resistance develops when doctors and patients overuse antibiotics — the more antibiotics are used, the more likely it is that bacteria will become resistant to them.

2) Antibiotic resistance stops antibiotics from working properly, making it more difficult to treat some diseases. This has increased the levels of disease and the time taken for patients to recover.

Some people use **Alternative Treatments**

1) Mistrust of modern medicine and technology means some people use alternative therapies instead.

- **Acupuncture** is the method of putting needles in specific points of the patient's skin to relieve pain.
- **Homeopathy** is treatment using extremely weak solutions of natural substances.

2) Unlike mainstream treatments, alternative therapies aren't based on evidence gathered from scientific research. As a result, there is little scientific evidence that alternative treatments work effectively, and some doctors believe that they might do more harm than good.

3) However, some doctors are now working with alternative therapists to see if using a mix of alternative and mainstream medicine might result in benefits to the patient.

The pharmaceutical industry researches and develops new drugs

Write a paragraph describing changes in the treatment of disease during the 20th century. Explain whether you think individuals or advances in technology were the most important factor.

Modern Surgery

Surgery improved rapidly during the 20th century. Surgery has become much <u>less risky</u> and <u>transplants</u> have been made possible. Nowadays the emphasis is on <u>precision</u> — technology has been an important factor here.

Transplants have been made more Successful

1) In 1905, the first successful <u>transplant</u> of the <u>cornea of the eye</u> was performed.
   During the First World War, surgeons developed techniques for <u>skin transplantation</u>.

2) The first complete organ to be successfully transplanted was the <u>kidney</u>.
   <u>Livers</u>, <u>lungs</u>, <u>pancreases</u> and <u>bone marrow</u> can now also be transplanted.

3) The first successful <u>heart</u> transplant was carried out by the South African surgeon
   <u>Christiaan Barnard</u> in 1967. The patient only survived for <u>18 days</u> — he died of pneumonia.

- The problem for transplants is <u>rejection</u>. The <u>immune system</u> attacks the implant as if it were a virus.

- The success of early transplant operations was limited because doctors lacked effective <u>immunosuppressants</u> — drugs that <u>stop</u> the immune system attacking.

- Since the 1970s, researchers have developed <u>increasingly effective</u> immunosuppressants, making transplants <u>safer</u> and more likely to be <u>successful</u>.

Technology has improved modern surgery

1) Advances in <u>science and technology</u> have led to improvements in the treatment of diseases like <u>cancer</u>. The discovery of <u>radiation</u> in 1896-1898 by <u>Antoine Henri Becquerel</u>, <u>Marie Curie</u> and <u>Pierre Curie</u> led to the creation of <u>radiation therapy</u>. Radiation therapy is the use of <u>radiation</u> to kill cancer cells.

2) The development of <u>lasers</u> since the 1950s led to their widespread use in medicine in the 1980s. <u>Laser surgery</u> is used to correct <u>vision problems</u>, and lasers are also used in <u>cancer</u> treatment and <u>dentistry</u>.

3) Advances in <u>technology</u> since the 1980s have led to the development of <u>robot-assisted surgery</u> and <u>keyhole surgery</u>.

Robot-Assisted Surgery

- The first <u>surgical robot</u> was introduced in 1985 but robot-assisted surgery only became widely used after 2000 with the launch of the da Vinci system.
- Robot-assisted surgery allows surgeons to make <u>smaller</u> cuts. This means less <u>scarring</u>, less <u>infection</u> and <u>quicker healing</u> of wounds.

Keyhole Surgery

- A type of camera called an <u>endoscope</u> is put through a <u>small cut</u>, letting the surgeon see inside the body. Other surgical instruments are then introduced through even smaller cuts in the skin.
- Keyhole surgery is useful for <u>investigating</u> the causes of pain or infertility. It's also used for vasectomies, removing cysts or the appendix, mending hernias and other minor operations.
- Keyhole surgery leaves patients with <u>smaller scars</u> and allows them to recover more <u>quickly</u>, with less risk of infection.

4) These new surgical methods have improved surgeons' <u>precision</u>, leading to less infection.

Changes in technology have driven improvements in surgery

Write a list of examples of technology playing a major role in changes in health and medicine. Which change do you think has been the most important and why?

The Liberal Reforms

In the 19th century, people believed government should have little involvement in public health.
This all began to change after 1900, when the Liberal social reforms were introduced to deal with poverty.

Booth and Rowntree showed the effects of Poverty

1) Slums and other poor, overcrowded housing were still common in industrial towns in 1900. The poor worked long hours for low wages. Many people couldn't afford doctors or medicine — they could barely provide their children with three decent meals a day.

> There was no unemployment benefit, or pensions for the elderly. Workhouses were the only help — they provided basic food and lodging in exchange for working long hours in brutal conditions.

2) Two reports showed how widespread poverty was:

Booth's Report

Charles Booth's 1889 'Life and Labour of the People in London' showed that 30% of Londoners were living in severe poverty, and that it was sometimes impossible for people to find work, however hard they tried. He showed that some wages were so low they weren't enough to support a family.

Rowntree's Report

Seebohm Rowntree had a factory in York. He didn't believe the problem was as bad there as in London — so he did a survey of living conditions. His report, 'Poverty, a Study of Town Life' (published 1901), showed that 28% of people in York couldn't afford basic food and housing.

3) The lack of access to good healthcare meant that most people's health was pretty poor. When the Boer War broke out in 1899, army officers found that 40% of volunteers were physically unfit for military service — mostly due to poverty-related illnesses linked to poor diet and living conditions.

4) The government realised that it needed to improve basic healthcare in order to have an efficient army.

The Liberal Reforms improved health by tackling Poverty

Booth, Rowntree and the Boer War showed that there was a link between poverty and ill health.
The newly-elected Liberal government and its Chancellor, David Lloyd George, realised it had to take action.

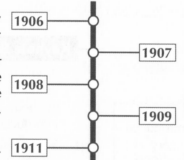

1906 — Free school meals were introduced, paid for by local council taxes.

1907 — Local Education Authorities started giving children at their schools free medical inspections.

1908 — Old age pensions were introduced for the first time — they were for people aged over 70. It was the first ever welfare scheme to be paid for by national taxes.

1909 — Labour exchanges were introduced to help unemployed people find work.

1911 — The National Insurance Act was passed.

The National Insurance Act introduced health insurance for workers — the worker, their employer and the government all contributed to a central fund that the workers could use for sick pay or to pay for a doctor.

Comment and Analysis

The Liberal reforms were the first real effort by the national government to improve people's living conditions as a way of improving their health. The reforms were a result of changing attitudes towards the role of government, and changed people's attitudes further.

The government intervened in public health by dealing with poverty

Create flashcards about the Liberal reforms — some with the dates and some with the names of the reforms. Match them up, then write a paragraph explaining why the reforms were important.

Public Health and the World Wars

After World War II, housing standards began to improve. The Beveridge Report argued that the state should provide support to people, resulting in the creation of the welfare state and the NHS.

The World Wars created Pressure for Social Change

The First World War (1914-1918) and the Second World War (1939-1945) broke down social distinctions and brought people together whose lives had been very separate.

- Raising mass armies made government and military officials more aware of the health problems of the poor, because so many recruits were in poor health. Powerful people were more concerned with solving these health problems when at war, because of the need for a strong army to defend the country.
- The evacuation of children during the Second World War increased awareness in richer rural communities of how disadvantaged many people were in other parts of the country.
- After the Second World War, people looked for improvements in society. Such feelings led to the 1945 victory for the Labour Party, which promised healthcare for everyone and full employment.

Housing and Health Improved after the Second World War

1) Towards the end of the First World War, Prime Minister David Lloyd George promised to tackle poor-quality housing by building 'homes fit for heroes' to tackle bad housing. Some new council houses were built in the 1920s and 1930s, but many of them were too expensive for the poorest families, who still lived in slums.
2) During the Second World War, destruction from bombing and a lack of construction led to severe housing shortages, making the situation worse.
3) After the war, the Labour government built 800,000 homes between 1945-51. In 1946, it passed the New Towns Act — this created completely new towns near major cities. Governments in the 1950s and 1960s demolished over 900,000 old, cramped slums — around 2 million inhabitants were rehoused.
4) In 1961, a report called 'Homes for Today and Tomorrow' gave specific standards for new housing, including adequate heating, a flushing toilet and enough space inside and outside. This was the final step in tackling the issues of overcrowding, poor nutrition and poor waste disposal that had caused major public health problems.

The Beveridge Report led to the Welfare State

1) In 1942, during the Second World War, economist and social reformer William Beveridge published his famous report. The Beveridge Report became a bestseller — it was widely read and hugely popular.

In his report, Beveridge called for the state provision of social security 'from the cradle to the grave.' Beveridge argued that all people should have the right to be free from want, disease, ignorance, squalor and idleness. He called these the five 'giants'.

2) Beveridge said that the government had a duty to care for all its citizens, not just the poor or unemployed. To achieve this, Beveridge suggested the creation of a welfare state — a system of grants and services available to all British citizens.
3) The 1945 Labour government was elected with the promise to implement Beveridge's proposals. One of their first acts was to pass a new National Insurance Act in 1946 to support anyone who couldn't work, whether as a result of sickness, pregnancy, unemployment or old age.

Comment and Analysis

The Labour Party's National Insurance Act went further than the one introduced by the Liberal government (see p.38) — anyone could apply for Labour's National Insurance without having to take a test to see if they were eligible.

The World Wars changed attitudes towards government intervention

You can use quotations from important public figures to back up your points. "Homes fit for heroes" (Lloyd George) and "from the cradle to the grave" (Beveridge) are two that are worth remembering.

The National Health Service

One of the most important changes in modern British medicine was the creation of the NHS.

The **National Health Service** was established in **1948**

1) In 1948, the Labour government implemented Beveridge's last proposal — a National Health Service.

2) Aneurin Bevan was the Labour Minister for Health who, after a lot of negotiation, introduced the National Health Service (NHS). The government nationalised hospitals and put them under local authority control. Treatment was made free for all patients. There were arguments for and against the NHS:

For the NHS

- During World War Two the government took control of all hospitals, creating the Emergency Medical Service. Its success led many to support the creation of the NHS.
- The NHS would make medical care free so it was accessible to everyone.
- The NHS guaranteed that hospitals would receive government money, rather than having to rely on charities for money.

Against the NHS

- Many Conservatives opposed the NHS as they believed the cost would be huge.
- Doctors saw themselves as independent professionals — they didn't want to be controlled by the government. They also worried that they would lose a lot of income. Many doctors threatened to go on strike in protest against the NHS.

The government finally convinced doctors by offering them a payment for each patient and letting them continue treating fee-paying patients.

The **NHS** was **Very Popular**

1) Although many Conservatives were opposed to the creation of the NHS, they couldn't abolish it when they came back into power in 1951 — it was too popular.

2) The NHS increased the number of people with access to healthcare — the number of doctors doubled between 1948 and 1973 to keep up with demand.

3) Today, the NHS provides a range of health services, most of which are free and accessible to everyone. They include accident and emergency care, maternity care and major surgery, as well as pharmacies, dentists, mental health services, sexual health services and general practitioners (GPs).

In the long term, the NHS has contributed to a dramatic improvement in people's health and a rise in life expectancy. In 1951, men could expect to live to 66 and women to 72 — by 2011 this had risen to 79 for men and 83 for women.

Today the **NHS** faces several **Challenges**

1) The increase in life expectancy means there are many more older people in Britain today than there were in 1948, who are more likely to suffer from long-term conditions like diabetes and heart disease. They need regular medical attention and require a lot of NHS time and resources.

2) Many people's lifestyle choices are putting strain on the NHS. Smoking, obesity and alcohol consumption can all harm people's health and may require expensive treatment — for example, smoking can cause lung cancer and drinking too much alcohol can cause serious liver disease.

3) Many modern treatments, equipment and medicines are very expensive, and the NHS has had to face rising expectations of what it can and should offer.

4) As a result of all these factors, the cost of the NHS is rising rapidly — in 2015/16 the NHS budget was £116 billion overall. In order to stay within its budget, the NHS sometimes has to make difficult choices about which treatments it can and can't provide.

A 2015 poll suggested that around 60% of British people are satisfied with the NHS, showing that it is still relatively popular.

The NHS has improved access to healthcare

REVISION TASK

Split your page in two. On one side, make a list of ways the NHS has improved public health since it was founded. On the other, write down all the problems and challenges that the NHS is facing today.

The Government's Role in Healthcare

Since 1900, the <u>government's role</u> in improving people's health has <u>grown and grown</u>.

Vaccination Campaigns have eradicated some Diseases

Since 1900, the government has launched several national <u>vaccination</u> programmes to <u>prevent</u> people from catching deadly diseases. These have been <u>successful</u> in reducing the number of deaths from such diseases.

Diphtheria

- <u>Diphtheria</u> is a contagious disease that is caused by bacteria in the <u>nose</u> and <u>throat</u>. It can eventually attack the heart muscles, causing <u>paralysis</u> or <u>heart failure</u>.
- Before the 1940s, diphtheria was a major killer disease — in 1940, there were over <u>60,000 cases</u> of the disease and over <u>3,000 deaths</u>.
- After fears that wartime conditions could lead to the spread of the disease, the government started a <u>vaccination campaign</u> in 1940.
- The government ran <u>publicity campaigns</u>, using posters, newspaper advertisements and radio broadcasts.
- The campaign was a success — by 1957, the number of diphtheria cases had dropped to just <u>38</u>, with only <u>six deaths</u>.

> In 1940, the easiest way to reach children was through <u>schools</u>, so <u>5-15 year olds</u> were vaccinated more than the youngest children who were most vulnerable. The establishment of the <u>NHS</u> in <u>1948</u> (see p.40) allowed the government to vaccinate <u>all</u> children by their <u>first birthday</u>.

Polio

- <u>Polio</u> is an infection that can attack the digestive system, bloodstream and nervous system. The disease can cause <u>paralysis</u>, and particularly affects <u>children</u>.
- In the late 1940s and early 1950s, Britain suffered a series of polio <u>epidemics</u> — the disease made over 30,000 children disabled between 1947 and 1958.
- The first vaccine was introduced in Britain in 1956 alongside a <u>national campaign</u>, aiming to vaccinate every person <u>under the age of 40</u>.
- The campaign was successful, with the disease all but <u>eradicated</u> by the late 1970s. In the period 1985-2002, only <u>40 polio cases</u> were reported in Britain.

Lifestyle Campaigns aim to improve people's Health

In the 20th century, scientists showed a link between people's <u>lifestyle choices</u> and their <u>health</u> (see p.33). The government ran several <u>campaigns</u> to make people aware of the dangers and to <u>change</u> their <u>lifestyles</u>.

1) In 1952, a <u>Great Smog</u> caused by coal fires resulted in <u>4,000 deaths</u> in London. It showed the dangers of <u>air pollution</u>, which can cause breathing conditions like <u>asthma</u> and <u>bronchitis</u>. The government passed laws in the hope of limiting air pollution.

2) An increase in <u>less active lifestyles</u> has led to an increase in <u>obesity</u>. In 2009, the government launched the <u>Change4Life</u> campaign, with the aim of <u>improving diets</u> and <u>promoting daily exercise</u>.

3) Excessive <u>alcohol</u> intake has been linked to several diseases, most notably <u>liver cirrhosis</u>. Alcohol intake <u>rose</u> between 1950 and 2004, but has since <u>fallen</u>. This may be due to the government's <u>Drinkaware</u> campaign, launched in 2004. The Drinkaware logo appears on many alcohol advertisements.

Comment and Analysis

These campaigns mark a <u>big shift</u> in the government's approach from the foundation of the NHS, and an even bigger shift from the <u>laissez-faire attitudes</u> of the 19th century, when people thought government shouldn't intervene at all in public health. Not only is the government trying to <u>treat</u> and <u>vaccinate against</u> known diseases, it is now <u>intervening in people's lives</u> in order to stop them getting particular illnesses in the first place.

REVISION TASK

The government took more responsibility for health in the 20th century

Draw a mind map of all of the ways the government has tried to improve health and medicine in Britain since 1900. Include vaccinations, lifestyle campaigns and the NHS in your diagram.

Lung Cancer

<u>Lung cancer</u> is a disease that was <u>much more common</u> after 1900 than before. The battle against lung cancer is an example of <u>science and technology</u> and <u>government campaigns</u> working side by side.

Lung Cancer can be caused by Smoking

1) Lung cancer was a rare disease in 1900, but became common by the 1940s. Today, around <u>20%</u> of all <u>cancer deaths</u> in the UK are due to lung cancer. Approximately <u>43,500</u> people are diagnosed <u>every year</u>.

2) Scientists have estimated that around 90% of lung cancer cases can be linked to <u>tobacco smoking</u>. The popularity of smoking increased during the <u>First World War</u>, particularly among soldiers. Smoking soon became popular among women too.

3) In 1950, the <u>link between smoking and lung cancer</u> was proven by Richard Doll and Austin Bradford Hill.

Lung cancer Diagnostics and Treatment have Improved

Advances in <u>science and technology</u> have made it easier to <u>diagnose</u> and <u>treat</u> lung cancer.

Diagnosis

- <u>Chest X-rays</u> are the first means of diagnosing lung cancer. The X-rays can't show whether the patient definitely has cancer, but can show if there is anything on the lung that <u>shouldn't be there</u>.
- <u>CT scans</u> (see p.34) can be used to give a more <u>detailed</u> image of the lungs.
- Doctors can now use <u>bronchoscopy</u> to diagnose lung cancer. This involves putting a <u>thin tube</u> into the lungs to take a sample of the suspected cells. It requires a <u>local anaesthetic</u> to numb the throat.

Treatment

- Lung cancer can be treated using <u>surgery</u>, for example by <u>removing</u> the affected lung.
- Modern treatments like <u>radiation therapy</u> (see p.37) and <u>chemotherapy</u> (see p.36) are also used to treat lung cancer. Radiotherapy involves directing <u>radiation</u> at the lungs. Lung cancer chemotherapy uses a <u>combination</u> of several drugs, which are normally injected directly into the <u>bloodstream</u>.

Government Campaigns have reduced smoking

When the link between <u>smoking</u> and lung cancer became clear, the government warned people of the risks.

1) In 1962, the <u>Royal College of Physicians</u> recommended a ban on tobacco advertising. Shortly afterwards, in 1965, <u>cigarette adverts were banned</u> from television. In 1971, tobacco companies were forced to put a <u>health warning</u> on cigarette packets.

2) In recent years, the government has put a <u>ban on smoking in public places</u> — this was introduced in Scotland in 2006, and in England and Wales in 2007.

3) Recent government campaigns have focused on helping people to <u>give up smoking</u> and on discouraging smoking in cars, homes and in front of children.

4) In March 2015, Parliament passed a law requiring all cigarette companies to use <u>plain packaging</u> on boxes of cigarettes.

These measures have contributed to a <u>decline in smoking</u>. The percentage of men who smoke cigarettes has fallen from 65% in 1948 to around 20% in 2010 and for women it's dropped from 41% to 20% in the same period.

Comment and Analysis

Lung cancer prevention is a good example of an area of health where the government has been increasingly <u>active</u> — the large number of <u>television campaigns</u> and pieces of <u>legislation</u> show that the government is now taking health seriously, which is in contrast to its attitude before 1900.

Government and technology have helped combat lung cancer

Draw a mind map of how lung cancer has been tackled over the past one hundred years.

Worked Exam-Style Question

This sample answer will help you to write longer answers that focus on the importance of different factors. You need to write a balanced argument that comes to a judgement — look at the comments for help.

Q1 'Technology has been the most significant factor in the development of health and medicine in Britain.'

Explain how far you agree with this statement. You should refer to technology and other factors in your answer. [16 marks]

It's a good idea to include a short introduction summarising your argument.

I do not agree that technology has been the most significant factor in the development of health and medicine in Britain. Although technology has had a major impact on health and medicine since the 1800s, other factors were more important in earlier periods.

This paragraph explains why technology has been significant.

Use specific and relevant examples to support your points.

Technology was important to the development of medicine in the 1800s as it allowed people to make new medical discoveries. Louis Pasteur's discovery that germs cause disease (published as the Germ Theory in 1861) was made possible by developments in microscope technology. The microscope was invented by Antonie van Leeuwenhoek in the 17th century and improved designs were created in the 1800s. These improvements allowed Pasteur to see clearer images of germs for the first time.

Explain how the factor in the question had an impact on health and medicine.

Technology has also been significant in improving diagnosis and treatment, especially in the late 1800s and the 1900s. The invention of diagnostic technology like X-rays (discovered in 1895) and CT scans (invented in 1972) has allowed doctors to diagnose illnesses more effectively and intervene before a disease becomes too advanced. For example, X-rays and CT scans have both been used to improve the diagnosis of lung cancer. Since the 1980s, new technology, like the endoscope, has led to the development of keyhole surgery. This allows surgeons to be more precise and use smaller cuts when operating, which means that patients recover more quickly and with less risk of infection. Technological advances like these have had a huge impact on the development of health and medicine by improving the ability of surgeons and doctors to diagnose patients and provide safer and more effective treatment.

Include specific dates to show you have a good knowledge of the period.

You need to show you know the order of events.

Even if you agree with the statement, it's important to consider both sides of the argument.

However, before the 1800s, other factors were more important to the development of health and medicine. For example, in the Renaissance period, war was a key factor in the development of medicine — many of the surgical techniques invented by Ambroise Paré in the 16th century, such as using ligatures to prevent blood loss after amputation, were devised in response to the injuries he encountered during his time as an army surgeon.

Don't just focus on the factor in the question — you should also write about other factors.

Worked Exam-Style Question

Start a <u>new paragraph</u> every time you introduce a <u>new factor</u>.

→ Another key factor in the development of medicine in the Renaissance period was the <u>advancement of medical knowledge</u>. Many doctors began to use dissection and experimentation in this period to improve their understanding of the human body. <u>Vesalius' work on human anatomy laid the foundations for improvements in diagnosis and treatment of disease, while Sydenham's observation of symptoms allowed him to develop more effective treatments for many ailments, including the use of iron to treat anaemia.</u>

You should include examples from <u>throughout</u> the thematic study in your answer.

Technology did have a minor impact on the development of medicine in the Renaissance period. For example, <u>William Harvey's discovery that blood circulated around the body was informed by new technology</u> — his ideas about the function of the heart were inspired by the way a new type of water pump worked. The invention of the printing press also allowed new ideas like those of Vesalius to be shared. However, technology was not the most important factor in this period.

Explain how each point you make is <u>relevant to the question</u>.

Moreover, while technology has been important since the 1800s, <u>it cannot be considered the most important factor because it has often required economic investment from large institutions like the government in order to have an impact</u>. For example, in the mid-19th century, Bazalgette's new sewer system, which helped to stop cholera in London by cleaning up the city's drinking water, was only built because the government supported the project. Similarly, since the mid-20th century, access to modern medical technology like MRI scans and ultrasounds has relied on funding from the National Health Service. Founded in 1948, the NHS provides free access to a range of medical services, including expensive medical equipment. In <u>2015/16 the NHS budget was £116 billion</u>, showing how much it invests in resources, including technology. <u>This demonstrates that technology has mainly had an impact on the development of health and medicine when it is supported by the economic resources of large institutions like the government</u>.

Use specific <u>facts</u> and <u>figures</u> that are relevant to your argument.

Remember to explain the <u>significance</u> of each factor you write about.

Make sure you give a <u>clear answer</u> to the question in your conclusion.

In conclusion, <u>technology has not been the most important factor in the development of health and medicine in Britain, because before the 1800s other factors, such as war and advances in medical knowledge, were more important</u>. Even though technology has had a major impact on health and medicine since the 1800s, it is still not the most significant factor, because <u>its impact in this period has relied on other factors, especially government funding</u>.

Summarise your argument in your <u>conclusion</u>.

Exam-Style Questions

Q1

Give one way that hospitals in the 20th century were different to those in the Middle Ages. Explain your answer.   [4 marks]

You'll need to use information from other parts of the Health and Medicine section to answer question one properly.

Q2

Explain the importance of the First and Second World Wars in the development of health and medicine.   [8 marks]

Q3

Has the government been the most important factor in the improvement of people's health in Britain since the Middle Ages?

You should refer to the government as well as other factors in your answer.   [16 marks]

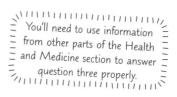

You'll need to use information from other parts of the Health and Medicine section to answer question three properly.

Revision Summary

Well, that was a <u>healthy</u> amount of information to revise. Now <u>treat</u> yourself to these <u>revision questions</u>.
- Try these questions and <u>tick off each one</u> when you <u>get it right</u>.
- When you've done <u>all the questions</u> for a topic and are <u>completely happy</u> with it, tick off the topic.

c.1000-c.1500: Medicine in Medieval Britain (p.4-10) ☑

1) Give two supernatural causes of disease believed by people in medieval Britain. ☑
2) Briefly describe two natural explanations for disease believed by people in medieval Britain. ☑
3) Describe two medical discoveries made by Islamic doctors. ☑
4) Name six treatments for disease used by people in medieval Britain. ☑
5) List three types of people you might visit if you felt ill in medieval Britain. ☑
6) List two approaches to health in towns and two approaches to health in monasteries. ☑
7) Give three ways people tried to prevent the spread of the Black Death. ☑

c.1500-c.1700: The Medical Renaissance in Britain (p.12-17) ☑

8) Describe the impact of the printing press on people's understanding of medicine. ☑
9) How did the Royal Society change perceptions of medicine? ☑
10) Describe how Paré found a better way to treat wounds. ☑
11) List five ways in which there was continuity between medieval and Renaissance medical treatments. ☑
12) What was Vesalius' discovery and why did it help improve surgery? ☑
13) Explain why Thomas Sydenham was important in Renaissance medicine. ☑
14) What did Harvey discover and why did he have a limited impact on diagnosis and treatment? ☑
15) List four treatments and four prevention methods people used against the Great Plague in 1665. ☑

c.1700-c.1900: Medicine in 18th and 19th Century Britain (p.20-29) ☑

16) List three reactions by Parliament to Jenner's discovery of the smallpox vaccine. ☑
17) In what year did Louis Pasteur publish the Germ Theory? ☑
18) Name the first two magic bullets, who discovered them and the dates they were discovered. ☑
19) Explain how Florence Nightingale changed nursing. ☑
20) Name the year that chloroform was discovered and explain why it led to a higher death rate initially. ☑
21) What is the difference between antisepsis and asepsis? ☑
22) Describe John Snow's 1854 investigation and explain what he showed. ☑
23) Give three things that the 1875 Public Health Act forced local councils to do. ☑

c.1900-Present: Medicine in Modern Britain (p.32-42) ☑

24) When were X-rays discovered? How are they used in medical diagnosis? ☑
25) Describe three causes of disease that have been discovered since Pasteur's Germ Theory. ☑
26) What did Watson and Crick discover in 1953 and how did it help medical diagnosis? ☑
27) Explain how the following individuals or institutions contributed to the production of penicillin: Fleming, Florey and Chain, the United States government. ☑
28) State three ways in which housing and public health were improved as a result of World War II. ☑
29) List two ways that the government has tried to change people's lifestyles. ☑
30) Give five ways in which lung cancer diagnosis and treatments have improved. ☑
31) List four ways that the government has tried to reduce smoking. ☑

North American Geography

Knowing a bit about the <u>geography</u> of America is really <u>important</u> to understanding this topic.

Many US citizens wanted to settle land in the **West**

North America can be divided into several different geographical <u>regions</u>. European settlers initially lived only on the <u>east coast</u>, leaving many regions of America <u>unsettled</u>.

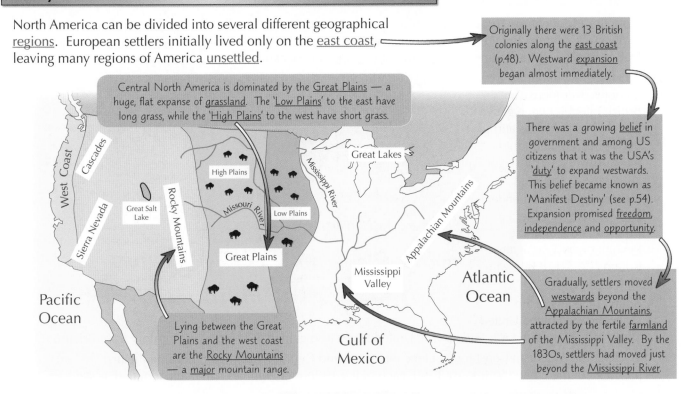

Originally there were 13 British colonies along the <u>east coast</u> (p.48). Westward <u>expansion</u> began almost immediately.

Central North America is dominated by the <u>Great Plains</u> — a huge, flat expanse of <u>grassland</u>. The '<u>Low Plains</u>' to the east have long grass, while the '<u>High Plains</u>' to the west have short grass.

There was a growing <u>belief</u> in government and among US citizens that it was the USA's '<u>duty</u>' to expand westwards. This belief became known as 'Manifest Destiny' (see p.54). Expansion promised <u>freedom</u>, <u>independence</u> and <u>opportunity</u>.

Lying between the Great Plains and the west coast are the <u>Rocky Mountains</u> — a <u>major</u> mountain range.

Gradually, settlers moved <u>westwards</u> beyond the <u>Appalachian Mountains</u>, attracted by the fertile <u>farmland</u> of the Mississippi Valley. By the 1830s, settlers had moved just beyond the <u>Mississippi River</u>.

Map labels: West Coast, Cascades, Sierra Nevada, Great Salt Lake, Rocky Mountains, Missouri River, High Plains, Low Plains, Great Plains, Great Lakes, Mississippi River, Appalachian Mountains, Mississippi Valley, Atlantic Ocean, Pacific Ocean, Gulf of Mexico

Geographical Obstacles separated the East from the West Coast

The <u>west coast</u> was attractive to settlers. The land is <u>fertile</u> and it has a <u>temperate</u> climate — temperatures don't vary hugely between summer and winter. But between would-be settlers and the west coast were the <u>Great Plains</u> and other geographical <u>obstacles</u>.

The Great Plains Have a Hostile Climate

- The Great Plains become <u>drier</u> and more desert-like the further <u>south</u> you go. US citizens didn't think they could <u>live</u> on the Great Plains — they called it the '<u>Great American Desert</u>'.
- The <u>mountains</u> on either side of the Plains produce <u>rain shadows</u> (regions with little rain). You often get <u>droughts</u> in the summer and <u>severe snow</u> in the winter.
- Being so far from the sea means there's a huge <u>difference in temperature</u> between summer and winter.

There was a widespread view among the white settlers that the Great Plains were <u>wild</u> and <u>harsh</u> — many believed they were <u>unsuitable</u> for living and farming because of the extremes of <u>weather</u>, sparse <u>rainfall</u> and <u>hard ground</u>. However, attitudes towards the Plains would later <u>change</u> (see p.54 and p.71). Understanding these changing <u>attitudes</u> is important for understanding America's expansion.

The Rocky Mountains Form a Barrier Across America

- The <u>slopes</u> on either side of the Rockies are <u>heavily wooded</u> — especially in the South.
- At the centre of the Rockies is the <u>Plateaux region</u>. It's fairly flat but has areas of <u>desert</u>. Water can get trapped here, only escaping by evaporation. This has created the Great Salt Lake (see p.56).

America's plains and mountains made it hard to get to the west coast

Yep, you're still studying history, but geography was really important in the story of the expansion of the USA. So make sure you learn it to show you have a good grasp of the topic in the exam.

Early Territorial Expansion

When America gained <u>independence</u> from Britain in 1783, westward expansion began almost <u>immediately</u>.

Most of the American population used to live along the **East Coast**

1) From the 15th century, European countries such as Britain, France and Spain <u>colonised</u> America. By the 18th century, Britain had <u>13 colonies</u> on the <u>east coast</u>. After winning the <u>Seven Years' War</u> against France in <u>1763</u>, Britain gained the <u>Northwest Territory</u> and became the <u>dominant</u> power in North America.

2) <u>Tension</u> grew in the British colonies over increasing British <u>interference</u>, e.g. tax and trade regulations and outlawing <u>migration</u> into the Northwest Territory.

3) The colonies declared themselves the independent <u>United States of America</u> in 1776 and fought the <u>Revolutionary War</u> against Britain (1775-1783) to gain their <u>independence</u>.

4) Britain <u>recognised</u> the independence of the United States in <u>1783</u> and the war <u>ended</u>. The United States also gained the <u>Northwest Territory</u> from Britain.

5) In 1789, the American <u>Constitution</u> came into force and <u>George Washington</u> became the first <u>president</u> of the United States. By 1790, each of the 13 former colonies had been admitted as <u>states</u>.

The <u>Northwest Ordinance</u> of 1787 agreed that in time the Northwest Territory should be cut up into <u>states</u> and that these should be admitted to the Union (the United States of America).

Comment and Analysis

The Northwest Ordinance was important because it laid out <u>plans</u> for <u>westward expansion</u> into the Northwest Territory (Ohio was the first state to be created in the Territory). It also established a <u>process</u> for adding <u>new states</u> to the Union.

The Louisiana Purchase **Doubled** the size of America

1) In 1803, the US bought the Louisiana Territory from France — it covered <u>over 800,000 square miles</u> of land, but its boundaries <u>weren't clear</u>. It was a <u>vast</u> amount of land — all or part of <u>15 states</u> would be formed from it.

The US claimed that the Louisiana Purchase included <u>West Florida</u>, which belonged to <u>Spain</u> — but Spain <u>disagreed</u>. In <u>1810</u>, the people of West Florida <u>revolted</u> against Spanish rule — US soldiers <u>occupied</u> the area and President Madison declared it to be part of the <u>US</u>. Spain officially gave Florida to the US in the <u>Adams-Onis Treaty</u> of <u>1819</u>.

2) The Louisiana Purchase encouraged westward <u>migration</u>. Settlers had already started to move westwards, but the Purchase provided even <u>more land</u> for people to settle on.

3) It gave the US control of the <u>Mississippi River</u>, which was important for <u>trade</u>, especially as the nation expanded westwards.

4) President Thomas Jefferson commissioned the <u>Lewis and Clark Expedition</u> in 1803 to <u>explore</u> the Louisiana Territory and the land beyond. The group reached the <u>west coast</u> in <u>1805</u> and returned with their findings. The expedition resulted in greater <u>geographic</u> and <u>scientific</u> knowledge of the West.

Comment and Analysis

The Louisiana Territory was a huge amount of land, which increased the <u>confidence</u> of the USA and its <u>power</u> on the world stage.

The Louisiana Purchase helped the US establish itself as a nation

Try scribbling down a map of America without looking at the maps on pages 47-49. Label the main regions and write a little about each one, using the information you can remember.

Early Territorial Expansion

A second war with Britain in 1812 made expansion <u>easier</u> for the US. Many US citizens <u>supported</u> expansion.

War **Weakened** Native American **Resistance** to western expansion

1) America <u>declared war</u> on Britain in <u>1812</u>. The government was angry that the British were <u>restricting</u> American trade, <u>forcing</u> American sailors to join the British Navy and <u>supporting</u> the Native American fight against western expansion.

> America <u>asserted</u> itself during the war — it was seen as a <u>second war of independence</u>.

2) The war ended in 1815. There was <u>no clear winner</u> and neither side <u>lost territory</u> — the <u>Treaty of Ghent</u> agreed to return things to how they were <u>before</u> the war.

3) However, <u>Native Americans</u> in the East were <u>badly affected</u> by the war:

- Native Americans felt <u>threatened</u> by westward expansion. Britain <u>supported</u> them in halting expansion, but at the end of the war Britain <u>withdrew</u> this support.
- The Shawnee war chief <u>Tecumseh</u> managed the difficult task of <u>uniting</u> different Indian tribes. But he <u>died</u> helping the British in the war and there was no-one to replace him.

Comment and Analysis

After the war, the Native Americans were <u>less able</u> to resist expansion — they were no longer united and had lost their external ally. Following Tecumseh's death, the USA made more than <u>200 treaties</u> with eastern tribes, which resulted in the tribes <u>losing</u> their <u>land</u>.

White Americans wanted to **Expand Westwards**

1) The US government and American people increasingly believed it was America's <u>duty</u> to expand westwards. Thomas <u>Jefferson</u>, president from 1801-1809, believed land ownership and farming would create a <u>healthy</u>, <u>virtuous</u> population. To American people, expansion promised <u>freedom</u>, <u>independence</u> and <u>opportunity</u>.

2) Better <u>transport links</u> were created which enabled western expansion.

- Construction of the 620 mile long <u>National Road</u> began in 1811, connecting the <u>east coast</u> to <u>Illinois</u>.
- The 353 mile long <u>Eerie canal</u> opened in 1825, connecting <u>New York</u> to the <u>Great Lakes</u>.

3) These transport links connected <u>farmers</u> who had moved westwards with <u>markets</u> in the <u>East</u>, creating profit-making opportunities for them.

> <u>Steamboats</u>, introduced in 1807, provided <u>faster</u> transportation along waterways.

4) <u>New technology</u> also made farming <u>profitable</u> and <u>attracted</u> settlers to move westwards, e.g. the <u>mechanical grain reaper</u> was invented in 1831, which allowed farmers to harvest crops more <u>efficiently</u>.

By 1838, <u>26 states</u> had been created from territory belonging to the United States.

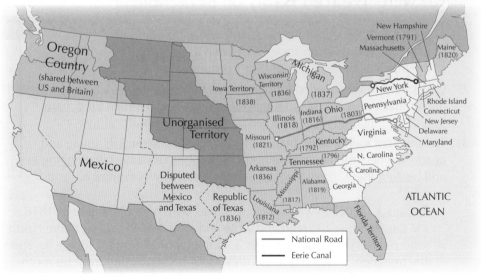

Expansion provided many Americans with new opportunities

REVISION TASK Make a timeline of the important events from 1789 to 1838. If you're feeling adventurous, keep adding to it throughout this section all the way up to 1900 — it'll give you a good overview of the period.

Cotton Plantations and Slavery

As cotton became more and more profitable, cotton plantations and slavery expanded in the South.

Cotton and slavery Weren't always Dominant in the South

~ time of slavery

1) Plantations were established in the South of America in the 17th century. Plantations were large farms which harvested crops such as sugar, tobacco and cotton — these were labour intensive crops, so large numbers of workers were needed to harvest them.

2) At first, indentured servants were the main source of labour on these plantations, but they were gradually replaced by African slaves. Plantation owners got these slaves through the Atlantic slave trade — Africans were forced into slavery and transported to America on ships where they would be bought at market.

> Indentured servants agreed to work for a certain number of years in return for passage to America from overseas.

3) Tobacco was more profitable than cotton in the 18th century. Cotton picking was a time consuming business — the cotton fibres had to be separated from the seeds by hand.

Technology increased the importance of Cotton and Slavery

More profit

1) Britain experienced an industrial revolution in the early 19th century. New machines were developed which allowed factories to process much more cotton. As a result, demand for cotton in Britain increased enormously, which meant US planters could export much larger quantities of cotton to Britain.

2) In the US, the mechanical cotton gin was invented by Eli Whitney in 1793. It removed the cotton fibre from the seeds mechanically.

3) The cotton gin hugely increased the speed at which cotton on plantations could be processed. This allowed planters to expand their cotton production. They increased their labour force, which resulted in the expansion of slavery.

> The end of the Atlantic slave trade in 1808 meant that the price of existing slaves in the US increased. (Although the slave trade ended, slavery and slave trading continued in the USA.)

4) Cotton became the South's most important crop — the economy of the South came to rely upon cotton exports and the South became dependent on slavery.

5) Only a small number of wealthier southerners owned plantations and slaves, but many southerners saw slavery as part of their way of life — they called it their 'peculiar institution'.

large profit

Slaves were Treated Badly on plantations

1) Many white Americans saw black Africans as inferior to white people. African slaves were seen as property of the planters and had no rights or freedom.

2) Cheap labour was needed for plantations to be profitable, which meant that slaves had poor living conditions. They worked long, hard hours, were not fed well and lived in small, poorly built cabins.

3) Treatment of slaves on plantations varied, but was often inhumane and cruel. Owners tried to maintain strict discipline of slaves by whipping and beating them. Sexual abuse of female slaves was common.

Comment and Analysis

It's important to recognise slaves' efforts to resist this inhumane treatment. Some ran away and some even rebelled. Others worked slowly, damaged farm machinery and kept African culture alive through religion and music.

Frederick Douglass was a slave who was born on a plantation in 1818. He taught himself to read and write and managed to escape to the North where slavery was banned. His autobiography is a useful source for showing the treatment of slaves — he writes about his separation from his mother at an early age and the brutal whippings and beatings he suffered on one plantation.

> Plantation owners tried to keep slaves like Douglass in ignorance by not allowing them to learn to read or write.

EXAM TIP

The benefits of cotton for the South came at a human cost

It's important to understand the relationship between the expansion of cotton and the expansion of slavery. The success of cotton meant that slavery became a way of life in the South.

Exam-Style Questions

Q1 Describe two ways that the geography of America made it difficult for settlers to travel from the East to the West.   [4 marks]

Q2 Write a summary explaining the reasons for the expansion of US territory between 1789 and c.1830. Give examples to support your answer.   [9 marks]

Q3 Why did slavery expand in the South of America between 1789 and c.1830? Use examples to support your answer.   [10 marks]

The West, c.1830–c.1861

The Removal of Indigenous People from the East

A number of <u>Native American</u> tribes lived on <u>land</u> in the East which US citizens <u>wanted</u> to settle and farm on.

Washington aimed to 'Civilise' eastern Native American tribes

1) President <u>George Washington</u> pursued a policy of '<u>civilising</u>' Native Americans living east of the Great Plains — many US citizens saw Native American society as <u>inferior</u> and <u>savage</u> and believed that they needed to be <u>taught</u> how to live like white settlers.

2) Washington claimed he wanted to <u>respect</u> the Native Americans' <u>right</u> to their homeland as long as they <u>assimilated</u> into society.

> <u>Assimilation</u> meant changing their <u>lifestyle</u> to fit in with that of white Americans.

3) <u>Five tribes</u> were considered '<u>civilised</u>' as a result of this policy, because they took on aspects of white culture — the <u>Cherokee</u>, <u>Chicksaw</u>, <u>Choctaw</u>, <u>Creek</u> and <u>Seminole</u>.

Jackson **Moved** eastern tribes onto the **Great Plains**

1) Some of the land that settlers wanted to farm was <u>occupied</u> by Native American tribes. The five 'civilised' tribes lived on land in the <u>South</u>, which settlers wanted for growing <u>cotton</u>. Settlers <u>harassed</u> these Indian tribes and <u>pressured</u> the government to take their tribal land.

> The <u>Cherokee</u> lived in European-style <u>houses</u> and published their own <u>newspaper</u>, but people still didn't see them as <u>equal</u>.

2) In 1830, the <u>Indian Removal Act</u> was passed under President <u>Andrew Jackson</u> — this authorised the president to grant tribes land on the <u>Great Plains</u> in <u>exchange</u> for their land <u>in the East</u>. Jackson claimed that it would <u>benefit</u> the tribes to be moved <u>away</u> from settlers where they could live in <u>peace</u>.

3) The Removal Act was supposed to be <u>voluntary</u>, but when some tribes in the south-east <u>resisted</u>, the US government <u>forced</u> them to leave:

- The <u>Cherokee</u> resisted removal through <u>legal</u> means, but they were eventually <u>forcefully</u> marched by US soldiers to the Plains in 1838. It was <u>winter</u> and it's been estimated that <u>4000</u> Cherokee out of around 15,000 died on the march. This journey became known as the <u>Trail of Tears</u>.
- The <u>Seminole</u> fought a guerilla war against the US army from <u>1835-42</u>. The war was <u>costly</u> for both sides, but the Seminole eventually <u>surrendered</u> and were moved onto the Plains.

4) By 1840, most of the eastern tribes had been moved onto the Plains — around <u>70,000-100,000</u> people in total.

5) The intention was that Native Americans would live on the Great Plains, while settlers farmed land in the East — the Plains would be like one <u>large Indian reservation</u>. The boundary between the two regions was known as the <u>Permanent Indian Frontier</u>.

6) At this point, white Americans viewed the Plains as the '<u>Great American Desert</u>'. They believed that its <u>harsh</u> climate and lack of <u>wood</u> and <u>water</u> made it unsuitable for settling.

Comment and Analysis

The government gave the Native Americans the Great Plains, but <u>only</u> because white settlers <u>didn't</u> want the land themselves. Because they saw Native Americans as <u>inferior</u>, they felt it was <u>acceptable</u> to give them land they themselves didn't think was <u>fit</u> to live on.

EXAM TIP

White Americans didn't see the Native Americans as equals

Use this page to understand how and why the Permanent Indian Frontier was created. It was actually a lot less permanent than the name suggests — more about this later.

The Plains Indians

Other Native American tribes already lived on the Great Plains — they're known as the Plains Indians.

The **Plains Indians** lived in different groups called **Tribes**

1) The Plains Indians weren't a single group with a single culture — there were many different tribes.

2) These tribes had things in common, but they were diverse in appearance, lifestyle and language.

> E.g. The Cheyenne led a nomadic lifestyle — they regularly moved from place to place, following the buffalo which they hunted for food. In contrast, the Mandan farmed and lived in permanent villages.

The Plains Indians led **Very Different Lifestyles** to white settlers

The Lakota Sioux are an example of a nomadic Plains Indian tribe who lived very differently to settlers. They had broadly similar beliefs and practices to other nomadic Plains Indian tribes.

1) The Lakota Sioux were the largest of the three Sioux-speaking tribes and were split into seven bands. Each band had a chief and a council of elders. The chief didn't have complete control, but he would have earned loyalty over the years by demonstrating courage and generosity — this gave him influence over the tribe.

2) Buffalo were vital for the Lakota Sioux. They used almost every part of the animal — meat for food, skin for clothing and tents, and bones for weapons and tools. Living in tipis (family tents) allowed the Lakotas to quickly follow buffalo herds — tipis are easy to take down and put back up.

3) The Lakota Sioux didn't see land as something that could be bought and sold — land belonged to everyone. Even other, more settled tribes believed agricultural land belonged to the tribe as a whole.

Tribal Warfare

- Tribal warfare was common — it was a way for men to gain prestige. The aim wasn't necessarily to kill or seize land, but to perform acts of bravery such as stealing horses or counting coup (getting close enough to an enemy to touch him).

- The Lakota Sioux were skilled warriors. Their main enemies were the Crow and the Pawnee. Taking the scalp of an enemy was important to the Lakota Sioux for religious reasons. But scalping and killing were less important to them than counting coup.

Religion

- Native American religion was closely linked with nature — humans were believed to be part of nature, not masters over it. The Lakota Sioux believed that a Great Spirit called Wakan Tanka created the world, and that everything in nature contained spirits which they needed to keep on their side.

- The Lakota Sioux performed rituals such as the Vision Quest, Sweat Lodge Ceremony and Sun Dance to contact the spirits.

4) Women did most of the work in the village or camp, while the men hunted and fought. The Lakota Sioux were a male-dominated warrior society and men were the heads of their families, but women were respected. They owned the tipi and its contents, which gave them status.

5) The Lakota Sioux practiced polygamy (having more than one wife) — the dangers of hunting and warfare meant there were often more women than men in tribes.

Comment and Analysis

Settlers failed to understand the culture of the Plains Indians because it was so different to their own. This led to tension and conflict.

Hunting became easier for the Lakota Sioux when they began to use horses, which were brought over by the Europeans in the 16th century.

Different Native American tribes had different identities

Make a list summarising the different features of the Plains Indians' way of life. For each point you make, think about how it's different from the lifestyle and beliefs of the settlers.

Journeys of Early Migrants

Settlers decided to make the long and dangerous journey to the <u>west coast</u> for a variety of <u>different reasons</u>.

People went to the west coast in **Large Numbers** from the **1840s**

1) The first people to explore the West were <u>mountain men</u> who hunted animals in the <u>1820s</u> and <u>1830s</u> to sell their skins. They <u>didn't settle</u> in the West, but established westward <u>trails</u> that settlers would later use.

2) <u>Missionaries</u> were among the earliest settlers on the <u>west coast</u> in the <u>1830s</u>.
Their aim was to <u>convert</u> the Native Americans there to <u>Christianity</u>.

3) Later, <u>larger</u> groups of people who wanted to make new lives for themselves went to the west coast. The first of these was the <u>Peoria Party</u> in 1839. Others followed in the 1840s — their routes became known as the <u>Oregon and California Trails</u>.

They had many **Different Reasons** for heading west

<u>The Great Migration</u> of <u>1843</u> saw a sudden <u>increase</u> in settlers — a party of around <u>1000</u> people moved to the west coast. This was because life in the East was <u>hard</u>, and there was promise of <u>better</u> things in the West.

Problems in the East (Push Factors)

- **Economic problems** — <u>Recession</u> in 1837 caused banks to collapse and businesses to fail. <u>Wages</u> and <u>profits</u> fell and <u>unemployment</u> rose.
- **Overpopulation** — High levels of European immigration, particularly from Ireland and Germany from 1846-1854, led to <u>overcrowded</u> cities, <u>fewer jobs</u> and a lack of <u>land</u> for people to farm.
- **Disease** — Overcrowding and poor sanitary systems led to epidemics of <u>yellow fever</u> and <u>cholera</u>.

Attractions of the West (Pull Factors)

- **A new start** — Land was <u>fertile</u> and <u>cheap</u>.
- **Government encouragement** — The government passed <u>acts</u> which allowed settlers to <u>claim land</u> in Oregon. They wanted people to settle in the West to <u>strengthen</u> the USA's claim to the land there.
- **Gold** — Gold was found at John Sutter's sawmill in California in January <u>1848</u> (see p.57). In December, President Polk confirmed that there was gold in the area. In <u>1849</u> there was a <u>gold rush</u>, as tens of thousands of people made the journey to California, hoping to make their <u>fortune</u>.

In 1841, Congress passed the <u>Distributive Preemption Act</u>, which allowed settlers to buy <u>160 acres</u> of land at a very low cost if they'd lived there for 14 months.

Only about <u>8%</u> of early migrants to California during the Gold Rush were <u>women</u>. More followed later as their husbands and families settled in California.

Settlers also moved west because of a belief in '<u>Manifest Destiny</u>':

- Many <u>US citizens</u> believed that they were destined to <u>occupy</u> and <u>govern</u> all of North America. They saw it as their <u>god-given right</u>.
- They believed they were <u>superior</u> to Native Americans and that they should <u>civilise</u> the continent.

The term 'Manifest Destiny' was coined by John L. O'Sullivan in <u>1845</u>.

Paintings which created a <u>romantic</u>, idealised image of moving west <u>promoted</u> expansion and 'Manifest Destiny'. For many, the journey wouldn't have been as <u>pleasant</u> as this image suggests (see p.55).

Migrants crossing the plains towards the Rocky Mountains.

Reasons why people went west can be split into push and pull factors

EXAM TIP

You should be able to explain the reasons why people went west. For example, there wasn't enough land in the East, but there was the promise of fertile land in the West.

Journeys of Early Migrants

Settlers faced many <u>challenges</u> on their journey to the west coast — it was a <u>long way</u> and it was <u>hard work</u>.

The journey to the west coast was **Difficult**

1) It took around <u>5 months</u> to complete the <u>2000 mile</u> overland journey to the west coast. The journey had to be completed <u>before</u> winter. People travelled in <u>wagons</u> and formed wagon trains with other settlers.

2) The journey was <u>dangerous</u> — as many as <u>10%</u> would die on the way.

> About <u>half</u> of the estimated <u>100,000</u> people who went to California during 1849 did so by <u>sea</u>. This journey also took around <u>5 months</u> and had its own <u>difficulties</u> — <u>crowded</u> conditions, <u>sickness</u> and <u>storms</u>.

- There were <u>mountains</u> and <u>rivers</u> to cross — this was difficult with <u>heavy</u> wagons.
- People suffered from <u>food</u> and <u>water</u> shortages, and <u>diseases</u> such as typhoid and cholera.
- <u>Accidents</u> were common, such as falling under wagon wheels and accidental shootings.

3) Travellers were <u>wary</u> of Native Americans — some killings did occur, but conflict was <u>rare</u>. Native Americans <u>traded</u> food with travellers and offered them <u>guiding</u> services, but they became more <u>hostile</u> with the rise in settlers in the <u>1850s</u> (see p.58). Travellers also had <u>disputes</u> among themselves.

4) Women did all of the <u>domestic chores</u> at this time, and this was made <u>harder</u> by trail life. Some women had to give birth on the journey, while children were vulnerable to <u>accidents</u>, e.g. falling off wagons.

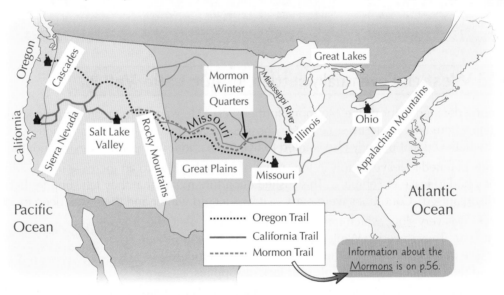

Information about the <u>Mormons</u> is on p.56.

The **Donner Party** had a **Disastrous** journey

1) In 1846 the Donner Party, heading for California, tried to take a <u>shortcut</u>, but they ended up <u>trapped</u> in deep snow in the <u>Sierra Nevada</u> mountains.

2) They had to <u>camp</u> in the mountains over winter. They had <u>low</u> supplies and many of the party <u>starved</u> to death.

3) Of the <u>87</u> migrants, less than <u>50</u> survived till the next spring — by <u>eating</u> those who had died.

> 'Still <u>snowing</u>; now about three feet deep; wind west; killed my last <u>oxen</u> today.'
> Extract from the diary of Patrick Breen, 27th November 1846. The Donner Party had to kill and eat the animals which pulled their wagons because they ran out of food.

Comment and Analysis

Once settlers had reached the west coast, life was still <u>hard</u> — they had to create farms and homes by <u>hand</u> from <u>scratch</u>. However, the <u>fertile</u> land meant that a <u>good living</u> could be made.

REVISION TASK

For the settlers, heading west was a big risk

Scribble down a brief description of the difficulties settlers faced on their journey to the west coast.

The Mormons

Another group of settlers were the <u>Mormons</u> — members of 'The Church of Jesus Christ of Latter Day Saints'.

The Mormons were **Persecuted** because of their beliefs

1) This religion was started by <u>Joseph Smith</u>, who published the <u>Book of Mormon</u> in <u>1830</u>. It claimed that Jesus had <u>visited</u> America and that <u>Native Americans</u> were <u>descended</u> from the lost tribes of <u>Israel</u>.

- Mormons <u>separated</u> themselves from American society and called non-Mormons '<u>gentiles</u>'.
- Some Mormons formed a <u>militia</u> called the <u>Danites</u> and there was violence against non-Mormons and dissenters (Mormons who questioned or abandoned the Mormon faith).
- Mormons were against <u>slavery</u> and tried to convert <u>Native Americans</u> to Mormonism.

2) Many US citizens <u>disliked</u> the Mormons, and repeatedly <u>drove</u> them out of their homes. They didn't agree with the Mormon practice of <u>polygamy</u> (having more than one wife), feared the <u>expansion</u> of the Mormon <u>faith</u> and felt threatened by the Mormons' <u>political</u> and <u>economic</u> power.

Ohio, 1831: The Mormons first settled in Kirtland, Ohio. They faced violence — Joseph Smith was <u>tarred and feathered</u> in 1832. The bank which Smith founded <u>collapsed</u> in <u>1837</u> — users of the bank were angry and drove the Mormons to <u>Missouri</u>.	**Missouri, 1837**: The Mormons' <u>anti-slavery</u> stance annoyed slave-owners, and the Danites were suspected of <u>plotting</u> with Native Americans. Many leaders were <u>arrested</u>, so <u>Brigham Young</u> led the Mormons to Illinois.	**Illinois, 1839**: The Mormons created their own city called <u>Nauvoo</u>, with its own <u>army</u> and <u>laws</u>. Joseph Smith declared his candidacy for <u>President</u>. Smith was eventually <u>killed</u> in jail by an angry mob and Brigham Young took over as <u>leader</u>.

They moved **West** and eventually settled in **Salt Lake Valley**

1) Brigham Young decided to move the Mormons further west. He wanted to create an <u>independent</u> Mormon state where they could live <u>freely</u>. He chose Salt Lake Valley — conditions there were <u>dry</u> and <u>harsh</u>, but he believed that <u>nobody else</u> wanted to live there and it was part of <u>Mexico</u>, not the US.

2) The Mormons planned to leave Illinois in the <u>spring</u> of 1846, but due to an <u>increase</u> in anti-Mormon violence they had to leave in <u>February</u>. This <u>rushed</u> departure meant that they left <u>supplies</u> behind and were <u>disorganised</u>. Conditions were hard — it was a <u>cold</u> winter and there was <u>deep mud</u>.

3) Their progress was very <u>slow</u>, which meant they couldn't complete the journey that year. They stayed in <u>Winter Quarters</u> by the Missouri River over winter (see map on p.55) — by the spring of 1847, around <u>400</u> Mormons had died from disease, the cold and lack of supplies.

> Although the journey was hard, the Mormons planted <u>crops</u> and built <u>way stations</u> along the trail to feed and help later travellers.

4) They set off again in April 1847 and <u>organisation</u> improved. They were divided into <u>groups</u> led by captains under the <u>strict</u> overall command of Young. They finally reached Salt Lake Valley in <u>July</u>.

5) The conditions in Salt Lake Valley were <u>tough</u>, but Young led the Mormons in <u>solving</u> their problems:

- There was little <u>rain</u> or other <u>water</u> sources, so they dug <u>irrigation</u> ditches.
- There were no trees for <u>wood</u>, so they built houses from bricks of <u>earth</u>.
- They needed to become <u>self-sufficient</u> but there weren't enough of them, so Young <u>encouraged</u> Mormons from all over the <u>world</u> to move to Salt Lake.

> <u>Tensions</u> were high — later in 1857, 140 non-Mormon settlers were killed in the <u>Mountain Meadows Massacre</u>. Mormons blamed the <u>Indians</u>, but others suspected the <u>Danites</u>.

6) In 1848, Mexico gave Salt Lake City to the US — it became the territory of <u>Utah</u> and was subject to American <u>laws</u>. The Mormons <u>ignored</u> these laws and the Danites <u>attacked</u> US officials. In <u>1857</u>, the US appointed a <u>non-Mormon governor</u> who arrived with 2500 US troops.

> The American government put <u>pressure</u> on the Mormons to <u>abandon polygamy</u>. The US only allowed Utah to become a <u>state</u> in <u>1896</u> after the Mormons had abandoned polygamy in <u>1890</u> — the Mormons <u>successfully settled</u> Salt Lake Valley, but they had to <u>compromise</u> their <u>beliefs</u>.

The Mormons had their own reasons for moving west

Make sure you understand that different groups of people had different experiences.
The Mormons went west to escape persecution — a very different motivation to other settlers.

Gold Miners

Migration to the west coast during the 1840s was <u>gradual</u>, but the California Gold Rush <u>changed</u> everything.

Gold was found in California in 1848

1) <u>James Marshall</u> found gold while working at John Sutter's sawmill in January <u>1848</u>. News of this spread <u>slowly</u> to the <u>east coast</u>, until President Polk made a speech in December <u>confirming</u> that gold had been found. As a result, <u>tens of thousands</u> of people made the journey west during <u>1849</u>.

2) People were <u>excited</u> at the prospect of making their <u>fortune</u>. Many hoped to find gold and then return <u>home</u>. James Carson, an army sergeant in California, abandoned his post to look for gold, writing later that he had 'a very violent attack of <u>gold fever</u>.'

3) People came to California from all over the <u>world</u> — e.g. China, Mexico and South America, as well as from other parts of North America.

A miner panning for gold.

The California Gold Rush presented many Challenges

1) Life as a miner was <u>hard</u>, even before reaching California. There were many <u>deaths</u> from <u>cholera</u> on the journey to California between 1849 and 1853.

2) Only a <u>lucky few</u> found gold in California. Surface gold (found using the simple method of panning) was <u>limited</u> and soon grew <u>scarce</u>. Some miners returned <u>home</u>, but others couldn't <u>afford</u> to.

> Some people ran <u>service</u> industries, e.g. <u>stores</u> and <u>saloons</u>. Unsuccessful miners often stayed on in California as <u>farmers</u> and <u>merchants</u> and started <u>families</u>.

3) Living and working conditions were <u>poor</u>. There was little <u>hygiene</u>, <u>disease</u> was common and <u>nutrition</u> among miners was poor. Miners who couldn't find gold worked for mining companies in <u>dangerous</u> conditions for <u>low</u> wages. When not working, people turned to <u>drinking</u> and <u>gambling</u> which often led to <u>trouble</u>.

4) The <u>rapid</u> migration of mostly <u>male</u> gold seekers and the quick <u>development</u> of <u>mining towns</u> meant that society was <u>unstructured</u> — there were no stable <u>families</u> or <u>communities</u>. There were <u>no laws</u> at first — miners had to enforce the law themselves but their justice wasn't always <u>fair</u> (see p.76).

5) There was frequent <u>racial conflict</u>. White Americans considered themselves <u>superior</u> to foreign miners and more <u>entitled</u> to the gold, especially when it began to grow scarce.

6) <u>Native American tribes</u> living in California suffered as a result of the Gold Rush. The Native American population in California <u>dropped</u> from around <u>150,000</u> to less than <u>30,000</u> during 1845-1870. This was the result of <u>violent attacks</u>, <u>epidemics</u> and being <u>driven off</u> their land.

California and the US as a whole felt the effects of the rush

1) Mining harmed California's <u>environment</u>. Timber for mine supports used up <u>forests</u>, chemicals such as mercury caused <u>pollution</u>, and the technique of <u>hydraulic mining</u> (the use of high powered jets of water to wash away hillsides and reach the gold beneath) <u>destroyed</u> the landscape.

2) But mining also kick-started California's <u>development</u>. The non-Native American population rose from around <u>14,000</u> to about <u>225,000</u> between 1848-1852. Mining towns such as <u>Sacramento</u> and <u>Stockton</u> expanded. <u>San Francisco</u> became the <u>economic centre</u> of California.

3) The Gold Rush <u>accelerated</u> the economic growth of the US. The wealth generated by gold mining gave America an important role in <u>world trade</u>. Settlement in California increased the need for <u>better links</u> between the east and west of the country, leading to improved <u>mail services</u> and a <u>transcontinental railroad</u> (see p.72).

Comment and Analysis

Mining had a <u>negative</u> impact on many individuals, especially the <u>Native Americans</u>.

Mining played an important role in the expansion of the USA
Write a quick summary of all of the positive and negative impacts of the California Gold Rush.

The Clash of Cultures

As more settlers started to cross the Great Plains, tension grew between them and the Plains Indians.

There was a **Lack** of **Understanding** between settlers and Indians

1) To settlers, it seemed that the Plains Indians had no system of government, that their warfare was cowardly and their religion just superstition (see p.53).

2) They had different views on land ownership. Native Americans believed that the land was for everyone, but settlers wanted to own, farm and exploit land.

3) Settlers thought that the Plains Indians' nomadic lifestyle was uncivilised and that they wasted the land. Native Americans thought that the settlers ruined the land.

> Horace Greeley, a newspaper editor, wrote in 1859 that 'God has given this earth to those who will subdue and cultivate it'.

Native Americans and Settlers Increasingly Came into Contact

- Significant numbers of settlers moved beyond the Permanent Indian Frontier (see p.52) and across the Plains to reach lands in the West from 1843. Many more came with the California Gold Rush of 1849.

- The settlers disrupted buffalo herds which the Plains Indians relied on, and polluted water sources, bringing diseases such as cholera.

- As a result, Plains Indians became more hostile. They sometimes attacked wagon trains, which increased the settlers' fear and distrust. The settlers also felt threatened by the Indians' inter-tribal conflict.

The **Reservation System** replaced the Permanent Indian Frontier

1) To reduce conflict on the Plains, the government pursued a policy of concentration — the Plains Indians would be concentrated onto specific areas of the Plains called reservations. The Indian Appropriations Act (1851) allocated funds to do this — it encouraged Native Americans to farm and build houses.

2) The Fort Laramie Treaty (1851) was the government's first attempt to concentrate the Plains Indians in certain areas. It defined the territory of each tribe to try to minimise inter-tribal conflict.

3) Tribes agreed to remain in their territory, allow settlers to cross the Plains, and allow the government to build roads and forts along the trails. In return, the government promised the tribes that they would have permanent rights to their lands, and that tribes would receive $50,000 of goods a year for 50 years.

4) Neither side kept to the treaty. Not all tribes agreed with it and many didn't even know it existed. The US government didn't keep its side of the deal either — it couldn't ensure settlers kept to the agreement, and in 1852 it reduced the yearly payments from 50 years to 10.

> The government never allowed existing treaties to prevent settlement it was in favour of — it simply negotiated new ones. For example, thousands of people encroached on Cheyenne land in Colorado during the Pike's Peak Gold Rush (1858-1861). The government then negotiated the Fort Wise Treaty, reducing Cheyenne land to make room for white settlers, and moving the Cheyenne to poor quality land on the Sand Creek Reservation. Some Cheyenne later claimed that they didn't understand the terms of the treaty when they signed it.

5) The treaty had a large impact:

- Settlement increased in California and Oregon.
- Restricting Native Americans to reservations threatened their way of life, as did the building of roads and forts in their territory.
- Broken promises increased Native American resentment towards government and settlers.

Comment and Analysis

The Fort Laramie Treaty is significant because it marked the end of the Permanent Indian Frontier — the Native Americans could no longer live freely on the Plains. It paved the way for further treaties in the 1850s and 1860s which resulted in tribes losing land, e.g. in 1853 treaties were made with tribes in Kansas and Nebraska to make room for settlers in those areas — these tribes lost nearly 17 million acres.

> Native Americans had been given the Great Plains when they were considered uninhabitable. This changed when settlers decided that they wanted the land.

The promises made in the Fort Laramie Treaty were quickly broken

For key laws and treaties, think about why they were introduced and what their consequences were.

Worked Exam-Style Question

This worked answer will give you some tips on answering questions that ask you to discuss the role of different factors in an event or development. Look at the way it considers both factors in detail.

Q1

> Which factor was the more important reason for increasing tension between US citizens and Native Americans from c.1830 to c.1860?
> - Government policy
> - Increasing settlement in the West
>
> Explain your answer, referring to both factors. [12 marks]

This gives a <u>basic answer</u> to the question in the <u>first sentence</u>.

<u>Government policies and increasing settlement in the West were both key factors</u> in the growing tension between US citizens and Native Americans between c.1830 and c.1860, but <u>government policy was a more important reason for this development</u>.

<u>Government policy</u> towards Native Americans and the territory they were allowed to occupy played a key role in increasing tension. For example, the <u>Indian Removal Act of 1830 removed Native Americans from lands in the East and instead granted them land on the Great Plains</u>. This policy increased tension, since many tribes resisted being moved onto the Plains. <u>The Seminole fought a guerilla war against the government for seven years from 1835 until they finally surrendered and moved west in 1842</u>.

This uses <u>relevant details</u> to explain the point that's being made.

This explains <u>how</u> this government policy <u>caused tension</u> by describing one of its <u>consequences</u>.

This develops the argument by bringing in <u>another relevant aspect</u> of government policy.

The government's <u>later policy of concentration, which was introduced in 1851, increased tension</u> between US citizens and Native Americans even further. This policy forced Native Americans onto smaller reservations on the Great Plains so that US citizens could occupy the rest of the land. <u>This created more tension because it broke the government's promise, made in the Indian Removal Act, that the Native American tribes could have the Great Plains to live on</u>.

This explains how later <u>government policies</u> caused tension to <u>increase</u>.

You have to talk about <u>both factors</u> to get high marks.

<u>Increasing settlement in the West</u> also caused tension between Native Americans and US citizens. The development of the Oregon and California Trails in the 1840s and the discovery of gold in California in 1848 meant that more US citizens began to move beyond the Permanent Indian Frontier. <u>These settlers didn't understand the Native Americans' way of life and disrupted the buffalo herds that the Plains Indians relied on. As a result, Native Americans became more hostile towards US citizens</u> — some Native Americans began to attack wagon trains. This caused tension as it damaged any trust that had existed between the two groups.

This gives an example of the <u>impact</u> of increasing settlement in the West.

Worked Exam-Style Question

This explains how <u>increasing settlement in the West</u> and <u>government policies</u> were <u>linked</u>.

The tension caused by increasing settlement in the West was made worse by government policies, because <u>the government often failed to uphold treaties that would have protected Native Americans from settlers</u>. For example, during the Pike's Peak Gold Rush in Colorado between 1858 and 1861, the terms of the Fort Laramie Treaty of 1851 were broken when settlers encroached on Cheyenne land. <u>Instead of enforcing the existing treaty, the government negotiated the Fort Wise Treaty, which reduced Cheyenne territory and gave their land to settlers</u>. This increased tension as the <u>government's willingness to break its treaties in order to secure land for US citizens made many Native Americans feel angry and resentful</u>.

This explains why government policies were <u>responsible</u> for increasing tension.

Make sure you give a <u>clear answer</u> to the question in the conclusion.

Overall, <u>government policies were a more important reason for the development of tension between Native Americans and US citizens</u>. Increasing settlement in the West did cause tension as settlers and Native Americans struggled to coexist peacefully. However, government policies made this tension worse as the government repeatedly failed to uphold the rights of Native Americans or protect them from the effects of increasing settlement. Furthermore, <u>the government's willingness to break its promises made it almost impossible for Native Americans to trust US citizens</u>. It was this behaviour by the government that played the biggest role in causing tension.

This <u>sums up</u> the points that have been made in the answer and comes to an <u>overall judgement</u>.

Exam-Style Questions

Q1
Describe two ways in which the traditional lifestyle of the Plains Indians differed from the lifestyle of white settlers.   [4 marks]

Q2
What played the most important role in encouraging settlers to migrate to the west coast from the 1840s: problems in the East or new opportunities in the West?

Explain your answer, referring to both factors.   [12 marks]

Q3
Give an account that analyses the ways in which the relationship between the Native Americans and white settlers changed between 1830 and 1850.

You could mention the Permanent Indian Frontier and the Great Migration of 1843 in your answer.   [8 marks]

Q4
Examine:

a) the significance of the California Gold Rush (1849) for the expansion of America.   [8 marks]

b) the significance of the Fort Laramie Treaty (1851) for the relationship between Native Americans and the American government.   [8 marks]

The Causes of the Civil War

The North and the South developed in <u>different</u> ways. They developed <u>economic</u> and <u>political</u> differences that grew more significant over time. These divisions caused tensions that eventually led to the <u>Civil War</u>.

The **North** and **South** had **Different Economies**

1) In the early 19th century, the <u>South's economy</u> was heavily based on <u>cotton exports</u>. Cotton was produced <u>cheaply</u> using slave labour on <u>plantations</u> (p.50).

2) Slavery wasn't as important in the <u>North</u> — it had a more <u>diverse economy</u> that was based on lots of <u>different industries</u> and <u>agricultural crops</u>.

> The North didn't necessarily want <u>racial equality</u>. They were more worried about the South gaining political power and spreading slavery into new territories (see p.63).

3) By <u>1804</u>, all of the <u>northern</u> states had <u>abolished slavery</u> (banned it). This created a <u>division</u> between southern '<u>slave states</u>' and northern '<u>free states</u>'.

4) As time went on, the North became even <u>more industrialised</u>, while the South <u>relied</u> more and more on <u>cotton cultivation</u>. By the <u>1860s</u>, the <u>North</u> had <u>six times</u> as many <u>factories</u> as the South. The North was now <u>more wealthy</u> than the South as a result of its <u>diverse</u> and <u>industrialised</u> economy.

Comment and Analysis

Some historians point out that the <u>South</u> didn't <u>need</u> to <u>industrialise</u>, because they made lots of money out of <u>plantation agriculture</u>. This might have been true, but it was a bad idea to <u>rely</u> on <u>one industry</u> (cotton) to keep the economy going.

5) Not <u>all</u> southerners were slave owners — in <u>1860</u>, only about <u>5%</u> of southerners <u>owned</u> slaves. <u>Less than 1%</u> of these slaveholders had <u>large slave plantations</u> with 200 or more slaves. However, because the southern <u>economy</u> was based on slave labour, southerners saw it as part of their <u>way of life</u>.

The **North** had a **Bigger Population** than the **South**

1) The <u>North's</u> population was <u>bigger</u> than the South's. A <u>big proportion</u> of the <u>South's population</u> were <u>slaves</u> — by <u>1860</u>, there were almost <u>4 million slaves</u> in the <u>South</u> compared to <u>8 million</u> free white Americans.

2) The North's population gave it more <u>political power</u>, as states with a bigger population could have <u>more representatives</u> in the <u>lower house</u> of Congress.

3) The <u>South</u> still had lots of <u>political power</u>, though.

- Each state had <u>two</u> representatives in the <u>Senate</u> (the upper house of Congress).
- Each <u>new state</u> that applied to join the Union had to <u>decide</u> whether to allow or ban slavery.
- As long as the number of <u>free</u> and <u>slave</u> states in Congress was <u>balanced</u>, the <u>South</u> could use its votes in the <u>Senate</u> to <u>protect slavery</u>.

> <u>Slaves</u> were counted as <u>three-fifths of a person</u>. This gave southerners <u>more power</u> than they would've had if only <u>free people</u> were counted.

The North had a much more diverse economy than the South

Write a bullet point list of the differences between the North and the South. Include the differences in economics, population and political power.

The Causes of the Civil War

One of the main points of disagreement between North and South was the issue of <u>slavery</u>. The North was <u>against</u> slavery, while the South was <u>in favour</u>. Each side did not want the other to gain an <u>advantage</u> on the issue.

Westward expansion **Increased** the **Tension** over **Slavery**

1) <u>Slavery</u> became so important in the <u>South</u> that many southerners believed there would be <u>economic</u> and <u>social chaos</u> if it was abolished. They were keen to <u>protect</u> their way of life.

2) As <u>westward expansion</u> continued, <u>northern senators</u> tried to stop <u>new states</u> becoming slave states. They wanted to use <u>land</u> in the West for their <u>own economic development</u>.

3) This caused <u>tension</u> between the North and the South, which came to the surface when <u>new states</u> asked to join the Union.

Comment and Analysis

The North and the South were <u>suspicious</u> of each other. They both feared that the other's way of life would be <u>forced</u> upon them.

- The <u>southern states</u> feared that admitting more free states would give the North enough <u>power</u> to pass a law abolishing slavery in <u>all states</u>.

- The <u>northern states</u> worried that they would be <u>outvoted</u> in the Senate if <u>too many slave states</u> were admitted. Both sides wanted the <u>balance</u> to tip in their <u>own favour</u>.

The **Missouri Compromise** helped to **Settle Tension**

1) In <u>1820</u>, the <u>Missouri Compromise</u> was created to try and <u>reduce tension</u> over slavery.

2) An <u>imaginary line</u> was drawn from the southern border of Missouri to the western edge of US territory. All <u>future states</u> that formed <u>north</u> of the <u>Missouri Line</u> were to be <u>banned</u> from becoming <u>slave states</u>.

3) The <u>Missouri Compromise</u> worked well for about <u>twenty years</u> and Congress stayed balanced. However, the debate started up again in <u>1846</u> after the USA gained <u>more territory</u> in the West.

Free State Abolitionists wanted Slavery to End

Some people in northern free states campaigned for slaves to be <u>freed</u> — they were called <u>abolitionists</u>. At first, abolitionists wanted slavery to be <u>ended slowly</u> and for owners to be <u>compensated</u> for losing their slaves.

<u>Attitudes</u> to slavery <u>varied</u> in the North — not everyone was opposed to it. But this didn't make the South feel any less <u>threatened</u> — they believed that the North was <u>united</u> against them to <u>end slavery</u>.

1) Opposition became more <u>radical</u> in the 1830s — abolitionists began to call slavery a moral evil which should end <u>immediately</u>. They became more organised, forming the <u>American Anti-Slavery Association</u> in <u>1833</u>.

2) Abolition gained <u>some support</u> in the <u>North</u>. However, many northerners <u>didn't support</u> abolition — they worried about the impact of <u>freed slaves</u> coming to the North in big numbers. <u>Southerners</u> felt that their <u>way of life</u> was being attacked, so there was <u>little support</u> for the movement in the South.

3) In <u>1851</u>, abolitionist Harriet Beecher Stowe wrote a novel attacking slavery called '<u>Uncle Tom's Cabin</u>'. It sparked <u>support</u> for abolition by making many in the <u>North</u> more aware of the <u>immorality</u> of slavery.

EXAM TIP

Slavery was an important factor in the outbreak of the Civil War

There were lots of different factors that led to the outbreak of the Civil War. For example, slavery and the tension it caused was a key factor, but economic and political factors were important too.

The Causes of the Civil War

Tensions over slavery and expansion continued to build, and Lincoln's election as President was the final straw for the South. It decided to secede (withdraw) from the Union, prompting a Civil War between North and South.

The Missouri Compromise was Broken in 1854

The Kansas-Nebraska Act of 1854 ended the Missouri Compromise (see p.63). Under the Compromise, slavery had been outlawed in the Kansas-Nebraska territory — but when the Act admitted Kansas and Nebraska to the Union, it allowed settlers to vote on whether they were to become free or slave states.

- Many northerners were angry with the Act. The Republican Party was formed as a result of this discontent — it aimed to stop the spread of slavery. By 1856, the Republicans had gained much support in the North, but the Democrats stayed popular in the South. This created more tension.

- The Act was designed to reduce tension, but it actually made things worse. Many in the North saw it as giving in to the South.

Lincoln's Election as President in 1860 triggered Secession

1) In 1860, Republican Abraham Lincoln won the presidential election. He thought slavery was immoral and opposed its spread into new territories, but said he didn't want to interfere with it in areas where it already existed.

> Lincoln was a minority president — he only got 40% of the overall vote and he didn't get any votes in 10 of the southern states.

2) Many Southerners felt that they didn't owe any loyalty to a man who threatened their way of life. His election triggered the secession (withdrawal) of seven states, and in February 1861 these states formed the Confederate States of America with Jefferson Davis as their president.

3) When Lincoln was sworn in as Union president in March 1861, he said that he wouldn't accept secession. Davis thought that states had the right to secede — he didn't want the Union to break up, but he also believed in the South's freedom to own slaves.

4) Lincoln refused to withdraw US government troops at Fort Sumter in South Carolina — the Confederates saw this as a lack of respect for their independence. Lincoln sent more supplies to the fort, but said that he would only attack if the South did so first. In April 1861, Confederate troops attacked the fort.

5) This triggered a Civil War between the Union and the Confederates. By August 1861, 11 southern states had seceded from the Union. Lincoln declared that the Confederate states were in rebellion.

Ending Slavery became a Main Aim of the Civil War for the North

1) Lincoln insisted that the aim of the war was to preserve the Union rather than abolish slavery — he knew that many northerners and citizens in the remaining loyal southern states wouldn't support abolition as a war aim.

2) The aim of the war changed with Lincoln's Emancipation Proclamation in 1863 — all slaves in rebellious states were to be emancipated (freed). This made ending slavery an aim of the war (in addition to preserving the Union).

3) Emancipation made military sense because it would strengthen the northern army. It also tied in with the moral beliefs of Lincoln, who was facing increasing pressure from fellow Republicans to make the war about slavery.

REVISION TASK

Tensions between North and South reached boiling point in 1861

Write a character profile of Abraham Lincoln. In your profile, you should include his attitude towards slavery and secession, his actions leading up to the Civil War and his aims during the war.

The Impact of the Civil War

The Civil War had a large economic and social impact on both the North and the South.

The War had a Negative Impact on the South's Economy

1) In 1861, the South introduced a ban on cotton exports to force Europe to side with them in the war. Europe had more cotton than they needed, so the ban failed and the South lost valuable income.

2) Southerners were cut off from northern markets during the war and the blockade made it hard to import food. Also, lots of farmland was destroyed by fighting. Things got worse in 1864 when the North started to target southern transport and civilian property to deliberately cause economic hardship.

3) Food shortages led to inflation (when prices go up and money loses value) — black markets formed and made inflation worse. In 1863, the Confederacy introduced new ways of collecting tax to help cover the costs of the war effort.

4) The Confederate government issued paper money in 1861. Once it became obvious that the South was losing the war and had printed too many notes, the value of the notes fell quickly and inflation increased.

> Lincoln knew the value of cotton exports, so he ordered a blockade of ships to be put in place. By July 1861, all Confederate ports were surrounded by Union ships. Even after the South ended their ban, they struggled to export cotton because of the blockade.

Comment and Analysis

Some historians criticise Davis's government for taking over the economy and then failing to protect it — its handling of paper currency and interference in the cotton industry made things worse.

The Economy in the North actually Benefited from the War

1) The North suffered from inflation too, but its economy was in a stronger position to deal with it. During the war, northern agricultural and industrial production increased, as the army needed a good supply of food and weapons. This created job opportunities and increasing prosperity for northerners.

2) Northerners were also taxed, but only those with incomes above a certain amount had to pay. The government borrowed a lot of money from richer northern citizens to fund the war.

The Social Impact of the War was Serious

> Around 260,000 Confederate soldiers and 360,000 Union soldiers died during the war. Historians reckon that about 50,000 southern civilians died because of the war too, though no one knows the full death toll.

1) Most of the fighting happened in the South — some areas were occupied by Union soldiers. Lots of property was destroyed, so many southerners became refugees. There was guerilla warfare too, where armed civilians fought against Union soldiers, raided their bases and cut their lines of communication. However, some guerilla groups also robbed and attacked other civilians.

2) People who weren't close to the fighting still knew quite a lot about what was going on — soldiers wrote letters to their families and newspapers ran stories about the war.

3) Civilians in both the North and South lost civil liberties during the war.

- Conscription (forcing civilians into the army) was introduced in the South by Davis in 1862 and in the North by Lincoln in 1863.
- Both sides suspended the right to a trial and introduced martial law (where a military commander takes control).

4) As men were fighting in the South, jobs were created for women and freed slaves in the North. This caused social tension — some felt that freed slaves were taking 'white jobs'.

5) In 1863, there were riots against conscription in New York. A lot of anger was directed at black citizens.

> During the 1864 election, a northern Democrat stirred up fears of mixed-race marriage as part of a racist campaign that played on this social tension.

An engraving from the Illustrated London News, August 1863. A black man is hanged by rioters during the New York Draft Riots in July 1863.

The Civil War had a devastating impact on the South
Draw a mind map of the effects of the Civil War, including its impact on both the North and the South.

African American Experiences of the Civil War

The Civil War was fought from <u>1861 to 1865</u>. The <u>North</u> won — seceded states <u>returned</u> to the <u>Union</u> and <u>slavery</u> was <u>abolished</u>. The Civil War had a <u>huge impact</u> on the lives of African Americans.

Many African Americans wanted to **Serve** in the **Union Army**

1) Many African Americans tried to join the army (enlist) at the outbreak of war, but they were <u>rejected</u>. Those who tried to enlist included <u>freemen</u> in the North and <u>slaves</u> who <u>escaped</u> from the South after the war started.

> Lincoln was worried he would lose the <u>support</u> of the remaining <u>loyal</u> southern states if he <u>allowed</u> African Americans to join the Union Army.

2) African Americans were eventually accepted into the Union Army with the <u>Emancipation Proclamation</u> of 1863 (see p.64). Thousands enlisted and formed <u>all-black</u> units. One of the first of these was the <u>54th Massachusetts Infantry Regiment</u>.

3) Around <u>180,000 African American soldiers</u> had joined the Union Army by the war's end.

4) African Americans also helped the war effort in <u>other</u> ways, e.g. as blacksmiths, nurses and cooks. Some served as <u>guides</u> and <u>spies</u> for the Union Army in the South.

Comment and Analysis

After the Emancipation Proclamation, the aim of the war became about <u>ending slavery</u> as well as preserving the Union — African Americans now had a <u>chance</u> to fight for their <u>own freedom</u>.

African Americans faced **Prejudice** from northerners

1) Although there was opposition to <u>slavery</u> in the North, many northerners <u>didn't</u> see African Americans as <u>equal</u>.

2) Black people faced <u>racism</u> and <u>discrimination</u> in the Union Army:

- They fought in <u>segregated</u> regiments led by white officers.
- Many people didn't believe that black men were as <u>skilled</u> or <u>brave</u> as white men — they were often given <u>menial</u> jobs.
- Black soldiers were paid <u>$10</u> a month — <u>$3</u> less than white soldiers.
- African Americans were given <u>poorer supplies</u> and worse <u>rations</u>.

A drawing of the 54th Massachusetts Infantry Regiment attacking Fort Wagner in 1863.

3) Black soldiers faced more <u>danger</u> than white soldiers if they were <u>captured</u> by the South in battle — the Confederates threatened to <u>enslave</u> them.

4) There was <u>racial tension</u> in the North. When <u>conscription</u> was introduced in 1863, many northerners were <u>angry</u> — they didn't want to be <u>forced</u> to fight to free slaves. This led to <u>riots</u> in New York in which African Americans were <u>killed</u>.

> Black troops proved their <u>bravery</u> during the Civil War — half the 54th Massachusetts Infantry Regiment were <u>killed</u> during the assault shown above.

Many African Americans **Unwillingly** helped the **South**

1) As white men left to fight in the Confederate Army, <u>discipline</u> on some plantations was <u>relaxed</u>. Many slaves began to <u>resist</u> by working at a <u>slower</u> pace, refusing to obey <u>orders</u> and breaking <u>rules</u>.

2) Many slaves and free African Americans were <u>forced</u> to support the Confederate war effort. They were made to build <u>fortifications</u>, work in <u>factories</u> or work as <u>nurses</u> and <u>cooks</u>.

3) Some free African Americans in the South did <u>volunteer</u> to help the Confederates — usually as skilled or manual <u>labourers</u> — but they were in the <u>minority</u>.

4) Confederates were <u>unwilling</u> to arm slaves because of fears of slave <u>rebellion</u>. Slaves were only accepted as troops in <u>1865</u>, when the South was coming close to <u>losing</u> the war.

EXAM TIP

The Civil War changed the lives of African Americans

Make sure you understand the effect of the Civil War on African Americans. Many fought for their own freedom. But many faced prejudice — their next battle would be one for equality.

The Reconstruction Era

After the Civil War, efforts were made to rebuild the United States — this is known as the Reconstruction Era, which lasted from around 1865 to 1877. It began with the abolition of slavery at the end of the Civil War.

Slavery was Formally Abolished after the War

After the Union won the war in 1865, over four million slaves were freed and the South's plantation economy was destroyed. Politicians started to rebuild the South and help freed slaves to become part of free society.

1) Securing freedom for African Americans was a key part of Reconstruction.

2) Many slaves in the South had already been freed by the Emancipation Proclamation in 1863, but slavery still existed in the border states (the slave states of Delaware, Kentucky, Maryland and Missouri which remained loyal to the Union).

The 13th Amendment

1) The 13th Amendment to the US Constitution was introduced by Lincoln when he was re-elected in 1864 — it abolished slavery in all states.

2) Lincoln was assassinated in April 1865, but his government had already laid the groundwork for the 13th Amendment.

3) The Amendment was ratified by most northern and border states, and some southern states, in December 1865.

> Ratification is when states formally accept changes to the Constitution. An amendment is ratified once three-quarters of states have agreed.

3) The 13th Amendment freed slaves, but it didn't give them equal rights. There was a debate over how far African Americans should be given civil rights during the Reconstruction Era.

4) The Freedmen's Bureau was set up in March 1865 to help freed slaves and poor southerners to rebuild their lives. It provided food and shelter, and legal and medical aid. It also helped communities to establish new schools. But it was poorly funded and limited by political issues — it closed in 1872.

Andrew Johnson began Presidential Reconstruction in 1865

Andrew Johnson was a Democratic senator from Tennessee. He was pro-slavery but strongly disagreed with southern secession. Johnson took over as President in April 1865 after Lincoln was assassinated. He took a lenient approach to the South:

- He pardoned all white southerners except Confederate leaders and wealthy planters, but many later received individual pardons.

- Property was returned to its original owners instead of being redistributed. Many African Americans rented land from white people (sharecropping) — sometimes they rented from their former masters.

- Some of the southern elite regained power — many had been in the Confederate government and army.

- Some southern states created the Black Codes, which limited the freedom of African Americans. For example, South Carolina made black people pay a tax if they were not farmers or servants.

The South was treated leniently during Presidential Reconstruction

When you're writing about Reconstruction, think about how the North and the South's different attitudes to slavery might have influenced the way that they wanted the South to be rebuilt.

The Reconstruction Era

Johnson's <u>lenient approach</u> towards the South <u>annoyed</u> some radical Republicans. Following Johnson's <u>veto</u> of the Civil Rights Act, Republicans in Congress believed it was time to <u>take control</u> of Reconstruction.

Johnson **Opposed** the **Civil Rights Act**

1) Johnson <u>didn't support equal rights</u> for African Americans, so he did <u>nothing</u> to stop the <u>Black Codes</u> (see p.67).

2) In <u>1866</u>, he tried to <u>veto</u> (reject) the Civil Rights Act. However, his veto was <u>overturned</u> and the Civil Rights Act became <u>law</u> in 1866:

> ### The Civil Rights Act
>
> The <u>Civil Rights Act</u> gave <u>citizenship</u> and <u>equal rights</u> to <u>all</u> who were <u>born</u> in the <u>US</u> — it excluded <u>Native Americans</u> and people who were under the control of a <u>foreign power</u>. The Act was designed to <u>protect</u> the rights of <u>African Americans</u>.

Some **Republicans** disagreed with **Johnson's Approach**

1) Some <u>radical Republicans</u> wanted <u>racial equality</u> and greater <u>punishment</u> of Confederate leaders.

2) <u>Moderate Republicans</u> didn't agree with Johnson's <u>veto</u> of the <u>Civil Rights Act</u>. They created an <u>alliance</u> with the radicals and <u>overturned</u> his veto to ensure that the Act became law.

3) Congress passed the <u>14th Amendment</u> in 1868 — Johnson <u>opposed</u> it and the southern states <u>refused</u> to ratify it. Many in the North began to think that a <u>tougher</u> approach was needed in the South.

> ### The 14th Amendment
>
> The <u>14th Amendment</u> had a '<u>Citizenship Clause</u>', which guaranteed <u>citizenship</u> to all males born in the US regardless of <u>race</u>. It also had an '<u>Equal Protection Clause</u>', which gave black people the same rights as white people to <u>state protection</u>.

Radical Republicans took over **Reconstruction** in **1867**

1) The <u>First and Second Reconstruction Acts</u> were passed by Congress in March <u>1867</u>. These acts placed the South under <u>military rule</u>. Before rebel states could <u>rejoin</u> the Union, they were forced to <u>ratify</u> the 14th Amendment and <u>rewrite</u> their state constitutions to allow <u>black people</u> to vote.

2) Congress's approach to the South was <u>more forceful</u> than Johnson's — they sent <u>troops</u> to the South to keep the <u>peace</u> and <u>protect</u> freed slaves and their right to <u>vote</u>. Leading rebels were <u>removed</u> from office.

3) Johnson tried to <u>obstruct</u> Radical Reconstruction — he vetoed both Reconstruction Acts, so radicals <u>impeached</u> him (put him on trial). He <u>wasn't convicted</u>, but he lost power and <u>Ulysses Grant</u> was elected President in <u>1869</u>. The <u>15th Amendment</u> was passed in 1869 and ratified in 1870.

> ### The 15th Amendment
>
> The <u>15th Amendment</u> ruled that citizens of the USA could not be <u>denied</u> the right to vote based on their '<u>race, colour, or previous condition of servitude</u>'.

The Republicans began to take control of Reconstruction

In the exam, rather than saying 'the government', try to identify which person or group of people was pushing for a particular change. Johnson's aims were very different to those of the radical Republicans.

The Reconstruction Era

The Republicans <u>introduced policies</u> to try to build a <u>better society</u> in the South. The problem was that by the <u>end</u> of the Reconstruction Era, the <u>attitudes</u> of many white people in the South <u>hadn't changed</u>.

The South became part of the Union again

1) By <u>1870</u>, all states had been <u>re-admitted</u> to the Union. The <u>southern</u> states had Republican governments made up of <u>white southerners</u> who supported Reconstruction, <u>northerners</u>, and <u>African Americans</u>.

2) Northerners who went to carry out the government's <u>Reconstruction policies</u> in the South were called 'carpetbaggers' by southerners. They were accused of being <u>corrupt</u> and <u>exploiting</u> the South.

3) Three <u>Enforcement Acts</u> were passed between <u>1870</u> and <u>1871</u>. They made it <u>illegal</u> to use terror, force or bribery to stop black people from <u>voting</u>, and they gave the government powers to <u>quickly suppress</u> the <u>Ku Klux Klan</u>.

The Ku Klux Klan

- The Ku Klux Klan was a <u>white supremacist</u> group that formed in 1865. They murdered, lynched, beat and threatened <u>African Americans</u>, white <u>Republicans</u> and their <u>supporters</u>.

- The Klan also <u>burned</u> churches, homes and schools.

- Many Klan members were <u>arrested</u> and put on <u>trial</u> under the Enforcement Acts.

Comment and Analysis

<u>Radical Reconstruction</u> was a period of <u>hope</u> and <u>idealism</u> for many, in spite of southern grievances. Radicals believed that <u>equality</u> could be achieved.

The Reconstruction Era ended in 1877

1) By <u>1873</u>, political support for Reconstruction had <u>weakened</u> in the <u>North</u>. <u>Economic depression</u> in 1874 caused <u>high unemployment</u>, so northerners <u>lost interest</u> in the South.

2) Supreme Court decisions also <u>weakened</u> the power of the <u>14th Amendment</u> to protect <u>black civil rights</u>. In <u>1876</u>, the Supreme Court ruled that only states, not the federal government, could prosecute people under the <u>Enforcement Acts</u> — this resulted in many <u>violent crimes</u> going <u>unpunished</u> in the South.

3) The depression, and <u>corruption</u> and <u>scandal</u> under President Grant, meant that Republicans <u>lost support</u>. The <u>Democrats</u> won <u>control</u> of the lower house of Congress in <u>1874</u> for first time since the Civil War.

4) Republican <u>Rutherford B. Hayes</u> was elected President in <u>1876</u>, but the election results were disputed. In return for recognition of his election, he <u>accepted</u> the <u>Democrats' control</u> of the <u>South</u> and <u>ended</u> federal <u>military involvement</u> there. The Reconstruction Era was <u>over</u>.

5) The Reconstruction Era <u>improved rights</u> for African Americans, but many issues were <u>unresolved</u> by <u>1876</u>:

- More than <u>700,000</u> black people were registered to <u>vote</u> and over <u>1500</u> were elected to <u>state</u> and <u>national</u> offices. However, while they had <u>representation</u>, it <u>wasn't in proportion</u> to their population.

- Some southerners <u>ignored</u> laws like 15th Amendment — they tried to stop black people from voting using <u>literacy tests</u> and <u>poll taxes</u>.

- Many <u>Ku Klux Klan</u> members were <u>fined</u> and let off with a <u>warning</u>. Other violent groups emerged, like the <u>Rifle Clubs</u> and the <u>Red Shirts</u>, who carried on murdering and threatening southern Republicans.

Comment and Analysis

A key <u>barrier</u> to the success of Reconstruction was that the <u>attitude</u> of many southern whites <u>didn't change</u>. African Americans had <u>more independence</u> than under slavery, but in many ways, their <u>rights</u> were still <u>limited</u>.

Some southerners found ways to get around the law

REVISION TASK Write down a description of what these acts or amendments did to protect African Americans — the First and Second Reconstruction Acts, the 15th Amendment and the Enforcement Acts.

Exam-Style Questions

Q1

Explain how far you agree that Lincoln's election was the main cause of the American Civil War (1861-65).   [18 marks]

Q2

Give two consequences of the American Civil War (1861-65) and explain them.   [8 marks]

Q3

Write a summary explaining the different stages of Reconstruction from 1865 to 1877. Give examples to support your answer.   [9 marks]

Homesteaders

After the Civil War, large numbers of <u>settlers</u> began to move on to the <u>Great Plains</u> — an area once seen as <u>unsuitable</u> for living. The US government did a lot to encourage <u>homesteaders</u> and the building of the <u>railways</u>.

Different Groups of people moved to the Plains

1) Many settlers had <u>previously</u> viewed the Plains as a '<u>desert</u>' (see p.47). More began to move there from the 1840s (see p.54), but after 1865, <u>thousands</u> followed — this was a big <u>change in attitude</u>. This included:

- Migrants from <u>eastern</u> states who moved because of <u>growing population</u> and <u>high land prices</u>.

- Immigrants who'd come to America to escape <u>poverty</u> and religious and political <u>persecution</u>.

- <u>Slaves</u> who had been freed after the Civil War and ex-Civil War <u>soldiers</u> who wanted a <u>new start</u>.

2) After the end of the <u>Reconstruction Era</u> in 1877 (see p.67-69), African Americans faced growing <u>oppression</u> in the South. As a result, thousands <u>moved west</u> — e.g. approximately 20,000 black migrants known as '<u>Exodusters</u>' moved to Kansas in 1879.

The Government encouraged people to Settle on the Plains

1) The government encouraged people to move west and settle on the Plains by promoting the idea of '<u>Manifest Destiny</u>' (see p.54). They moved Indians onto <u>reservations</u>, which <u>freed up</u> land for settlement (see p.58).

2) Before the Civil War, southerners in Congress <u>opposed</u> acts which encouraged non-slave-owning settlers to move into new areas — southerners were <u>worried</u> that this would result in these areas eventually becoming <u>free states</u> (see p.62).

3) When the South seceded, the North was able to <u>pass</u> acts like the <u>Homestead Act</u> and the <u>Pacific Railroad Act</u> (see p.72) to encourage migration.

The 1862 Homestead Act gave settlers Free Land

1) The <u>Homestead Act</u> was passed in 1862. It gave each settler 160 acres of <u>free land</u> if they farmed it for five years.

2) This opened up <u>2.5 million</u> acres for settlement and was open to <u>everyone</u>, including immigrants, freed slaves and single women.

3) Between <u>1862</u> and <u>1900</u>, around <u>600,000</u> people claimed land under the Act.

4) The condition of farming the land for five years was meant to discourage <u>speculators</u> — those aiming to make a short-term <u>profit</u> on rising land prices rather than settling and living on the land. However, the Homestead Act was still <u>affected</u> by speculators and corruption.

Comment and Analysis

The Homestead Act was <u>important</u> because it opened up land ownership to <u>ordinary</u> people. Although there were <u>problems</u>, it helped to <u>establish</u> settlement on the Plains.

The role of the Great Plains was far from settled

The Homestead Act was an important development in the settlement of the Great Plains. Make sure you're able to explain why it was passed and what made it so significant.

Homesteaders

The Homestead Act made the Plains seem more attractive, but the 1862 Pacific Railroad Act made the Plains much more accessible to people living on the east coast. The Act introduced the first railway to join East and West.

The **Pacific Railroad Act** was passed in **1862**

1) The Pacific Railroad Act of 1862 approved the construction of the First Transcontinental Railroad — a railway which ran across the US from east to west.

2) The government believed the railway would make migration into unsettled land easier and create national unity by connecting the West and the East.

3) The railway was completed in 1869.

Railway Companies encouraged further Settlement of the West

1) Railway companies were granted huge areas of land on the Plains by the government — they sold this land cheaply to settlers to help fund their railway building.

2) Economic development was made easier because the West was now linked with markets in the East.

3) People could be transported more easily, as well as supplies which aided settlement, such as building materials and machinery.

4) Promotional posters made exaggerated claims about the good life on the Plains.

> 'The Location is Central, along the 41st parallel, the favorite latitude of America. Equally well adapted to corn or wheat; free from the long, cold winters of the Northern, and the hot, unhealthy influences of the Southern states...
>
> The Soil is a dark loam, slightly impregnated with lime, free from stone and gravel, and eminently adapted to grass, grain and root crops...
>
> The Climate is mild and healthful; the atmosphere dry and pure. Epidemic diseases never prevail; Fever and Ague are unknown...
>
> Timber is found on the streams and grows rapidly.'
>
> *Extract from a Union Pacific Railroad advertisement for farming lands in Nebraska, 1870.*

Life on the Plains was **Hard** for homesteaders

1) There was little or no wood for building or fuel.

2) The soil was fertile, but the thick top layer of earth (known as sod) was too hard for light ploughs.

3) Lack of water meant crops like maize failed and deep wells had to be dug.

4) Wind, extremes of weather, grasshopper plagues and prairie fires often destroyed crops.

Railroads made it easier for people to move west

On a sheet of paper, draw your own railroad company poster trying to tempt people to move west. Then, draw an honest poster detailing the difficult farming conditions that settlers might face.

America, 1789-1900

Farming Out West

The government was <u>encouraging</u> people to settle on the Plains, but homesteading was a <u>tough</u> life. As <u>more people</u> faced the difficulties of living and farming on the Plains, they found ways to <u>survive</u>.

Technology and Government Acts helped settlers farm the Plains

1) Conditions on the Plains made farming (and life generally) <u>difficult</u> (see p.72). But new developments in <u>technology</u> and <u>crops</u> helped:

- John Deere developed a stronger <u>steel plough</u> in the 1830s which could break through the tough soil. This was improved on by <u>James Oliver</u> who invented a <u>lower cost</u> iron plough called the 'sodbuster' in 1868.
- <u>Windpumps</u> increased the supply of <u>water</u> by pumping underground water to the surface.
- The introduction of <u>barbed wire</u> in 1874 meant that farmers could <u>cheaply</u> fence off their land to keep animals off their crops.
- <u>Turkey Red Wheat</u> was a hardy crop brought over from Russia in around 1874 which was <u>well-suited</u> to growing on the Plains. People also learned which crops were most <u>suitable</u> for growing on different types of land, e.g. people in Kansas and Nebraska realised that their land was more suited to growing <u>wheat</u> than <u>corn</u>.

2) The government helped people living in <u>less fertile</u> areas who struggled to make a living from the 160 acres given to them by the Homestead Act (see p.71).

Farming was still <u>hard</u> — not all settlers could <u>afford</u> new equipment.

3) For example, the <u>Timber Culture Act</u> of <u>1873</u> gave these settlers another <u>160 acres</u> for free — as long as they planted <u>trees</u> on one quarter of the land. This meant that <u>wood</u> eventually became more widely available on the Plains.

Settlers had to Adapt to survive everyday life on the Plains

1) Because of the lack of wood, people originally had to make houses out of <u>sod</u>. But these became <u>infested</u> with insects and were <u>unhygienic</u>. Settlers <u>whitewashed</u> the walls to try and stop insects coming into the house through the walls.

Women also <u>nursed</u> the sick and helped each other in childbirth — there weren't many <u>doctors</u> on the Plains.

2) <u>Women</u> were responsible for housework and their children's <u>education</u>. They had to collect buffalo dung for <u>fuel</u> and made a lot of what they needed, such as <u>clothes</u> and <u>soap</u>.

© The Art Archive / Granger Collection

Settlers with their sod house in Nebraska.

3) <u>Isolation</u> was a constant problem for early settlers, as towns and neighbours were often far away. Women formed <u>church groups</u> and other <u>social networks</u> to combat the loneliness.

4) As more settlers arrived, <u>communities</u> formed. This eventually led to the building of <u>schools</u> and <u>shops</u>.

REVISION TASK

The government wanted to make farming on the Plains more successful

Divide a piece of paper in half. On one side, make a list of the hardships faced by settlers on the Plains. On the other, write down how people tried to overcome them.

America, 1789-1900

Cattling and Cowboys

The popularity of beef in the 1850s led to the 'Beef Bonanza' — when the beef trade became very profitable. This was when ranchers started to drive their cattle along cattle trails to reach lucrative markets further north.

The **Beef Bonanza** began in **Texas**

1) Texas had been part of Mexico until 1845, when it became a US state. Many Mexicans were driven out, leaving their cattle to American ranchers. The famous Texas Longhorn cattle was the result of interbreeding between these Mexican cattle and cattle brought to the USA by Anglo-American settlers.

2) Numbers of Texas Longhorn grew massively during the Civil War. Many Texans left their ranches to fight, and while they were away, their cattle continued to breed. E.g. Charles Goodnight (who would become a key figure in cattle ranching) left behind 180 cattle, but returned in 1865 to find he owned 5000.

> **Comment and Analysis**
>
> Railroads were very important in the growth of the cattle industry — they connected ranchers with lucrative markets. Railroads had become established by the end of the Civil War and continued to expand afterwards (see p.72).

3) Beef grew in popularity in the 1850s — there was a large demand for it in northern markets. So ranchers drove their cattle to the railroads, which then transported them to these markets.

The great **Cattle Trails** linked supply with demand

1) The four main cattle trails were the Goodnight-Loving Trail, the Western Trail, the Chisholm Trail and the Shawnee Trail. Trails were between 1200 and 1500 miles long and progress of 15 miles was considered a good day's drive. Early cattle drives followed the Shawnee Trail, and cattle would then be taken east by rail to Chicago.

> 1871 was the peak year for the cattle drives — 600,000 cattle were driven north.

2) However, Oliver Loving and his partner Charles Goodnight decided to target western markets. They established the Goodnight-Loving Trail in 1866, making it possible to drive cattle from Texas to Wyoming. They sold their beef in New Mexico to the army, to growing numbers of settlers and to the US government to feed Indians on reservations. They then drove the cattle up to Colorado to sell to miners.

3) Some Indian tribes were being put on reservations in the 1860s (see p.77). Goodnight and Loving supplied beef to the Apache and Navajo Indian reservation at Fort Sumter in New Mexico.

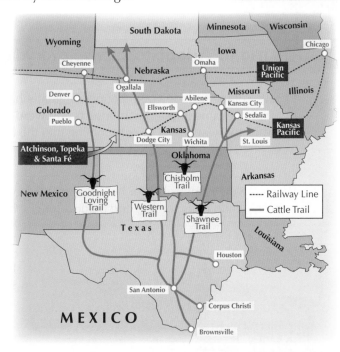

4) Instead of driving their herds all the way north from ranches in Texas, some cattlemen decided it would be better to set up ranches on the Plains.

5) The first man to do this was John Iliff, who set up open-range ranching in Wyoming in 1867. Open ranching meant there were no fences — cattle were free to graze where they liked.

6) In 1868, Goodnight drove cattle up to Iliff in Wyoming, which Iliff sold on to the transcontinental railroad construction gangs. Iliff also won a government contract in 1868 to supply beef to the Sioux reservation.

7) Some ranchers were very successful and became known as cattle barons. John Iliff became a powerful rancher, with 35,000 cattle in Colorado and Wyoming.

EXAM TIP

Cattle ranching was a profitable business

Make sure you know the key players and how they contributed to the growth of the cattle industry. You won't get any marks for getting your Goodnights and Lovings mixed up with your Iliffs.

Cattling and Cowboys

The cattle industry continued to develop and thrive with the emergence of cow towns. But it wasn't all plain sailing — cowboys had a tough job, and there was rivalry between ranchers and homesteaders.

The **Cattle Trails** led to the **Cow Towns**

1) The Shawnee Trail (see p.74) was threatened when homesteaders in Kansas and Missouri objected to ranchers' cattle crossing their land.

> The development of refrigerated rail carriages from 1878 meant that cattle could be slaughtered before transportation.

2) Joseph McCoy, a livestock trader and entrepreneur, saw the potential of moving beef cattle by rail to the eastern cities and Indian reservations. He decided to create a cow town away from homesteaders' land where cattle could be driven. He chose Abilene to be his cow town — the Kansas Pacific railway had pushed westward to run past Abilene and it was away from settled areas.

3) In sixty days in 1867, McCoy built Abilene up to a fully equipped cow town, with a stockyard, hotel, and bank. It was soon connected to Texas via the Chisholm Trail — McCoy persuaded ranchers to drive their cattle to Abilene, where they would be sold and transported to northern markets.

4) In a few years, about 3 million cattle had passed through Abilene. Soon, other cow towns such as Wichita, Ellsworth and Dodge City emerged, as the railway continued to advance westwards.

The **Cowboys'** job was **Very Tough** and **Badly Paid**

1) The men who drove the cattle on the trails were called cowboys. Cowboys had a tough job — they had to contend with storms, river floods and, worst of all, stampedes on the trail.

2) Many cowboys were Mexican or African Americans. Some were ex-soldiers from the Civil War, some were outlaws. Most cowboys were young and single with little time for a family life.

3) Boredom and discomfort were also part of the job. Winters were spent watching the cattle from line camps on the edges of the ranch. Trail life mostly involved breathing dust and staring at cows.

4) Longhorn cattle are big and aggressive, so rounding them up by 'cutting out' the correct cattle from mixed herds on the open range took skill.

> Cowboys' pay was low but tended to come in one lump at the end of a drive. Combined with the hardships of the trail, this led to many cowboys letting off steam and misbehaving once a cattle drive was over (see p.76).

5) Cowboys sometimes came into conflict with other people on the Plains. Native Americans and other rustlers could steal or stampede cattle. Diplomacy would help deal with some situations, but others ended in violence, so cowboys had to know how to use a gun.

6) Cowboys had to work as a team on the trail to succeed. They were highly disciplined and were kept in line as much by each other as by their bosses.

> The work of the cowboy changed as ranches became increasingly established on the Plains in the 1870s. It reduced the distance that cowboys had to drive cattle — the journey from Texas to the railroads could take up to two months, but from ranches on the Plains it could be done in around 35 days.

There was Rivalry Between Ranchers and Homesteaders

- Homesteaders living on the Plains weren't always delighted to see ranchers' cattle heading for their homes. The lack of wood on the Plains for fences meant that homesteaders' crops could be destroyed by the cattlemen's herds as they passed. Homesteaders' cattle sometimes died — the cattlemen's Longhorn herds carried a disease called Texas fever which they were immune to but homesteaders' cattle weren't.

- Homesteaders used barbed wire as a cheap way to fence off their land from 1874, but this reduced cowboys' access to water and made cattle drives much harder.

- As ranches moved onto the Plains there were clashes with homesteaders over land ownership. This would lead to violent confrontations later on, such as the Johnson County War (see p.84).

The life of a cowboy could be dangerous

REVISION TASK

Create a mind map of how the cattle industry developed. Make sure you have each of the main factors and then add detail to explain each one. You'll need to use the information from p.74 too.

Law and Order Problems

As more people settled in more areas of the West, it became a lot more difficult to maintain <u>law and order</u>.

Settled areas became **Territories**, which then became **States**

1) As the USA <u>expanded</u>, it brought more land and people under the control of its <u>government</u>.

2) The USA has a <u>federal</u> system of government — there's a <u>national</u> government in Washington, and then each <u>state</u> also has a government of its own, which is responsible for things such as <u>law and order</u>.

3) As the West developed, it was carved up roughly into <u>territories</u>. The <u>federal</u> government controlled these, and took <u>responsibility</u> for law and order by sending a <u>governor</u>, a <u>marshal</u> and three <u>judges</u> into each territory. As the population <u>increased</u>, people could <u>elect</u> some of the lawmen, such as <u>sheriffs</u>.

> Marshals sent in by the government looked after whole territories. They had <u>deputy marshals</u> to help them. Territories were split into counties and towns — <u>sheriffs</u> were in charge of counties and some <u>towns</u> elected <u>town marshals</u>.

4) Territories became <u>states</u> when the population reached <u>60,000</u>. On becoming a state, law and order decisions could be made <u>locally</u>, instead of relying on the federal government a long way away.

Many **Factors** led to **Crime** on the Plains

- **Gold** — Gold was discovered in <u>Montana</u> and <u>Nevada</u> in the 1860s and 70s. These areas had the same problems as <u>California</u> during the 1849 Gold Rush (see p.57). The areas grew <u>quickly</u>, and <u>criminals</u> were attracted by the potential riches, but it took <u>time</u> to establish systems of law and order.

- **Cow towns** — <u>Cowboys</u> would go to cow towns such as <u>Abilene</u> and <u>Dodge City</u> at the end of long cattle drives. These places grew to provide lots of <u>temptations</u> for cowboys who wanted to <u>relax</u> after their <u>hard work</u> on the trail. There was <u>drunkenness</u>, <u>gambling</u> and <u>gun fights</u>.

- **Homesteaders and cattlemen** — There was <u>conflict</u> as homesteaders and cattlemen <u>clashed</u> with each other (see p.84). They struggled to live <u>side-by-side</u> on the Plains.

> Many people carried <u>guns</u>, creating a culture of <u>violence</u>. <u>Poverty</u> and lack of stable <u>communities</u> to promote good behaviour in new settlements also contributed to <u>lawlessness</u>.

- **Gangs** — Outlaws formed <u>gangs</u>, which <u>robbed</u> trains and banks, and often committed <u>murders</u>. In the late 1860s, many of these men were <u>ex-Confederate soldiers</u> who turned to <u>crime</u> after the Civil War, e.g. the famous outlaw <u>Jesse James</u>.

- **Racial tensions** — Different <u>groups</u> of people including African Americans, Chinese, Europeans and Mexicans, created the potential for conflict.

Policing these areas was **Difficult**

1) The West was a <u>huge</u> area of land, and transport was <u>slow</u> — it could take a long time for marshals to reach remote areas.

2) Law officers such as sheriffs and marshals were sometimes <u>criminals themselves</u>. For example, <u>Henry Plummer</u> was elected <u>Sheriff</u> of the gold mining town of Bannack in Montana in 1863 while he was still the <u>leader</u> of a gang of <u>robbers</u>.

> Plummer was caught and hung by <u>vigilantes</u>. Vigilante groups could do some <u>good</u>, but their justice was <u>violent</u>, quick and not always fair.

3) For lawmen such as sheriffs, the work was <u>dangerous</u> and they were <u>poorly paid</u> — this made it difficult to <u>attract</u> new recruits. There was also a shortage of money to <u>train</u> anyone who wanted to do the job.

4) This lack of formal law enforcement meant that <u>vigilante</u> groups often sprang up. These were made up of ordinary citizens who tried to keep law and order — often <u>brutally</u>.

5) The <u>army</u> also tried to police the West. '<u>Buffalo soldiers</u>' were black soldiers whose job it was to keep order among <u>settlers</u> and fight <u>Native Americans</u> who raided white settlements.

The growth of the USA made it difficult to enforce law and order

Make a bullet point list of law and order problems on the Plains. Then write down the attempted solutions to these and how successful you think they were. Use evidence to back up your opinion.

The Indian Wars

The Plains Indians grew increasingly <u>threatened</u> as more people settled on the Plains — this led to <u>conflict</u>.

Railroads, Ranching and Gold angered the Plains Indians

1) <u>Railroad companies</u> often clashed with the Plains Indians. They encouraged the <u>settling</u> of the Plains as they expanded their networks and they frequently built railroads <u>through</u> Native American lands, even if it <u>violated</u> treaties.

2) Railroad companies also encouraged the <u>hunting</u> of buffalo — both to <u>feed</u> the railway construction gangs, and to make money by <u>transporting</u> hunters.

Buffalo hunting became a <u>popular</u> sport (see p.86).

Sioux raiding a train on the Great Plains.

© The Art Archive / Granger Collection

3) Buffalo were a hugely important <u>resource</u> for Native Americans (see p.53). Some tribes <u>derailed</u> trains and <u>ambushed</u> workmen. In response, the military built <u>forts</u> to safeguard the railroad.

4) <u>Ranchers</u> clashed with the Plains Indians when their <u>cattle drives</u> went through Indian land and when they built <u>ranches</u> on Indian territories. Again, this disrupted buffalo herds, leading to Indian <u>attacks</u> on ranchers and the cattle drives. <u>Oliver Loving</u> (see p.74) died in 1867 after a fight with <u>Comanches</u>.

5) When gold was discovered in <u>Montana</u> in <u>1862</u>, miners arrived in the area and prospected on Indian <u>reservation</u> land, breaking the treaties which had <u>promised</u> this land to the Native Americans.

Many Plains Indians were Unhappy with the Reservation Policy

1) More Indians were moved onto <u>reservations</u> as more settlers came to live on the Plains.

2) Life on reservations <u>varied</u>. The <u>Navajos</u> achieved <u>peace</u> and <u>prosperity</u> after 1868 when a treaty with the US allowed them <u>sufficient</u> reservation area in their <u>homeland</u>.

Many Plains tribes were still <u>able</u> to hunt <u>buffalo</u>, but only within <u>certain areas</u>.

3) Other tribes were moved off their <u>homeland</u> and onto <u>unfamiliar</u> territory. They were encouraged to <u>farm</u> the land, which went against their <u>culture</u> and <u>nomadic</u> lifestyle.

4) Often reservation lands were <u>insufficient</u> and <u>unsuitable</u> for farming — some tribes faced <u>starvation</u>.

5) If the lands were <u>good</u>, they were often <u>grabbed</u> by settlers, despite the <u>promises</u> in the government treaties. Many chiefs also lacked the <u>authority</u> to make their tribes keep to the agreements.

6) Many tribes wanted <u>peace</u>, but the situation had become <u>intolerable</u>. They were forced into <u>conflict</u> during the 1860s in a series of <u>Indian Wars</u>.

Comment and Analysis

It isn't <u>surprising</u> the Native Americans went to war. The government had given them the Great Plains (see p.52), but the government repeatedly <u>broke</u> their promises and <u>forced</u> tribes onto <u>ever-smaller</u> areas of land.

Little Crow's War was an uprising in Minnesota — 1862

1) The first major Indian War was Little Crow's War. Little Crow was the chief of the Santee Sioux, also known as the <u>Dakota</u>, who lived on a reservation in Minnesota.

2) They were peaceful and <u>accepted</u> reservation life. But they nearly <u>starved</u> as a result of Civil War <u>shortages</u>, a <u>delay</u> in their payment from the government, <u>cheating</u> by traders and a <u>poor</u> harvest.

3) In August 1862, four Dakota returning from an unsuccessful hunt <u>murdered</u> five settlers for a dare. Fearing <u>retaliation</u> on the entire tribe, Little Crow reluctantly led his warriors in an <u>uprising</u>. Hundreds of settlers and about 100 soldiers were killed, and the town of <u>New Ulm</u> was burned.

4) The uprising was ended when the Dakota were defeated at <u>Wood Lake</u> in September. 38 Dakota prisoners were <u>hanged</u> and most of the Dakota were <u>expelled</u> from what was left of their land.

REVISION TASK

Railroads didn't have a positive impact on everybody

Choose one cause of the Indian Wars. Write a short paragraph explaining why it helped cause conflict.

The Indian Wars

More <u>Indian Wars</u> followed during the 1860s. This led the US government to try a more <u>peaceful</u> approach.

The **Cheyenne Uprising** and the **Sand Creek Massacre** — **1864**

1) In 1863, the Cheyenne faced <u>starvation</u> because they couldn't grow enough food on their <u>infertile</u> reservation land at Sand Creek (see p.58) or find any <u>buffalo</u>. They decided to raid settlers' wagon trains for food. There was further <u>violence</u> between Indians and the army during <u>1864</u>.

2) Chief <u>Black Kettle</u>, who wanted peace, moved his band to a camp where he believed they would be safe. But in <u>November 1864</u>, Colonel <u>John Chivington</u> attacked the camp while most of the band's men were out <u>hunting</u>. Of the 500 people left in the camp, at least 163 were <u>killed</u> — mostly <u>women</u> and <u>children</u>.

3) The Cheyenne, Arapaho and Sioux <u>retaliated</u> by attacking ranches and other settlements, and killing those inside, including women and children. The central Plains erupted into <u>war</u>.

Red Cloud's War and the Bozeman Trail — 1866-1868

© The Art Archive / Granger Collection

1) The Bozeman Trail was established to link the gold fields in Montana with the Oregon Trail. However, this trail passed through the <u>hunting grounds</u> of the Sioux, which had been guaranteed to them by the <u>Fort Laramie Treaty</u> of <u>1851</u>.

2) The Sioux <u>attacked</u> travellers who used the trail, so the army wanted to build <u>forts</u> to protect them. Talks were held with <u>Red Cloud</u>, a Sioux chief, to negotiate the building of these forts, but they were <u>abandoned</u> when the Sioux saw soldiers marching out to begin building before any deal had been made.

3) The Sioux began to attack the <u>army</u>. In a major incident known as <u>Fetterman's Trap</u>, the Sioux <u>ambushed</u> Captain W.J. Fetterman and his troops — Fetterman and all 80 of his men were killed.

Red Cloud.

4) As a result, the US army <u>surrendered</u> and <u>abandoned</u> the forts. This was a <u>major defeat</u> for the army.

- Red Cloud eventually signed the 1868 <u>Fort Laramie Treaty</u>, which created a large <u>Sioux reservation</u> on an area that included the sacred <u>Black Hills</u> of Dakota. The government also agreed not to <u>rebuild</u> their forts on the Bozeman Trail.

- Red Cloud <u>promised</u> never again to make war on the settlers — and <u>kept</u> his promise. But <u>not all</u> of the Sioux bands agreed with the treaty. Sioux chiefs <u>Crazy Horse</u> and <u>Sitting Bull</u> would be involved in future conflict (see p.85).

Policies of **Separation** and **Assimilation** were tried

1) The Indian Wars made it clear to the government that their Indian policy <u>wasn't working</u>. The government wanted to move away from aggressive <u>military</u> actions.

2) In <u>1867</u>, the <u>Indian Peace Commission</u> tried to establish peace by negotiating the <u>Medicine Lodge Treaty</u> — this treaty moved southern Plains Indian tribes onto <u>smaller</u> reservations away from <u>settlers</u>.

3) Following on from this, <u>President Grant</u> established his 'Peace Policy' in 1868 — the aim was to <u>assimilate</u> the Indians peacefully into white society. But it was agreed that those who <u>resisted</u> the policy would face <u>military</u> action.

4) The policy <u>failed</u> — the Native Americans didn't want to give up their <u>lifestyle</u> and Grant didn't stop settlers <u>encroaching</u> on Indian land when <u>gold</u> was found on the Black Hills of Dakota in 1874. More <u>conflict</u> would follow (see p.85).

> Many <u>settlers</u> and <u>army</u> officers such as General Sherman thought the Native Americans should be <u>destroyed</u>. Many politicians took a more <u>humane</u> view.

EXAM TIP

The Indian Wars soured relations ever further

Remember that although President Grant's 'Peace Policy' had humane intentions, it still aimed to deny the Native Americans their way of life. Many Native Americans didn't want to be assimilated.

Worked Exam-Style Question

This worked answer shows how to explain the consequences of an event or development. Look at the way it uses knowledge of the facts and evidence from the period to explain the impact of the event in the question.

Q1

> The First Transcontinental Railroad was completed in 1869.
> Explain two consequences of this event. [8 marks]

This first sentence directly addresses the question.

This explains how the consequence was caused by the development of the railroad.

One consequence of the completion of the First Transcontinental Railroad (and other railroads that followed) was an increase in buffalo hunting. The railroad allowed hunters quick access to the Plains, where they shot buffalo for sport or their hides. The railroad also enabled hunters to transport buffalo skins to the East where there was a demand for buffalo robes, so it encouraged more people to make money from hunting buffalo. This increase in buffalo hunting angered the Native Americans, shown by the fact that the US army had to build forts to protect the railroads from Native American attacks.

Giving more detail shows a good knowledge of the period.

Another consequence of the completion of the First Transcontinental Railroad was increased settlement on the Plains. The railroad made it easier for people to migrate to the West and settle along the railroad, so more families moved to the Plains. This led to a growth in settler communities on the Plains, and schools, shops and churches were built to cater for their growing numbers. As a result, the settlers' quality of life improved, because they were less isolated than earlier settlers had been.

This introduces a second consequence.

This explains how and why things changed.

Exam-Style Questions

When civilisation and barbarism are brought in such relation that they cannot coexist together, it is right that the superiority of the former should be asserted and the latter compelled to give way. It is, therefore, no matter of regret or reproach that so large a portion of our territory has been wrested from its aboriginal inhabitants and made the happy abodes of an enlightened and Christian people.

Interpretation 1 — an extract from a report written by Luke Lea in 1852. Lea was the Commissioner of Indian Affairs for the American government between 1850 and 1853. The Office of Indian Affairs helped to manage the government's relations with Native Americans.

The President told me to work, and I have done it... Although other people often move from place to place, yet I have always stayed on our land. It is ours… I have sown wheat and planted corn and have performed all my promises to the President. I have raised enough on my farm to support myself, and now it seems just as though the government were trying to drown me when he takes my land away from me... The land is our own... I have broken no treaties, and the President has no right to take it from me.

Interpretation 2 — an extract from an interview with the Chief of the Ponca tribe, conducted in 1879. The Ponca tribe co-operated with the government's concentration policy and settled on a reservation that was located within their ancestral lands on the Great Plains. In 1877, they were forcibly relocated to a new, smaller reservation.

Q1

Explain how Interpretation 1 is different to Interpretation 2 concerning attitudes towards the government's policy of relocating Native Americans.   [4 marks]

Exam-Style Questions

Q2 Explain why the authors of Interpretation 1 and Interpretation 2 might have different viewpoints about the government's policy of relocating Native Americans. [4 marks]

Q3 Which interpretation do you think is more convincing about the government's policy of relocating Native Americans? Give reasons for your answer. [8 marks]

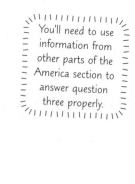

You'll need to use information from other parts of the America section to answer question three properly.

Q4 Give two consequences of the growth of cattle trails during the 1860s and explain them. [8 marks]

Q5 Examine:

a) the significance of changes in farming between c.1861 and c.1877 for the development of the Great Plains. [8 marks]

b) the significance of the Indian Wars (1862-67) for government policy towards Native Americans. [8 marks]

Changes in the Cattle Industry

The 1860s to the 1880s were the ranchers' heyday (see p.74-75) — but the Beef Bonanza didn't last forever.

Changing Tastes and Hard Winters ended the Beef Bonanza

1) Eastern markets eventually began to demand a higher quality of meat than the Longhorn could provide. This led ranchers like Iliff and Goodnight to start crossbreeding Longhorns with Herefords — the meat from these cattle was better quality, but the cattle were less resistant to harsh conditions.

2) States passed quarantine laws because settlers were concerned about diseases carried by the ranchers' cattle (see p.75) — from 1885 Kansas shut its borders to Texas cattle between March and November.

3) Ranchers overstocked their cattle and after 1885 there was less demand for beef — herds grew very large and prices fell. The herds became too large for the grazing area and the drought of 1886 meant there wasn't enough grass to feed the cattle.

> Ranchers had become greedy — they wanted to take advantage of the high demand for beef, but they allowed their herds to grow too large.

4) The over-grazed range meant that underfed cattle entered the terrible winter of 1886-87 in weakened condition. Thousands of cattle died. Homesteaders' fences became death traps as cattle piled against them during blizzards. Average losses were perhaps 30%. Many cowboys also died.

The end of the Beef Bonanza Transformed cattle Ranching

1) Ranchers had to adapt when the cattle boom ended.

2) Businesses which survived the 1880s economised by raising better-quality animals on smaller areas of land, shifting towards a more managed environment.

> The bad winter of 1886-87 had shown ranchers the importance of caring for their cattle in harsh weather, including being able to feed and shelter them.

3) More intensive ranching also favoured smaller scale operations — these were more likely to be family-owned than corporate.

4) Ranching now depended on the ability to feed livestock in winter. Ranchers grew crops such as hay so that they could feed their cattle and this meant that dependence on irrigation increased.

> Windpumps made it easier for ranchers to fence off their land. Previously, cattle had moved around to find water sources, but this invention allowed water to be pumped from underground.

5) Ranchers, like homesteaders, began to use barbed wire enclosures to fence off their land — this allowed them to control their herds and look after them. Cattle could no longer roam freely — it was the end of the open range.

The end of the open range had a large Impact on the Cowboy

1) The change from the open range to fenced pastures changed the role of the cowboy.

2) The expansion of the railroads made long drives unnecessary. Round-ups (herding cattle together) occurred less often and involved much smaller herds of cattle. This meant that fewer cowboys were needed and those who remained spent less time roaming the Plains on their horses.

3) Cowboys became domesticated ranch hands with more mundane jobs, such as mending fences. As ranchers were growing more crops, cowboys became more involved in farming.

4) As a whole, their lives became more settled — their living conditions on ranches were more comfortable than life on the trail, they had to follow ranch rules and their hours were more regular.

Comment and Analysis

The romantic image of the cowboy has remained strong in popular culture — it's a symbol of a wild and free existence.

5) The end of cowboy culture and the cattle trails helped bring some order to the Plains.

The winter of 1886-87 was the catalyst for change on the ranches

Write an account that explains how the cattle industry changed after the winter of 1886-87. Talk about these factors: the end of the beef bonanza, windpumps, barbed wire and the end of the open range.

Changes in Farming

Living and farming on the Great Plains was still <u>hard</u>, but the area was eventually <u>successfully</u> settled.

People continued to **Settle** on the Plains...

1) By 1880, people had started to move onto even <u>drier</u> areas of the Plains.
   <u>Different groups</u> of people were still helping to <u>settle the West</u>:

   - There were <u>10 million immigrants</u> to America during <u>1865-90</u> — many of these helped settle the West, such as the <u>Scandinavians</u> on the <u>Dakotas</u>. By 1900 there were 500,000 farms on the Plains.
   - At the end of the Reconstruction Era in 1877, <u>African Americans</u> faced growing oppression in the South (see p.69). As a result, thousands moved <u>west</u>. This mass migration is known as the <u>Exoduster movement</u>.

2) <u>Government</u> actions also helped:

   - **The Desert Land Act 1877** — Farmers who lived on <u>drier</u> land could buy up to <u>640 acres</u> at a low cost as long as they <u>irrigated</u> the land within three years.
   - **The Oklahoma Land Rush of 1889** — The government opened up <u>two million acres</u> of land in Oklahoma to settlers in 1889 — this had previously been <u>Indian</u> territory (see p.52). Thousands of people rushed into the territory to claim their land.

   > In <u>1893</u> another <u>6 million acres</u> was opened up. This land was known as the '<u>Cherokee Strip</u>' and had been promised to the <u>Cherokees</u> 60 years previously on their <u>removal</u> to the Plains.

3) By 1890, <u>six</u> railroads crossed the US from east to west.
   This helped to make the Plains a <u>less isolated</u> place and linked farmers on the Plains with wider <u>markets</u>.

4) People continued to <u>adapt</u> to life on the Plains. <u>Towns</u> developed and <u>communities</u> grew, as more people settled the Plains. Life was made more <u>comfortable</u> by luxury goods brought by railroads from the East.

5) There were still <u>hardships</u> though, and the <u>failure</u> rate for new farms was high.
   There were severe <u>droughts</u> in the <u>1870s</u> and <u>1880s</u>, and problems caused by <u>overgrazing</u>.
   Some people got into debt and <u>lost</u> their farms, while others gave up and moved on.

... and **Farming** continued to **Develop**

1) Farmers began to learn techniques to cope with the low rainfall and retain the moisture in the soil, e.g. '<u>dry farming</u>' involved turning the soil after rain.

2) Machinery — such as reapers, binders and harvesters — was <u>developed</u> and <u>improved</u> to harvest grain <u>faster</u>.

3) Initially only farmers making good profits could afford to buy new machinery, but it eventually became more <u>widespread</u> as it became more <u>affordable</u>. The <u>railroads</u> gave farmers greater access to machinery by transporting it to the Plains from the <u>East</u> — farmers who could afford to were using <u>steam-powered tractors</u> by the 1890s.

4) <u>Bonanza farms</u> were established. These were large farms which grew and harvested wheat on a <u>large scale</u>.

5) The Great Plains helped the US become a major world <u>wheat</u> producer. In <u>1895</u>, the US grew around <u>three times</u> as much wheat and corn as it did in <u>1860</u>.

Steam-powered wheat thresher, 1878. This image shows the productivity of the Plains and the growing use of new machinery.

Comment and Analysis

By the 1890s, farming was becoming increasingly <u>mechanised</u> — farm work took <u>less time</u>, required <u>less labour</u> and became <u>more productive</u>.

New technology and better farming techniques improved harvests

A lot of the problems faced by homesteaders had been solved by the 1890s. In the exam, make sure you can give specific examples of the technology and farming methods which helped settlers.

Wild West

It was known as the <u>Wild West</u> for a reason. <u>Lawlessness</u> was still a major problem for settler communities.

Conflicts over **Land** and **Power** led to **Violence** and **Lawlessness**

1) The <u>violence</u> in the late 1800s in the American West was partly due to changes in <u>society</u>. Cattle barons, railroads and other <u>corporations</u> — using the power and influence that their size gave them — were <u>taking over</u> from the homesteaders, small ranchers and prospectors. Some historians call the violence it sparked the '<u>Western Civil War of Incorporation</u>'.

2) There were conflicts called the <u>Range Wars</u> — the <u>Lincoln County War</u> and the <u>Johnson County War</u>.

3) The <u>Lincoln County War</u> of <u>1878</u> resulted in the murder of a <u>cattle baron</u> called <u>John Tunstall</u>. A gang of <u>outlaws</u> called the <u>Regulators</u> took the law into their own hands and got revenge on Tunstall's killers. One of the Regulators, <u>Billy the Kid</u>, escaped justice and later became a famous figure of the Wild West.

4) The <u>Johnson County War</u> took place in <u>1892</u>. Homesteaders in <u>Johnson County</u>, Wyoming, felt that the <u>cattle barons</u> were stealing their <u>land</u>. Cattle barons felt that homesteaders were blocking their use of the <u>open range</u> and accused them of <u>rustling</u> (stealing) their cattle.

In <u>1892</u>, the <u>Wyoming Stock Growers Association</u> (who represented the cattle barons) mounted a vigilante raid into <u>Johnson County</u>. They killed two alleged rustlers, but locals came out of <u>Buffalo</u> and laid siege to the vigilantes.	More locals gathered until there were about <u>250</u> men ready to kill the vigilantes. The <u>Stock Growers Association</u> had influence with the <u>government</u> via the <u>Republican Party</u> and the <u>President</u>. They used this to call out the <u>army</u>, who rescued the vigilantes.	There were <u>no prosecutions</u>, but the cattle barons lost their <u>power</u> and <u>influence</u> and the war marked the <u>end</u> of the open range in Wyoming.

Lawmen fought the **Outlaws**

1) A career as a lawman in the Wild West was open to <u>all sorts</u> of people. <u>Wyatt Earp</u> was a natural recruit for the forces of <u>incorporation</u> (corporations and big businesses) as he was a keen <u>entrepreneur</u> and an effective <u>gunman</u>.

> Earp had been <u>arrested</u> in 1871 for <u>stealing</u> horses in Missouri. He <u>fled</u> the state and the federal system did nothing to <u>prevent</u> his later career as a lawman.

2) Earp, his <u>brothers</u> and <u>Doc Holliday</u> killed three men who were accused of cattle rustling and other crimes at the <u>OK Corral</u> in Arizona in <u>1881</u>. The dead men were <u>typical</u> of the small ranchers/outlaws who opposed the growth of big business in the West.

3) Some people believed that the violence <u>wasn't justified</u> — the Earps and Holliday were charged with <u>murder</u>, but this was later <u>dropped</u>. A bloody <u>feud</u> followed the shootout. When Wyatt's brother Morgan was killed, Wyatt got his <u>revenge</u> by killing the men he believed responsible.

4) Other lawmen had successes in hunting down outlaws. <u>Pat Garrett</u>, who became sheriff of Lincoln County in 1880, hunted down and shot <u>Billy the Kid</u> after he escaped from jail in <u>1881</u>.

5) Some lawmen, such as <u>Bill Tilghman</u>, gained reputations for being <u>respectable</u> and <u>honest</u>. Unlike other lawmen, he wasn't quick to resort to <u>violence</u>. He became Deputy US Marshal in Oklahoma in 1892 and played a <u>major</u> part in stopping outlaw activity there.

Law and order in the West gradually **Improved**

1) The expansion of the <u>railroads</u> and improved <u>communication</u> (e.g. the telegraph) helped law enforcement — <u>news</u> travelled faster and lawmen could more <u>easily</u> reach areas where there was trouble.

2) More <u>homesteaders</u> arrived who wanted to make a successful life — they demanded <u>better</u> law and order.

3) As towns developed, <u>living conditions</u> improved — towns and roads were planned, with better <u>buildings</u> and <u>sanitation</u> systems. This created a more <u>civilised</u> atmosphere and encouraged <u>better</u> behaviour.

4) More <u>states</u> were created, so more areas were becoming <u>responsible</u> for their own law and order rather than <u>relying</u> on a distant federal government. <u>Seven</u> more territories became states between <u>1876</u> and <u>1890</u>, bringing the number of states up to <u>44</u>.

EXAM TIP

It took time to solve the problem of law and order in the West
When answering exam questions, remember that lawmen such as Wyatt Earp weren't squeaky clean.

War on the Plains

The government attempted a more 'peaceful' approach to Native Americans, but it only led to more conflict.

Fighting occurred at the battle of **Little Bighorn**

The Sioux and the US army came into conflict from 1874, sparking the 1876-77 Great Sioux Wars.

1) In 1874, troops under Lt. Col. George Custer confirmed the presence of gold in the Black Hills of Dakota and a gold rush began. The US government tried to buy the Black Hills from the Sioux, but they refused — the hills were sacred and belonged to them under the 1868 Fort Laramie Treaty.

2) Despite the Sioux's refusal to sell the Black Hills, miners arrived to search for gold. In protest, many of the Sioux left the reservation and gathered in Montana in the Bighorn Valley. The government ordered the Sioux back to their reservation, but they refused. By the start of 1876, Sitting Bull and Crazy Horse had raised the largest Native American force ever seen (several thousand men).

3) The US government sent soldiers to oppose the uprising. The Sioux launched a successful attack on the soldiers while they were resting, killing 28 of them. This became known as the Battle of the Rosebud.

4) Army commanders Sheridan and Terry planned an attack on the Sioux village at Little Bighorn, but Custer and his men arrived first and decided to attack alone.

5) Custer split his men into three groups — the other two were led by Reno and Benteen. When Custer approached the village with around 220 soldiers, they were surrounded by Indians — he and all of his men were killed. This was the greatest Native American victory in battle against the US army.

Different **Factors** explain the **Defeat** of the US army

Custer

He marched his men through the night and arrived at Little Bighorn a day early, so his men were tired. He ignored orders to wait for the rest of the army and warnings from his Indian scouts that the Sioux village was too large for them to fight alone. He also turned down the offer of extra men and guns, and weakened his force by splitting it into three.

Custer's commanders

Terry and Sheridan didn't try to find out how many Indians were in the village.

Reno and Benteen

Custer ordered them to come to his support but they didn't. They were under attack themselves and later argued that this was why they were unable to help Custer.

Bad luck

Quicksand stopped Custer from crossing the river to attack the village — he and his men were forced onto higher ground, where they were seen by the Sioux.

Native Americans

The Sioux were determined to save their territory. Instead of fleeing, which was their usual tactic, they stood and fought — Custer wasn't expecting this. He also wasn't expecting the Indians to have superior weaponry — many had repeating Winchester rifles, while Custer's soldiers had single shot Springfields. Sioux leaders such as Crazy Horse were experienced warriors, and they joined forces with their traditional enemies, the Cheyenne and Arapaho, to greatly outnumber the US army.

REVISION TASK

Custer was ambitious and after personal glory

Make a list of factors that explain why Custer lost at Little Bighorn. Write a short paragraph explaining which of these factors you think was the most important reason for Custer's defeat.

A Way of Life Destroyed

Little Bighorn was a big victory for the Native Americans, but it marked the beginning of the end for their freedom. The US army's strengthened resolve and the slaughter of the buffalo caused the Indians to accept reservations.

The Indians **Won** at **Little Bighorn** but it made things even **Worse**

1) Following their defeat at the battle of Little Bighorn (see p.85), the US army launched a winter campaign against the Sioux in 1876-77.

2) Facing hunger and the loss of their horses, the Sioux surrendered and were forced onto reservations.

3) Crazy Horse surrendered in May 1877 and was later killed by a US soldier while resisting arrest.

4) Sioux reservations were put under military control and, in 1877, the Black Hills were opened to white settlement.

5) Sitting Bull retreated to Canada, but returned and surrendered in 1881.

> The victory at Little Bighorn wasn't enough to turn the Native Americans' fortunes around and the US army's determination to defeat them increased following the battle.

Buffalo Slaughter forced Native Americans to accept **Reservations**

A buffalo skinner. Buffalo skins were much in demand. The rest of the animal would be left to decay on the Plains.

1) Millions of buffalo had once roamed the Plains. They were vital to the Native Americans' survival (see p.53) and were sacred to them.

2) Buffalo were slaughtered in large numbers by white settlers (see p.77). They were killed to feed soldiers and railroad construction workers. People also killed them for their skins — there was a demand for buffalo robes in the East from the 1850s, and from 1871 a process was developed to make buffalo hides into leather. Others just killed them for sport — men would shoot the animals from the windows of trains.

3) As a result of this, buffalo numbers decreased rapidly — it has been estimated that there were 13 million buffalo on the Plains in 1865, but by the end of the century they were almost extinct.

4) The effect on the Plains Indians was devastating — their main source of food was gone, as well as a major part of their culture. This caused many Indians to accept life on the reservations — they feared starvation.

5) It's not clear whether there was an official policy to exterminate the buffalo, but many people recognised that destroying them would help defeat the Indians.

General Sheridan is quoted as saying, 'let them kill, skin and sell until the buffalo is exterminated as it is the only way to bring lasting peace and allow civilisation to advance'.

EXAM TIP

Little Bighorn was only a short-term victory for the Native Americans

The destruction of the Native Americans' way of life happened gradually over time, not all at once. Make sure that you can talk about the important events that contributed to its decline.

A Way of Life Destroyed

America's population was growing — increasing the pressure on reservation land belonging to the Plains Indians.

Reservations destroyed Native American Culture

1) Many Plains Indians were nomadic. Confined to smaller areas, they could no longer feed or clothe themselves without government aid. Living on hand-outs, they became demoralised and there were high rates of alcoholism.

2) Many tribes were moved off their culturally significant ancestral lands and onto reservations elsewhere. The influence of chiefs declined because reservations were run by Indian agents, undermining tribal structure. Hostile tribes were sometimes put on reservations in close proximity.

3) Many children were taken away to be educated, for example at the Carlisle Indian School in Pennsylvania (founded in 1879). Polygamy (having more than one wife) and religious practices such as the Sun Dance, were banned. The threat of withholding rations was used to enforce co-operation.

> The government had always wanted the Indians to assimilate. As Indians living on the reservations were now dependent on the state, there was a way to force them to abandon their own culture.

The Dawes Act (1887) Parcelled Out tribal lands

1) The aim of the Dawes Act was to convert tribesmen into independent farmers. It was hoped this would help destroy tribal bonds and lead to the assimilation of Native Americans into white society.

2) The Dawes Act broke reservations up into allotments. Each head of family was assigned 160 acres, each single adult 80 acres, and each child 40 acres. US citizenship was also part of the deal.

3) When all the inhabitants of a reservation had been assigned their holdings, the remaining land was thrown open to white settlement. Indian schools were established from the sale of this surplus land.

US Reformers Supported the Act...

- Some reformers supported the Act because they wanted to stop Indian suffering on reservations.
- Some believed that reservation life encouraged idleness and reliance on government hand-outs.
- Others just wanted to open up reservation lands to settlers.

Comment and Analysis

> While many reformers may have believed they had good intentions, their actions were based on their prejudiced belief that Native Americans needed to be introduced to Christianity and western civilisation to improve themselves.

...but it was a Disaster for the Native Americans

- Their tribal communities were broken up and their culture almost destroyed — the idea of land ownership went against Native American tradition.
- The creation of allotments led to Indians losing their land — down from 138 million acres in 1887 to 78 million acres in 1900. They also lost land granted to them under the Act (nearly two thirds of it between 1887 and 1934) as a result of being cheated by land speculators.
- Lands belonging to the five eastern tribes that had been moved on to the Plains in the 1830s (see p.52) were exempt from the Dawes Act, yet through forced sales they too were eventually lost.
- Men found it difficult to adapt to farming — this had traditionally been seen as a woman's role. In Indian schools, children had to dress like white Americans and weren't allowed to speak tribal languages.
- In 1934, the government repealed the Dawes Act and encouraged tribal identities. But by that time, Native Americans had lost over 60 per cent of their original reservation lands and were suffering from high rates of poverty, alcoholism, illiteracy and suicide.

Assimilation destroyed the Native Americans' way of life

EXAM TIP

It's all very well knowing all the little facts about this period of American history, but to write a good answer you've got to know how they fit together too. Think about how developments were linked.

A Way of Life Destroyed

It seems as though the Plains Indians had always been fighting a <u>losing battle</u> against land-hungry settlers. By the time of the <u>Wounded Knee Massacre</u> in 1890 it was clear that they had lost and the settlers had won.

The **Wounded Knee Massacre** was the **End** of Indian resistance

1) Some armed resistance <u>continued</u> during the <u>1880s</u>, but it was finally <u>suppressed</u> in 1890 at the <u>Battle of Wounded Knee</u>. This was to be the <u>last</u> confrontation between Native Americans and the US army.

2) A Native American spiritual leader named <u>Wovoka</u> taught that a special <u>Ghost Dance</u> could raise the dead and bring a new world, <u>free</u> from the settlers. He was <u>opposed</u> to violence, but ghost dances built the dancers up into a <u>frenzy</u> — this <u>unsettled</u> whites who feared that the dance would lead to <u>rebellion</u>.

3) Tensions <u>peaked</u> at the <u>Pine Ridge Reservation</u> in Wounded Knee Creek, South Dakota. Troops tried to <u>disarm</u> a band of Sioux led by Chief Big Foot, but when a warrior fired a shot, the troops fired back, killing 52 people. Survivors went on to fight by hand.

4) The battle <u>escalated</u> when <u>more warriors</u> from nearby heard the gunfire and swarmed out, shooting at the soldiers, then disappearing into the prairie.

- The <u>Battle of Wounded Knee</u> cost the lives of some <u>150</u> Sioux (about 60 of them women and children) and <u>25</u> soldiers.
- It marked the <u>final suppression</u> of Native Americans by armed <u>force</u>. By mid-January 1891, the dispersed warriors had all <u>surrendered</u>.
- Some Sioux followers of the Ghost Dance movement had believed that special <u>shirts</u> would <u>protect them</u> from the bullets of the Americans. The sight of Ghost Dance shirts <u>pierced</u> by bullets after the battle destroyed the Indians' <u>faith</u> in a magical restoration of the old way of life. The reservation was reluctantly accepted as <u>home</u>.

Native Americans were **Unable** to fight back **Successfully**

It's <u>debatable</u> whether the Plains Indians could ever have <u>protected</u> their traditional way of life. There were many <u>factors</u> at work against them:

1) The US army usually had better <u>weapons</u> than the Native Americans — repeating rifles, machine guns and cannons.

2) The system of <u>forts</u> gave the US army control on the Plains. The <u>railroads</u> and <u>telegraph</u> system provided fast transport and communication.

3) <u>Divisions</u> between Native American nations meant that they had no <u>organised</u> resistance. Reservation life also made it more <u>difficult</u> for them to resist.

Comment and Analysis

It seems that <u>nothing</u> could halt the tide of white settlers — and <u>broken</u> government promises failed to <u>protect</u> the Indians from it.

Americans became aware of the **End** of the **Frontier**

1) In <u>1890</u>, census results revealed that, unlike in 1880, there was no longer a <u>definable western frontier</u> of settlement. The frontier was declared officially <u>closed</u>.

2) This didn't mean that there was no more land available for settlers, but what remained was in <u>isolated pockets</u> and the best areas had been taken.

3) The Native Americans were no longer a <u>barrier</u> to settlement — they'd been <u>subdued</u> and were in the process of being <u>assimilated</u> into white society.

EXAM TIP

The government failed to protect the Native Americans
Think about whether the Native Americans' way of life was doomed from the beginning.

Changes to the Lives of African Americans

After 1877, African Americans <u>lost</u> many of the <u>gains</u> they had made during <u>Reconstruction</u> (see p.67-69).

African Americans lost their **Civil** and **Political Rights**

1) African Americans had an <u>inferior</u> status in society as a result of <u>segregation</u>. This meant that they were <u>separated</u> from white people, for example in schools, shops, hotels, theatres and on public transport.

Civil Rights

- Southern states passed 'Jim Crow' laws which <u>legalised</u> segregation. <u>Intermarriage</u> also became illegal.
- In 1883, the <u>Supreme Court</u> ruled that the 1875 <u>Civil Rights Act</u>, which had outlawed <u>discrimination</u> in public places, was <u>unconstitutional</u> (against the constitution).
- The Supreme Court also <u>supported segregation</u>. In the <u>Plessy v. Ferguson</u> case of 1896, it ruled that a Louisiana law requiring <u>separate railway coaches</u> for African Americans was <u>constitutional</u>.

> There was an increase in <u>violence</u> against African Americans in the 1890s. <u>Lynchings</u> became more common — lynchings are killings <u>without trial</u>, often by <u>hanging</u>.

2) Democrats regained control of the South in <u>1877</u>. They tried to <u>remove</u> African American <u>voting rights</u> — rights which they had been guaranteed under the <u>15th Amendment</u> (see p.68).

Political Rights

- States passed new state <u>constitutions</u> which introduced voting <u>restrictions</u>, like <u>poll taxes</u> and <u>literacy tests</u>. This mostly affected African Americans because they were more likely to be <u>poor</u> or <u>unable</u> to read and write — the voting restrictions made it <u>difficult</u> or <u>impossible</u> for many of them to vote.
- People who couldn't vote weren't able to run for <u>office</u> or serve on <u>juries</u> — <u>reducing</u> African American <u>participation</u> in politics even further.
- The <u>Supreme Court</u> upheld these new constitutions. It ruled that Mississippi's 1890 constitution <u>wasn't</u> discriminatory and other southern states adopted <u>similar</u> constitutions between 1890 and 1908.

They faced **Economic Repression**

Many African Americans lived in <u>poverty</u> and were <u>prevented</u> from making money.

> White southerners felt <u>threatened</u> by African Americans and wanted to maintain <u>white superiority</u>. Many in the South were still <u>bitter</u> about the outcome of the <u>Civil War</u>.

1) Many worked as <u>sharecroppers</u>, harvesting cotton and tobacco, or in <u>low paid</u> jobs in the coal and iron industries. Sharecroppers were often <u>exploited</u> by landowners and became <u>trapped</u> in a cycle of poverty and debt.

2) They had few chances to <u>improve</u> their lives — legal restrictions and violence often <u>prevented</u> them from working in <u>skilled</u> professions. <u>Education</u> for African Americans was <u>poor</u> — African American schools were given <u>less funding</u> than white schools by state governments.

3) States passed laws which punished <u>small</u> crimes with <u>harsh</u> sentences, e.g. the <u>Pig Laws</u>, which punished people for stealing farm animals, and <u>vagrancy statutes</u>, which made it a crime to be unemployed. These laws targeted African Americans as they were <u>more likely</u> to be <u>poor</u> and <u>unemployed</u>.

Many African Americans **Moved** out of the South

1) Many African Americans moved to the <u>West</u>. For example, around 20,000 'Exodusters' moved to Kansas in 1879, creating all-black communities such as <u>Nicodemus</u>. Others moved to the <u>North</u>.

2) Even though there were no discriminatory laws in these areas, African Americans still faced <u>racism</u>. 'Sundown towns' were white communities which <u>excluded</u> African Americans — these towns existed all across America. In the North, African Americans and whites lived <u>separately</u>, and African Americans experienced racism from <u>European immigrants</u> who they competed with for housing and jobs.

The battle for equality wasn't over

Write a paragraph that summarises the ways the lives of African Americans changed after 1877. Explain how these changes went against acts that were passed during the Reconstruction Era.

Big Business, Cities and Mass Migration

The USA underwent huge economic growth between 1870 and 1900 — a few people became very wealthy. But this period is known as the 'Gilded Age' — beneath the appearance of wealth, there were problems.

America Industrialised and Big Business emerged

1) The period between 1870 and 1914 is known as the Second Industrial Revolution. It was a time of rapid industrial growth and technological change. America's economy changed from being mainly agricultural to industrial.

> The nature of industry changed from small businesses employing skilled craftsmen to big businesses using mass production techniques and employing unskilled workers.

2) Industries were developed such as steel and oil. New technologies like electricity emerged. Factories multiplied — they began to use machinery and production increased.

3) Successful businesses were created in these industries. Big businesses appeared when several businesses were merged to form one large corporation — these corporations forced out competition and took control of the market. The businessmen who owned these corporations became very wealthy.

- John Rockefeller founded the Standard Oil Company. He introduced new techniques which transformed the oil industry. He was the first American billionaire.

> These figures were seen as contributing to the prosperity of America. They were also philanthropists — they gave away much of their wealth to good causes such as schools and libraries.

- Andrew Carnegie created the Carnegie Steel Company. He used improved technology and methods to quickly and efficiently mass produce steel.

Industrialisation and mass Migration led to the Growth of Cities

1) Industrialisation was centred on the cities where factories were built. Growing numbers of factories created a demand for labour, attracting people to move to cities for jobs — migrants from rural areas in America and immigrants from Europe. Nearly 11 million immigrants arrived between 1870 and 1900.

> Initially, most immigrants came from north-west Europe, but after 1890, most came from southern and eastern Europe, e.g. Italy and Russia.

2) The US population nearly doubled between 1870 and 1900. It has been estimated that in 1870 25.7% of the population lived in cities, but this increased to almost 40% by 1900.

3) Cities like New York and Chicago grew and developed as more people moved to them. America began to build its first skyscraper in Chicago in 1884 — the first tall building to use steel in its frame.

4) New electric transport was introduced, such as electric streetcars (trams). This resulted in the growth of suburbs — people could now travel into cities quickly, which meant that those who could afford to didn't have to live in the cities themselves.

There was Corruption, Poverty and Inequality

1) While some businessmen grew very wealthy, many other people struggled in poverty. Some people called the wealthy 'robber barons' — accusing them of using unfair methods to gain their wealth.

- They put smaller competitors out of business, could control markets and had political influence.
- Workers were paid low wages and worked long hours, often in dangerous conditions.

2) The rich showed off their wealth while many others struggled with life in crowded and unsanitary cities — crime was common and there was a lot of racial conflict.

> Men at the Carnegie steelworks worked 12 hours a day, seven days a week with only one day off a year. Accidents and deaths were common.

3) Discontent among workers led to the rise of trade unions — organisations formed by workers which aim to improve their rights. Workers also went on strike.

4) Many of the elite believed in survival of the fittest — that people with the right skills would be successful in life. As a result, they didn't support measures to help the poor, such as improving working conditions.

There was a growing gap between the wealthy and the poor
Make a table listing the pros and cons of the growth of big business between 1870 and 1900.

Exam-Style Questions

Q1

What played the most important role in the loss
of the Native American way of life after 1877:
government policies or the actions of white settlers?

Explain your answer, referring to both reasons.   [12 marks]

You'll need to use information from other parts of the America section to answer question one properly.

Q2

Explain how the lives of African Americans were affected
by the end of the Reconstruction Era.   [8 marks]

Q3

Why did America undergo huge economic growth between c.1870 and c.1900?
Use examples to support your answer.   [10 marks]

Revision Summary

Now you've absorbed all of that <u>lovely knowledge</u>, here are some <u>revision questions</u> to get your teeth into.

- Try these questions and <u>tick off each one</u> when you <u>get it right</u>.
- When you've done <u>all the questions</u> for a topic and are <u>completely happy</u> with it, tick off the topic.

America's Expansion, 1789-c.1830 (p.47-50) ☑

1) Explain why many people viewed the Plains as the 'Great American Desert' before the 1860s. ☑
2) Give two reasons why the Louisiana Purchase was important for the expansion of the USA. ☑
3) How did the War of 1812 affect the Native Americans? ☑
4) Which part of the USA became reliant on slavery? ☑

The West, c.1830-c.1861 (p.52-58) ☑

5) What was the Permanent Indian Frontier? What was its purpose? ☑
6) Why were the buffalo important to the Plains Indians? ☑
7) Give a brief description of 'Manifest Destiny'. ☑
8) What difficulties did the Mormons face on their journey to Salt Lake Valley? ☑
9) How did the expectations of miners compare with the reality of life in California? ☑
10) Give three examples of settler activity on the Plains which caused tension with the Plains Indians. ☑

Civil War and Reconstruction, c.1861-c.1877 (p.62-69) ☑

11) Explain why westward expansion increased tension over slavery. ☑
12) What was the impact of Abraham Lincoln's election as President in 1860? ☑
13) Give two reasons why the South's economy suffered during the Civil War. ☑
14) How and why did African Americans help the Union war effort? ☑
15) Give two examples of Andrew Johnson's lenient approach to the South during Reconstruction. ☑
16) What were the Enforcement Acts? ☑

Development of the Plains, c.1861-c.1877 (p.71-78) ☑

17) What was the Homestead Act? ☑
18) List three things which helped settlers live and farm on the Plains. ☑
19) Why did the cattle trails develop? ☑
20) Explain why there was rivalry between ranchers and homesteaders. ☑
21) Why did many Native Americans dislike life on the reservations? ☑
22) Describe the events in 1863-1864 that led to war between settlers and Native Americans. ☑

Conflict and Conquest, c.1877-1900 (p.82-90) ☑

23) Why did ranchers begin to fence off their land? ☑
24) What was the Exoduster movement? ☑
25) What role did Wyatt Earp play in enforcing law and order? ☑
26) Explain five factors which led to the defeat of the US army at Little Bighorn. ☑
27) What impact did the destruction of the buffalo have on the Native Americans? ☑
28) What was the aim of the Dawes Act? ☑
29) Explain three ways that African Americans lost their rights after 1877. ☑
30) Why did cities grow between 1870 and 1900? ☑

Elizabeth's Background and Character

Elizabeth I became queen in <u>1558</u>. She reigned for <u>almost 45 years</u>, until her death in <u>1603</u>.

Queen Elizabeth I was from the House of Tudor

The <u>Tudor family</u> had ruled England since Henry VII became king in 1485. Here's their family tree:

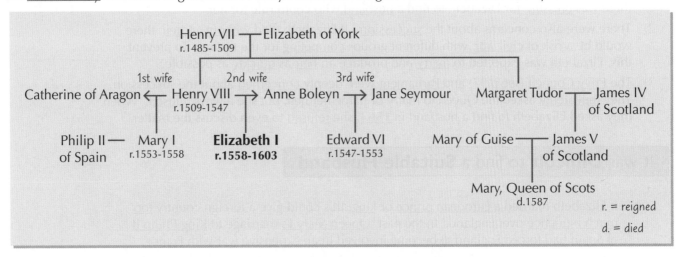

Elizabeth I was Cautious, Intelligent and Powerful...

1) Elizabeth was <u>Henry VIII's</u> second child, the daughter of his second wife, <u>Anne Boleyn</u>.
    As a child, she was <u>third</u> in line to the throne, so <u>no-one</u> really <u>expected</u> her to become queen.

2) Elizabeth was <u>very cautious</u> and only trusted a few <u>close advisers</u>. She could also be <u>indecisive</u>
    — she was reluctant to make decisions without carefully considering their possible <u>consequences</u>.

3) She was <u>intelligent</u>, <u>confident</u> and very <u>well educated</u>. Despite having had
    little training in how to govern, she became a <u>powerful and effective</u> leader.

...but some people Didn't Want her to rule

Gender

Most people believed the <u>monarch</u> should be a <u>man</u>. They thought that rule by a <u>woman</u> was
<u>unnatural</u>, and expected Elizabeth to be a <u>figurehead</u>, without any real power. They thought
she should let her <u>male counsellors</u> take control or find a <u>husband</u> to govern for her (see p.94).
Elizabeth was <u>determined to rule</u> in her own right and <u>refused</u> to let her counsellors take over.

Illegitimacy

When Henry VIII's marriage to Anne Boleyn was <u>dissolved</u> and Anne was <u>executed</u>
in 1536, Henry declared Elizabeth <u>illegitimate</u>. Although Henry later <u>changed his
mind</u> about this, some <u>Protestants</u> still questioned Elizabeth's <u>legitimacy</u>.

Elizabeth was a strong leader, despite her critics

It's important to understand what Elizabeth was like as a person and the early difficulties she
faced — her background and character shaped many of the decisions she made during her reign.

Marriage and Succession

One of Elizabeth's biggest headaches as queen was the issue of marriage and the succession.

Elizabeth was expected to Marry and produce an Heir

1) Because people believed that women couldn't rule effectively (see p.93), there was pressure for Elizabeth to find a husband who could rule for her.

2) There were also concerns about the succession. If Elizabeth died without an heir, there would be a risk of civil war, with different groups competing for the throne. To prevent this, Elizabeth was expected to marry and produce an heir as quickly as possible.

3) The Privy Council (see p.97) and Parliament were deeply concerned about the succession. They repeatedly asked the Queen to marry or name her heir, but she always refused. When they asked Elizabeth to find a husband in 1563, she refused to even discuss the matter.

It was Difficult to find a Suitable Husband

1) If Elizabeth married a European prince or king, this could give a foreign country too much influence over England. In the past, Queen Mary I's marriage to King Philip II of Spain had forced England to become involved in an expensive war with France.

2) If Elizabeth chose a member of the English nobility, this would create anger and resentment among those who weren't chosen.

3) The religious settlement had made England a Protestant country (see p.116), so it was difficult for Elizabeth to marry a Catholic. Growing anti-Catholic feeling in England would have made a Catholic husband unpopular and might have undermined support for Elizabeth's rule.

4) Elizabeth was reluctant to marry anyone — women were expected to obey their husbands, so she would lose much of her power and freedom if she married.

Elizabeth Considered many Suitors, but she Rejected them All

1) Early in her reign, Elizabeth received proposals from foreign rulers, including King Philip II of Spain, Archduke Charles of Austria and King Eric of Sweden. She and her Privy Council seriously considered King Eric's proposal, but in the end all these early suitors were rejected.

2) Elizabeth seems to have been in love with her 'favourite', Robert Dudley, and seriously considered marrying him. However, members of the Privy Council and the nobility, including William Cecil (see p.97), were strongly opposed to this match and it did not go ahead.

3) In the 1570s, Elizabeth was courted by Duke Francis of Anjou, brother of the King of France. Although there was some support for the match, there was also strong opposition to the idea of Elizabeth marrying a French Catholic, and in the end the marriage negotiations were abandoned.

Comment and Analysis

Marriage negotiations could be a useful tool in foreign policy. Anglo-Spanish relations were breaking down in the 1570s (see p.125), and England needed a new European ally. The proposed marriage to Duke Francis played an important role in efforts to create an alliance with France.

By the late 1570s, Elizabeth was in her mid-forties and it was clear that she would never have children. The issue of the succession still needed to be resolved, but Elizabeth refused to name a successor. She was concerned that a successor might become the focus of plots to overthrow her. Towards the end of her reign, her advisors began secret negotiations to make James VI of Scotland (son of Mary, Queen of Scots) heir to the throne. When Elizabeth died in 1603, James became king of England.

Elizabeth ruled without a husband

REVISION TASK

Scribble down a spider diagram showing all the reasons why it was difficult for Elizabeth to find a husband. Name two suitors Elizabeth considered and explain why she didn't marry them.

Problems at the Start of Elizabeth's Reign

Elizabeth also faced <u>other problems</u> — the <u>economy</u> was <u>weak</u> and there was a threat of a <u>French invasion</u>.

Elizabeth's reign began with a **French Threat** in **Scotland**

In 1557, <u>Mary I</u> took England to <u>war with France</u>. She did this to support her husband, Philip II of Spain, who was already fighting the French.

→

The war wasn't a success. In <u>January 1558</u>, the <u>French conquered Calais</u>, England's last territory on the European mainland. This made it <u>harder</u> for the English to <u>control the Channel</u>, and increased the risk of a <u>French invasion</u>.

→

When Elizabeth became queen in November 1558, she wanted to <u>end the war</u> with France as quickly as possible. <u>Peace</u> was agreed in <u>1559</u>.

Elizabeth tried to <u>avoid foreign wars</u> — a policy partly influenced by England's <u>financial weakness</u>. She feared that <u>raising taxes</u> to fund a war would be <u>unpopular</u> and might fuel <u>opposition</u> to her rule.

1) Elizabeth had <u>quickly ended</u> the war with France, but there was still a <u>French threat</u> in <u>Scotland</u>. When she became queen, <u>Scotland</u> was controlled by <u>France's Catholic royal family</u> and there were many <u>French troops</u> in the country. However, French rule was unpopular with many Scots.

2) In 1558 <u>Mary, Queen of Scots</u> (p.119) married the <u>heir to the French throne</u>. As Catholics, the French royal family disliked Elizabeth (a Protestant), and wanted England to be ruled by a <u>Catholic</u>. Mary's marriage <u>increased</u> the risk that the French might <u>invade</u> from Scotland to try and put her on the English throne.

3) In the late 1550s, <u>Scottish Protestants</u>, led by the preacher John Knox, <u>rebelled</u> against French rule. They asked England for support, and in <u>1560</u> English troops and ships were sent to help them.

4) The <u>French</u> were <u>defeated</u> and forced to <u>leave Scotland</u>. The departure of the French, combined with the death of Mary's French husband in 1560, greatly <u>reduced</u> the <u>threat of invasion</u>.

Comment and Analysis

There were many <u>Catholics</u> in England who wanted to be ruled by a <u>Catholic monarch</u>. There was a risk that they'd <u>betray</u> Elizabeth and <u>support the French</u> if they invaded.

The English **Economy** was **Weak**

1) Under <u>King Edward VI</u>, huge sums of money had been spent on <u>wars in Scotland</u>. Queen Mary I had also spent too much money. As a result, Elizabeth inherited <u>enormous debts</u> when she became queen.

2) Mary I had <u>sold off</u> lots of <u>land</u> owned by the Crown to cover her debts. This had raised money in the short term, but it also <u>reduced</u> the monarch's <u>income from rent</u>.

3) The tax system was <u>old-fashioned</u> and <u>ineffective</u>. Ordinary people paid <u>high taxes</u>, but it had become common for the <u>nobility</u> and <u>gentry</u> to pay <u>less</u> tax than they owed.

4) England was suffering high levels of <u>inflation</u> (when <u>prices rise</u> and wages don't). The <u>poor</u> (see p.103-104) and those living in <u>urban areas</u> were hit hardest by inflation.

Elizabeth was <u>reluctant</u> to reform the tax system and raise taxes because she feared it would <u>upset</u> the nobility and gentry who <u>supported</u> her.

There were **Social** and **Economic Divisions**

1) England's <u>population</u> had been <u>rising</u> steadily since around 1500. Most people lived and worked in <u>rural areas</u>, but <u>towns and cities</u> were <u>growing</u> rapidly. <u>London</u> was by far the <u>largest</u> and most important city.

2) The economy was dominated by <u>agriculture</u>, but farming was <u>changing</u> (p.103). The export of <u>woollen cloth</u> to <u>Europe</u> was a key part of the economy, but merchants were also starting to trade with the <u>Americas</u> and <u>Asia</u> (p.109-111).

3) Elizabethan society was dominated by a small, <u>land-owning aristocracy</u> of nobility and gentry (see p.105). There was also a growing number of wealthy men who made a living as <u>lawyers</u> or <u>merchants</u>.

4) There was great <u>inequality</u>, and the divide between rich and poor was growing. <u>Poverty</u> became a <u>major problem</u> in Elizabethan England (see p.103-104).

EXAM TIP

Foreign wars were a luxury Elizabeth couldn't afford

Include plenty of specific information in your answers. For example, don't just say that Elizabeth had lots of problems at home and abroad — explain the different challenges she faced.

Political Power in Elizabethan England

Elizabeth's <u>court</u> was the heart of <u>social</u> and <u>political</u> life — everyone who was anyone could be found there.

The **Court** was the **Centre** of Elizabethan **Social Life**

1) The royal <u>court</u> was a large group of people who <u>surrounded</u> the monarch at all times. More than <u>1000 people</u> attended the court, including Elizabeth's personal servants, members of the Privy Council (see p.97), members of the nobility, ambassadors and other foreign visitors, and Elizabeth's 'favourites'.

Elizabeth's 'Favourites'

- Early in her reign, Elizabeth was very close to <u>Robert Dudley</u>. She made him <u>Earl of Leicester</u> in 1564 and may have considered <u>marrying</u> him (see p.94).
- <u>Christopher Hatton</u> was another of her 'favourites'. In <u>1587</u>, she made him <u>Lord Chancellor</u>, even though he had <u>little relevant experience</u>.
- <u>Sir Walter Raleigh</u> came to Elizabeth's court in 1581. Elizabeth gave him many <u>valuable gifts</u>, including the right to colonise the <u>New World</u> (see p.111).

2) Courtiers were expected to <u>flatter</u> Elizabeth, shower her with <u>gifts</u> and pretend to be in <u>love</u> with her.

3) Courtly <u>pastimes</u> included plays, concerts, hunting, jousting and tennis. There were also balls and grand meals.

4) Members of the court <u>travelled</u> with Elizabeth when she moved between her <u>palaces</u>, and when <u>great processions</u> were held. They also went with her when she went on her '<u>royal progresses</u>' (see p.99).

> **Comment and Analysis**
>
> The <u>entertainments</u> and <u>fashionable clothes</u> on show at court were a way for Elizabeth to <u>impress</u> her subjects and foreign visitors by <u>displaying</u> her <u>wealth</u> and <u>power</u>.

Political Power relied on **Access** to the **Queen**

1) The Queen was the <u>centre</u> of <u>government</u>, and political power revolved around her. This meant that those <u>closest</u> to Elizabeth had the <u>greatest influence</u> and power.

2) The <u>court</u> was the centre of <u>political life</u>. Anyone who wanted to <u>get ahead</u> and increase their political power had to have a place at <u>court</u>.

3) Courtiers didn't necessarily hold government positions — they became <u>powerful</u> through their <u>close relationship</u> with the Queen.

> <u>Courtiers</u> had to <u>compete</u> with one another for the Queen's <u>attention</u> and <u>favour</u>. Towards the end of Elizabeth's reign, this <u>competition</u> led to growing <u>conflict</u> at court (p.100).

Patronage helped to ensure **Loyalty**

<u>Patronage</u> involved handing out <u>titles</u> and <u>offices</u> which gave men a source of <u>income</u>. Elizabeth had <u>lots</u> of these to give away, including high positions in the Church. Patronage was distributed at <u>court</u>.

1) Elizabeth's use of <u>patronage</u> helped to ensure <u>loyalty</u>. Those who received patronage became <u>dependent</u> on Elizabeth for some or all of their <u>income</u> and <u>status</u>, so they were likely to be <u>loyal</u> to her.

2) Elizabeth <u>distributed</u> patronage very <u>widely</u>. This helped to ensure political <u>stability</u> — all members of the elite felt they had a chance to be <u>rewarded</u> by the Queen, so they were <u>unlikely</u> to <u>rebel</u> against her.

> **Comment and Analysis**
>
> Traditionally, the <u>elite</u> was <u>dominated</u> by <u>noble families</u>. Their power mainly came from <u>land</u> that they <u>inherited</u>. By promoting men who <u>relied</u> on her for their wealth and influence, Elizabeth <u>limited</u> the power of the traditional <u>noble families</u> and made the new elite <u>more loyal</u> to her.

The court was the centre of political power in England

Jot down a quick description of Elizabeth's court, including the names of some of her favourite courtiers. Write an explanation of how Elizabeth used patronage to ensure her courtiers were loyal.

Elizabethan Government

The Queen was the head of government. She was advised by her Privy Council, which included her key ministers. Laws made at the national level were enforced by local government.

Local Government enforced National Laws

1) The role of local government was to supervise the running of each county and enforce the law there.

2) Most local government positions were unpaid. Members of the nobility and gentry (see p.105) often volunteered for them because being a part of the local government was a symbol of status and power.

3) An important local government position was Justice of the Peace. They were in charge of administering national policies like poor laws (see p.104) and taxation in their counties, and enforcing law and order. They also looked after local issues like maintaining sewers and roads.

4) Most counties had a Lord Lieutenant, appointed by the Queen. Lord Lieutenants were in charge of the Justices of the Peace, and had an important military role. For example, they maintained defences and managed the training of the militia (ordinary people called to fight alongside the army in an emergency).

> After England went to war with Spain in 1585 (p.125), there was a higher demand for Lord Lieutenants, as military preparations in each county became more important. Elizabeth also needed more Justices of the Peace to collect extra taxes to fund the war.

5) Towards the end of the 16th century, the number of Justices of the Peace and Lord Lieutenants increased.

The Privy Council was Central to Elizabethan Government

1) The Privy Council had two main roles. It gave advice to the Queen and managed the administration of government.

> This involved making sure that Elizabeth's policies were enforced. The council oversaw many different areas of government, including religion, the economy, the military, foreign policy and the Queen's security.

2) The Council was made up of around twenty men, all chosen by Elizabeth. Members of the Privy Council were the Queen's closest and most trusted advisors. Some key ministers served on the Council for many years.

3) The Queen didn't have to follow the advice of the Privy Council. Councillors were expected to carry out her instructions, even when doing so went against their advice.

William Cecil was Elizabeth's Closest Advisor

1) When she became queen in 1558, Elizabeth made William Cecil her Principal Secretary. He became her closest advisor, leading the Privy Council and making sure the government ran smoothly.

2) In 1571, Elizabeth gave Cecil the title Lord Burghley. The next year she made him Lord High Treasurer, giving him greater control over royal finances. Cecil continued to serve Elizabeth until his death in 1598.

3) Elizabeth's other key ministers included Nicholas Bacon, who was Lord Chancellor from 1559 to 1579, and Francis Walsingham, who became Principal Secretary in 1573.

Comment and Analysis

Cecil was a highly skilled politician and administrator. Some historians argue that Elizabeth's success as queen was as much due to Cecil's remarkable skills as it was to Elizabeth's own talents.

EXAM TIP

Elizabeth was very powerful, but she didn't rule alone

To really ace the exam, you need to understand the key features of Elizabethan government. Make sure you know the role of the Queen, the Privy Council, Parliament and local government.

Elizabethan Government

Unlike today, in the 16th century the monarch held <u>more power</u> than Parliament, which was only a <u>secondary</u> part of government. Its sessions were <u>temporary</u> and <u>occasional</u>, and its <u>powers</u> were <u>limited</u>.

There were **Two Chambers** of **Parliament**

The **House of Lords** was <u>not elected</u> — it was made up of members of the <u>nobility</u> and senior <u>churchmen</u>.

The **House of Commons** was <u>elected</u>, but only <u>men</u> who owned <u>property</u> over a certain value were allowed to <u>vote</u>. Elections <u>weren't free</u> — the <u>Crown</u> controlled who got elected in some areas, and in others <u>powerful local figures</u> controlled who was chosen.

Parliament's main functions were **Advice**, **Taxation** and **Legislation**

Advice

Parliament was an important point of <u>contact</u> between <u>central government</u> and the leading figures in <u>local government</u> throughout the country. It enabled the Queen and her councillors to gauge the <u>mood</u> of the country and levels of <u>support</u> for their <u>policies</u>.

Taxation

When the Queen needed <u>extra revenue</u>, she had to ask <u>Parliament's permission</u> to raise <u>taxes</u>.

Legislation

The Queen needed <u>Parliament's approval</u> to pass <u>new laws</u>. However, she could <u>bypass</u> this function by issuing <u>royal proclamations</u> instead.

Comment and Analysis

Elizabeth took <u>little interest</u> in the <u>advice</u> of Members of Parliament (<u>MPs</u>), and she could <u>bypass</u> Parliament's role in passing <u>new laws</u>. For Elizabeth, Parliament's <u>main purpose</u> was to grant her <u>taxes</u>.

Parliament's **Powers** were **Limited**

1) Elizabeth had the power to <u>summon</u> and <u>dismiss</u> Parliament. She <u>disliked</u> working with Parliament and tried to use it <u>as little as possible</u> — she only called <u>13 sessions</u> of Parliament during her 44-year reign.

2) Parliament was <u>not free</u> to decide what topics it debated. It had to have <u>permission</u> from the <u>Queen</u> to discuss <u>matters of state</u> (e.g. religion, the succession, foreign policy).

3) As a result, most parliamentary business focused on <u>local matters</u> and <u>social</u> or <u>economic issues</u>, which it could discuss without royal permission.

Comment and Analysis

Elizabeth believed in <u>Divine Right</u> — that <u>rulers</u> were sent by <u>God</u> to govern their country. She believed that this gave her a <u>royal prerogative</u> — the right to <u>decide</u> about <u>matters of state</u> without <u>interference</u> from Parliament.

Elizabeth I in Parliament.

Parliament had very few powers compared to the Queen

REVISION TASK Split your page in two. On the left-hand side, write a list of Parliament's main functions and powers. On the other side, list all of the ways in which Parliament's powers were limited.

Elizabethan Government

There were many disagreements in Parliament, which could prove a challenge for the Queen. However, through the Privy Council and public propaganda, Elizabeth managed to remain in control.

The Privy Council helped Elizabeth to Manage Parliament

1) The Privy Council managed relations between Elizabeth and Parliament very effectively. In particular, Cecil was highly skilled at convincing MPs to support the Queen's policies.

2) Some members of the Privy Council sat in Parliament. They acted as royal spokesmen and helped to steer debates in favour of royal policies.

3) The Speaker, who kept order in the House of Commons, was chosen by the Queen and closely monitored by members of the Privy Council. This helped the Queen's councillors to control Parliament and convince MPs to support royal policy.

4) Elizabeth was a strong public speaker. She made a number of powerful speeches in Parliament which helped to persuade MPs to obey her wishes.

There were some Disagreements, but Elizabeth stayed In Control

During Elizabeth's reign, Parliament didn't always agree with her policies:

- Throughout her reign, MPs were concerned about who would rule England after Elizabeth's death — they repeatedly tried to persuade her to marry or name an heir (see p.94).
- Some Puritan MPs challenged the religious settlement (see p.116-117) and tried to make England more Protestant.
- MPs were worried about the threat from Mary, Queen of Scots, and the Catholic plots surrounding her (see p.119). They tried to convince Elizabeth to take action against Mary.

Occasionally, MPs tried to force the Queen to change her mind by threatening to refuse taxation. Elizabeth never gave in to this kind of parliamentary pressure. Effective management by the Privy Council, combined with Elizabeth's powers to dismiss Parliament and select the topics it debated, meant that she remained firmly in control.

Elizabeth used Propaganda to maintain Public Support

Public support helped to make Elizabeth's position more stable, especially as some people doubted her. She and her councillors used propaganda to ensure she had a positive public image.

1) Portraits were commissioned showing Elizabeth as a powerful queen who was pure and chaste (a virgin) — they suggested she was married to her people and was concerned with their welfare above all else.

2) Plays which emphasised Elizabeth's wealth and power were performed at court (see p.96). These helped to combat courtiers' fears that an unmarried woman was too weak to rule England properly.

3) Elizabeth was careful to make ordinary people feel recognised by the state. She often went on 'royal progresses' — she journeyed across different parts of England, allowing the public to see and praise her. Their public displays of affection helped her seem popular and loved by her subjects.

Elizabeth remained powerful through personality and propaganda

Using information on pages 96-99, write a list of the ways Elizabeth was able to maintain control despite opposition. You can use details from the rest of the section to expand your points.

The Elizabethans, 1558-1603

The End of Elizabeth's Reign

The last 15 years or so of Elizabeth's rule were so different to her early years that they're sometimes called her 'second reign'. One of the main differences was the growth of competing groups at court.

Elizabeth's **Court** split into **Rival Groups** in the **1590s**

1) The make-up of Elizabeth's Privy Council changed towards the end of her reign. Several of her key ministers, including Christopher Hatton and Francis Walsingham, died around 1590. William Cecil died in 1598 and was succeeded by his son, Robert Cecil.

2) In 1593, Elizabeth made Robert Devereux, Earl of Essex, a member of the Privy Council. Essex's rise led to the growth of two conflicting groups at court, one around the Earl of Essex and the other around William and Robert Cecil.

3) The two groups were constantly competing for royal patronage and influence. They also disagreed over important matters, especially strategy in the war with Spain (see p.125). Elizabeth's inability to control this conflict undermined her authority.

Essex was the stepson of Elizabeth's earlier 'favourite', Robert Dudley. He came to court in 1584 and quickly became a 'favourite' himself. He was extremely ambitious for military success and could be arrogant and disrespectful, even towards the Queen.

Essex launched a **Rebellion** in **1601**

1) In 1599, Elizabeth sent Essex to Ireland at the head of a huge army. His task was to crush Tyrone's Rebellion (also known as the Nine Years' War), which had been going on since 1594.

2) Essex made some limited attempts to fight the rebels, but when these were unsuccessful, he made a truce with them. He then abandoned his post and returned to England without the Queen's permission.

3) As a punishment, Elizabeth put Essex under house arrest for a time, banished him from court and took away most of his public offices. In November 1600, she also took away Essex's role as the sole distributor of sweet wines, his main source of income.

4) The loss of his political power and his income drove Essex to revolt. On 8th February 1601, he launched a rebellion in London. Essex aimed to seize the Queen and force her to replace her closest advisers, especially Cecil, with himself and his followers.

5) Essex's rebellion failed within just a few hours. He received no support from ordinary Londoners, and most of his own supporters quickly abandoned him too. Essex was arrested, tried for treason and executed on 25th February 1601.

Comment and Analysis

In her later years, Elizabeth rarely appointed new men to the Privy Council, which created resentment among some courtiers. These men became frustrated at Elizabeth's refusal to promote them to government posts, and so they encouraged Essex's rebellion.

The **Conflict** at court **Undermined** Elizabeth's **Authority**

1) The lack of popular support for Essex's rebellion shows that it wasn't a serious threat to Elizabeth's rule. She was still a popular and respected queen, and there was no desire to overthrow her or her government.

2) However, the rebellion does suggest that Elizabeth's authority over her court became weaker towards the end of her reign. By the 1590s, she was no longer using patronage as effectively as she had in the past.

3) Instead of balancing the different groups at court, she let the Cecils become too powerful, while failing to promote many others. This led to a build-up of anger and resentment, which risked fuelling challenges to her authority — like Essex's revolt.

4) The conflict at court in the 1590s also made Elizabeth's government less effective. Constant competition and in-fighting between groups made it more difficult to make decisions and get things done.

EXAM TIP

Essex's rebellion showed that many courtiers were unhappy

Make sure you know the order of the key events in Elizabethan England. If something happens at the end of Elizabeth's reign, don't write about it as if it happened at the same time as earlier events.

Worked Exam-Style Question

This sample answer will give you an idea of how to answer questions that ask you how far you agree with a statement or interpretation. Look at the way that the answer clearly states an opinion at the beginning and end.

Interpretation 1

Elizabeth I orders the arrest of the Earl of Essex after his return from Ireland in 1599.

Q1 To what extent is Interpretation 1 convincing about the Earl of Essex's career? [8 marks]

Interpretation 1 is convincing because it shows Essex's loss of Elizabeth's favour following his failure to crush Tyrone's Rebellion in Ireland in 1599 and his abandonment of his duty there. It shows Essex being held by the guards, who are ready to act on Elizabeth's authority. This shows one of the lowest points in Essex's career, when Elizabeth had him placed under house arrest, banished him from court and eventually took away his main source of income. These punishments ultimately led to his rebellion and execution in 1601.

> *This refers to the details of the image to work out what it is trying to show or say.*

The image does not, however, convincingly represent Essex's career as a whole. For example, there is no hint of Essex's role on the Privy Council, his rivalry with Robert Cecil for Elizabeth's favour, or Elizabeth's support and patronage of him in the decade or so before the events in the image. As a result, this image is more convincing as a representation of the end of Essex's career and does not visually represent the more positive side of his career.

> *This uses knowledge of Essex's career to show what is missing from the interpretation.*

> *This judges how accurately the image represents Essex's career.*

While this image shows a specific, low moment in Essex's career, it also hints that there were occasions when Essex successfully pleaded for Elizabeth's forgiveness. The interpretation focuses on their gestures towards one another. Essex extends his arm towards Elizabeth as if asking for her forgiveness or mercy, while Elizabeth points towards the door, banishing Essex from her presence and favour. Essex had been disrespectful and arrogant towards Elizabeth before, yet she had still allowed him to serve her. This is reflected in the image, as Essex clearly hopes that Elizabeth will forgive him yet again.

> *This looks at what the image emphasises to decide what it is trying to say.*

> *This makes a final judgement about how convincing the image is as a depiction of Essex's career.*

Therefore, while the interpretation only shows a specific moment in Essex's career, it is still convincing as a symbolic representation of the role of Essex's personal relationship with Elizabeth in his career as a whole.

Exam-Style Questions

Q1 Describe two aspects of Elizabeth's character.   [4 marks]

Q2 'When she became queen in 1558, the greatest challenge Elizabeth faced was the question of the succession.' Explain how far you agree with this interpretation.

You could mention the English economy and Elizabeth's legitimacy in your answer.   [16 marks]

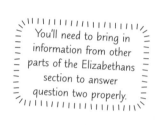
You'll need to bring in information from other parts of the Elizabethans section to answer question two properly.

Q3 Why was patronage an important part of Elizabeth's rule? Explain your answer.   [8 marks]

Q4 Give an account of the challenges Elizabeth faced in the last 15 years of her rule and how they affected her authority.   [8 marks]

Poverty

The growing number of people living in <u>poverty</u> was a major problem in Elizabethan society.

Religious Changes meant there was Less Support for the Poor

1) Between 1536 and 1541, Henry VIII had <u>closed down</u> England's <u>monasteries</u> and sold off most of their land (this was called the 'dissolution of the monasteries').

2) The monasteries had performed important <u>social functions</u>, including providing <u>support</u> for many <u>poor</u>, <u>ill</u> and <u>disabled</u> people. The dissolution of the monasteries <u>removed</u> a valuable source of <u>assistance</u> for people need.

Population Growth led to Rising Prices

1) In the 16th century, England's birth rate increased and the death rate fell. This led to huge <u>population growth</u> — during Elizabeth's reign, the English population grew from around 3 million people to at least <u>4 million</u>.

2) Food production <u>didn't</u> keep pace with the growth in population. As a result, <u>food prices rose</u> and sometimes there were <u>food shortages</u>.

3) Prices for food and other goods rose much <u>more quickly</u> than <u>wages</u>. <u>Standards of living fell</u> for many workers as they struggled to afford the necessities — many were forced into <u>poverty</u>.

4) Because of the rapid population growth, there was growing <u>competition</u> for <u>land</u>, and so <u>rents increased</u>. This trend was made worse by changes in <u>farming practices</u>.

Developments in Agriculture left many people Unemployed

1) <u>Traditional</u> farming methods involved many <u>farmers</u> renting strips of land in large <u>open fields</u>. This was <u>subsistence-level</u> farming — each farmer only grew enough crops to supply himself and his family.

2) This kind of farming was very <u>inefficient</u>, and in the 16th century landowners began <u>changing</u> their <u>farming techniques</u> to try and make <u>more money</u> from their land. Instead of sharing open fields among many farmers, they <u>enclosed</u> these fields to create a <u>few large farms</u>.

3) These new, enclosed farms required <u>fewer labourers</u>, so farmers who rented land were <u>evicted</u>, leaving them <u>unemployed</u> and <u>homeless</u>.

4) Exporting <u>wool</u> to Europe was <u>more profitable</u> than selling grain, so many landowners <u>stopped</u> growing <u>grain</u> and began <u>sheep farming</u>. This <u>fall</u> in <u>grain production</u> contributed to <u>rising food prices</u>. It also meant that there was a higher risk of <u>food shortages</u> when there was a <u>bad harvest</u>.

Comment and Analysis

These <u>enclosures</u> of farm land forced many people to <u>leave</u> their <u>villages</u> and migrate to <u>towns</u> or <u>cities</u> in search of <u>work</u>. The government viewed these migrant workers as '<u>vagabonds</u>' and feared that they would encourage <u>riots</u> and <u>rebellions</u>.

Poverty got Worse in the 1590s

The problem of poverty reached a <u>crisis point</u> towards the end of Elizabeth's reign. In the <u>late 1580s</u> and <u>1590s</u>, England suffered several <u>failed harvests</u>, which led to <u>food shortages</u> and even <u>higher</u> food prices. This pushed even <u>more</u> people into <u>extreme poverty</u> — in some areas people <u>starved</u> to <u>death</u>.

Poverty was a growing problem in Elizabethan England

Make a spider diagram of the reasons for poverty in Elizabethan England. Underneath, write a short paragraph explaining what you think was the most important cause of increasing poverty.

Poverty

Elizabeth's government introduced a series of <u>Poor Laws</u> to try and tackle the problem of <u>poverty</u>.

The **Government** became **More Involved** in **Poor Relief**

1) Traditionally, the <u>main</u> source of <u>support</u> for the poor was <u>charity</u> — rich people made <u>donations</u> to hospitals, monasteries and other organisations that helped the poor. However, during Elizabeth's reign the problem of <u>poverty</u> became <u>so bad</u> that these <u>charitable donations</u> by individuals were <u>no longer enough</u>.

2) People began to realise that <u>society as a whole</u> would have to take <u>responsibility</u> for helping the poor, and so the <u>government</u> began to take <u>action</u> to tackle the problem of <u>poverty</u>.

Comment and Analysis

The government feared that the rising poverty levels were a <u>serious threat</u> to <u>law and order</u>. As poverty levels rose, <u>crime</u> rates <u>increased</u> and there were <u>food riots</u> in some places. The government feared that the poor might <u>rise up</u> in <u>rebellion</u> if the problem of poverty wasn't tackled.

People believed the **Poor** could be split into **Three Categories**

The Helpless Poor

Those who were <u>unable</u> to support themselves — including young <u>orphans</u> and the <u>elderly</u>, <u>sick</u> or <u>disabled</u>.

The Deserving Poor

People who <u>wanted to work</u>, but weren't able to find a job in their home town or village.

The Undeserving Poor

<u>Beggars</u>, <u>criminals</u> and people who <u>refused to work</u>. Also <u>migrant workers</u> ('<u>vagabonds</u>') who left their homes and travelled around looking for work.

The **Poor Laws** gave **Help** to the **Helpless** and **Deserving Poor**

1) From the <u>1560s</u> onwards, the government brought in a series of <u>Poor Laws</u> to deal with the growing problem of <u>poverty</u>.

2) Because <u>voluntary donations</u> were <u>no longer sufficient</u> to fund poor relief, in the <u>1560s</u> the government passed a Poor Law which introduced a <u>tax</u> to raise money for the poor (known as the '<u>poor rate</u>').

3) Further Poor Laws were passed in <u>1597</u> and <u>1601</u> in response to the <u>poverty crisis</u> of the <u>1590s</u> (see p.103). Under these laws, the poor rate became a <u>national</u> system of <u>compulsory taxation</u>. It was collected locally by an official called the <u>Overseer of the Poor</u>.

4) Poor rates were used to provide <u>hospitals</u> and <u>housing</u> for the elderly, sick and disabled. Poor children were given <u>apprenticeships</u>, which usually lasted at least seven years, and local authorities were expected to provide <u>financial support</u> or <u>work</u> for the <u>deserving poor</u>. Poor people could be sent to <u>prison</u> if they <u>refused</u> to take work.

Comment and Analysis

The Privy Council <u>researched</u> how <u>local government</u> had tackled the problem of poverty. They based the <u>national Poor Laws</u> on the <u>local policies</u> that seemed to be <u>most effective</u>. For example, towns like London, Norwich, Ipswich and York had been using <u>compulsory poor rates</u> to pay for poor relief since the <u>mid-16th century</u>.

The **Undeserving Poor** were treated **Harshly**

1) Under the Poor Laws of the 1590s, the <u>undeserving</u> poor were to be publicly <u>whipped</u> and then <u>forced</u> to return to their <u>home parish</u>. Repeat offenders could be sent to <u>prison</u>.

2) The <u>undeserving poor</u> were treated so <u>harshly</u> because they were seen as a <u>threat</u> to <u>society</u>. Many people believed that poor <u>criminals</u> and <u>vagabonds</u> had encouraged the <u>Northern Rebellion</u> in 1569 (see p.120).

3) In <u>response</u> to the Rebellion, the government introduced particularly <u>harsh punishments</u> for the undeserving poor in <u>1572</u>.

The Poor Laws helped some, but punished others

Include plenty of specific information in your answers. For example, don't just write about the Poor Laws in general, give the dates of specific laws and explain the changes they brought in.

A 'Golden Age'

Despite the very high levels of poverty, Elizabeth's reign is often seen as a 'Golden Age'.
The growing prosperity of the elite contributed to a flourishing in architecture, the arts and education.

The **Gentry** became **Richer** during Elizabeth's reign

1) Population growth and changes in farming practices (see p.103) were good for landowners, especially members of the gentry.

> The gentry were part of the social elite in Elizabethan England, below the level of the nobility. Members of the gentry were people who owned land and lived off the income it provided. They didn't have to do other work to survive.

2) The enclosures meant that land was farmed more efficiently. At the same time, rents were increasing and prices of agricultural products like grain were rising, so landowners were earning a lot more money from their land.

3) As a result, the land-owning gentry became much wealthier during Elizabeth's reign, and members of the nobility also saw their incomes increase.

4) The growth of towns and the development of national and international trade allowed some merchants to become very rich. They often used their money to buy land and become part of the gentry.

Some members of the **Elite** built **New Houses**

1) From the 1570s, many members of the gentry and nobility improved their homes or built new ones. This is sometimes called the 'Great Rebuilding'.

2) These building projects enabled members of the elite to show off their wealth. New houses often had many large windows — glass was very expensive, so using a lot of it was a sign of prosperity. Large landscaped gardens were also a popular way to display wealth.

> Some members of the nobility built huge, elaborate houses. Burghley House in Peterborough, built for William Cecil, is a well-known example.

3) The 'Great Rebuilding' improved living standards for the wealthy, because the new houses were much more comfortable. The large windows made them lighter, and bigger chimneys and fireplaces meant they were better heated.

Art, Literature and Education were all highly Fashionable

1) The nobility and gentry had money to spend on elaborate decorations for their homes. Portraits, miniatures (very small portraits), tapestries and embroidery were all popular.

2) It was also fashionable to take an interest in literature — some people collected large libraries, and members of the elite supported the work of poets and playwrights. Elite support for playwrights and acting companies contributed to the flourishing of Elizabethan theatre (see p.109).

3) More people could afford to give their children an education (see p.107).

A miniature of Queen Elizabeth's 'favourite', Robert Dudley, painted by Nicholas Hilliard.

The Art Archive / Granger Collection

> Members of the elite wore elaborate clothing to show off their wealth and status. Their clothes were often made of expensive fabrics like silk, satin, velvet and lace, and were decorated with detailed embroidery. Women's dresses had very full sleeves and a large skirt, supported by a hoop-skirt, which gave it shape (see the portrait of Elizabeth on p.99). Both men and women wore wide, ruffled collars, called ruffs.

Comment and Analysis

Many elite fashions started at the royal court. For example Nicholas Hilliard was employed as Queen Elizabeth's miniaturist in the 1570s and painted many miniatures of Elizabeth and her courtiers. This encouraged the growing popularity of miniatures among the nobility and gentry.

REVISION TASK

Culture bloomed in Elizabethan England

Write a sentence or two to explain why the gentry got richer during Elizabeth's reign. Then make a quick spider diagram showing some things that members of the elite spent their wealth on.

Family Life

Families were at the <u>heart</u> of Elizabethan society, and were usually <u>positive</u> and <u>loving</u> environments. Family life taught children important <u>morals</u> and reinforced Elizabethan <u>social structures</u>.

Families played an **Important Role** in **Elizabethan Society**

1) Elizabethan families were usually <u>loving</u>, and <u>close relationships</u> with family members were <u>encouraged</u>.

2) Elizabethan family life was <u>hierarchical</u> — some members of the family had <u>more authority</u> than others. The father was the <u>head</u> of the family. The mother <u>assisted</u> him, and the children <u>obeyed</u> their parents.

3) <u>Wider kinship</u> (extended family) was also important. <u>Kin</u> formed part of a family's <u>social life</u> and could be called upon to provide <u>financial</u> help.

Comment and Analysis

This hierarchical structure <u>reflected</u> the structure of larger organisations in society like the <u>Church</u> and the <u>state</u>. Elizabethans believed that families were essential for <u>maintaining</u> the idea of hierarchy, which helped to <u>strengthen</u> and <u>stabilise</u> the country.

4) Having important or rich ancestors was a source of <u>pride</u> and <u>status</u>. Noble families would often hang <u>portraits</u> or <u>miniatures</u> (very small portraits) of their kin or ancestors in their homes.

5) Kin also provided useful <u>political</u> and <u>social</u> connections, particularly in wealthy families, e.g. children's education in other households (see below) was sometimes arranged using <u>wider family connections</u>.

People got **Married** for **Different Reasons**

1) In Elizabethan England, marriage could be a way of increasing a family's <u>wealth</u> or <u>social standing</u>. Husbands usually owned all of their wife's <u>money</u> and <u>property</u> once they were married.

2) For members of the <u>nobility</u> and <u>gentry</u>, the right marriage could <u>advance</u> a man's career at <u>court</u> or in <u>government</u>. But marriage wasn't always about money or status — many Elizabethans married for <u>love</u>.

3) A husband was the <u>head</u> of the household, and was responsible for providing an <u>income</u> for his family. He was expected to <u>care</u> for his wife and children.

4) A wife's main role was to run the <u>household</u> and look after her <u>children</u> and <u>husband</u>.

5) If their husbands went away, women were often left <u>in charge</u> of all household staff and servants. In some poor families, wives had to <u>work</u>. Women could help their husbands with <u>farm work</u> and sometimes even took on <u>separate jobs</u>, e.g. as midwives or shop assistants.

Children often **Left Home** to learn **New Skills**

1) Childbirth was extremely <u>dangerous</u> in Elizabethan times. Many women died giving birth, and infant mortality rates (the number of children who died) were <u>high</u>, especially amongst the <u>poor</u>.

2) The Elizabethans expected parents to <u>love</u> and <u>take care</u> of their children. Parents were also responsible for teaching children <u>morals</u> and <u>social expectations</u>.

3) <u>Richer</u> Elizabethan children were often <u>sent away</u> from the family home. Some went to <u>school</u>, but many became <u>skilled apprentices</u>. Children of the nobility were often sent to <u>noble households</u> to train for <u>knighthoods</u>.

4) Most <u>poor</u> and <u>middle-class</u> children stayed at home to work, but some were servants in other <u>households</u> or did an <u>apprenticeship</u>.

5) In poorer families, life was often a <u>struggle</u> for both parents, who had to work hard to <u>feed</u> and <u>clothe</u> their children.

Comment and Analysis

The <u>affection</u> between parents and children was demonstrated by the regular practice of giving a '<u>parental blessing</u>'. Every morning and evening children would <u>kneel</u> before their parents, who would reach out, place their hands on them and <u>bless</u> them.

The Elizabethans tried to create loving families

Using the information on this page, write an account of an Elizabethan household from the point of view of one of the family members. Remember to include what each family member's role is.

Education

During Elizabeth's reign, people increasingly began to recognise the importance of education.

Children received a **Basic Education** at **Home**

1) Children received their early education at home. Most parents probably taught their children how to behave correctly and gave them a basic religious education. From the age of six, all children had to go to Sunday school, where they learnt things like the Lord's Prayer, the 10 Commandments and the Creed (a basic statement of the Christian faith).

2) From a young age, boys were trained in simple work skills, while girls helped their mothers with household activities.

3) Some children from noble households were taught at home by a private tutor. Others were sent to live with another noble family and educated there.

> This kind of education was intended to teach children how to behave in noble society and give them the skills to be successful at court.

More children went to **School**

Only a small minority of children in Elizabethan England went to school, but the number was growing. Education was increasingly important for many careers, including trade and government administration.

Petty Schools

1) Petty schools were small, local schools that provided a basic education. Many were run by the local parish priest. Others were attached to grammar schools, or were set up by private individuals.

2) The schools taught basic reading and writing, and sometimes a little maths. There wasn't a set curriculum, although lessons usually had a strong religious focus. The schools didn't usually have any books — instead the main teaching aid was the hornbook, a wooden board showing the alphabet and the Lord's Prayer.

3) Most pupils were boys, although some petty schools admitted a few girls. There was no fixed age for pupils to start school, but they usually started at about six and stayed until they could read and write.

Grammar Schools

1) Grammar schools had existed for centuries, but there was a big expansion during Elizabeth's reign, with the foundation of around 100 new grammar schools. There was no state education system at this time. Instead, most schools were set up by wealthy individuals.

2) It was very rare for girls to go to grammar school — most pupils were boys from the upper and middle classes. Some schools offered free places to bright boys from poorer backgrounds, but few poor boys were able to attend because their parents needed them to work at home.

3) Children usually started grammar school around the age of seven. Lessons focused mainly on Latin and classical literature (literature from Ancient Greece and Rome). A few schools also taught Greek.

The number of **University Students** was **Increasing**

1) When they left grammar school, some boys went on to study at one of the two English universities, Oxford and Cambridge. The growing prosperity of the upper and middle classes meant that the number of university students increased during Elizabeth's reign.

2) University courses were conducted almost entirely in Latin. Students studied advanced written and spoken Latin, before moving on to study arithmetic, music, Greek, astronomy, geometry and philosophy. After completing an undergraduate degree, students might specialise in law, theology or medicine.

> **Comment and Analysis**
>
> The printing press had been introduced to England in the late 15th century. As printing spread, it encouraged increased literacy levels because it made books much cheaper and more widely available.

Education became more important in Elizabethan England

REVISION TASK

Write down these headings: Home, Petty School, Grammar School, University.
Under each heading, jot down the main things pupils were taught in that place.

Popular Culture

Some Elizabethan pastimes, including tennis, fencing, football and the theatre, are still popular today.

Hunting and Sports were an Important part of Court Life

1) Elizabeth and her courtiers often hunted deer and other wild animals. As well as being a form of entertainment, hunting was an important source of food for the court. The Queen was skilled at hawking, spending many hours with her trained falcons as they hunted. Only the rich could afford to train falcons.

2) Elizabeth's courtiers and other nobles practised fencing from a young age. Tennis and bowls were also becoming more popular. These sports needed expensive equipment, so they were only played by the rich.

3) Most ordinary people worked six days a week and went to church on Sundays, so they had little leisure time. However, there were several festival days in the calendar, including Midsummer's day and Ascension day. On these days, people were free to enjoy sports, feasting and other pastimes.

4) Football was a popular sport, often played between two villages. An unlimited number of players could take part, and there were few rules — games often descended into long and violent fights.

5) Blood sports like cockfighting and bull- or bear-baiting were also very popular.

The Theatre became Very Popular later in Elizabeth's reign

1) There were no permanent theatres in England at the start of Elizabeth's reign. Instead, actors travelled around, performing in village squares or inn courtyards.

2) The first theatres were built in London in the 1570s. They included The Theatre and The Curtain. They were usually round, open-air buildings with a raised stage that stretched out into the audience.

> Lots of plays were written in the Elizabethan era. Famous Elizabethan playwrights include William Shakespeare, Christopher Marlowe and Ben Johnson.

3) The theatre appealed to both rich and poor. Poorer audience members, known as groundlings, stood around the stage, while richer people sat under cover around the theatre's walls.

4) Elizabeth enjoyed plays and often had them performed at court. She supported her favourite performers and even set up an acting company, The Queen's Men. Members of the elite (including some Privy Councillors) also supported theatre companies.

5) The London authorities and the Puritans opposed the theatre because they saw it as a source of crime and immorality. As a result, many theatres were built just outside the City of London in Southwark.

Elizabethans became More Hostile towards Witches

A woodcut of witches hanged after a trial at Chelmsford in 1589.

1) Elizabeth banned Catholic rituals like charms, blessings or exorcisms, which were used to cleanse someone of the Devil or evil spirits. This made some Elizabethans feel more vulnerable.

2) In 1562, Elizabeth passed the Witchcraft Act, which made all acts of witchcraft a crime. Accused witches were given a trial in a court. Witches found guilty of causing death would be hanged. Less serious offences, like providing herbal remedies, carried a prison sentence of one year.

> People believed that witches acted on the Devil's orders and wanted to cause harm to others.

3) Those accused of witchcraft were usually older women who didn't fit in to society. These included mothers with illegitimate children, spinsters (unmarried women) and women who were rude or outspoken

4) Formal accusations against witches reached their height at the end of the 16th century. Between 1570 and 1609, 263 people were accused of being witches, but only 64 were executed.

EXAM TIP

People's pastimes depended on whether they were rich or poor

Remember that there were social distinctions in leisure activities — the rich and the poor mostly enjoyed different pastimes and even at the theatre the two groups didn't mix.

Elizabethan Sailors

Elizabeth's reign was an <u>exciting</u> time to be a sailor. Developments in <u>navigation</u> and <u>ship-building</u> were finally opening up the <u>oceans</u> and enabling explorers to discover the world <u>beyond Europe</u>.

The **English** were **Slow** to take an interest in **Exploration**

1) The <u>Portuguese</u> and <u>Spanish</u> were the first to explore the world beyond Europe. In the <u>1400s</u>, their fleets began to set out on <u>voyages of discovery</u> to Africa, the Americas and Asia. By the time Elizabeth became queen in 1558, both Portugal and Spain had established many <u>colonies</u> in the <u>Americas</u>.

2) However, it was only from the <u>1560s</u> that <u>English sailors</u> began to take an interest in <u>global exploration</u> and set out on their own voyages of discovery.

Explorers were **Attracted** by **Economic Opportunities**

1) <u>Spanish trade</u> with its <u>colonies</u> was very <u>profitable</u>. This attracted <u>English privateers</u> (men with their own ships) — they hoped to profit by <u>trading</u> with Spain's colonies and <u>raiding</u> Spanish settlements and ships.

2) <u>John Hawkins</u> was the <u>first</u> English privateer to join the <u>Atlantic slave trade</u>. In the <u>1560s</u>, he made <u>three</u> slave-trading voyages. He bought slaves in <u>west Africa</u> and sold them to <u>Spanish colonies</u>. The Spanish <u>didn't</u> want the English to <u>trade</u> with these <u>colonies</u>, so his actions fuelled <u>tensions</u> between England and Spain (see p.125).

3) Hawkins' first two voyages were very <u>profitable</u>, but on his last expedition he was confronted by Spanish ships in the battle of <u>San Juan de Ulúa</u> and most of his fleet was <u>destroyed</u>.

> Elizabeth encouraged English merchants to take part in <u>long-distance trade</u> and <u>privateering</u>, and to try and establish English <u>colonies</u> in the <u>Americas</u> (see p.111). She wanted England to <u>compete</u> with Spain globally.

4) From the 1570s, English merchants also looked for <u>routes</u> to <u>Asia</u>, like the <u>North West passage</u> around the top of North America. In 1591, <u>James Lancaster</u> sailed to India around the <u>Cape of Good Hope</u> (the southern tip of Africa). After this, the <u>East India Company</u> was set up in <u>1600</u> to trade with Asia.

New Technology made **Longer Journeys** possible

1) As the Portuguese and Spanish began to explore the seas, they developed <u>better navigational techniques</u>. They learnt how to navigate by the position of the <u>stars</u> or the <u>Sun</u> using an instrument called a <u>sea astrolabe</u>.

2) In 1561, a key Spanish book, '<u>The Art of Navigation</u>' by <u>Martin Cortés</u>, was translated into English. This gave English sailors detailed information about how to navigate across the <u>Atlantic</u> using a <u>sea astrolabe</u>.

> Other <u>innovations</u> improved navigation. The <u>log and line</u> helped sailors to estimate their <u>speed</u> with more <u>accuracy</u> from the 1570s. English navigator <u>John Davis</u> invented the <u>backstaff</u> in the 1590s, which was <u>easier</u> to use and <u>more accurate</u> than the sea astrolabe. There were also <u>improvements</u> in <u>map-making</u>, which made maps and naval charts more <u>detailed</u> and reliable.

3) From the 1570s, the English built <u>larger</u>, <u>longer</u> ships. These were <u>better-suited</u> to long ocean voyages, as they were <u>faster</u>, <u>more stable</u> and <u>easier to navigate</u>. They could also carry <u>larger cargoes</u>, making their voyages <u>more profitable</u>.

New technology made it easier for sailors to explore the world

Write a short paragraph explaining whether you think economic opportunities or new technology was the most important factor in English sailors' growing involvement in global exploration.

Elizabethan Sailors

One of the most significant sailors of the Elizabethan era was <u>Francis Drake</u>. Drake is perhaps best remembered for <u>sailing all the way around the world</u>, which was a tremendous feat at the time.

Francis Drake was the Second man ever to sail Around the World

<u>Francis Drake</u> was John Hawkins' <u>cousin</u>, and had travelled with Hawkins on two of his <u>slave-trading</u> expeditions. Between <u>1577</u> and <u>1580</u>, Drake circumnavigated the world (sailed all the way around it).

1) Drake probably <u>wasn't</u> trying to sail around the world. It seems that he was sent by <u>Elizabeth</u> to <u>explore</u> the coast of <u>South America</u>, looking for opportunities for English <u>colonisation</u> and <u>trade</u>.

2) Drake <u>explored</u> the South American coastline, <u>raiding</u> many Spanish settlements as he went. In the <u>Pacific</u>, he captured two very valuable <u>Spanish treasure ships</u>. In order to get this treasure safely home, Drake had to return by a <u>different route</u> — the Spanish were <u>blocking</u> the way that he had come.

3) Instead, Drake sailed <u>west</u>, across the <u>Pacific</u> to <u>Indonesia</u>. He then made his way across the <u>Indian Ocean</u>, went round the <u>Cape of Good Hope</u> and back to <u>England</u>.

4) Drake was <u>knighted</u> by Elizabeth on his ship, the <u>Golden Hind</u>. This <u>royal recognition</u> and the <u>wealth</u> that Drake brought back <u>encouraged</u> more English sailors to go on long-distance journeys.

Drake was involved in many other important <u>naval expeditions</u>. E.g. in <u>1587</u> he led a raid on the Spanish port of <u>Cadiz</u> (p.126), and in <u>1588</u> he played a key role in the <u>defeat</u> of the <u>Spanish Armada</u>. He <u>died</u> of disease in <u>1596</u> while trying to conquer Spanish colonies in the Americas.

Drake's Circumnavigation was a Huge Achievement

Drake's expedition was only the <u>second successful global circumnavigation</u>, and the first by an English sailor. He and his crew had to overcome some <u>major challenges</u> in order to complete the expedition.

1) <u>Navigating</u> across vast <u>oceans</u> was extremely <u>difficult</u>. Elizabethan sailors knew how to use the <u>Sun</u> and <u>stars</u> to work out how far north or south of the equator they were (their <u>latitude</u>), but they <u>couldn't</u> measure how far east or west they had travelled (their <u>longitude</u>).

2) Many of the places Drake visited had <u>never</u> been <u>explored</u> by European sailors before, so there were <u>no detailed maps</u> or charts to help him navigate.

> The challenges of <u>navigation</u>, <u>bad weather</u> and <u>disease</u> had to be faced by <u>all</u> Elizabethan sailors who set out on <u>long-distance</u> voyages.

3) Many sailors <u>died</u> of <u>disease</u> during long journeys — one of Drake's ships had to be <u>abandoned</u> after crossing the Atlantic because so many of the crew had <u>died</u>.

4) <u>Bad weather</u> could blow ships <u>off course</u>, or even <u>sink</u> them. Storms <u>destroyed</u> one of Drake's ships as it attempted to sail around the bottom of South America, and forced another to <u>turn back</u> to England.

EXAM TIP

Drake faced many hardships on his journey around the globe

Remember that Drake was an important figure for many different reasons. As well as circumnavigating the globe, he also played a part in the defeat of the Spanish Armada (see p.126-127).

Elizabethan Sailors

After Drake's circumnavigation, England tried to challenge Spain's dominance as an imperial power by establishing a colony in North America. But creating a permanent settlement turned out to be very difficult.

Raleigh's attempts to Colonise Virginia were Unsuccessful

Walter Raleigh was a member of a gentry family from Devon. His family were involved with international exploration, and Raleigh first visited America in 1578. From the early 1580s, Raleigh had a powerful position at court as one of Elizabeth's 'favourites'.

1) In 1584, Elizabeth gave Raleigh permission to explore and colonise unclaimed territories. She wanted him to establish a colony on the Atlantic coast of North America.

Comment and Analysis

An English colony would have challenged Spain's dominance in the Americas and could be used as a base for attacking Spanish treasure ships. The colony might also provide opportunities for trade.

2) In 1585, Raleigh sent 108 settlers to establish a permanent colony on Roanoke Island, Virginia (Raleigh named his colony after Elizabeth, who was known as the 'Virgin Queen').

3) However, the settlers (or planters) soon ran low on supplies, and when Francis Drake visited Roanoke in 1586, most of them abandoned the colony and returned to England.

Roanoke Island, Virginia

4) A second group of planters reached Roanoke in 1587. They were expecting supplies from England in 1588, but the fleet was delayed by the Spanish Armada (see p.126).

5) When the supply ships reached Roanoke in 1590, all the planters had disappeared. They were never found, and Roanoke became known as the 'Lost Colony'.

6) Raleigh was partly responsible for the colony's failure — his funds were too limited and the whole project was poorly planned. However, other factors like bad luck and a lack of supplies also played a part.

Raleigh's Career had Ups and Downs

1) Despite the failure of the Roanoke colony, Raleigh remained one of Elizabeth's 'favourites'.
2) However, in 1592 he was disgraced when Elizabeth found out that he had secretly married one of her ladies-in-waiting. As a punishment, Raleigh was banished from court and briefly imprisoned.
3) This wasn't the end of his career though — after his release he continued to play an important role in politics. He became a Member of Parliament and was still heavily involved with the Royal Navy.

REVISION TASK

Raleigh was an important sailor and courtier

Make a timeline of Walter Raleigh's career. Include all the key events of his attempts to colonise Virginia and details of what happened to him after the failure of the Roanoke colony.

Worked Exam-Style Question

This sample answer will show you how to identify differences between two interpretations and explain why two authors might have different ideas or approaches to the same topic.

John walked quickly along the muddy road to the market town. His children ran on ahead of him, weaving through fields full of dying crops. The harvest had all but failed for the second year in a row, and John was struggling to feed his half-starved children. There wasn't enough food for everyone, and prices had risen so high that most people couldn't afford to buy food from the market. John worried that his children would never escape their life of hunger. After a while, John came upon a traveller further up the road who warned him that there was illness in the town. There were dreadful rumours that the plague had returned. John called his children and hurried home, hoping that this time his family would be spared.

Interpretation 1 — an extract from a fictional story about a poor Elizabethan farmer and his family, set in the 1590s.

In [Shakespeare's] day many of the gentry could trace their ancestors to enterprising yeomen who... had raised their incomes from about £100 a year to £200 or £300. Their sons in turn dressed in velvet breeches... and called themselves gentlemen. But even more of the new gentry came from trade, industry, law and government. Having made their fortunes in these professions, they bought manors and joined the gentry. Not only did the numbers of the gentry swell, so did the wealth of the class as a whole...

The nobility and gentry lavished their new wealth on the building of country houses that were more spacious, more comfortable, more impressive, and more elegant than those in which their fathers had lived.

Interpretation 2 — an extract from a textbook about the history of England, published in 2016.

Q1

Read the interpretations above about life in Elizabethan England. How different are they? Why do you think they might differ?   [12 marks]

Address the question directly in the first sentence.

> Both interpretations discuss social mobility, but they have different views on this issue. Interpretation 2 discusses the social mobility of tradesmen and professionals, who used their growing wealth to buy land and join the gentry. It highlights that the children of the gentry were able to prosper from their parents' wealth and dress in 'velvet breeches'. Interpretation 1, however, suggests that poor children were stuck in a cycle of poverty, as they might 'never escape their life of hunger' and had to face starvation and serious illness as part of their daily lives, especially during the crisis years of the 1590s when several harvests failed and poverty increased.

This shows <u>how</u> the interpretations <u>differ</u> in their approach to a <u>specific topic</u>.

Use your <u>own knowledge</u> to add <u>relevant detail</u> to your explanation.

Worked Exam-Style Question

This paragraph explains why the interpretations take a <u>different view</u> on a <u>similar issue</u>.

A <u>key reason</u> for this difference between the two interpretations is that they <u>are discussing two different classes who had very different lifestyles and experiences</u>. <u>Interpretation 1 focuses on the experiences of a poor farmer in Elizabethan England</u> and the uncertainty that his family faced as a result of bad harvests, plague and poverty. However, <u>Interpretation 2 discusses the increasing prosperity of the gentry</u>, who greatly improved their living conditions by building <u>'elegant' and 'comfortable'</u> country houses that displayed their wealth.

This shows how the <u>main focus</u> of each interpretation differs.

Use <u>evidence</u> from the interpretations to <u>back up</u> your points.

You can talk about the <u>way the interpretations are written</u>, as well as what they say.

While both interpretations focus on developments in living conditions in Elizabethan England, <u>Interpretation 1 is very descriptive and Interpretation 2 focuses on causes and consequences</u>. For example, <u>Interpretation 1 paints a picture</u> of Elizabethan poverty by attempting to show <u>what daily life was like</u> in Elizabethan England for a farmer and his family. As a result, it describes the impact of worsening poverty on ordinary Elizabethans, focusing on settings where the majority lived, like the countryside and market towns. On the other hand, <u>Interpretation 2 describes the development</u> of the gentry in a more detached way.

This describes how the <u>style</u> of the interpretations <u>differs</u>.

This suggests <u>reasons</u> why the styles might differ by talking about the <u>purpose</u> of each text.

This difference may be because the two books have different purposes. Interpretation 1 comes from a fictional story that is <u>designed to entertain the reader, so it focuses more on creating an image of Elizabethan life</u>, rather than a historical analysis. <u>Interpretation 2 is from a historical textbook, so it aims to explain rather than describe the rise of the gentry and its consequences</u>. As a result, it offers an account of the lives of the gentry as a whole class and focuses more on historical concepts like causes and consequences.

In your conclusion, give a <u>clear answer</u> to the question that judges <u>how far the interpretations differ</u>.

<u>Overall, Interpretations 1 and 2 focus on similar topics, like living conditions and life chances, but the details and tone of these interpretations differ significantly</u>. This is mainly <u>because the interpretations focus on two different social groups</u>, but the fact that the texts have different aims has also played a part in creating this difference.

<u>Explain why</u> you think these differences might have occurred.

Exam-Style Questions

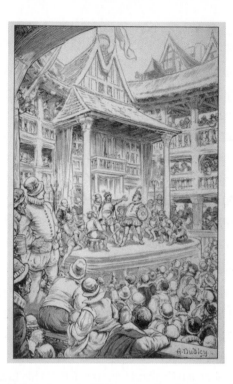

Interpretation 1 — an illustration by Ambrose Dudley
of a performance at the Globe Theatre in London.

Q1

a) Explain one way that the artist of Interpretation 1 shows the
popularity of the theatre in Elizabethan England.   [3 marks]

b) If you had to investigate another aspect of Interpretation 1, what
would it be? Explain how your choice would help historians
understand more about Elizabethan theatre.   [5 marks]

Q2

Do you find this interpretation of Elizabethan theatre convincing?
Use the picture and your knowledge of the period to explain your answer.   [8 marks]

Exam-Style Questions

Q3 Why was poverty a growing problem in Elizabethan England? Explain your answer.

You could mention England's growing population
and its agriculture in your response.   [12 marks]

Q4 Give an account of the ways in which people's living
standards changed during Elizabeth I's reign.   [8 marks]

Q5 'Francis Drake was the most successful English sailor of Elizabeth's reign.'

Explain how far you agree with this statement.   [16 marks]

The Religious Settlement

By 1558, England had experienced decades of dizzying <u>religious changes</u>. Elizabeth's <u>religious 'settlement'</u>, passed in <u>1559</u>, aimed to put a stop to these changes and bring <u>religious stability</u> to England.

There had been constant **Religious Changes** since the **1530s**

1) When Elizabeth became queen in <u>1558</u>, England had suffered <u>30 years</u> of <u>religious turmoil</u>, with the national religion switching repeatedly between <u>Catholicism</u> and <u>Protestantism</u>.

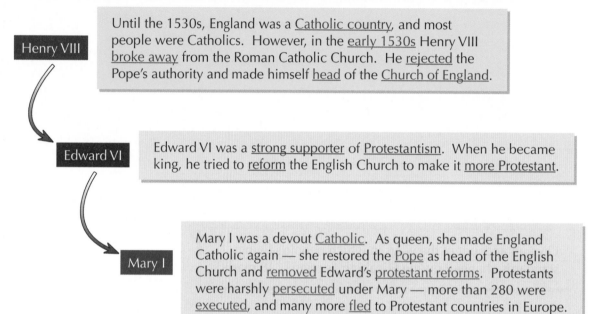

Henry VIII

Until the 1530s, England was a <u>Catholic country</u>, and most people were Catholics. However, in the <u>early 1530s</u> Henry VIII <u>broke away</u> from the Roman Catholic Church. He <u>rejected</u> the Pope's authority and made himself <u>head</u> of the <u>Church of England</u>.

Edward VI

Edward VI was a <u>strong supporter</u> of <u>Protestantism</u>. When he became king, he tried to <u>reform</u> the English Church to make it <u>more Protestant</u>.

Mary I

Mary I was a devout <u>Catholic</u>. As queen, she made England Catholic again — she restored the <u>Pope</u> as head of the English Church and <u>removed</u> Edward's <u>protestant reforms</u>. Protestants were harshly <u>persecuted</u> under Mary — more than 280 were <u>executed</u>, and many more <u>fled</u> to Protestant countries in Europe.

2) Elizabeth had been raised as a <u>Protestant</u>. She was <u>deeply religious</u> and <u>committed</u> to Protestantism.

3) However, she was also determined to end the constant religious changes of the last 30 years by creating a <u>stable</u> and <u>lasting religious settlement</u>.

Protestants Challenged Many Catholic Beliefs and Practices

*   Protestants <u>questioned</u> the authority of the <u>Pope</u> and <u>rejected</u> some <u>Catholic beliefs</u> — e.g. they believed that Christians were <u>saved by faith</u>, not by good deeds.
*   They encouraged ordinary people to read the <u>Bible</u> by <u>translating</u> it from Latin.
*   They also thought churches should be <u>plain</u> and <u>simple</u>, unlike highly decorated Catholic churches.

The **Act of Supremacy** gave Elizabeth **Control** over the **Church**

1) Henry VIII and Edward VI had both used the title Supreme Head of the Church of England.

2) In her <u>Act of Supremacy</u> (passed in <u>1559</u>), Elizabeth altered this title to make herself the <u>Supreme Governor</u> of the English Church.

3) This gave Elizabeth <u>control</u> of the English <u>Church</u>, without actually calling her its 'Head'. This <u>compromise</u> satisfied those who believed a <u>woman</u> couldn't lead the Church.

EXAM TIP

The religious settlement was an important break with the past

Religious tension had a huge impact on Elizabethan England. Understanding the tensions that existed when Elizabeth came to power will help you get to grips with the effects of the religious settlement.

The Religious Settlement

As well as the <u>Act of Supremacy</u>, Elizabeth also introduced the <u>Act of Uniformity</u> and the <u>Royal Injunctions</u> in 1559. They introduced some <u>Protestant reforms</u>, but they didn't go far enough for the <u>Puritans</u>.

The **Act of Uniformity** made **Moderate Protestant Reforms**

The <u>Act of Uniformity</u> and the <u>Royal Injunctions</u>, both passed in <u>1559</u>, imposed <u>moderate Protestant reforms</u> on the English Church, but they also made some <u>concessions</u> to English <u>Catholics</u>:

Reforms

- Going to <u>church</u> was <u>compulsory</u> — there were <u>fines</u> for missing a church service.
- A new <u>Book of Common Prayer</u> was issued, which had to be used in all churches.
- All parishes had to have a copy of the <u>Bible</u> in <u>English</u>.

Concessions

- The wording of the <u>communion service</u> (an important Christian ceremony) was kept <u>deliberately vague</u>, so that it could be accepted by both <u>Protestants</u> and <u>Catholics</u>.
- Churches were allowed to keep some <u>decorations</u>, and priests had to wear certain Catholic <u>vestments</u> (robes).

Comment and Analysis

The <u>religious settlement</u> made England a <u>Protestant country</u>, but allowed some elements of <u>Catholic belief and practice</u> to continue. This '<u>middle way</u>' was designed to satisfy the <u>majority</u>, who held <u>moderate religious beliefs</u> and were willing to make some <u>compromises</u> for the sake of <u>peace and stability</u>. But it <u>couldn't</u> win over the more <u>extreme Catholics</u> or the <u>Puritans</u>.

The **Puritans** challenged the **Religious Settlement**

1) The Puritans were committed Protestants. For them, Elizabeth's religious settlement was only a <u>first step</u>, and they wanted her to make <u>further reforms</u> to remove all traces of Catholicism from the English Church.

> Many of the <u>Protestant bishops</u> appointed from 1559 <u>supported</u> the Puritans and were in favour of <u>further reforms</u>. However, the Archbishop of Canterbury, <u>Matthew Parker</u>, was a <u>moderate</u> who helped Elizabeth to uphold the '<u>middle way</u>' of the religious settlement.

2) Many <u>Puritans</u> had fled England when Mary I was in power (see p.116). While in exile in Protestant parts of Europe, some had come into contact with the teachings of leading reformers like <u>Martin Luther</u> and <u>John Calvin</u>.

3) The <u>Vestment Controversy</u> of the 1560s was a serious Puritan challenge to the religious settlement. Puritan priests <u>refused</u> to wear the <u>surplice</u>, a white vestment used by Catholics, which the Royal Injunctions had made compulsory.

4) Elizabeth tolerated this at first, but in <u>1565</u> she ordered the Archbishop of Canterbury to ensure that all priests wore the surplice. Those Puritans who still refused <u>lost their jobs</u> or were <u>imprisoned</u>.

5) The Puritans challenged the religious settlement <u>again</u> later in Elizabeth's reign — see p.124.

The religious settlement was designed for religious stability

Divide a piece of paper into two. Jot down the key features of the Act of Supremacy (see p.116) on one side and the Act of Uniformity and the Royal Injunctions on the other.

The Religious Settlement

As well as the Puritans (see p.117), Elizabeth's religious settlement faced many other challenges in the 1560s.

Many members of the **Nobility** continued to practise **Catholicism**

1) A large proportion of the nobility were still Catholic. The compromises in the religious settlement won some of them around, but others refused to attend church services — they were known as recusants.

2) The Catholic nobility was influential in areas outside the south-east, especially Lancashire. They used their strong local power bases to protect Catholics and maintain their traditional religious practices.

> The threat posed by the Catholic nobility became more serious when Mary, Queen of Scots, (a Catholic claimant to the English throne) arrived in England in 1568 (p.119).

3) These Catholic nobles posed a potential threat to the religious settlement — there was a risk that they might try to overthrow Elizabeth and restore Catholicism.

4) To minimise this threat, Elizabeth did not force the Catholic nobility to attend church services. As long as they didn't make a public show of their beliefs, they were allowed to continue practising Catholicism.

France and Spain were **Distracted** by **Domestic Difficulties**

1) There was a risk that the Catholic rulers of France or Spain might try to reverse the religious settlement and replace Elizabeth with a Catholic monarch. However, neither country was really in a position to challenge the religious settlement during the 1560s.

2) The threat of a French invasion was serious in the first years of Elizabeth's reign, but faded with the start of the French Wars of Religion in 1562.

3) In the 1560s, Spain was facing a growing revolt in the Netherlands. To prevent an alliance forming between England and the Protestant Netherlands, Spain tried to stay on good terms with Elizabeth and avoided challenging her religious settlement.

Comment and Analysis

The Catholic aspects of the settlement encouraged Catholic countries and the Pope to think that Elizabeth might eventually return to Catholicism. This helped to reduce the threat of a foreign challenge during the early years of the settlement.

The Papacy **Lacked Military Support**

1) The Pope had the power to excommunicate Elizabeth (expel her from the Catholic Church). This might encourage Catholic countries to invade England. It could also encourage rebellion at home by releasing Elizabeth's Catholic subjects from their duty of loyalty to her.

2) However, neither France nor Spain had the military resources to invade England, and there was no clear support for a revolt against Elizabeth at home, so the Pope didn't take any action against her in the 1560s.

EXAM TIP

The religious settlement was under threat from the beginning

The religious settlement was a major cause of opposition to Elizabeth throughout her reign. It's important to remember that different groups of people had different reasons for disliking it.

Mary, Queen of Scots

Elizabeth and Mary, Queen of Scots, were <u>cousins</u>, but Elizabeth wasn't too pleased when Mary arrived in England.

Mary, Queen of Scots, had a **Strong Claim** to the **English Throne**

Mary was the only child of <u>James V of Scotland</u>. She was related to the <u>Tudors</u> through her grandmother, <u>Margaret Tudor</u>. Margaret was Henry VIII's sister, the wife of James IV and mother of James V (see p.93).

1) As a granddaughter of Margaret Tudor, Mary had a <u>strong claim</u> to the <u>English throne</u>. Because Mary was a Catholic, her claim was <u>supported</u> by many <u>English Catholics</u>.

2) Mary became <u>queen of Scotland</u> in 1542 when she was just six days old. Her mother acted as regent (she ruled on Mary's behalf), while Mary was raised in <u>France</u>.

3) In 1558, when Mary was 15 years old, she married the heir to the French throne. However, her husband died suddenly in <u>1560</u>, and Mary <u>returned to Scotland</u>.

Comment and Analysis

Mary wanted to be named as <u>heir</u> to the <u>English throne</u>, but Elizabeth was <u>unwilling</u> to do this. She feared that making Mary her heir would <u>encourage Catholic plots</u>, both at home and abroad, to overthrow her and make Mary queen.

Mary **Fled** to **England** in 1568

1) In <u>1565</u> Mary married the Scottish nobleman <u>Lord Darnley</u>. The marriage was not a happy one. Darnley hated Mary's personal secretary, <u>David Rizzio</u>, and became convinced that the two were having an <u>affair</u>. In 1566 a group of Scottish nobles, accompanied by Darnley, <u>stabbed Rizzio to death</u>.

2) In <u>1567</u>, Darnley was <u>murdered</u>. Many people believed <u>Mary</u> and her close friend, the <u>Earl of Bothwell</u>, were behind the murder. Their suspicions seemed to be confirmed when <u>Mary married Bothwell</u> a few months later.

3) This marriage was <u>unpopular</u> with the Scottish nobles, who <u>rebelled</u> against Mary. They <u>imprisoned</u> her and forced her to <u>abdicate</u> (<u>give up the throne</u>) in favour of her one-year-old son, James. In <u>1568</u>, Mary <u>escaped</u> from prison and raised an army. Her forces were <u>defeated</u> in battle and she <u>fled</u> south to <u>England</u>.

Some people (including <u>Elizabeth</u>) thought the Scottish nobles had <u>no right</u> to <u>overthrow</u> Mary. As a result, they <u>didn't accept</u> her <u>abdication</u>, and still viewed her as the <u>legitimate</u> queen of Scotland.

Mary was **Imprisoned**, but still posed a **Threat**

1) Mary hoped that Elizabeth would help her <u>regain control</u> of <u>Scotland</u>. Elizabeth was <u>not</u> willing to do this — Mary's <u>claim</u> to the <u>English throne</u> meant that there would be a constant <u>threat of invasion</u> from the north if Mary regained power in Scotland.

2) Instead, Elizabeth had Mary <u>imprisoned</u> and set up an <u>inquiry</u> to investigate whether she had been involved in <u>Darnley's murder</u>.

3) Elizabeth <u>didn't</u> want the inquiry to find Mary <u>guilty</u>. A guilty verdict would lend <u>support</u> to the actions of the <u>Scottish nobles</u>, who had <u>overthrown</u> Mary, their <u>legitimate queen</u>.

The so-called '<u>Casket Letters</u>' were presented to the inquiry. They included several letters apparently written by Mary to Bothwell, which <u>implicated</u> the pair in Darnley's murder. Mary's supporters insisted that the letters were <u>forgeries</u>, but most members of the inquiry believed they were <u>genuine</u>.

4) However, Elizabeth <u>didn't</u> want a <u>not-guilty</u> verdict either, because this would force her to <u>release</u> Mary. Once free, Mary might use her claim to the English throne to try and <u>overthrow Elizabeth</u>.

5) In the end, the inquiry <u>didn't</u> reach a <u>verdict</u> — this enabled Elizabeth to keep Mary in <u>captivity</u>. Elizabeth hoped that <u>imprisoning</u> Mary would <u>prevent</u> her becoming the centre of <u>Catholic plots</u>, but Mary's presence caused <u>problems</u> for Elizabeth throughout the next <u>20 years</u> (see p.120-123).

 Mary's strong claim to the English throne made her a serious threat
Write a character profile of Mary, Queen of Scots. Include her religion, family and actions.

The Northern Rebellion

Mary, Queen of Scots, had barely been in England five minutes when she began causing trouble for Elizabeth.

The **Northern Nobles** were unhappy for **Several Reasons**

1) Many northern nobles were still committed Catholics. They wanted to see the restoration of Catholicism in England under a Catholic monarch. The arrival of Mary, Queen of Scots, in 1568 (see p.119) gave them hope that Elizabeth could be replaced with Mary.

2) Elizabeth had confiscated large areas of land from the Earl of Northumberland and shared them between Northumberland's main rival in the north and a southern Protestant. Northumberland was also angry that Elizabeth had claimed all the profits from copper mines discovered on his estates.

3) Elizabeth had reduced the power of the northern nobles and increased her control in the north. In part, she did this through the Council of the North, which helped to govern the region. Under Elizabeth, the Council was controlled by southern Protestants. The northern nobles deeply resented this.

4) The northern nobles blamed Elizabeth's advisors for these policies. They believed that some Privy Councillors, especially William Cecil (see p.97), had become too powerful. They wanted to remove these 'evil counsellors' and replace them with men who would be more sympathetic to their interests.

The **Northern Rebellion** broke out in **November 1569**

1) In 1569, the Duke of Norfolk (the wealthiest landowner in England) hatched a plan to marry Mary, Queen of Scots, and have her recognised as Elizabeth's heir. This plan was supported by Catholic nobles, including the Earls of Northumberland and Westmorland, because it meant that Elizabeth would be succeeded by a Catholic queen.

2) When the plan was uncovered, the Earls feared they would be executed for their involvement. In a desperate attempt to escape punishment, they rebelled and tried to overthrow Elizabeth.

3) In November 1569, the Earls captured Durham, where they celebrated Catholic Mass in the cathedral. They then marched south, probably making for Tutbury in Derbyshire, where Mary was imprisoned.

4) Before the rebels reached Tutbury, a large royal army forced them to retreat. Many of their troops deserted, and the two Earls fled to Scotland. Elizabeth showed the rebels little mercy. Westmorland fled abroad, but Northumberland was executed, as were at least 400 rebel troops.

The revolt was a **Serious Threat** to Elizabeth's rule

The Northern Rebellion was the most serious rebellion of Elizabeth's reign. It posed a major threat to her rule and showed the danger that Mary, Queen of Scots, represented as a rallying point for English Catholics.

- News of the rebellion created widespread fear among English Protestants about the threat posed by Catholics, and contributed to growing anti-Catholic feelings. These views were fuelled by memories of the harsh persecution of Protestants during the reign of Queen Mary I.

- There was little support for the revolt among the rest of the Catholic nobility and ordinary people — when given a choice between Elizabeth and their religion, most Catholics chose to support the Queen. 1569-70 was the last time that English Catholics tried to remove Elizabeth by force.

Comment and Analysis

The Northern Rebellion sought to protect the long-standing independence of the northern nobles, but in the end it increased government control in the north of England. After the revolt, many rebels had their lands confiscated. The Council of the North was also strengthened under the leadership of the Puritan, Henry Hastings, Earl of Huntingdon.

EXAM TIP

The Northern Rebellion was about politics as well as religion

As well as knowing what happened in Elizabethan England, you also need to know why things happened — so be sure to learn what caused events like the Northern Rebellion.

The Catholic Threat

The Catholic threat got even <u>worse</u> throughout the <u>1570s</u> and early <u>1580s</u>.
As a result, Elizabeth and her government became less and <u>less tolerant</u> of Catholicism.

The Pope **Expelled** Elizabeth from the **Catholic Church**

1) In <u>1570</u>, Elizabeth was <u>excommunicated</u> (<u>expelled</u> from the Catholic Church) by the Pope. This meant Catholics no longer had to <u>obey</u> the Queen and were encouraged to <u>overthrow</u> her.

> The excommunication was meant to <u>strengthen</u> the <u>Northern Rebellion</u>, but news of it didn't arrive until <u>after</u> the revolt had <u>collapsed</u>.

2) Together with the Northern Rebellion (see p.120), the excommunication <u>changed</u> Elizabeth's <u>attitude</u> towards Catholics. They were now seen as potential <u>traitors</u>, so Elizabeth and her government became <u>less tolerant</u> of <u>recusancy</u> (refusal to go to church) by Catholics.

3) In response to the excommunication, <u>Parliament</u> passed the <u>Treasons Act</u> in <u>1571</u>. Under this Act, anyone who claimed that Elizabeth <u>wasn't</u> England's <u>legitimate ruler</u> could face the <u>death penalty</u>.

Missionary Priests strengthened English Catholicism

1) In <u>1568</u>, William Allen founded a <u>missionary college</u> at <u>Douai</u> (now in France) to train English Catholic priests. Once trained, these missionary priests would return to England and <u>secretly</u> minister to English Catholics. The first missionary priests reached England in <u>1574</u>.

2) In <u>1580</u>, the missionaries <u>Robert Parsons</u> and <u>Edmund Campion</u> (who had both trained at a missionary college in <u>Rome</u>) entered the country. Campion was <u>executed</u> for <u>treason</u> in December <u>1581</u>.

3) In the <u>1560s</u>, Elizabeth had <u>tolerated recusancy</u> because she believed that English Catholicism would gradually <u>die out</u> as the religious settlement became more firmly established.

4) However, the arrival of the <u>missionary priests</u> from the 1570s <u>changed</u> things — with the support of these highly-committed missionaries, it was now <u>unlikely</u> that Catholicism in England would just <u>fade away</u> on its own. This <u>strengthening</u> of Catholicism was a <u>major threat</u> to the religious settlement.

Parliament passed two **Anti-Catholic Acts**

In response to the threat from missionary priests, Parliament passed two <u>anti-Catholic Acts</u> in <u>1581</u>. These Acts:

- Massively <u>increased</u> the <u>fines</u> for <u>recusancy</u>, making them too expensive for most ordinary Catholics.

- Introduced <u>fines</u> and <u>prison sentences</u> for people who said or attended <u>Catholic Mass</u>.

- Made it treason (which was punishable by death) to <u>convert</u> to Catholicism or persuade others to convert.

- Introduced <u>prison sentences</u> and the <u>death penalty</u> for anyone who encouraged <u>rebellion</u>.

The Catholic threat intensified after the Pope's intervention

Write a couple of sentences to explain why each of the following factors was a threat to Elizabeth and her religious settlement: excommunication, missionary priests and Mary, Queen of Scots (see p.119).

The Catholic Threat

There were Catholic plots against Elizabeth — she reacted by passing stricter laws that persecuted Catholics.

Catholic Plots aimed to put Mary on the English Throne

1) Between 1571 and 1585, there were several Catholic plots to assassinate Elizabeth and replace her with Mary, Queen of Scots. They included the Ridolfi Plot (1571), the Throckmorton Plot (1583) and the Babington Plot (1586, see p.123).

> Letters sent by Mary implicated her in the Ridolfi Plot. In 1572 Parliament urged Elizabeth to execute Mary for her part in the plot. Elizabeth refused — she was reluctant to execute someone she saw as a legitimate monarch (p.119).

2) The plots involved Catholic conspirators in England and Europe. They were supported by the Pope and Catholic rulers, especially King Philip II of Spain.

3) The plots were a real threat to Elizabeth's rule and her religious settlement (p.116-118). Mary's strong claim to the throne (p.119) made them seem credible, and Philip II's involvement meant there was a risk they would lead to a Spanish invasion.

4) However, none of the plots succeeded. This was partly because there was little public support for a Catholic revolution (as the Northern Rebellion had shown).

By the 1580s Elizabeth's Principal Secretary, Francis Walsingham, had established a highly efficient spy network, which ensured that the plots were uncovered before they were carried out.

Comment and Analysis

Missionary priests supported the Catholic plots to assassinate Elizabeth. They wanted England to return to Catholicism and believed this could only be achieved if Elizabeth was removed.

Persecution of Catholics Increased in the 1580s

1) In 1584, the Dutch Protestant leader, William the Silent, was assassinated by a Catholic (see p.125). Combined with the arrival of missionary priests and the Catholic plots against Elizabeth, this assassination made the government even more concerned about the Catholic threat in England.

2) As a result, persecution of Catholics increased. Anti-Catholic laws were enforced more strictly than they had been earlier in Elizabeth's reign, and in 1585 Parliament passed two new laws:

1585 Anti-Catholic Laws

- Mary, Queen of Scots, wouldn't be allowed to become queen if Elizabeth was assassinated. It was hoped that this would put a stop to the plots involving Mary.

- Missionary priests had 40 days to leave the country. Any priests who didn't leave could be executed, as could anyone who tried to help them.

3) The anti-Catholic laws of 1581 (see p.121) and 1585 led to the execution of more than 120 Catholic priests and the deaths of many more in prison.

The Anti-Catholic laws persecuted Catholics

Using relevant dates can make a good impression on the examiner. For example, remembering the year that each Catholic plot took place shows you have good knowledge of the period.

The Catholic Threat

In 1586, <u>Walsingham</u> used his <u>spy network</u> to prove that <u>Mary</u> had supported the <u>Babington Plot</u>. His evidence persuaded Elizabeth to put Mary on <u>trial</u> and <u>execute</u> her for <u>treason</u>.

The **Babington Plot** led to the **Execution of Mary, Queen of Scots**

1) In 1586, <u>Francis Walsingham</u> (see p.122) used his <u>spy network</u> to gather evidence of Mary, Queen of Scots' involvement in the <u>Babington Plot</u>. He intercepted and decoded Mary's <u>letters</u>, including one which <u>approved</u> plans to <u>assassinate</u> the Queen and <u>free</u> Mary from prison.

2) Mary had been <u>implicated</u> in Catholic plots before, but Elizabeth had always <u>refused</u> to take action against her.

- Elizabeth was <u>reluctant</u> to execute Mary because she was <u>queen of Scotland</u>.

- Elizabeth believed that monarchs ruled by <u>Divine Right</u> (see p.98), so she felt she had <u>no right</u> to execute a <u>legitimate monarch</u>.

- She also feared that <u>executing</u> Mary would <u>undermine</u> her own claim to rule by Divine Right and might fuel <u>more plots</u> against her.

3) The <u>evidence</u> gathered by <u>Walsingham</u> finally <u>persuaded</u> her to put Mary on <u>trial</u>. In <u>October 1586</u>, Mary was found <u>guilty</u> of <u>treason</u> and sentenced to death.

- Despite the guilty verdict, Elizabeth was very <u>reluctant</u> to execute Mary.

- <u>Parliament</u> and the <u>Privy Council</u> believed that the execution was <u>vital</u> to <u>weaken</u> the Catholic threat and <u>protect</u> the religious settlement, so they put <u>pressure</u> on Elizabeth to sign Mary's death warrant.

4) After <u>hesitating</u> for several months, Elizabeth eventually <u>agreed</u> to the execution. Mary was <u>executed</u> on <u>8th February 1587</u>.

Mary's execution **Reduced** the **Threat** from Catholics at **Home...**

1) The <u>execution</u> of Mary, Queen of Scots, <u>removed</u> the <u>Catholic threat</u> to Elizabeth at home.

2) English Catholics now had <u>no-one</u> to <u>rally around</u>, and they <u>lost hope</u> of ever overthrowing Elizabeth and reversing the religious settlement. There were <u>no more major Catholic plots</u> during Elizabeth's reign.

...but it **Increased** the **Threat** from **Abroad**

1) In 1587, relations with <u>Spain</u> were at a <u>low point</u> — the two countries were now at <u>war</u> over the <u>Netherlands</u>, and King Philip II had been <u>preparing</u> for an <u>attack</u> on England since 1585 (see p.125). Mary's execution made the situation <u>worse</u>. Philip was now even more <u>determined</u> to <u>invade</u>.

2) There was also a danger that Mary's son, <u>James VI of Scotland</u> might seek <u>revenge</u> for his mother's death. There were fears that he would form an <u>alliance</u> with other <u>Catholic powers</u> in order to <u>invade</u> England.

Elizabeth found the decision to execute Mary difficult

REVISION TASK

Write a summary discussing whether Elizabeth was right to execute Mary, Queen of Scots. First, suggest reasons why Elizabeth made the right decision, and then suggest reasons why she was wrong.

The Puritan Threat

Puritans were dedicated to Protestantism and they wanted to purify the English Church.

The Puritans wanted to make the English Church More Protestant

1) As committed Protestants, the Puritans were strongly anti-Catholic. They thought that the English Church should be free from all traces of Catholicism.

2) The Puritans believed that preaching (explaining the word of God) was very important. They thought that all priests should be well educated so that they'd be able to preach. At the time, this was unusual — many priests lacked education and didn't preach at all.

3) The Puritans encouraged the education of ordinary people, so they would be able to read and understand the Bible for themselves. They were very strict about godly living (obeying all of God's commandments).

4) Some Puritans were more radical. They wanted to get rid of the Church hierarchy of archbishops, bishops, etc. This view was a threat to Elizabeth because it called into question her authority as Supreme Governor of the Church — the head of the hierarchy.

Comment and Analysis

For Elizabeth, the religious settlement of 1559 was final and couldn't be changed. She wanted everyone to accept the settlement, so she saw Puritan demands for further reforms as a serious threat.

Puritans believed that Christians should live a restrained lifestyle. They opposed anything encouraging playfulness or idleness. This included sports and popular pastimes, like cock-fighting and drinking. They also disliked public celebrations, even for religious events like Christmas.

The 'Prophesyings' taught Priests how to Preach

1) By the 1570s, the Puritans were concerned about the lack of educated priests who were able to preach. So they introduced the 'prophesyings' — a kind of training to teach priests how to preach.

2) Elizabeth thought that the 'prophesyings' would encourage more Puritan opposition to the religious settlement. In 1576, she ordered the Archbishop of Canterbury, Edmund Grindal, to put a stop to them.

3) Grindal (a moderate Puritan) thought the 'prophesyings' were good for the Church, so he refused to obey Elizabeth's order. This made Elizabeth furious. She suspended Grindal and put him under house arrest.

Archbishop Whitgift tried to Suppress Puritanism

1) In 1583, Grindal died and Elizabeth made John Whitgift Archbishop of Canterbury. With Elizabeth's support, Whitgift launched an attack on Puritan clergy — all priests had to accept the regulations of the Church of England or face suspension. Between 200 and 300 Puritan priests were suspended.

2) Whitgift's campaign made some Puritans feel that there was no hope of reforming the Church of England. Instead, they decided to break away and form a separate church.

3) These Puritan separatists were seen as a major threat to the religious settlement. The government introduced censorship laws to prevent them spreading their ideas, and in 1590 several of their leaders were arrested.

4) The threat from Puritan separatists probably wasn't as serious as Elizabeth and her government thought. There weren't many separatists and they didn't have the support of any powerful members of the elite. Most Puritans were moderates who worked within the Church of England.

Whitgift's campaign faced some opposition from the Privy Council and Parliament. Elizabeth overcame this by threatening to dismiss any council members who opposed it, and refusing to let Parliament discuss the matter.

EXAM TIP

The Puritans wanted the Church to be pure and simple

The different religious groups in Elizabethan England can be confusing. You need to know what the Puritans believed, and how they were different from Catholics and moderate Protestants.

War with Spain

England and Spain tried to stay on <u>good terms</u>, but the <u>growing tensions</u> between them eventually led to <u>war</u>.

There were **Political**, **Religious** and **Economic** tensions with Spain

<u>King Philip II</u> of Spain had been married to <u>Queen Mary I</u> of England, and the two countries had been allies. Elizabeth and Philip tried to maintain <u>good relations</u>, but tensions between them gradually began to grow.

Political

Spain was a great <u>imperial power</u>. In Europe, Philip ruled <u>Spain</u>, the <u>Netherlands</u>, parts of <u>Italy</u> and (from 1581) <u>Portugal</u>. He also had a large <u>empire</u> in the <u>Americas</u>. By the 1570s, England was starting to have <u>ambitions</u> for an empire of its own (p.109-111). This led to growing <u>rivalry</u> and tension between the two countries.

Religious

Philip was a <u>devout Catholic</u> and disliked Elizabeth's religious settlement. He became involved in several <u>Catholic plots</u> against Elizabeth in the 1570s and 1580s (p.122-123), which <u>damaged</u> Elizabeth's <u>trust</u> in him.

Economic

*   Elizabeth encouraged <u>privateers</u> to <u>trade illegally</u> with Spanish colonies, <u>raid</u> Spanish ships and <u>attack</u> the treasure fleets carrying gold and silver from the New World (the Americas) to Spain.
*   In the <u>1560s</u> an English fleet, commanded by <u>John Hawkins</u>, traded with Spanish colonies (see p.109), even though Spain had <u>banned</u> them from doing so. This led to the <u>Battle of San Juan de Ulúa</u> in <u>1568</u>.
*   <u>Francis Drake</u> also <u>raided</u> many Spanish colonies in South America during his round-the-world voyage of <u>1577-80</u> (p.110).

England and Spain eventually went to War over the Netherlands

1) In 1581, <u>Protestant rebels</u> in the Netherlands declared independence from Spain. In <u>1584</u> the rebel leader, <u>William the Silent</u>, was assassinated, and the revolt was in danger of being <u>defeated</u>.

2) Elizabeth decided to help the rebels — in <u>1585</u> she signed the <u>Treaty of Nonsuch</u>, which promised <u>military assistance</u>. <u>Religious</u>, <u>economic</u> and <u>military</u> factors influenced her decision:

Religious

Elizabeth wanted to protect <u>Dutch Protestantism</u> and <u>prevent</u> Philip forcing <u>Catholicism</u> on the Netherlands.

Military

If the rebels were <u>defeated</u>, Philip might use the Netherlands as a base for an <u>invasion</u> of England.

Economic

English <u>exports</u> to Europe were <u>vital</u> to the English economy, and many English goods reached the European market via Dutch ports, especially <u>Antwerp</u>. Elizabeth needed to <u>ensure</u> that English merchants would have <u>access</u> to the <u>Dutch ports</u>.

3) Philip saw the Treaty of Nonsuch as a <u>declaration of war</u> on Spain. In response, he began building a <u>huge fleet</u> (an <u>Armada</u>) that he planned to use to <u>invade England</u>.

EXAM TIP

England was beginning to challenge the supremacy of Spain

England's relationship with Spain was a large problem for Elizabeth throughout her reign. Make sure you understand how and why the relationship changed over time.

The Spanish Armada

The Spanish Armada was launched in 1588, but right from the start, things didn't go according to plan.

Drake was sent to Disrupt Spanish Preparations for the Armada

1) Elizabeth sent Francis Drake to spy on Spanish preparations and attack their ships and supplies. In April 1587, Drake attacked the Spanish port of Cadiz. He destroyed around 30 ships and seized many tonnes of supplies.

2) This delayed the Armada by more than a year. Obtaining fresh supplies and weapons was very expensive and seriously strained Spain's finances.

3) During his raid, Drake captured planks made from seasoned wood, which were needed to make the barrels used to carry food and water.

4) As a result, the Spanish had to make their barrels from unseasoned wood, which couldn't preserve food and water very well. This caused supply problems for the Armada and affected the morale of Spanish troops and sailors. Fresh water supplies were lost and many tons of food rotted as the fleet sailed to England in 1588.

Drake described his raid on Cadiz as 'singeing the King of Spain's beard'. He meant that he had inflicted temporary damage on King Philip's Armada, but hadn't destroyed it entirely — it would 'grow back' in time.

The Armada Planned to meet the Duke of Parma at Dunkirk

1) By the spring of 1588, the Spanish Armada was complete. The Armada was a huge fleet of around 130 ships, manned by approximately 8000 sailors and carrying an estimated 18,000 soldiers.

2) Philip appointed the Duke of Medina Sidonia to lead the Armada. Philip respected the Duke's high social status and trusted him to obey instructions. However, the Duke had little military or naval experience.

3) The Spanish had thousands more soldiers stationed in the Netherlands under the leadership of the Duke of Parma. Philip's plan was for the Armada to meet Parma's army at Dunkirk. The combined forces would then sail across the Channel to England under the protection of the Armada's warships.

The English managed to Scatter Spain's ships

1) The Armada set out in May 1588. In July, it was sighted off Cornwall. English ships set sail from Plymouth to attack the Armada, but they caused little damage. Only two Spanish ships were lost, and they were destroyed by accident.

2) The Armada sailed up the Channel in a crescent formation. This was an effective defensive strategy, which used the large, armed galleons to protect the weaker supply and troop ships.

3) Having sailed up the Channel, Medina Sidonia anchored at Calais to wait for Parma's troops. However, Parma and his men were being blockaded by Dutch ships and weren't able to reach the coast in time.

The Spanish Armada sailing up the Channel in its crescent formation.

English sailors made things difficult for the Armada

Use the information on pages 125 and 126 to write an account describing the events leading up to the Armada setting sail in May 1588. Make sure you explain how these events were linked to each other.

The Spanish Armada

Medina Sidonia may have thought his ships were safe in Calais, but his problems were only beginning.

Things went from **Bad** to **Worse** for Spain

1) That night, England sent eight fireships (ships loaded with flammable materials and set alight) among the anchored Spanish ships. The Spanish sailors panicked and headed for the open sea. The weather made it impossible for them to return to their defensive position at Calais.

2) The English advanced, and the following battle lasted for many hours. Five Spanish ships were sunk, and the rest of the fleet was forced to sail away from the French coast into the North Sea.

The Armada's **Journey** back to **Spain** was a **Disaster**

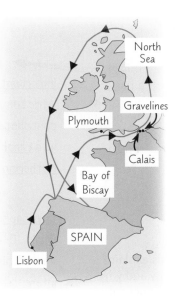

1) Medina Sidonia decided to call off the attack on England and return to Spain by sailing round Scotland and Ireland.

2) The Spanish sailors were unfamiliar with this very dangerous route, and they encountered several powerful Atlantic storms. Many ships sank or were wrecked on the Scottish and Irish coasts.

3) Those ships that completed the journey ran short of supplies, and many men died of starvation and disease. Less than half the fleet and fewer than 10,000 men made it back to Spain.

The war with Spain **Continued** until **1604**

Despite the defeat of the Armada, continued tension between England and Spain helped to sustain the war.

1) The victory of 1588 encouraged England's development as a strong naval power to rival Spain. It also boosted Elizabeth's popularity and strengthened the Protestant cause — it was seen as a sign that God favoured Protestantism.

2) Spain was determined to end the Protestant rebellion in the Netherlands and bring the country back under Spanish control. Elizabeth continued supporting the rebels, which angered Philip.

3) England was still attacking Spanish ships off the coast of Spain and in the Caribbean (see p.110), while Spain launched two more unsuccessful Armadas in 1596 and 1597.

4) However, by the end of the 16th century, the conflict was beginning to drain English and Spanish resources. In 1604, they signed a peace treaty, which brought an official end to the war.

The defeat of the Armada was a great victory for Elizabeth

The Armada was an important event in the war with Spain — you need to learn the story well, including its consequences for England and the resulting relationship with Spain.

Worked Exam-Style Question

This sample answer will give you an idea of how to answer questions that ask you how far you agree with a statement or interpretation. Look at the way that the answer clearly states an opinion at the beginning and end.

Q1 'Commercial rivalry was the most important reason for the outbreak of war with Spain in 1585.'

Explain how far you agree with this statement. [16 marks]

This gives a basic answer to the question in the first sentence.

I disagree that commercial rivalry was the most important reason for the outbreak of war with Spain in 1585. While commercial rivalry was one of the long-term factors that contributed to growing tension between England and Spain, it was Elizabeth's involvement in the Protestant rebellion in the Netherlands that caused war to break out in 1585.

This gives a basic reason for disagreeing with the statement.

Commercial rivalry was an important long-term factor that caused growing tension and conflict between England and Spain. This is because England's increasing interest in trade and colonisation in the Americas threatened Spain's economic interests overseas. For example, in the 1560s, English privateers were encouraged by Elizabeth to trade illegally with Spanish colonies, despite being banned from doing so by Spain. This resulted in the traders and Spanish forces coming into direct conflict in the Battle of San Juan de Ulúa in 1568. Furthermore, Francis Drake's circumnavigation of the globe between 1577 and 1580 caused more disruption to Spanish interests, because he raided Spanish settlements while searching for new colonisation and trading opportunities.

This explains how and why commercial rivalry caused tension.

This directly addresses the issue in the statement.

This uses to relevant details to explain the consequences of commercial rivalry in the Americas.

This shows that tension developed further because of commercial rivalry.

Since Elizabeth encouraged this behaviour by knighting Drake upon his return, it is clear that Elizabeth wanted English sailors to challenge Spanish interests in the Americas. Indeed, Elizabeth's support for Walter Raleigh's attempts to colonise Virginia represented a direct challenge to Spanish commercial and imperial power, since a colony in North America would have given England a base from which to attack Spanish treasure ships. This commercial and imperial rivalry was a growing source of tension that strained relations between Spain and England and made war more likely.

This links commercial rivalry to imperial rivalry between Spain and England.

This shows how rivalry in the Americas created an atmosphere over time where war was more likely.

The Elizabethans, 1558-1603

Worked Exam-Style Question

Even if you agree with the statement, it's important to look at <u>other factors</u> — this shows that you've considered <u>alternative arguments</u>.

However, there was another long-term factor that contributed to the growing tension. <u>The deep religious divide between Protestant England and Catholic Spain</u> was a key factor that contributed to the outbreak of war in 1585. As a devout Catholic, Philip disapproved of Elizabeth's religious settlement of 1559, which made England a Protestant country. As a result, in the 1570s and the 1580s, he <u>supported many of the Catholic plots against Elizabeth and her religious settlement, like the Ridolfi plot of 1571</u>. This was <u>directly responsible for damaging relations between England and Spain, as it made it very difficult for Elizabeth to trust Philip</u>.

Use <u>accurate details</u> from your <u>own knowledge</u> to <u>back up</u> your points.

This gives an <u>example</u> of how religious conflict <u>strained relations</u>.

This introduces a <u>short-term factor</u> that <u>directly caused</u> the outbreak of war.

While all of these long-term factors played a key role in creating an atmosphere of tension, they did not directly provoke war. In fact, <u>war only broke out when Elizabeth signed the Treaty of Nonsuch in 1585</u>. Philip saw this as a declaration of war on Spain, because the treaty <u>interfered with Spain's imperial power by promising military aid to Protestant rebels</u> fighting against Spanish rule in the Netherlands. It also showed Philip that Elizabeth was prepared to directly intervene in Spanish affairs in order to protect Protestantism in Europe. <u>The religious tension that had been growing between England and Spain since 1559 thus turned into open conflict in 1585 because Elizabeth's decision to support Protestantism now posed a threat to Spain's power in Europe</u>.

This <u>links</u> the <u>long-term factors</u> that have been discussed to the event that <u>triggered</u> the war.

Make sure you end by <u>clearly stating</u> your opinion in the <u>conclusion</u>.

Overall, while commercial rivalry was an important factor that contributed to the build up of tension between England and Spain, it did not directly cause war to break out in 1585. Instead, <u>the religious divide between England and Spain was the most important reason for the outbreak of war, because Elizabeth's decision to protect Dutch Protestantism directly triggered the opening of hostilities in 1585</u>. It also played a big role in creating the <u>atmosphere of tension and mistrust that led Philip to respond to the Treaty of Nonsuch as if it were a declaration of war</u>.

This <u>sums up</u> why religious division was the <u>most important reason</u> for the outbreak of war.

Exam-Style Questions

Q1
Describe two aspects of Puritan opposition to Elizabeth I's religious settlement.   [4 marks]

Q2
Explain how the presence of Mary, Queen of Scots, in England affected Elizabeth I's rule.   [8 marks]

Q3
Give an account of the ways that the actions of missionary priests affected Elizabethan England.   [8 marks]

Q4
'Luck was the main reason why England managed to defeat the Spanish Armada'. Explain how far you agree with this statement.

You could mention Francis Drake and English naval tactics in your answer.   [16 marks]

Revision Summary

That's the Elizabethans all done and dusted — time to test your knowledge with a quick revision summary.

- Try these questions and tick off each one when you get it right.
- When you've done all the questions for a topic and are completely happy with it, tick off the topic.

Elizabeth's Court and Parliament (p.93-100) ☑

1) Describe Queen Elizabeth I's character. ☑
2) Why was Elizabeth under pressure to find a husband? ☑
3) Explain what the term 'patronage' means. ☑
4) What was the role of the Privy Council? ☑
5) Name three of Elizabeth's key ministers. ☑
6) What were Parliament's main functions? ☑
7) Give three ways in which Elizabeth and her Privy Council managed Parliament. ☑
8) How did Elizabeth's Privy Council change towards the end of her reign? ☑
9) Who was Robert Devereux? Briefly describe his rebellion against Elizabeth. ☑

Life in Elizabethan Times (p.103-111) ☑

10) Why was the problem of poverty growing in Elizabethan England? ☑
11) What were the three categories of poor people in Elizabethan England? ☑
12) Describe how the Poor Laws of 1597 and 1601 treated the deserving and undeserving poor. ☑
13) Give four ways in which members of the Elizabethan elite spent their growing wealth. ☑
14) Give two reasons that family was considered important to Elizabethan society. ☑
15) What was a petty school? ☑
16) Why were some people opposed to the theatre? ☑
17) Who was John Hawkins? ☑
18) What did Francis Drake do between 1577 and 1580? Why was this a major achievement? ☑
19) Who organised the attempted colonisation of Virginia in the 1580s? ☑

Troubles at Home and Abroad (p.116-127) ☑

20) Name the two Acts of the Elizabethan religious settlement. ☑
21) Why did the Puritans oppose the religious settlement? ☑
22) Why did Mary, Queen of Scots, have a strong claim to the English throne? ☑
23) Give three reasons for the 1569 Northern Rebellion. ☑
24) How did Elizabeth's government respond to the threat posed by missionary priests? ☑
25) Name three Catholic plots against Elizabeth. ☑
26) Why was Elizabeth reluctant to execute Mary, Queen of Scots? ☑
27) Explain how radical Puritans wanted to change the Church. ☑
28) Who was John Whitgift? What was his role in dealing with the Puritan threat? ☑
29) Why were there growing tensions between England and Spain in the 1570s and 1580s? ☑
30) Why did England and Spain go to war in 1585? ☑
31) Explain what the phrase 'the singeing of the King of Spain's beard' means. ☑
32) Give two consequences of the defeat of the Spanish Armada for England. ☑

Kaiser Wilhelm II

The German Empire was created in 1871 and lasted until 1918. It was ruled by Kaiser Wilhelm II from 1888.

The **Constitution** made the **Kaiser** very **Powerful**

When the German Empire was created in 1871, its constitution made the Kaiser the most powerful figure in government. A German parliament called the Reichstag was also created, but in reality it held little power.

> **Kaiser**
> * Inherits his position and rules like a king.
> * Has personal control of the army and foreign policy.
> * Appoints and dismisses the Chancellor.
> * Can dissolve the Reichstag at any time.

The Kaiser held ultimate power. He could dismiss the Chancellor, bypass the Bundesrat and dissolve the Reichstag.

The Bundesrat was more powerful than the Reichstag. It was only accountable to the Kaiser.

> **Chancellor**
> * Runs the government and proposes new legislation.
> * Doesn't need the support of the Reichstag or the Bundesrat to stay in power.

> **Bundesrat**
> * Members are representatives from each state in the German Empire.
> * Its consent is needed for all legislation (but can be overruled by the Kaiser).

The Chancellor had more influence than the Bundesrat and the Reichstag.

> **Reichstag**
> * Members elected by the public every three years (and every five years after 1888).
> * Members pass or reject legislation handed down by the Bundesrat.

The Reichstag couldn't put forward its own legislation and had no say in who became Chancellor or who served in government.

Kaiser Wilhelm disliked **Democracy**

1) Kaiser Wilhelm II didn't believe in democracy and disliked working with the Reichstag. He preferred to place his trust in the army, and often relied on military advisors to help him make important decisions.

2) The Prussian army played an important role in Germany's unification in 1871. Wilhelm II was strongly influenced by its prestige and power, and adopted a system of militarism — this meant strengthening Germany's military (e.g. its army and navy) and using it to increase Germany's influence.

Before 1871, Germany was made up of lots of independent states — one of these was called Prussia.

3) Wilhelm II wanted to make Germany a world power. He also believed in Germany's traditional class system, where the upper classes held the most power.

Kaiser Wilhelm wanted the upper classes to stay in control

EXAM TIP Even though the Reichstag was elected by the people, it didn't have much power. The Kaiser thought his authority was secure, so he focused on making Germany strong on the world stage.

The Monarchy Under Threat

In the late 1800s and early 1900s, a lot of <u>changes</u> took place in Germany's <u>economy</u> and <u>society</u>. These changes gave the <u>working classes</u> and their representatives more <u>power</u>, and caused a headache for the Kaiser.

Germany experienced Economic and Social change

In the <u>early</u> 20th century, Germany's economy was <u>modernised</u> and the working classes <u>grew</u>.

1) Germany's economy <u>expanded</u> massively between <u>1890</u> and <u>1914</u>. Production of iron and coal <u>doubled</u>, and by 1914 Germany produced <u>two-thirds</u> of Europe's steel. It was also successful in <u>new</u> industries like chemical manufacturing.

2) As a result of <u>industrialisation</u>, new <u>jobs</u> were created and the population in Germany's <u>cities</u> grew. The working classes <u>expanded</u> and the upper classes had <u>less</u> economic power.

3) The working classes played a <u>larger</u> part in German society, but their working conditions were <u>poor</u>. They had a growing sense of <u>identity</u> and wanted better <u>representation</u>.

4) This contributed to a rise in <u>socialism</u> — a political ideology promoting <u>equality</u>, and <u>public ownership</u> of industry. This led to a growth in <u>support</u> for the <u>Social Democratic Party</u> (SPD) in Germany (see below).

Social problems Increased and Germans wanted Reforms

1) The growing population in cities and towns created new <u>social problems</u>. The working classes wanted better <u>working</u> and <u>living</u> conditions, and new and growing industries needed more <u>regulation</u>.

2) Initially, the government didn't want to pass reforms because it was <u>afraid</u> of encouraging <u>socialist</u> ideas. This meant that groups promising <u>change</u> became more <u>popular</u>.

3) In 1887, the Social Democratic Party (SPD) had just <u>11</u> seats in the Reichstag, but by 1903 it had <u>81</u>. Trade unions (organisations set up by employees to defend their rights) became more popular too — by 1914, membership stood at around <u>3.3 million</u>.

The Growth of Socialism Worried the Kaiser

- The SPD had very <u>different</u> political views to the Kaiser. It wanted to improve conditions for the <u>working classes</u> and disagreed with the <u>privileges</u> held by elites like the <u>military</u> and the <u>monarchy</u>.

- The German aristocracy and Kaiser Wilhelm worried that the SPD wanted a <u>revolution</u> to overthrow the <u>monarchy</u> and <u>destroy</u> the German class system.

- Even though the SPD and trade unions promised to work <u>with</u> the government to introduce reforms, the Kaiser still saw them as a <u>threat</u>. He didn't want to give more <u>power</u> to the German public.

The Kaiser saw the SPD as a threat

In the exam, make it clear that different people or groups had different aims. For example, in 1890-1914, the SPD wanted to give more power to workers, while the Kaiser wanted it all for himself.

The Monarchy Under Threat

Social and economic changes were <u>good</u> for industry, but German politics became <u>unpredictable</u>. The growth of the working classes and the rise of socialism made ruling Germany increasingly <u>difficult</u> for Kaiser Wilhelm II.

German **Politics** became more **Unstable**

1) German politics had become more <u>radical</u>. The upper classes feared the <u>growth</u> of the working classes and thought rapid industrialisation threatened their <u>wealth</u> and <u>social status</u>. As the SPD's popularity increased, extreme <u>nationalist</u> groups also grew.

2) This made it harder for the Kaiser to govern Germany. He was under <u>pressure</u> to introduce socialist reforms, but knew that doing so would risk <u>angering</u> his supporters.

3) To make matters worse, the popularity of the SPD made it more difficult for the government to get legislation <u>passed</u> in the Reichstag.

> Chancellors found it hard to get <u>support</u> in the Reichstag, so they <u>struggled</u> to pass new laws. The Reichstag had <u>more</u> <u>influence</u> over German politics than it had <u>ever</u> had before.

Wilhelm tried to **Divert Attention** away from **Socialism**

1) The Kaiser tried to reduce <u>discontent</u> among the working classes by introducing some limited <u>social reforms</u>, e.g. in 1891 the <u>Workers' Protection Act</u> was introduced to <u>improve safety</u> in the workplace.

2) In 1897, the Kaiser adopted a foreign policy called '<u>Weltpolitik</u>' — this focused on expanding Germany's <u>territory</u> and boosting the size of Germany's <u>army</u> and <u>navy</u>.

3) The Kaiser hoped this would <u>distract</u> attention from socialism and <u>increase</u> support for the <u>monarchy</u> and the <u>military</u>. It would also help to make Germany a <u>world power</u>.

The **Navy Laws** made people feel **Patriotic**

1) In <u>1898</u>, the first Navy Law was passed. Its eventual aim was to build up Germany's navy to <u>rival</u> Great Britain's. It increased Germany's fleet to include <u>19 battleships</u>.

2) In <u>1900</u>, the Reichstag passed another Navy Law, which put a <u>17 year</u> navy expansion programme into place.

3) The government used propaganda to promote the Navy Laws and inspire <u>patriotism</u> among the German people. The laws were popular, and socialist opposition to them was seen as <u>unpatriotic</u>. In the elections of 1907, the SPD <u>lost</u> 36 seats in the Reichstag.

Comment and Analysis

Despite the Kaiser's best efforts, by 1912 the SPD was the <u>largest</u> party in the Reichstag. The Kaiser had managed to <u>keep</u> his power, but the <u>growth</u> of the SPD showed an increasing desire for <u>democracy</u> amongst the German people.

The Navy Laws increased support for the Kaiser

Fold a piece of paper in half. Jot down all the problems the Kaiser faced between 1890 and 1914 on one half, and write how he tried to solve them on the other.

The War Ends

World War I lasted from 1914-1918. During the war, political parties agreed to support the government. However, by 1918 Germany was experiencing widespread unrest, which eventually resulted in a revolution.

World War I had a **Devastating Impact** on **Germany**

1) Towards the end of the war, people in Germany were undergoing severe hardship. The Allies had set up naval blockades which prevented imports of food and essential goods — by 1918, many people faced starvation.

2) Public opinion had turned against Kaiser Wilhelm II and there were calls for a democracy. Germany's people were war-weary — they were tired of fighting and wanted an end to the war. There was widespread unrest:

In Germany---Now

- In November 1918, some members of the German navy rebelled and refused to board their ships.
- In Hanover, German troops refused to control rioters.
- A Jewish communist called Kurt Eisner encouraged a general uprising, which sparked mass strikes in Munich.

In this British cartoon from 1917, German civilians queue for food as an over-fed official walks past them. The cartoonist is highlighting the difference between the lifestyle of Germany's rich officers and that of the rest of its struggling population.

Social Unrest turned into Revolution

1) By November 1918, the situation in Germany was almost a civil war. A huge public protest was held in Berlin, and members of the SPD (Social Democratic Party) called for the Kaiser's resignation.

2) Kaiser Wilhelm abdicated (resigned) on 9th November 1918. On the same day, two different socialist parties — the Social Democratic Party and the Independent Social Democratic Party (USPD) — declared a republic. A republic is a country ruled without a monarch — power is held by the people via elected representatives.

3) On November 10th, all the state leaders that had been appointed by the monarchy left their posts. New revolutionary state governments took over instead. The monarchy had been abolished and Germany had the chance to become a democracy.

> Germany was made up of 18 states, and each had its own government. The national government decided national affairs, and state governments dealt with more local affairs.

The Signing of the Armistice

- On 11th November 1918, a ceasefire to end the First World War was agreed. The Allies (Britain, France and the USA) signed an armistice (truce) with Germany.
- The new republic was under pressure to sign. The government didn't think Germany could continue fighting — its people were starving and military morale was low.
- The armistice wasn't supported by some right-wing Germans, who saw the truce as a betrayal. They believed Germany could still win the war.

The **Socialists** set up a **Temporary Government**

After the abdication of the Kaiser, Germany was disorganised. Different political parties claimed control over different towns. A temporary national government was established, consisting of the SPD and the USPD. It was called the Council of People's Representatives. It controlled Germany until January 1919, when elections were held for a new Reichstag (parliament) — see p.136.

REVISION TASK

The Kaiser fled, leaving Germany in disarray

Draw a timeline of all the important events that led to the German Revolution of 1918.

The Weimar Republic

The Weimar Republic was the first time Germany had ever been governed as a democracy. It was designed to give the German people a voice. However, there were major flaws in its constitution that made it weak.

The **Weimar Republic** was formed

1) The Council of People's Representatives organised elections in January 1919 to create a new parliament. Germany was now a democracy — the people would say how the country was run.

2) Friedrich Ebert became the first President, with Philip Scheidemann as Chancellor. Ebert was leader of the SPD, a moderate party of socialists.

3) In February 1919, the members of the new Reichstag met at Weimar to create a new constitution for Germany. This was the beginning of a new period of Germany's history that historians call the Weimar Republic.

> The constitution decided how the government would be organised, and established its main principles.

The **Weimar Constitution** made Germany **More Democratic...**

The new constitution reorganised the German system of government.

> Proportional representation is where the proportion of seats a party wins in parliament is roughly the same as the proportion of the total votes they win.

President
- Elected every 7 years.
- Chooses the Chancellor and is head of the army.
- Can dissolve the Reichstag, call new elections and suspend the constitution.

> The President was elected by the German people, and so were the parties in the Reichstag. The President had the most power, but the Chancellor was in charge of the day-to-day running of government.

Reichstag
- The new German Parliament.
- Members are elected every 4 years using proportional representation.

Reichsrat
- Second (less powerful) house of parliament.
- Consists of members from each local region.
- Can delay measures passed by the Reichstag.

1) The new constitution was designed to be as fair as possible. Even very small political parties were given seats in the Reichstag if they got 0.4% of the vote or above.

2) The constitution allowed women to vote for the first time, and lowered the voting age to 20 — more Germans could vote and the German public had greater power.

...but the **Constitution** had **Weaknesses**

Even though the new constitution was more democratic, it wasn't very efficient.

1) Proportional representation meant that even parties with a very small number of votes were guaranteed to get into the Reichstag. This meant it was difficult to make decisions because there were so many parties, and they all had different points of view.

2) When a decision couldn't be reached, the President could suspend the constitution and pass laws without the Reichstag's consent.

> The President's ability to force through his own decision was known as 'Article 48'.

3) This power was only supposed to be used in an emergency, but became a useful way of getting around disagreements that took place in the Reichstag. This meant it undermined the new democracy.

EXAM TIP

The Weimar Republic was vulnerable from the beginning
When you're writing an answer in the exam, make sure you develop the points you make. For example, don't just say that Weimar Republic was weak — explain why it was weak.

Early Unpopularity

The Treaty of Versailles was signed in June 1919. The treaty was very unpopular in Germany and many Germans resented the new government for accepting its terms — it wasn't a good start for the Republic.

President Ebert signed the Treaty of Versailles

1) After the armistice, a peace treaty called the Treaty of Versailles was imposed on Germany.

2) The terms of the treaty were mostly decided by the Allied leaders — David Lloyd George (Britain), Georges Clemenceau (France) and Woodrow Wilson (USA).

Comment and Analysis

Since the President had signed the Treaty of Versailles, the Weimar Republic became associated with the pain and humiliation it caused.

The new German government wasn't invited to the peace conference in 1919 and had no say in the Versailles Treaty. At first, Ebert refused to sign the treaty, but in the end he had little choice — Germany was too weak to risk restarting the conflict. In June 1919, he accepted its terms and signed.

The Terms of the Versailles Treaty were Severe

1) Article 231 of the treaty said Germany had to take the blame for the war — the War-Guilt Clause.

> Many Germans didn't agree with this, and were humiliated by having to accept total blame.

2) Germany's armed forces were reduced to 100,000 men. They weren't allowed any armoured vehicles, aircraft or submarines, and could only have six warships.

> This made Germans feel vulnerable.

3) Germany was forced to pay £6600 million in reparations — payments for the damage caused by German forces in the war. The amount was decided in 1921 but was changed later.

> The heavy reparations seemed unfair to Germans and would cause lasting damage to Germany's economy.

4) Germany lost its empire — areas around the world that used to belong to Germany were now called mandates. They were put under the control of countries on the winning side of the war by the League of Nations — an organisation which aimed to settle international disputes peacefully.

> People opposed the losses in territory, especially when people in German colonies were forced to become part of a new nation.

5) The German military was banned from the Rhineland — an area of Germany on its western border with France. This left Germany open to attack from the west.

Germany Felt Betrayed by the Weimar Republic

The Treaty of Versailles caused resentment towards the Weimar Republic.

1) Germans called the treaty a 'Diktat' (a treaty forced upon Germany), and many blamed Ebert for accepting its terms.

> The Weimar politicians involved in signing the armistice became known as the 'November Criminals'.

2) Some Germans believed the armistice was a mistake and that Germany could have won the war. They felt 'stabbed in the back' by the Weimar politicians, who brought the Treaty of Versailles upon Germany unnecessarily.

Comment and Analysis

The Treaty of Versailles played an important part in the failure of the Weimar Republic. It harmed the Republic's popularity, and created economic and political unrest that hindered the government for years.

This German cartoon demonstrates Germany's feelings towards the Treaty of Versailles. The Allies are shown as demons, out for revenge.

Germans felt 'stabbed in the back' by the government

Scribble down as much as you can remember about the terms of the Treaty of Versailles. Include how Germans felt about it and its consequences for the Weimar Republic.

Years of Unrest

The first four years of the Weimar Republic (1919-1923) were dominated by political, social and economic unrest. This unrest created hardship for the German people, and fuelled criticism of Ebert's government.

There was **Widespread Discontent** in **Germany**

1) By 1919, thousands of Germans were poor and starving, and an influenza epidemic had killed thousands.

2) Many Germans denied they had lost the war and blamed the 'November Criminals' who had agreed to the armistice and the Treaty of Versailles.

3) Others who were blamed for losing the war included communists and Jews.

4) The government was seen as weak and ineffective — the Treaty of Versailles made living conditions worse.

5) The government faced threats from left-wing and right-wing political groups:

The Extreme Left Wanted a Revolution

- In January 1919, communists led by Karl Liebknecht and Rosa Luxemburg tried to take over Berlin. They took control of important buildings like newspaper headquarters, and 50,000 workers went on strike in support of the left-wing revolution. This became known as the Spartacist Revolt.

- Ebert asked for help from the right-wing Freikorps (ex-German soldiers) to stop the rebellion. Over 100 workers were killed. The Freikorps' use of violence caused a split on the Left between the Social Democratic Party and the communists.

The Right Also Rebelled Against the Weimar Government

- In March 1920, some of the Freikorps themselves took part in the Kapp Putsch ('Putsch' means revolt) — led by Wolfgang Kapp. They wanted to create a new right-wing government.

- The Freikorps marched into Berlin to overthrow the Weimar regime. But German workers opposed the putsch and staged a general strike. Berlin was paralysed and Kapp was forced to give up.

- Even after the putsch failed, threats to the government remained. In 1922, some former Freikorps members assassinated Walter Rathenau — he'd been Foreign Minister and was Jewish.

> As Germany's economic problems got worse after the war, anti-Semitic (anti-Jewish) feelings increased.

In 1923 Germany **Couldn't Pay** its **Reparations**

1) By 1923, Germany could no longer meet the reparations payments set out by the Treaty of Versailles.

2) France and Belgium decided to take Germany's resources instead, so they occupied the Ruhr — the richest industrial part of Germany. This gave them access to Germany's iron and coal reserves. The occupation led to fury in Germany, and caused a huge strike in the Ruhr.

3) German industry was devastated again. Germany tried to solve her debt problem by printing more money, but this plunged the economy into hyperinflation.

> Hyperinflation happens when production can't keep up with the amount of money in circulation, so the money keeps losing its value.

4) In 1918, an egg cost ¼ of a Mark. By November 1923, it cost 80 million Marks.

The Consequences of Hyperinflation

- Germany's currency became worthless. Nobody wanted to trade with Germany, so shortages of food and goods got worse.

- Bank savings also became worthless. The hardest hit were the middle classes.

> By 1923, even basic necessities were hard to get hold of. The German people were undergoing immense hardship, which they'd now come to associate with the rise of the Weimar Republic.

Money became worthless as a result of hyperinflation

Draw a spider diagram of all of the problems the Weimar Republic faced in the early 1920s.

Early Stages of the Nazi Party

Hitler entered German politics around the time the Weimar Republic was formed. By the time the Nazi Party was founded in 1920, he was growing in influence. In 1923, he tried to overthrow the Weimar government.

Adolf Hitler became the Voice of the German Workers' Party

Hitler began his political career in the German Workers' Party — a nationalist party led by Anton Drexler.

1) Hitler joined the German Workers' Party in January 1919, when he was still in the German army. He became known for his talent as a passionate and skilled speaker, and crowds gathered to hear him talk.

2) In 1920, the party was re-branded as the National Socialist German Workers' Party (the Nazi Party). In July 1921, Hitler became its leader.

3) The party had around 60 members in 1919. By the end of 1920, it had around 2000.

4) As the Nazi Party grew in popularity, it established an identity that appealed to as many people as possible:

- In February 1920, the Nazi Party promoted its policies in the 'Twenty-Five Point Programme'. The Programme stressed German superiority and promoted anti-Semitism (prejudice against Jews).

- The party wanted to raise pensions and improve health and education — but only for Germans. It also rejected the Treaty of Versailles. Promoting German greatness gave the party a nationwide appeal.

- In 1921, Hitler founded his own party militia called the SA ('storm troopers'). The SA were political thugs — they carried out violent anti-Semitic attacks and intimidated rival political groups. Many people were scared of them, but some Germans admired them. The militia also gave many ex-soldiers a job and a purpose.

Hitler tried to Overthrow the Government in the Munich Putsch

1) In 1923, things were going badly for the Weimar Republic — it seemed weak:
- Hyperinflation was at its peak and there were food riots.
- Many Germans were angry at the French and Belgian invasion of the Ruhr (see p.138). When the government stopped resisting by ending the strike there in 1923 (see p.140), discontent increased.

2) Hitler thought the time was right to attempt a putsch (revolt). In November 1923, the Nazis marched on Munich:

- Hitler's soldiers occupied a beer hall in the Bavarian city of Munich where local government leaders were meeting. He announced that the revolution had begun.

- The next day, Hitler marched into Munich supported by his storm troopers. But news of the revolt had been leaked to the police, who were waiting for Hitler. The police fired on the rebels and the revolt quickly collapsed.

3) Hitler was imprisoned for his role in the Munich Putsch and the Nazi Party was banned. However, his trial gave him publicity. He wrote a book in prison called 'Mein Kampf' ('My Struggle') describing his beliefs and ambitions.

4) 'Mein Kampf' spread Nazi ideology — millions of Germans read it. It introduced Hitler's belief that the Aryan race (which included Germans) was superior to all other races, and that all Germans had a right to 'Lebensraum' (more space to live).

5) In 1926, Hitler held a conference with the Nazi leadership at Bamberg. He was worried that the party had become divided — some members wanted the party to go in a more socialist direction. He made it clear that the party would only follow his agenda.

> The ban on the Nazi Party was lifted in February 1925. However, it suffered a dip in support from 1924 to 1928 due to the improving economic situation in the mid 1920s (see p.140). Economic unrest was a key reason why people supported Nazi ideology.

REVISION TASK

Historians disagree over whether the Munich Putsch was a failure
Some historians interpret the Munich Putsch as a failure for the Nazi Party, but others think it ended up helping Hitler. Jot down a couple of reasons in support of each view.

Recovery

In 1923, Gustav Stresemann became <u>Chancellor</u> of the Weimar Republic. His <u>domestic</u> and <u>international</u> policies helped the German economy to recover, resulting in the '<u>Golden Years</u>' of the Weimar Republic.

Stresemann introduced a New Currency

1) Gustav Stresemann was <u>Chancellor</u> of the Weimar Republic between <u>August</u> and <u>November 1923</u>. He made important changes to help Germany to recover from its economic crisis.

2) In September 1923, he <u>ended the strike</u> in the Ruhr. This <u>reduced tension</u> between Germany, France and Belgium, and meant the government could stop <u>compensation payments</u> to strikers.

3) In November 1923, Stresemann replaced the German Mark with the <u>Rentenmark</u> to stabilise Germany's currency.

4) Stresemann created the '<u>great coalition</u>' — a group of moderate, pro-democracy socialist parties in the Reichstag who agreed to <u>work together</u>. This allowed Parliament to make decisions <u>more quickly</u>.

Stresemann wanted International Co-operation

In November 1923, Stresemann became <u>Foreign Minister</u>. He tried to co-operate more with other countries and build better <u>international relationships</u>. Germany's economy prospered as a result.

1) **The Dawes Plan** was signed in 1924. Stresemann secured France and Belgium's <u>withdrawal</u> from the <u>Ruhr</u> and agreed more <u>realistic</u> payment dates for the reparations. The USA <u>lent</u> Germany £40 million to help it pay off its other debts.

2) **The Young Plan** was agreed in 1929. The Allies agreed to <u>reduce</u> the reparations to a <u>quarter</u> of the original amount, and Germany was given <u>59 years</u> to pay them.

3) **The Locarno Pact** was signed in October 1925. Germany, France and Belgium agreed to respect their <u>joint borders</u> — even those created as a result of the Treaty of Versailles.

4) **The League of Nations** (see p.137) allowed Germany to join in <u>1926</u>. Germany was <u>re-established</u> as an international power.

5) **The Kellogg-Briand Pact** was signed by Germany in 1928, alongside 65 other countries. They promised <u>not</u> to use <u>violence</u> to settle disputes.

> The Dawes Plan helped Germany's <u>economy</u>, but meant its success was <u>dependent</u> on American loans.

The Structure of the Dawes Plan

The USA could <u>afford</u> to <u>loan</u> out money to other countries.

The USA lent <u>Germany</u> money to help it pay off its debts.

Germany was able to pay its reparations to <u>Britain</u> and <u>France</u>.

<u>Britain</u> and <u>France</u> used the money they'd received to pay off their <u>own debts</u> to the USA.

Germany had begun to Recover — but Depended on US Money

1) Life was beginning to <u>look better</u> for Germany thanks to the work of Stresemann.

2) But he <u>died</u> in October <u>1929</u>, just before the disaster of the <u>Wall Street Crash</u> — a massive stock market crash in the USA which started a global economic depression.

3) The plans he had agreed would only work if the <u>USA</u> had <u>enough money</u> to keep lending to Germany — but after the crash, it didn't. Things were suddenly going to <u>get worse again</u> (see p.145).

Comment and Analysis

Germany's economic recovery helped <u>restore faith</u> in the Weimar Republic — there was strong support for pro-Weimar political parties in the <u>1928 elections</u>.

Stresemann boosted the German economy

Stresemann had a positive impact on the Weimar Republic and on the lives of many Germans, but he didn't solve all of Germany's problems — the economy was still very unstable.

Changes Under the Weimar Republic

Despite political, social and economic unrest, life did <u>improve</u> for some under the Weimar Republic.

Living standards **Improved** for the **Working Classes**

During the '<u>Golden Years</u>', living standards improved in the Weimar Republic. This was a result of Germany's <u>economic prosperity</u>, but also of the <u>reforms</u> which took place throughout the 1920s.

What Improved	How It Improved
Unemployment	The unemployed were <u>more protected</u>. In 1927, the government introduced <u>unemployment insurance</u>. Workers could pay into the scheme and would receive <u>cash benefits</u> if they became unemployed.
Wages	The <u>working classes</u> became more <u>prosperous</u>. Wages for industrial workers rose quickly in the late 1920s.
Housing	The government launched mass <u>housing projects</u>. More than <u>2 million</u> new homes were built between 1924 and 1931. This also provided <u>extra employment</u>.

Comment and Analysis

Not everyone benefited from higher standards of living. The middle classes felt <u>ignored</u> by the Weimar government and their <u>resentment</u> made it easier for the government's <u>political opponents</u> to gain <u>support</u>.

Despite these changes, some problems remained:

1) Higher living standards could only be maintained with a strong economy, and Germany's was <u>fragile</u>.

2) The changes mainly helped the <u>working classes</u> — the <u>middle classes</u> couldn't access the <u>welfare benefits</u>.

Women gained more **Freedoms**

Women were given <u>more freedom</u> and greater access to <u>public life</u> under the Weimar Republic.

1) Politically, women were given <u>more representation</u>. They were awarded the <u>vote</u> and could enter politics more easily — between 1919 and 1932, <u>112 women</u> were elected to the Reichstag.

2) Women showed that they were <u>capable workers</u> during the war, and the number of young women working <u>increased</u>.

3) The <u>traditional role</u> of women began to change. New female <u>sports clubs</u> and societies sprang up, and women had more <u>opportunities</u>.

4) <u>Divorce</u> became easier, and the number of divorces rose.

Comment and Analysis

These changes fuelled <u>right-wing criticism</u> — some German nationalists thought giving women more power and freedom <u>threatened</u> traditional family life and values in Germany.

The Weimar Republic had many **Cultural Achievements**

1) The Weimar Republic was a period of <u>creativity</u> and <u>innovation</u> in Germany. <u>Freedom of expression</u> generated <u>new ideas</u>. Artists began to question traditional forms and styles, especially ones that focused on <u>authority</u> and <u>militarism</u>.

2) There were advances in the <u>arts</u> — some developments were <u>bold</u> and <u>new</u>, like the drama of <u>Bertholt Brecht</u>. The <u>Bauhaus School</u> of <u>design</u> was highly influential, especially in fine arts and architecture.

3) There were also important changes in <u>music</u>, <u>literature</u> and <u>cinema</u>. German films were successful — e.g. 'Metropolis' directed by <u>Fritz Lang</u>.

4) The Weimar Republic encouraged new ways of <u>critical thinking</u> at places like <u>Frankfurt University</u>, and a <u>cabaret culture</u> developed in Berlin.

Not all Germans liked the rejection of <u>traditional forms</u> and <u>values</u> in Weimar culture. Some were <u>afraid</u> it symbolised a <u>loss</u> of German <u>tradition</u>.

The Weimar Republic had a lot of important successes

Split a piece of paper in two. On one side, write down all of the ways people's lives improved under the Weimar Republic. On the other side, write down all of the ways their lives got worse.

Worked Exam-Style Question

This sample answer will give you an idea of how write an answer that explains causation.

Q1

> Explain why the Weimar Republic was unpopular between 1919 and 1923.
> You could mention reparations and political weaknesses in your answer. [12 marks]

The prompts in the question are only there as a guide. To get a high mark, you'll also need to include ideas of your own that go beyond the prompts.

This links back to the question by explaining how this factor affected the Republic's popularity.

The Weimar Republic was very unpopular in Germany between 1919 and 1923. From the outset, many Germans distrusted its politicians because of their involvement in the 1918 Armistice Agreement, which ended the First World War. Some Germans felt betrayed by these 'November Criminals', as they believed Germany could have continued fighting and won the war. This undermined the popularity of the Weimar Republic before it had even begun.

Make sure your points are relevant to the question.

Another important cause of the Weimar Republic's unpopularity was President Ebert's decision to sign the Treaty of Versailles (June 1919). Many Germans were angry with President Ebert for accepting the treaty's conditions, which were seen as very unfair. Germany lost its empire, its military was significantly reduced and German forces were banned from the Rhineland, leaving Germany open to attack from the west. Germans also felt humiliated by Article 231, which forced Germany to accept total blame for the war. In the eyes of the German public, signing the Treaty of Versailles was a betrayal and a display of the Weimar Republic's weakness.

Giving specific examples shows you know the topic well.

The first sentence in each paragraph links back to the question.

The Weimar Republic was also unpopular because Germans came to associate it with the crippling reparations payments laid down in the Treaty of Versailles. Many Germans were living in poverty by 1919 and reparations placed huge financial pressure on Germany, making living conditions even worse. The government was unable to pay the £6600 million demanded in reparations, and tried to solve the problem by printing more money. This resulted in hyperinflation, which hit the middle classes particularly hard, as bank savings became worthless. However, by 1923 everyone was affected because even basic items were hard to get hold of. Between 1918 and 1923, the cost of an egg rose from 1/4 of a Mark to 80 million Marks. People blamed the Weimar Republic for failing to cope effectively with the consequences of the reparations.

This explains why reparations made the Republic unpopular.

Worked Exam-Style Question

The Weimar Republic's domestic political weaknesses also played a part in its unpopularity. The Weimar constitution introduced a system of proportional representation, which meant that lots of different parties were represented in the Reichstag. This often made the Reichstag slow to come to decisions, which frustrated the German public.

Think about how one factor might have <u>affected</u> another.

The Republic's political weakness fuelled political instability, which further harmed its popularity. The government was unable to stop the left-wing Sparticist Revolt (1919) on its own, so it had to rely on the help of the right-wing Freikorps to prevent it. <u>In 1920, the Freikorps themselves attempted a coup, and in 1923 Hitler attempted to gain power in the Munich Putsch</u>. Although these challenges were all unsuccessful, they created political instability in the Weimar Republic and emphasised the weaknesses of its government.

Including <u>dates</u> shows that you can provide <u>accurate</u> information.

<u>The Republic also had a reputation for being weak internationally when dealing with the Allies, which was made worse by its response to the French and Belgian invasion of the Ruhr in 1923</u>. Many Germans were angry at the invasion and held a large strike in the Ruhr, but the government called the strike off. This made the government seem unpatriotic, as it appeared unwilling to defend Germany from further humiliation. Many Germans felt betrayed by the fact that the government didn't want to stand up for its country at a time when Germany was particularly vulnerable.

It's important to include factors that <u>weren't mentioned</u> as prompts in the question.

Exam-Style Questions

Q1
What was the most important reason for the growth of socialism in Germany between 1890 and 1918: economic change or social problems?

Explain your answer, referring to both reasons.   [12 marks]

Q2
Explain why the German economy experienced a recovery between 1924 and 1929.

You could mention the Rentenmark and the Dawes Plan in your answer.   [12 marks]

Q3
Explain how the lives of Germans changed under the Weimar Republic between 1919 and 1928.   [8 marks]

The Great Depression

In 1929, the <u>Great Depression</u> hit Germany. The <u>desperation</u> it caused in the 1920s and 1930s meant that the German people were willing to consider any political party that promised something <u>different</u>.

The Wall Street Crash **Ended** economic **Recovery**

In October 1929, the Wall Street stock market in America <u>crashed</u>. It sparked an international economic <u>crisis</u> (the Great Depression) and meant the USA couldn't afford to <u>prop up</u> the German economy any longer.

1) Germany's economic recovery between 1924 and 1929 was built on <u>unstable</u> foundations. The biggest problem was that it was <u>dependent</u> on loans from the <u>USA</u>, which had been agreed in the Dawes Plan (see p.140).

2) After the Wall Street Crash, the USA <u>couldn't afford</u> to lend Germany money anymore. It also wanted some old loans to be <u>repaid</u>.

- Germany's economy <u>collapsed</u> without US aid. Industrial production <u>declined</u> — factories closed and banks went out of business.

- There was <u>mass unemployment</u>. In October 1929 <u>1.6 million</u> people were out of work, and by February 1932 there were over <u>6 million</u>.

- The government also <u>cut</u> unemployment benefits — it couldn't afford to <u>support</u> the large numbers of Germans out of work. This made many Germans <u>angry</u> with the government.

3) By 1932, many parts of society were <u>discontent</u> with the Weimar government. Its failure to deal with unemployment meant it <u>lost</u> some backing from the working classes who'd been a <u>key part</u> of its support.

Extremist parties became **More Popular**

Popular discontent with the Weimar <u>government</u> and economic <u>instability</u> created an <u>opportunity</u> for extremist parties to grow. The KPD (the Communist Party of Germany) increased in influence.

1) The KPD was founded in December 1918 and wanted a <u>workers' revolution</u>. The communists promised to represent workers' needs and make German society more <u>fair</u>.

2) This helped the KPD to gain a lot of support from <u>unemployed</u> Germans during times of economic <u>crisis</u>.

3) When the Great Depression hit Germany in 1929, the KPD <u>competed</u> with the Nazi Party for the <u>support</u> of Germans who had been hit <u>hard</u> by the economic crisis.

4) Between 1928 and 1932, membership of the KPD grew from <u>130,000</u> to almost <u>300,000</u>. However, Nazi Party membership grew <u>even more</u> rapidly — soon the KPD got left behind.

> **Comment and Analysis**
>
> Some historians think the Nazi Party's rise to power <u>wasn't</u> guaranteed — in the 1930s, both left <u>and</u> right-wing political parties <u>increased</u> in popularity in Germany.

Federal Election Results in Germany, 1928-32

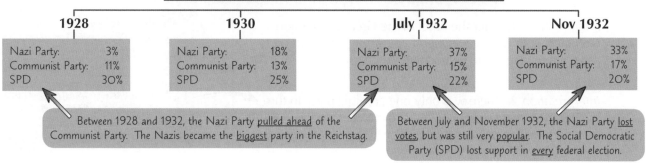

	1928	1930	July 1932	Nov 1932
Nazi Party:	3%	18%	37%	33%
Communist Party:	11%	13%	15%	17%
SPD	30%	25%	22%	20%

Between 1928 and 1932, the Nazi Party <u>pulled ahead</u> of the Communist Party. The Nazis became the <u>biggest</u> party in the Reichstag.

Between July and November 1932, the Nazi Party <u>lost votes</u>, but was still very <u>popular</u>. The Social Democratic Party (SPD) lost support in <u>every</u> federal election.

The Great Depression changed the course of German politics

Describe the changes in federal election results between 1928 and 1932.
What do they show about the changing popularity of the three different political parties?

The Nazi Rise

The Nazi Party was able to take advantage of the discontent and anger created by the Great Depression.

The Nazi Party Appealed to many Different Groups in Society

The Nazis promised a more prosperous and less humiliating future, which was very popular among the German people — by 1930, membership had grown to over 300,000.

1) After the onset of the Depression, the Nazi Party's popularity soared. Hitler's promise to make Germany great again appealed to the growing ranks of unemployed and young people who wanted a brighter future.

2) Some people also supported the Nazis' anti-communist and anti-Jewish views. Communists and Jews were useful scapegoats for Germany's economic problems and gave Germans someone to blame.

3) Some wealthy businessmen who had lost out in the Great Depression turned to the Nazi Party. They approved of the Nazis' anti-communist stance and wanted the economic prosperity Hitler had promised.

> **Comment and Analysis**
>
> After the Depression hit Germany, more Germans began to vote. Participation in elections increased by around 10% between 1928 and 1932. Many of these new voters were attracted by the changes the Nazi Party promised.

The Nazi Party was Well Organised

- Hitler's private army, the SA (see p.139), gave the party a military feel, which made it seem organised and disciplined. His authority over the SA and his undisputed role as head of the Nazi Party made the Nazis seemed strong in comparison to the Weimar government.

- Propaganda was very efficient. It often focused on regional issues and targeted specific groups. This made individuals feel valued by the Nazi Party and stole votes from smaller parties.

Hitler's Personality attracted Support

A Nazi election poster from April 1932. The text reads 'Our last hope: Hitler'.

Interviews with Germans who lived through this period suggest that Hitler's personality was an important factor in the Nazis' popularity.

1) Hitler was patriotic and energetic, and was able to effectively get across his enthusiasm to his supporters. His speeches brought hope to those who listened.

2) In the 1932 election campaigns, Hitler was depicted as Germany's saviour. He stood up to the Weimar government and opposed communism.

3) He came across as a strong leader, which created a sharp contrast with the politicians of the Weimar governments. Hitler's authority over the SA and his undisputed role as head of the Nazi Party attracted support — many Germans had now lost faith in democracy.

4) Here are two different interpretations of Hitler's rise to power. There's evidence to support both opinions:

Interpretation 1: After the onset of the Great Depression, Germans were willing to support any strong extremist party as an alternative to the democratic Weimar government.

> After the Great Depression, both the Nazi Party and the Communist Party became more popular, and support for moderate parties like Social Democratic Party dropped off.

Interpretation 2: There was only one credible party to turn to after the Great Depression hit — the Nazi Party. It was the only party with a charismatic leader who had mass appeal.

> The Nazi Party grew more rapidly than any other party after 1928. Hitler's passion and energy made the Nazis stand out, and support for the KPD simply couldn't keep up.

Hitler's personality helped him to win the support of many Germans

If you're asked to discuss interpretations or statements then it's a good idea to read through them carefully and think about what each one suggests. For more advice, see p.198.

Establishing a Dictatorship

As the Depression got worse, political instability grew. Several parties were competing for power in the elections of 1932 (see p.145). In 1933, the Nazis would emerge on top. Hitler's rise continued.

Hitler **Gained Power** with the aid of a **Political Deal**

1) By April 1932, conditions had worsened. The country was desperate for a strong government.

2) President Hindenburg had to stand for re-election because his term of office had run out. He was a national hero, but Hitler decided to run against him. Despite claiming he'd win easily, Hindenburg didn't win a majority in the first election. In the second ballot he won 53%, beating Hitler's 36.8%.

3) In July 1932, the Nazis won 230 seats in the elections for the Reichstag — more than any other party. Hitler demanded to be made Chancellor, but Hindenburg didn't trust Hitler and refused to appoint him.

4) Then in the election of November 1932, the Nazis seemed to be losing popularity — they lost 34 seats.

5) But Hitler struck a deal with another politician, Franz von Papen — if Papen would persuade Hindenburg to make Hitler Chancellor, Hitler would make Papen Vice-Chancellor.

6) Hindenburg agreed to Papen's suggestion, thinking that he could control Hitler. But Hitler used his new powers to call another election in March 1933, hoping to make the Nazis even stronger in the Reichstag.

> **Comment and Analysis**
>
> Hindenburg hoped that Hitler would be less extreme once he was actually in power. He also hoped that Hitler wouldn't be able to repair the economy — meaning he (Hindenburg) might be able to regain popularity and power.

January 1932		July 1932			January 1933
There are 6 million unemployed.	Hitler uses the Depression to promise better things.	Hitler stands against Hindenburg in 1932 and loses.	July 1932 — the Nazis are the largest party in the Reichstag with 230 seats.	The Nazis lose seats in November 1932 but are still the largest party.	Hitler is finally offered the Chancellorship in January 1933.

The Nazis used **Dirty Tricks** to **Win** in 1933

1) In the elections of 1933, the Nazis took no chances:

- They controlled the news media, and opposition meetings were banned.

- They used the SA to terrorise opponents.

- When a fire broke out in the Reichstag building, Hitler blamed the communists. He used the fire to claim that communists were a threat to the country and to whip up anti-communist feelings. Hitler was even given emergency powers to deal with the supposed communist threat — he used these powers to intimidate communist voters.

2) The Nazis won 288 seats but didn't have an overall majority. So Hitler simply made the Communist Party (who had 81 seats) illegal.

3) This gave him enough support in Parliament to bring in the Enabling Act, passed with threats and bargaining in March 1933. This let him govern for four years without Parliament.

4) Trade unions were banned in May 1933. Then in July 1933, all political parties, apart from the Nazi party, were banned. Germany had become a one-party state.

> **Comment and Analysis**
>
> The emergency powers granted to Hitler were a turning point — they mark the first step towards making Germany a dictatorship. Hitler justified them by saying that they were necessary to protect the German people. This meant he faced little opposition from the German public.

The Nazis cheated their way to power

In the exam, remember to consider people's circumstances and the limited knowledge they had at the time. Most Germans had no idea what the Nazi Party would grow into after it gained power.

Achieving Total Power

Hitler was more powerful, but he still had <u>enemies</u>. He wanted to <u>remove</u> them to secure his <u>dictatorship</u>.

The **SA** was a **Threat** to Hitler

1) The <u>SA</u> had <u>helped</u> Hitler come to power (see p.139), but Hitler now saw it as a <u>threat</u>.

2) Its members were very loyal to <u>Ernst Röhm</u>, the SA's leader. Hitler was worried that Röhm was becoming <u>too powerful</u> — by 1934 the SA had more members than the German army.

3) The SA was also <u>unpopular</u> with the leaders of the <u>German army</u> and with some <u>ordinary Germans</u>.

The **'Night of the Long Knives'** — Hitler removes his enemies

1) <u>Ernst Röhm</u> was the biggest threat to Hitler, but Hitler was also worried about <u>other members</u> of the Nazi Party who <u>disagreed</u> with his views.

2) On the 29th-30th June 1934, Hitler sent men to <u>arrest</u> or <u>kill</u> Röhm and other leaders of the SA. Hitler also used this opportunity to remove some of his <u>political opponents</u>. Altogether, several hundred people were <u>killed</u> or <u>imprisoned</u>.

3) Hitler claimed that those who had been killed had been <u>plotting</u> to <u>overthrow</u> the government, so he declared their murders legal.

- This became known as the '<u>Night of the Long Knives</u>', and was a triumph for Hitler.
- It stamped out all potential <u>opposition</u> within the Nazi Party and sent a powerful message to the party about Hitler's <u>ruthlessness</u> and <u>brutality</u>. It also showed that Hitler was now free to act <u>above the law</u>.

Comment and Analysis

Most Germans <u>wouldn't</u> have known exactly what had happened on the 'Night of the Long Knives' until a few days later, when Hitler declared the events legal. Even then, there was <u>little outcry</u>. It's likely that some people <u>believed</u> Hitler's claims that the violence was necessary to <u>protect</u> the country. Others were <u>too scared</u> to speak out.

Hitler took full control of **National** and **Local** government

1) In August 1934, <u>Hindenburg died</u>. Hitler used the opportunity to <u>combine</u> the posts of Chancellor and President, and also made himself Commander-in-Chief of the army.

2) He called himself <u>Der Führer</u> (the leader) — this was the beginning of the <u>dictatorship</u>.

3) At this point, Germany was <u>reorganised</u> into a number of provinces. Each province was called a <u>Gau</u> (plural: Gaue), with a Gauleiter (a loyal Nazi) in charge of each.

4) Above them were the <u>Reichsleiters</u>, who <u>advised</u> Hitler, e.g. <u>Goebbels</u> who was in charge of propaganda, and <u>Himmler</u> who was chief of the German police.

5) At the top and in absolute <u>control</u> was the <u>Führer</u> — Hitler.

6) Every aspect of life was carefully <u>controlled</u>, and only <u>loyal</u> Nazis could be <u>successful</u>.

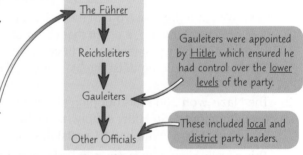

Gauleiters were appointed by <u>Hitler</u>, which ensured he had control over the <u>lower levels</u> of the party.

These included <u>local</u> and <u>district</u> party leaders.

Comment and Analysis

When the Nazis took over, some Germans were glad that someone was at last <u>taking control</u> after the chaos and political weaknesses of the Weimar years.

The <u>army</u> had to swear an <u>oath of allegiance</u> to Hitler, instead of pledging to protect Germany. Some <u>German workers</u> were also forced to take an <u>oath of obedience</u>, promising loyalty to Hitler. Those who refused could lose their jobs.

Hitler eliminated anyone who might have threatened his power

You need to know how Hitler secured his power to become the Führer. Write a summary of the steps he took to consolidate his position between January 1933 and August 1934.

Worked Exam-Style Question

This sample answer will help you to explain the usefulness of some sources.

Source A — a photograph of a German girl decorating a picture of Adolf Hitler with flowers. It was taken in Germany in 1935.

Source B — an extract from a public speech made by Adolf Hitler in July 1932.

> The German peasant has become impoverished... the social hopes of many millions of people are destroyed; one third of all German men and women of working age is unemployed... If the present parties seriously want to save Germany, why have they not done so already? Had they wanted to save Germany, why has it not happened?

Q1

Explain how useful Sources A and B are for an investigation into what the Nazi Party offered the German people. Use both sources, as well as your own knowledge. [8 marks]

Make it clear <u>which source</u> you're talking about.

You can use <u>relevant information</u> from other parts of the section to explain the source's <u>wider context</u>.

Remember to write about <u>both sources</u>.

Use <u>evidence</u> from the source to <u>support</u> the points that you've made.

<u>Source A</u> is partially useful because it shows that the Nazi Party was offering the German people a strong leader who was admired and loved by his people. <u>The photo was taken by an unknown photographer in 1935 — two years into Hitler's Chancellorship</u>, when he was consolidating his dictatorship. <u>By 1935, the Nazi Party had established a system of censorship to control the image of the party</u>, so it is possible that this photograph was taken as a propaganda image, which limits its usefulness. The photo's suggestion that the Nazi Party offered a strong and loved leader isn't necessarily false — Hitler's charisma and patriotism were undoubtedly a factor in the Nazi Party's popularity. However, it's unlikely that photos published at that time would challenge Nazi Party ideology, making Source A unreliable in showing what German people felt the Nazi Party offered them. <u>Because of this, Source A is only partially useful</u>.

<u>Source B</u> is from a speech made by Hitler himself in July 1932. The fact that the speech was made by the leader of the Nazi Party is useful because it shows what Hitler was directly offering the people of Germany. Hitler talks about the need to '<u>save Germany</u>', which suggests that the Nazi Party wanted to be seen by the German people as offering hope. <u>In mid-1932, the Nazi Party was trying to appeal to as many people as possible before elections in November</u>. This view is from the Nazi Party's perspective, and as a result is biased and only partially useful. Both sources focus on the impression the Party was trying to give — <u>not on what Germans themselves believed</u>. This means that both sources are only partially useful at best.

Ask yourself about the source — <u>who</u> made it, <u>when</u> they made it, and <u>where</u>.

Remember to say how <u>useful</u> you think each source is.

Think about <u>when</u> the sources were created, and how that affects their <u>usefulness</u>.

You can also write about what the sources <u>don't</u> <u>include</u>.

Exam-Style Questions

Q1

Explain why Hitler's personality attracted support from the German public. You could mention patriotism and strong leadership in your answer. [12 marks]

You'll need to use information from other parts of the Germany section to answer question one properly.

Q2

What was the most important reason for the growing appeal of the Nazi Party in the early 1930s: the policies of the Nazi Party or the weaknesses of the Weimar Republic?

Explain your answer, referring to both reasons. [12 marks]

Q3

'The granting of emergency powers (1933) was the most important turning point in Hitler's consolidation of power between January 1933 and August 1934.'

Explain how far you agree with this statement. [18 marks]

The Machinery of Terror

The Nazis aimed to make Germany a totalitarian state (where the government controls all aspects of life).

Germany became a **Police State**

1) The Nazis wanted complete control over the machinery of government and people's lives.

2) Hitler's Enabling Act of 1933 (see p.147) allowed the government to read people's mail, listen in on their phone calls, and search their homes without notice.

3) The Law for the Reconstruction of the Reich (1934) gave the Nazis total power over local governments.

4) There were laws to sack civil servants who didn't support the Nazis and accept their rules.

5) The Nazis also made changes to the justice system. Judges didn't have to be 'fair' and unbiased. Instead, they were expected to make rulings that were in line with Nazi Party policy.

6) The Sicherheitsdienst (SD) was the Nazi intelligence service. It was initially run by Reinhard Heydrich — he aimed to bring every German under continual supervision.

The Legal System Was Far From Fair

- In 1933, the Nazis set up special courts where the basic rights of those accused were suspended — they couldn't appeal or question evidence given against them.

- In 1934, Hitler established the People's Court in Berlin, which held trials for important political crimes. Defendants were nearly always found guilty.

People could be **Terrorised** into **Conforming**

The government was also prepared to use terror and even violence against the German people.

1) The SS (Schutzstaffel) began as a bodyguard for Hitler. It expanded massively under the leadership of Himmler during the 1930s. Its members were totally loyal to Hitler, and feared for their cruelty.

2) Himmler was also in charge of the secret police — the Gestapo. The Gestapo's job was to protect the German public, but their methods included harsh interrogations and imprisonment without trial.

3) Local wardens were employed to make sure Germans were loyal to the Nazis. Members of the public were encouraged to report disloyalty. Many were arrested by the Gestapo as a result.

4) After 1933, concentration camps were created across Germany and its territories to hold political prisoners and anybody else considered dangerous to the Nazis. Some of these were later turned into death camps.

Security Police search a car in Berlin on the orders of the Gestapo.

Not everyone lived in **Constant Terror**

1) Most Germans were prepared to go along with the new regime. Some people accepted the new rules out of fear.

2) Others went along with them because they believed in their aims, even if they didn't approve of the Nazis' brutal methods.

Comment and Analysis

For those that didn't fit in with the Nazi ideals (e.g. Jews), life under the SS and the Gestapo could be terrifying. But Hitler was supported, not feared, by many Germans.

The Nazis exercised control using any means necessary

Turn this page over, then scribble down as much as you can remember about the Nazi police state. If you get stuck, think how you might've been treated if you were a political enemy.

Nazi Propaganda

The Nazis also used a wide range of propaganda to help them control all aspects of German people's lives.

Propaganda aims to Control how people Think

1) Propaganda means spreading information that influences how people think and behave.

2) It gives only certain points of view and often leaves out important facts.

3) The Nazis used powerful propaganda to get the support of the German people. Dr Joseph Goebbels was in overall charge of the Nazis' 'propaganda machine'.

Nazi propaganda took Simple Ideas and Repeated them

1) Nazi propaganda was used to unite the German people and convince them that the Nazis would make Germany strong.

2) Germans were encouraged to hate the countries that signed the Treaty of Versailles (see p.137). The Nazis said Germany should fight to get back the territory 'stolen' by the treaty.

3) Goebbels created the 'Hitler Myth', which made Hitler seem like a god and the saviour of Germany. This was the 'cult of the Führer'. A popular slogan was 'One people, one empire, one leader'. Many Germans devoted their lives to Hitler.

4) The Nazis' propaganda also said that Jews and communists were the biggest cause of Germany's problems. One Nazi paper claimed that Jews murdered children for the Passover Feast.

5) The Nazis encouraged a return to traditional German values and a revival of traditional German culture.

The Government had to Approve all Artistic Works

Goebbels founded the Ministry of Public Enlightenment and Propaganda in 1933. It had departments for music, theatre, film, literature and radio. All artists, writers, journalists and musicians had to register to get their work approved.

Nazis used the Media as a tool of Propaganda

1) The Nazis wanted to surround people with their propaganda. They used censorship to prevent Germans from seeing or hearing anything that gave a different message.

> According to Goebbels, radio was a 'weapon of the totalitarian state' — it was a way to control the German people.

2) They sold cheap radios and controlled broadcasts. By 1939 approximately 70% of households had a radio, which gave the Nazis a voice in most people's homes.

3) In 1933, only 3% of German daily newspapers were controlled by the Nazis. By 1944, this had risen to 82%. This meant the Nazis could decide what was published in the papers.

4) The Nazis also produced hundreds of films. Many films showed the strengths of the Nazis and Hitler, and the weakness of their opponents. An important German director was Leni Riefenstahl.

5) Another method of spreading propaganda was through posters showing the evil of Germany's enemies and the power of Hitler. Propaganda also let Germans know what was expected of them.

Nazi propaganda poster, 1935. It states that 'the German student' fights for the Führer and for the German people.

EXAM TIP — Goebbels understood that the media could be a powerful tool

In the exam, you might need to think about why propaganda had such a big impact on many Germans. Think about why it was attractive, who it targeted and how powerful it was.

Nazi Propaganda

Nazi propaganda was <u>sophisticated</u> and it was <u>everywhere</u> — Germans were constantly exposed to Nazi ideas.

Nazi propaganda could involve **Spectacular Displays**

Hermann Göring at a Nuremberg Rally, as shown in 'Triumph of the Will'.

1) The Nazis used <u>public rallies</u> to spread their propaganda. The annual <u>Nuremberg Rallies</u> focused on speeches by leading Nazis, like Hitler and Goebbels. The 1934 Nuremberg Rally was recorded by Riefenstahl in her film '<u>Triumph of the Will</u>'.

2) One million people attended the 1936 rally. There were displays of <u>lights</u> and <u>flags</u> to greet the arrival of Hitler. These made him look <u>more powerful</u>.

3) Sporting events like the <u>1936 Berlin Olympics</u> were used to show off German wealth and power. But the success of non-Aryan athletes like African-American <u>Jesse Owens</u> (who won four gold medals) undermined Hitler's message.

4) Nazi power was also shown through <u>art</u> and <u>architecture</u>, and grand new buildings appeared in Nuremberg and Berlin.

Propaganda was used to change **Culture** and **Society**

1) The Nazis promised an empire that would last a <u>thousand years</u> — based on <u>traditional values</u>.

2) <u>Modern art</u> was banned, in favour of realistic paintings that fit with Nazi ideology. Modern art was labelled '<u>degenerate</u>' and exhibitions were created to show people how 'bad' it was. The Nazis celebrated the works of '<u>German</u>' composers, such as Wagner, but much <u>modern classical music</u>, works by <u>Jewish composers</u>, and <u>jazz</u> were all attacked.

3) <u>School textbooks</u> were rewritten to make Germans look successful. Children were taught to believe in <u>Nazi doctrines</u> (see p.157).

4) The '<u>Strength through Joy</u>' programme sought to show ordinary workers that the Nazi regime cared about their living conditions (see p.156).

Propaganda was most **Effective** when **Reinforcing Existing Ideas**

Surprisingly, it's quite <u>difficult</u> to tell how <u>effective</u> Nazi propaganda was.

1) Some historians say Nazi propaganda was better at <u>reinforcing</u> people's <u>existing attitudes</u> than making them believe <u>something different</u>.

2) Many Germans felt angry and humiliated by the <u>Treaty of Versailles</u>, so Hitler's promises to reverse the treaty and make Germany great again were very <u>popular</u>.

3) After the <u>political weakness</u> of the Weimar Republic, people found the image of Hitler as a <u>strong</u> leader appealing. So the '<u>Hitler Myth</u>' was very effective and made Hitler an extremely <u>popular</u> leader.

4) <u>Anti-Jewish</u> and <u>anti-communist</u> attitudes already existed in Germany <u>before</u> the Nazis came to power.

5) The <u>Weimar Republic</u> was seen as too <u>liberal</u> by many — they thought standards in Germany had slipped. These people liked the promise of a return to <u>traditional</u> German values.

6) The Depression had left many German people in <u>poverty</u>. This made them easier to <u>persuade</u>, and the Nazis' promises of help extremely <u>popular</u>.

Comment and Analysis

However effective their propaganda was, the Nazis' <u>control</u> of the media made it almost <u>impossible</u> for anyone to publish an <u>alternative</u> point of view.

Nazi propaganda invaded nearly every aspect of daily life

Write a list of all the Nazis' different methods of propaganda. Write a short paragraph explaining which method you believe was the most effective and why.

Nazis and the Church

The Nazi Party publicly <u>supported</u> religious freedom, but in reality Hitler saw Christianity as a serious <u>threat</u>.

Hitler wanted to **Reduce** the Church's **Power**

1) In the 1930s, most Germans were <u>Christians</u> and the Church was very <u>influential</u>. During the Weimar Republic, the state and the Church had worked <u>closely</u> together and the Church was involved in national matters like <u>education</u>.

2) Some prominent Nazis were <u>anti-Christian</u> and Nazi ideology disagreed with the <u>role</u> the Church had traditionally had in society.

3) Hitler thought religion should comply with the <u>state</u> and wanted churches to promote <u>Nazi ideals</u>. He was also worried that some members of the Church might publicly <u>oppose</u> Nazi policies.

4) The Nazi Party was careful to maintain <u>support</u> from the <u>Catholic</u> and <u>Protestant</u> Churches during its rise to power because they were so <u>popular</u>. However, as Hitler consolidated his totalitarian state, his <u>control</u> over churches <u>increased</u>.

The **Catholic Church** was **Persecuted**

1) In July 1933, an agreement called the <u>Concordat</u> was signed between the <u>Pope</u> and the <u>Nazi government</u>. Hitler promised <u>not</u> to interfere with the Catholic Church if the Church agreed to <u>stay out</u> of German politics.

2) The Catholic Church was now <u>banned</u> from speaking out against the Nazi Party, but Hitler soon <u>broke</u> his side of the deal.

> **Comment and Analysis**
>
> The Concordat reassured Christians that Hitler was <u>consolidating</u> ties with the Catholic Church, but he was actually <u>restricting</u> its power.

- The Nazi Party started to <u>restrict</u> the Catholic Church's role in <u>education</u>.
- In 1936 all crucifixes were removed from <u>schools</u>. By 1939 <u>Catholic education</u> had been destroyed.
- The Nazis began arresting <u>priests</u> in 1935 and put them on trial.
- Catholic newspapers were <u>suppressed</u> and the Catholic Youth group was <u>disbanded</u>.

3) In 1937, the Pope <u>spoke out against</u> Hitler in a letter to Catholic Churches in Germany. The view of the Church had <u>changed</u>, but many German Catholics were <u>too scared</u> to speak out against the Nazi Party. They tried to protect their religion by <u>avoiding confrontation</u> with the Nazis.

The Nazi Party **Controlled** the **Protestant Church**

The Protestant Church was <u>reorganised</u> and fell under <u>Nazi control</u>.

1) When Hitler became Chancellor in 1933, there were 28 independent Protestant Churches. These Churches were politically <u>divided</u> — some formed a group known as the '<u>German Christians</u>'. They supported Hitler and favoured an <u>anti-Semitic</u> version of Christianity.

2) The Nazi Party <u>backed</u> this version of Christianity and believed all Christians should follow its <u>principles</u>. In 1936, all Protestant Churches were <u>merged</u> to form the <u>Reich Church</u>.

3) The Reich Church '<u>Nazified</u>' Christianity:

> The Reich Church replaced the symbol of a <u>cross</u> with the Nazi <u>Swastika</u>, and the Bible was replaced by '<u>Mein Kampf</u>' (see p.139). Only <u>Nazis</u> could give sermons and the Church <u>suspended</u> non-Aryan ministers.

> **Comment and Analysis**
>
> Not everyone supported the Reich Church — it was opposed by a Protestant group called the '<u>Confessing Church</u>' (see p.155).

4) The Reich Church was an attempt to increase <u>state control</u> over the Protestant Church and make a <u>National Socialist</u> version of Christianity.

The Nazis wanted the state to come first

You might get sources in the exam that give different viewpoints on Nazi religious policies. Don't forget that Catholic and Protestant Christians were treated differently by the Nazis.

Opposition to the Nazis

The Nazis had a <u>tight grip</u> on Germany, but there was <u>opposition</u> from the left wing, the Church and young people.

The **Political Left** opposed Hitler, but was **Divided** and **Weak**

1) Once in power, the Nazis had <u>banned</u> other political parties, including those on the political left, such as the <u>Communist Party</u> (<u>KPD</u>) and the <u>Social Democratic Party</u> (<u>SPD</u>).

2) But members of these parties formed <u>underground groups</u> to try and organise <u>industrial unrest</u> (e.g. <u>strikes</u>). These networks were often <u>infiltrated</u> by the Gestapo, and party members could be <u>executed</u>.

3) Their impact was also limited because the different parties of the left were <u>divided</u> and <u>didn't co-operate</u>.

Some members of the **Church Opposed** the Nazis

There was <u>little opposition</u> to the Nazis in Germany from <u>Christian groups</u>. But a number of Church members did <u>oppose</u> the Nazis, even though they risked being sent to <u>concentration camps</u> (see p.151):

1) <u>Martin Niemöller</u> was a Protestant pastor, a former U-boat (submarine) captain, and a one-time Nazi supporter. He objected to Nazi interference in the Church, and was one of the founders of the <u>Confessing Church</u>. He used a sermon in 1937 to protest against the <u>persecution of Church members</u>, and as a result spent several years in concentration camps.

> The <u>Confessing Church</u> protested against Hitler's attempt to unite the different Protestant Churches into one <u>Reich Church</u> (see p.154).

2) Another key member of the Confessing Church was <u>Dietrich Bonhoeffer</u>, a Protestant philosopher and pastor who <u>opposed</u> the Nazis from the beginning. He joined the resistance, helped Jews escape from Germany and planned to assassinate Hitler. He was caught and imprisoned, then <u>executed</u> just weeks before the fall of the Nazis.

3) <u>Clemens August von Galen</u> was the Catholic Bishop of Münster, who used his sermons to <u>protest</u> against Nazi racial policies and the murder of the disabled. His protests <u>didn't stop</u> the killing, but they did force the Nazis to keep them <u>secret</u>. Only the need to maintain the support of <u>German Catholics</u> stopped the Nazis from <u>executing</u> him.

The **Edelweiss Pirates** and **Swing Kids** were **Youth Movements**

1) The <u>Edelweiss Pirates</u> was the name given to groups of rebellious youths who rejected <u>Nazi values</u>.

- They helped <u>army deserters</u>, <u>forced labourers</u> and escaped concentration camp <u>prisoners</u>.
- At first the Nazis mostly ignored them, but cracked down after they started distributing <u>anti-Nazi leaflets</u>. Many members were <u>arrested</u>, and several were publicly <u>hanged</u>.

2) The <u>Swing Kids</u> (or Swing Youth) were groups of young people who rebelled against the <u>tight control</u> the Nazis had over <u>culture</u>, acting in ways considered '<u>degenerate</u>' by the Nazi regime (e.g. listening to American music and <u>drinking alcohol</u>). They were mostly considered a <u>nuisance</u> rather than a <u>threat</u>, but some members were <u>arrested</u> and even sent to <u>concentration camps</u>.

3) Other Germans expressed their dissatisfaction with the Nazi regime in '<u>low level</u>' ways — e.g. by <u>grumbling</u> about the government or <u>spreading rumours</u>. Not everyone considers this genuine <u>opposition</u>, but even this was probably <u>risky</u>.

> **Comment and Analysis**
>
> German opposition to the Nazis didn't really <u>threaten</u> their <u>dominance</u>, but it did mean the <u>Gestapo</u> was <u>kept busy</u> tracking down people who had distributed anti-Nazi leaflets, held secret meetings, committed acts of sabotage, etc.

If you weren't with the Nazis, you were against them

Write the headings 'political opposition', 'religious opposition' and 'opposition from youths' on a piece of paper. Cover this page, then jot down as much as you can remember about each one.

Work and Home

The Nazis encouraged <u>women</u> to be <u>homemakers</u> and tried to provide <u>jobs</u> for <u>men</u>.

Women were expected to raise **Large Families**

1) The Nazis didn't want <u>women</u> to have too much freedom. They believed the role of women was to provide <u>children</u> and support their families <u>at home</u>.

2) Women were <u>banned</u> from being <u>lawyers</u> in 1936, and the Nazis did their best to stop them following other professions.

3) The <u>League of German Maidens</u> spread the Nazi idea that it was an honour to produce <u>large families</u> for Germany. Nazis gave <u>awards</u> to women for doing this and encouraged more women to marry by offering <u>financial aid</u> to married couples.

4) Women were expected to dress <u>plainly</u> and were <u>discouraged</u> from wearing make-up and smoking. At school, girls studied subjects like <u>cookery</u>. It was stressed that they should choose 'Aryan' husbands.

> This didn't quite go to plan for the Nazis — after 1939, the war caused a <u>shortage of workers</u>, which meant lots of women had to <u>go back to work</u> (see p.164).

Public Works and **Rearmament** meant **Unemployment Fell**

1) Hitler started a huge <u>programme</u> of <u>public works</u>, which helped to reduce unemployment — e.g. from 1933 jobs were created as a result of the construction of <u>autobahns</u> (motorways).

2) <u>All</u> men between 18 and 25 could be <u>recruited</u> into the <u>National Labour Service</u> and given jobs. Industrial output increased and <u>unemployment</u> fell.

3) Hitler also brought in <u>military conscription</u> and encouraged German <u>industry</u> to manufacture more <u>ships</u>, <u>aircraft</u>, <u>tanks</u> and <u>weapons</u> for the military. This <u>rearmament</u> meant further falls in <u>unemployment</u>.

4) Trade unions were banned (see p.147), and workers had to join the Nazis' <u>Labour Front</u> instead. The Labour Front acted like one big trade union, but it was controlled by the Nazis. Workers <u>couldn't</u> go on <u>strike</u> or campaign for better conditions, and <u>wages</u> were relatively <u>low</u>.

> **Comment and Analysis**
>
> Although <u>unemployment fell</u> after the Depression, the Nazis <u>fiddled</u> with the <u>statistics</u> to make it look lower than it really was — e.g. they didn't count <u>women</u> or <u>Jewish</u> people without jobs in the official unemployment statistics.

Many groups in society **Felt Better Off**

1) The Nazis made efforts to maintain the support of German <u>workers</u>. They wanted workers to feel <u>important</u> and believe that they were an essential part of the <u>Volksgemeinschaft</u>.

> 'Volksgemeinschaft' means a <u>community</u> of people working hard towards the same <u>aims</u>.

- The Nazis introduced the <u>Volkswagen</u> (the 'people's car') as a luxury people could aspire to own.
- They also introduced '<u>Strength through Joy</u>' — a scheme which provided workers with <u>cheap holidays</u> and leisure activities.
- The '<u>Beauty of Labour</u>' scheme encouraged factory owners to <u>improve conditions</u> for workers.

2) Many in the <u>middle classes</u> also felt <u>better off</u>, e.g. small-business owners were able to advance more in society than previously.

3) But even though many people felt better off, workers and small-business owners had <u>lost out</u> in some ways:

- The cost of living rose by about <u>25%</u> — but wages didn't go up.
- Workers didn't have the <u>right</u> to <u>strike</u> or <u>resign</u>.
- <u>Small businesses</u> had to pay <u>high taxes</u>.

> **Comment and Analysis**
>
> During the <u>Depression</u>, one third of all workers had been <u>unemployed</u>. Many Germans had been <u>desperate</u>, so life under the Nazis did feel genuinely <u>better</u> for them.

Hitler reduced unemployment — and gained popularity

It's important to remember that for some Germans life really did get better under the Nazi Party.

Young People

An important key to Nazi success was controlling the minds of <u>German youth</u> through youth groups and education.

Youth Movements helped produce Committed Nazis

1) Hitler knew that <u>loyalty</u> from <u>young people</u> was essential if the Nazis were to remain <u>strong</u>.

2) <u>Youth movements</u> were a way of teaching children <u>Nazi ideas</u> —
so they would be <u>loyal</u> to the Nazi Party when they grew up.

The Hitler Youth Seemed Exciting

- The <u>Hitler Youth</u> was founded in 1926. <u>Boys</u> aged fourteen and over were recruited to the movement. It became all but <u>compulsory</u> in <u>1936</u> and lasted until <u>1945</u>.

- Boys wore <u>military-style uniforms</u> and took part in physical exercise <u>preparing</u> for <u>war</u>. High-achieving boys might be sent to <u>Hitler Schools</u> to be trained as loyal <u>Nazi leaders</u>.

- They also went on camping trips and held sports competitions. Some of those who took part said the organisation was <u>fun</u>, made them feel <u>valued</u> and encouraged a sense of <u>responsibility</u>.

The League of German Maidens Was For Girls

- The <u>League of German Maidens</u> was the <u>female</u> branch of the Hitler Youth, aimed at <u>girls</u> aged between fourteen and eighteen.

- Girls were trained in <u>domestic skills</u> like sewing and cooking.

- Sometimes they took part in <u>physical activities</u> like camping and hiking. This gave girls <u>new</u> opportunities that were normally reserved for <u>boys</u>.

Comment and Analysis

After 1936, all other youth organisations were <u>banned</u> and it was almost impossible for children to avoid joining the Hitler Youth. However, towards the end of the 1930s, attendance actually decreased as activities adopted an increasingly <u>military</u> focus.

Education across Germany was 'Nazified'

1) Education in schools meant learning <u>Nazi propaganda</u>. Most teachers joined the <u>Nazi Teachers' Association</u> and were trained in Nazi methods. Children had to <u>report</u> teachers who did not use them.

2) Subjects were <u>rewritten</u> to fit in with Nazi ideas. Children were taught to be <u>anti-Semitic</u> (prejudiced against Jews) — for example, Biology courses stated that Jews were biologically inferior to 'Aryans'. History courses explained that the <u>First World War</u> was lost because of Jews and communists.

3) <u>Physical education</u> became more important for boys to prepare them for joining the army. They sometimes even played <u>games</u> with live ammunition.

4) In universities, students <u>burned</u> anti-Nazi and Jewish books, and <u>Jewish lecturers</u> were sacked. Jewish teachers were also dismissed from <u>public schools</u>.

German children were always being <u>bombarded</u> with Nazi propaganda. Erika Mann, a German who opposed the Nazis, described <u>Nazi education</u> in Germany. 'Every child says 'Heil Hitler!' from 50 to 150 times a day...[it] is <u>required by law</u>; if you meet a friend on the way to school, you say it; study periods are opened and closed with [it]...[The Nazis'] <u>supremacy</u> over the German child...is complete.'

German Youth eventually became involved in Fighting the War

1) During the <u>Second World War</u>, members of the Hitler Youth contributed to the <u>war effort</u> — for example, helping with air defence work, farm work and collecting donations for Nazi charities.

2) Towards the end of the war, many Hitler Youth members ended up fighting <u>alongside adults</u>. They were known for being <u>fierce</u> and <u>fanatical</u> fighters.

The Nazis' attempts to impose their ideology on children <u>weren't</u> always effective. See p.155 for more about how unofficial youth movements <u>resisted</u> Hitler and the Nazis.

The Nazis tried to control what children thought

Imagine you're a teacher in Nazi Germany who has experienced the Nazification of education. Write an account of how your job might have changed after the Nazis gained power in 1933.

Nazi Racial Policy

The Nazi idea of a 'master race' caused a huge amount of harm to groups who were labelled as 'non-Aryan'.

The Nazis **Oppressed** people they **Didn't Like**

1) Most Nazis believed that Germans were members of a superior ancient race called the 'Aryans'. Hitler thought people who were not pure Aryans (e.g. Jews) did not belong in Germany, and had no part to play in the new German Empire.

2) He wanted to 'cleanse' the German people by removing any groups he thought 'inferior'. Jews were especially targeted, but action was also taken against other groups:

> Hitler always claimed the Jews were responsible for many of Germany's problems.

- Many Romani (gypsies) and Slavs (an ethnic group from central and eastern Europe) were sent to concentration camps. The Nazis believed that they were racially inferior.
- The Nazis practised eugenics policies — they wanted to create a strong race by removing all genetic 'defects' from its gene pool. Many people with mental and physical disabilities were murdered or sterilised. Many people of mixed race were also sterilised against their will.
- Homosexual people were sent to concentration camps in their thousands. In 1936 Himmler, Head of the SS, began the Central Office for the Combating of Homosexuality and Abortion.

Nazis **Changed the Law** to **Discriminate** against Jews

1) In 1933, the SA organised a national boycott of Jewish businesses, which resulted in Nazi-led violence against Jews. The violence wasn't popular with the German people, so the Nazis decided to use the legal system to persecute Jews instead.

2) Over time, the number of jobs that Jews were banned from gradually increased.

3) The Nuremberg Laws of 1935 were based on the idea that Jews and Germans were biologically different. They removed many legal rights from Jews and encouraged 'Aryan' Germans to see them as inferior.

- The Nuremberg Laws stopped Jews being German citizens.
- They banned marriage between Jews and non-Jews in Germany.
- They also banned sexual relationships between Jews and non-Jews.

> Some Jews were given passports enabling them to leave Germany but preventing them from returning.

> The Nazis' racial policies aimed to isolate Jews from the rest of society. 'Aryan' Germans were even encouraged to break off friendships with Jews and avoid any contact with Jewish people.

4) Jews were later forced to close or sell their businesses, and they were banned from all employment.

5) By 1938, all Jewish children had been banned from attending German schools and Jews were no longer allowed in many public places, including theatres and exhibitions.

Kristallnacht — the '**Night of the Broken Glass**'

1) In November 1938, a German diplomat was murdered in Paris by a Jew.

2) There was anti-Jewish rioting throughout Germany — thousands of Jewish shops were smashed and almost every synagogue in Germany was burnt down. In the days that followed, thousands of Jews were arrested and sent to concentration camps.

3) The Nazis claimed that the events of Kristallnacht were a spontaneous reaction by the German people to the Paris murder. In fact, they had been planned and organised by the Nazi government. Few ordinary Germans had participated.

Comment and Analysis

Kristallnacht was a turning point in the Nazi persecution of Jews — it was the first widespread act of anti-Jewish violence in Nazi Germany. After Kristallnacht, conditions for German Jews got even worse.

There was a climate of cruelty and fear in Nazi Germany

Fold a piece of paper in half. On one side, jot down all the different types of people who were persecuted as a result of the Nazis' racial policies, and on the other list how they were treated.

Worked Exam-Style Questions

The sample answers on the next three pages will show you how to answer questions that ask you to analyse interpretations. Make sure you read both interpretations carefully before reading through the answers.

> ...once Hitler came to power, it was wonderful. Everybody had a job and there weren't any more unemployed people. They were happy to have a job and the foodstuffs were cheaper and the wages were raised a bit. Somehow, things were going better in the first years.

Interpretation 1 — an extract from an interview with a German woman who lived through the Nazi regime. It was published in 2005.

> By the end of 1934, the Reichstag had no power, authority or influence... Not content with taking over all branches of government, and then of the state, the NSDAP [the Nazis] had taken power over the agencies of civil society. As a result, there was almost no association which people could join or activity in which they could engage that was not a branch of the NSDAP or in some way sponsored by, administered by or monitored by the Nazis.

Interpretation 2 — an extract from a history textbook about Germany, written by Nick Pinfield. It was published in 2015.

Q1
> Look at Interpretations 1 and 2. Explain how their opinions differ about what life was like in Germany after Hitler came to power. Refer to both interpretations in your answer. [4 marks]

Identify the main opinion given in each interpretation.

Interpretation 1 presents a very positive view of life in Germany after Hitler came to power. The author claims that 'things were going better' in the first few years. She emphasises the economic benefits that some Germans initially experienced after the Nazi Party gained power by mentioning that there were higher levels of employment and lower food prices.

Use evidence from the interpretations to back up your points.

This answer highlights more than one feature of the interpretation.

In contrast, Interpretation 2 suggests that life in Germany was oppressive. It doesn't focus on economic improvements, but instead looks at the lack of freedom Germans had in their daily lives. The author emphasises that Germans had no democratic voice by stating that the Reichstag had 'no power, authority or influence' under the Nazi regime. He also highlights that it was difficult for Germans to avoid being associated with, or monitored by, the Nazi Party, as many aspects of their social and professional lives were overseen by the state.

Make sure you clearly state how the opinions in each interpretation are different.

Worked Exam-Style Questions

Q2 Explain why the authors of Interpretations 1 and 2 might have different views about what life was like in Germany after Hitler came to power. Use your own knowledge and both interpretations in your answer. [4 marks]

The first sentence directly addresses the question.

Although both interpretations focus on the first few years of Nazi rule in Germany, the authors have two very different perspectives. Interpretation 1 is from a German woman who lived under the Nazi regime. She claims that 'once Hitler came to power, it was wonderful'. She would have been able to compare life in Germany before and after Hitler became Chancellor in January 1933, and would have personally experienced the devastating impact that the American Wall Street Crash had on Germany in 1929. As a result, her positive view of life shortly after the Nazis gained power isn't surprising — life did initially improve for many Germans.

A very quick summary of the interpretation shows you've understood the message.

The answer talks about the authors' different experiences.

Interpretation 2 is an extract from a history textbook published in 2015. Unlike Interpretation 1, the author's opinion isn't based on personal experience. This could be why the author takes a more negative view of life in Nazi Germany than the author of Interpretation 1 — he did not experience the economic hardships of the 1920s or the initial economic benefits of the Nazi regime. Instead, he focuses on issues that had a more important long-term effect on the lives of Germans, e.g. a lack of freedom.

Interpretation 2 may also have a more negative view because it is a textbook and is trying to give an accurate overview of what life was like for the majority in Nazi Germany. In contrast, because Interpretation 1 is an extract from an interview, it only recalls the experience of one individual who had a positive experience of the first few years of the Nazi regime.

The answer analyses the purpose of each interpretation and what effect it may have had.

Worked Exam-Style Questions

Q3 Do you think Interpretation 1 or Interpretation 2 is more convincing about what life was like in Germany after Hitler came to power? Use both interpretations and your own knowledge to explain your answer. [8 marks]

This addresses the question straight away.

Interpretation 1 offers a first-hand account of what life was like in Germany after Hitler came to power. Its view that 'things were going better in the first years' is partially convincing, as that certainly was the experience of some Germans. The Nazi Party did reduce unemployment through a series of public works, e.g. the construction of new autobahns, and through the creation of the National Labour Service, which offered employment to all men between the ages of 18 and 25.

Use your own knowledge to help you decide whether the interpretation is convincing or not.

Highlight any limitations or inaccuracies that you find.

However, these changes only benefited some Germans and, for many people, life wasn't 'wonderful' like Interpretation 1 suggests. The claim that 'everybody had a job' is untrue — the Nazis did not achieve full employment. The cost of living for many Germans rose by around 25% and workers lost the right to resign or strike. As a result, Interpretation 1 is only partially convincing about what life was like in Nazi Germany.

Give a clear opinion about how convincing the interpretation is.

On the other hand, Interpretation 2 focuses on the more general experiences of many Germans in Nazi Germany. This makes its view on what life was like in Nazi Germany more convincing because it offers a wider perspective than Interpretation 1. It addresses the high level of state involvement in the lives of civilians, stating that 'there was almost no association which people could join' that was not under Nazi influence or control. The existence of Nazi associations like the Hitler Youth (which all young people were required to join from 1936) and the Labour Front (which all workers had to join) supports this view.

This makes a direct comparison between the two interpretations.

You can use relevant information from throughout the Germany section to support your answer.

Interpretation 2's claim that 'By the end of 1934, the Reichstag had no power, authority or influence' also demonstrates how undemocratic life in Germany became after Hitler came to power. After Hitler passed his Enabling Act in March 1933, he no longer needed the Reichstag's consent to pass new laws. The banning of all other political parties (July 1933) marked the end of democracy and the emergence of a one-party state. Whilst this lends support to Interpretation 2's view, it also makes Interpretation 1 less convincing. Although some Germans were pleased about the economic improvements that the Nazis achieved after they came to power, Nazi rule became a dictatorship so quickly that it probably was not widely viewed as 'wonderful', even in the first few years. Overall, I find Interpretation 2 more convincing because it gives a more accurate view of what life was like for most people living in Nazi Germany.

Including specific details like dates shows good knowledge of the topic.

Say which interpretation you think is more convincing.

Worked Exam-Style Questions

This sample answer will give you an idea of how to answer a source-based question.

> The government has ordered that the Hitler Greeting is to be used in conversation between teachers and pupils. Every day at the beginning of the first lesson, the pupils will get up from their places as soon as the teacher enters the class, stand to attention and each raise their outstretched arm level with their eyes. The teacher will go to the front of the class and offer the same greeting accompanied by the words 'Heil Hitler!' The pupils will reply 'Heil Hitler!'

Source A — a translated extract from a German newspaper. It was published in the mid-1930s.

Q4 What does Source A reveal about Nazi education policies? Use evidence from the source and your own knowledge to explain your answer. [7 marks]

Source A reveals that education policies were used by the Nazi Party to control the actions of pupils and teachers. It discusses the requirement for teachers and pupils to greet one another using the 'Hitler Greeting'. This suggests that education policies exposed schoolchildren to Nazi propaganda, in an attempt to build Nazi beliefs and values in children from a young age. The Nazis also did this through curriculum changes, for example science courses taught that Jews were biologically 'inferior' to Aryans. Youth organisations, like the Hitler Youth and the League of German Maidens, helped to build on the loyalty and idolisation of Hitler that was encouraged in the classroom.

This gives a direct answer to the question straight away.

The answer doesn't just repeat what the source says — it explains what it reveals about the Nazis' education policies.

Your own knowledge can also be used to back up a point you've made. This will show a good understanding of the topic.

Source A says that teachers also had to use the greeting, which demonstrates that Nazi policies in education were far-reaching — the Nazis wanted the whole education system (not just schoolchildren) to follow National Socialist principles. The establishment of Nazi organisations like the Nazi Teachers' Association also supports this view. Hitler wanted every aspect of education to be under Nazi control.

This explains where the source is from, and what this reveals.

Source A was taken from a German newspaper, which reveals that the Nazi Party was open with the German public about its policy of using propaganda in schools. However, newspapers were censored by the Nazis after Hitler became Chancellor in 1933. This means that Source A reveals how the Nazi Party hoped pupils and teachers would act, but it doesn't show how effectively Nazi education policies were carried out.

Exam-Style Questions

Q1
Explain why Nazi propaganda was effective.
You could mention censorship and traditional values in your answer.   [12 marks]

Q2
Explain how the lives of Jewish people in Germany were affected
by Nazi racial policies between 1933 and 1939.   [8 marks]

Q3
'German opposition to the Nazis between 1933 and
1939 didn't pose a significant threat to Hitler's regime.'

Explain how far you agree with this statement.   [18 marks]

Germany's War Economy

Hitler had always planned a <u>war</u> to provide <u>Lebensraum</u> (more space to live) for the German people. But Germany's economy <u>wasn't</u> at <u>full strength</u> when the <u>Second World War</u> broke out in 1939.

The **Nazi Economy** had to **Prepare** for **War**

1) Hitler transformed the German <u>economy</u> to prepare the country for war.

2) A <u>Four-Year Plan</u> was started in 1936, concentrating on <u>war preparations</u>. The Nazis needed to quickly build up industries making <u>weapons</u> and <u>chemicals</u>, and increase Germany's <u>agricultural output</u>.

3) <u>Hermann Göring</u> was put in charge of the <u>economy</u>. He aimed to make Germany <u>self-sufficient</u> — this meant producing enough goods to <u>not need</u> imports from other countries. ⟵

> Supplies to Germany had been blocked during the First World War, causing <u>severe shortages</u>. By becoming self-sufficient, Hitler hoped to <u>avoid</u> this problem in future wars.

4) Many workers were <u>retrained</u> to do jobs that would help the war effort, such as producing <u>weapons</u> and working in <u>chemical plants</u>.

5) But Hitler knew that ultimately Germany would need to <u>conquer</u> new territories and <u>capture</u> their <u>resources</u> to become genuinely <u>self-sufficient</u>.

The **Outbreak of War** forced **Changes** in the **Economy**

1) When war broke out in 1939, the German economy <u>wasn't ready</u>. More changes were needed.

2) A <u>quarter</u> of the workforce was already working in <u>war industries</u>, especially <u>weapons production</u>. Two years later this had become <u>three-quarters</u>.

3) A lot of German workers were <u>conscripted</u> into the army, so the Nazis had to use <u>foreign workers</u> to keep the economy going. This included <u>civilians</u> from occupied territories, <u>prisoners of war</u> and <u>slave labourers</u> — see p.167.

4) Eventually, in <u>1942</u>, after several years of fighting, Hitler put <u>Albert Speer</u> in charge of the <u>war economy</u>.

- Speer focused the economy completely on the <u>war effort</u>.
- He improved efficiency and greatly <u>increased</u> weapons production.
- Germany also used <u>raw materials</u> from <u>occupied lands</u> to support its production.

Daily Life in Germany was **Affected** by the **War**

Germans had to make <u>sacrifices</u> to help the war effort:

1) Wages were <u>less</u> than they had been before the Nazis took control and working hours <u>increased</u>.

2) <u>Rationing</u> affected people's <u>quality of life</u>. <u>Food</u> and <u>clothes</u> rationing began in <u>1939</u>, but while Germany was winning the war, most goods could still be bought easily.

- Rationing meant that some people ate <u>better</u> than they had before the war, though it soon became <u>impossible</u> to eat meat every day.
- Later in the war, things became <u>harder</u> for ordinary Germans. ⟵ By 1942, German civilians were living on rations of bread, vegetables and potatoes — these rations <u>decreased</u> as the war progressed (and were much less than British rations).

> <u>Toilet paper</u> and <u>soap</u> became difficult to get hold of too. And to save fuel, the use of <u>warm water</u> was restricted to two times per week. Germans also made use of '<u>ersatz</u>' (or '<u>substitute</u>') goods. For example, <u>ersatzkaffee</u> ('substitute coffee') was made from acorns or other types of seed.

3) More <u>women</u> and <u>children</u> had to work, especially after 1941 when German forces suffered some heavy defeats in Russia. By 1944, <u>50%</u> of the German workforce were women (up from 37% in 1939).

EXAM TIP

Life became more difficult for German civilians as the war went on

Remember that Germany was made up of diverse groups of people. Try to write about specific groups when explaining the impact of Nazi policies on people's lives.

The Impact of Total War

Food rationing was one thing. But the impact of <u>total war</u> on German civilians went way beyond that.

'Total War' involves **Soldiers** and **Civilians**

1) A lot of wars are fought between two <u>armies</u>. The term '<u>total war</u>', on the other hand, is often used to describe conflicts where <u>all</u> of a country's resources are considered part of the war effort.

2) So a total war is also a battle between countries' <u>economies</u>, their <u>scientists</u>, their <u>industries</u>, and their <u>civilians</u>. World War II is usually considered to have been a total war.

Germans were **More Heavily Affected** later in the war

1) After some <u>heavy defeats</u> in 1942, Germany prepared itself for <u>total war</u>. In a speech at the <u>Berlin Sportpalast</u> (sports arena) in February 1943, <u>Goebbels</u> stated: '<u>Total war</u> is the demand of the hour... The danger facing us is enormous. The <u>efforts</u> we take to meet it must be just as <u>enormous</u>... We can no longer make only partial and careless use of the war potential <u>at home</u> and in the <u>parts of Europe that we control</u>. We must use our <u>full resources</u>.'

> Hitler had hoped that the wars he was starting would be <u>short</u> (quick victories). This would have meant <u>less disruption</u> to normal life.

2) This meant that <u>all</u> of Germany's resources had to be directed to help with the <u>war effort</u>.

- <u>Non-essential</u> production (production that wasn't vital to the war effort) stopped, and small non-essential businesses closed. Workers were used in <u>war-related</u> industries instead.
- <u>Civilian clothes</u> and <u>consumer goods</u> were no longer manufactured.
- <u>Rationing</u> was a fact of life in Germany from the very start of the war (see p.164). Food supplies for ordinary families became much more <u>restricted</u> later on.
- More <u>women</u> were expected to <u>work</u> or join the <u>army</u>.

> German women never fought on the <u>front line</u> — they took mainly <u>clerical</u> and <u>administrative</u> roles. However, many women did help to operate Germany's <u>anti-aircraft</u> defences and served in <u>signals units</u> on the front line.

- Eventually, males between the ages of 13 and 60 who weren't already serving in the military had to join the <u>Volkssturm</u> — a part-time defence force (a sort of German 'Dad's Army').

Bombings Killed Thousands and left many more **Homeless**

1) From <u>1940</u>, Germany <u>rapidly prepared</u> for <u>bombing</u>. Hundreds of community <u>air raid shelters</u> were built.

2) <u>Auxiliary hospitals</u> and emergency <u>first-aid stations</u> were also established to care for civilian injuries.

3) From <u>1942</u>, the British and American air forces began bombing German cities more <u>heavily</u>. Around <u>half a million</u> German civilians were killed, and many more were made <u>homeless</u>.

4) Germany was later flooded with <u>refugees</u> from other <u>German territories</u> and from cities like Dresden, Berlin and Hamburg, which were all <u>heavily bombed</u>.

5) Germany struggled to deal with the growing number of <u>refugees</u>. There was <u>little help</u> for people displaced by the war — most struggled to find <u>food</u> and <u>shelter</u>.

> German cities were attacked using <u>incendiary bombs</u> — these were designed to cause huge <u>fires</u>. Hamburg and Dresden were both fire-bombed.

Dresden, after an Allied air raid in February 1945.

Germany had to throw everything behind the war effort

Remember, total war wasn't what the Nazis had wanted. They had hoped for short wars and prepared accordingly. But things hadn't gone at all as the Nazis had planned.

Growing Opposition

As the <u>war</u> went on, and especially as things started to go <u>worse</u> for Germany, <u>opposition</u> to Hitler grew.

There were some anti-Nazi **Protest Movements**

1) The <u>Kreisau Circle</u> was an anti-Nazi movement led by <u>Helmuth von Moltke</u> and <u>Yorck von Wartenburg</u>.

- The group was <u>against</u> violence, so they didn't <u>actively resist</u> the Nazis. Instead they discussed how to make Germany a <u>better country</u> after the Nazis had fallen. Some members of the Circle tried to <u>inform</u> Allied governments about the <u>dangers</u> and <u>weaknesses</u> of Nazi control.
- In <u>1944</u>, members of the Kreisau Circle, including <u>Moltke</u>, were <u>arrested</u> and <u>executed</u>.

2) The <u>Rosenstrasse protest</u> took place in Berlin after the authorities had rounded up some of the last Jewish men left in the city — many of them married to 'Aryan' German women.

- When the men's wives discovered what had happened, they went to the building in <u>Rosenstrasse</u> ('Rose Street') where their husbands were being held.
- For several days, the women gathered outside the building and <u>protested</u>. Eventually Goebbels ordered the Jewish men to be <u>released</u>.

Comment and Analysis

This was one of the few <u>successful</u> anti-Nazi public protests. It's thought that the men were released because Goebbels saw it as the <u>simplest way</u> to quickly end the protest without attracting too much attention. He also thought the Jews would soon be <u>killed</u> anyway.

3) Underground networks of <u>communists</u> operated in Germany after 1941. They mostly <u>gathered information</u> about Nazi brutality and <u>distributed leaflets</u>.

Some young people joined the **White Rose** group

1) The <u>White Rose</u> group (active between 1942 and 1943) was an opposition movement of students and lecturers from <u>Munich University</u>. Among the leaders were brother and sister <u>Hans</u> and <u>Sophie Scholl</u>.

2) Some male members of the group had served in the army and had been horrified by the <u>atrocities</u> carried out by the German army, including the <u>mass killing</u> of Jews.

3) The group used <u>non-violent</u> methods to protest against Nazi <u>discrimination</u> against <u>minorities</u> — they wrote anti-Nazi <u>graffiti</u> and distributed anti-Nazi <u>leaflets</u> to encourage opposition. In <u>1943</u>, the group organised the first <u>public</u> anti-Nazi <u>demonstration</u>.

4) Many of the group were later <u>arrested</u> by the Gestapo. Several were tortured and <u>executed</u>, including <u>Hans</u> and <u>Sophie Scholl</u>.

Comment and Analysis

At her trial, Sophie Scholl stated that everything she had written in the leaflets was also known by <u>many others</u>, but they <u>didn't dare</u> to say anything about it.

Resistance in the **Army** grew during the war

There had been <u>plots against Hitler</u> by army officers before the war. These became <u>more serious</u> when some became convinced Hitler was going to lead Germany to <u>defeat</u>.

July 1944 Plot

- One of the most famous army plots was the <u>July plot</u> of <u>1944</u>. <u>Claus von Stauffenberg</u> (along with other German officers) <u>planned</u> to <u>kill Hitler</u> and install a <u>moderate</u> government, which would include members of the Kreisau Circle.
- During a meeting, Stauffenberg left a <u>bomb</u> in a <u>briefcase</u> by Hitler's chair. However, someone <u>moved</u> the briefcase. The bomb exploded, but Hitler was <u>unhurt</u>.
- Most of the plotters were quickly <u>captured</u> and <u>executed</u>.

It wasn't easy to stand against the Nazis

Write a list of all of the acts of resistance mentioned on this page. For each one, write down a short summary of who the resistors were and whether they were successful or unsuccessful.

Nazi Rule in Eastern and Western Europe

The Nazis conquered territory to the west and east of Germany, but they didn't treat all areas equally.

Nazi rule in the **West** was **Relatively Humane**

1) Hitler had hoped to be able to quickly knock western European countries like France and Britain out of the war, before invading countries in the east to provide Germany with Lebensraum (see p.139). But the western countries didn't all surrender — e.g. Britain fought on. So a long occupation of Western countries followed.

2) Life in any Nazi-occupied country was far from pleasant, and Jews were especially persecuted in all territories under Nazi rule. But the Nazis didn't attempt to exterminate occupied countries' entire populations in the west. However, the Nazis would certainly respond brutally to any resistance, and arrests, detentions and imprisonment in concentration camps were common.

3) It was the resources of these occupied countries in the west that Germany most wanted — raw materials, agricultural produce, and industrial goods. This led to extreme shortages for the inhabitants of those countries.

4) Germany also needed manpower. Citizens of occupied countries were forced to work for the Nazis in Germany. The work was hard, but conditions were generally reasonable for workers from western Europe.

5) There were also other rules that people in occupied countries had to live by:

- Being hostile to Germans was forbidden.
- Listening to foreign propaganda or communicating with Germany's enemies was forbidden.
- Owning a weapon or a radio, taking photographs outdoors, gathering with other people without permission and displaying flags were all forbidden.

Nazi rule in the **East** was **Brutal** and **Cruel**

1) In occupied countries in eastern Europe, life could be much harder.

- The Nazis thought of the east as Lebensraum for the 'Aryan master race' — it was intended eventually to become part of the Greater Germanic Reich.

- This meant it had to be 'cleansed' of non-Aryan populations. Jews and Slavic populations (e.g. Poles and Russians) were especially targeted.

  > In 1939, Hitler told his commanders to kill 'without pity or mercy, all men, women, and children of Polish descent or language'.

- Although the Nazis thought some members of these populations might be suitable for 'Germanisation' (absorption into the German population), those considered unsuitable would be killed.

  > In 1940, Himmler said, 'All Poles will disappear from this world. It is imperative that the great German nation considers the elimination of all Polish people as its chief task'.

2) When Germany invaded the Soviet Union in 1941, Einsatzgruppen (see p.169) followed the German army with orders to kill every Jew they found.

3) Forced labourers from the east were essentially slaves, and endured terrible conditions. About 2 million non-Jewish Poles were forced into slave labour.

Comment and Analysis

The different treatment stemmed from the Nazis' belief that people in the west were of Germanic origin (they were 'Aryans', just like the Germans). People in the east, on the other hand, were thought to be 'biologically inferior'.

The Nazis didn't treat everyone in the same way

Write a paragraph comparing the how the Nazis ruled in Western Europe compared to how they ruled in Eastern Europe. In what ways were they the same, and in what ways were they different?

Responses to Nazi Rule

As the war went on, and especially as things started to go worse for Germany, opposition to Hitler grew.

People **Resisted** or **Collaborated** in different ways

1) There was some resistance to Nazi rule in Nazi-occupied Europe. Other people collaborated with the occupiers, and a lot of people just accommodated them (put up with them).

2) The types of action people took can be grouped into different categories:

Acts of Genuine Resistance

- These are actions that tried to hinder the Nazi war effort, or help Jews or the Nazis' enemies — using either violent or non-violent methods.

- French and Polish resistance movements supplied information to the countries fighting Germany, and disrupted German communications by destroying train lines and cutting telephone wires.

- Some people offered to hide Jews from the Nazis. For example, in the Netherlands, Anne Frank and her family hid for over two years with the aid of several helpers. These helpers would have known how serious the penalties were for hiding Jews, but they still chose to help.

- In some countries there was armed resistance by guerrilla movements (e.g. 'partisans' in eastern Europe).

- In some ghettos, underground movements supplied hot food to help the Jews survive the harsh conditions.

> Minor acts of resistance are sometimes called non-cooperation (e.g. workers in a factory deliberately working slowly).

- Jews sometimes rose up against the Nazis. For example, in the Warsaw ghetto in 1943, Jews launched an armed revolt against the Nazis. It took almost a month for the Nazis to regain control.

- Penalties for resistance varied between countries — e.g. people in Poland could expect to be more harshly treated than those in Denmark (see p.167).

Acts of Collaboration

- These are actions that helped the Nazis.

- Whole governments could collaborate (e.g. the Vichy government in southern France, which voluntarily persecuted Jews, deporting tens of thousands of them to Nazi death camps), or it could be individuals.

- Acts of collaboration ranged from doing German soldiers' laundry and denouncing fellow citizens, through to taking part in mass killings.

Acts of Accommodation

These are actions that didn't help the Nazis, but didn't do anything to hinder them or help their victims either. It's often called being a bystander.

People in occupied countries had a **Difficult Choice**

1) Given the scale of the crimes being committed by the Nazis, some people are surprised that more people didn't resist Nazi rule.

2) But not everyone would have been aware of what the Nazis were doing, and the penalties for resistance could be extremely harsh.

3) People faced a difficult choice — for example, they might have thought it more important to do what they could to look after their family than to resist the Nazis. Or they might just have wanted to survive the war.

> Primo Levi, a survivor of Auschwitz, has explained that resistance was especially difficult for Jews, partly because the Nazis had taken away any hope of rescue or of finding a place of safety.

Resistance was extremely risky and often futile

This course is partly about understanding people's lives and experiences — using what you've learnt, jot down a list of reasons for why some Germans might have accommodated the Nazis.

The Holocaust

The <u>Holocaust</u> is the name given to the <u>mass murder</u> of Jews by the Nazis. The Nazis built several <u>death camps</u> and used them to murder as many Jews as possible. They called this plan to kill Europe's Jews the '<u>final solution</u>'.

The **Final Solution** was the **Genocide** of Europe's Jews

1) Large numbers of German <u>Jews</u> had been sent to concentration camps since the Nazis came to power. After the conquest of countries in <u>western Europe</u>, many more Jews had been deported to camps. When Germany invaded Poland and the Soviet Union, even <u>more Jews</u> fell under Nazi control.

2) The Nazis planned to deport them to a <u>Jewish reservation</u> in German-occupied Poland — but the idea was dropped because the area couldn't possibly hold all of Europe's Jews. Instead Jews were to be <u>killed</u>. This was described as the '<u>final solution</u> to the Jewish question.'

3) As a temporary measure, the Nazis created <u>ghettos</u> — <u>small</u> areas of towns and cities where Jews were to be <u>gathered together</u>, away from the rest of the population.

4) Conditions in the ghettos were <u>terrible</u>. Many people died of <u>disease</u> or <u>starved</u>. Some were used for <u>slave labour</u>, e.g. in <u>weapons factories</u>.

5) After the Nazis invaded the Soviet Union, <u>Einsatzgruppen</u> followed the German army. These were units of SS soldiers whose job was to <u>murder</u> 'enemies' of the Nazi state in occupied eastern Europe. They were a key part of the final solution and killed in huge numbers, especially in <u>Poland</u> and the <u>Soviet Union</u>.

The largest ghetto was in Warsaw. In this picture, Jewish police are separating different members of the population.

Death Camps were built to **Kill People** on an **Industrial Scale**

1) To slaughter on the scale the Nazis required, <u>death camps</u> were built in Eastern Europe. <u>Heinrich Himmler</u>, head of the SS, was in overall charge of this operation.

2) The camps included <u>gas chambers</u> to carry out the <u>mass murder</u>, and <u>crematoria</u> to burn the bodies.

3) The plan was to kill around 11 million people — <u>all</u> of the Jews living in Nazi-controlled territory.

4) People were transported to the camps from <u>all over</u> Nazi-occupied Europe. They could take <u>luggage</u> and even <u>paid</u> for their own train tickets — the Nazis wanted to <u>hide</u> their intentions to prevent <u>panic</u>.

5) Mainly <u>Jewish</u> people were killed, but <u>other</u> groups were targeted as well, for example <u>Slavs</u> (e.g. Russians and Poles), <u>Romani</u>, <u>black people</u>, <u>homosexuals</u>, <u>disabled people</u> and <u>communists</u>.

It's **Hard** to understand **How** this **Mass Murder** happened

1) By the end of the war, the Nazis had killed approximately <u>6 million Jews</u> and countless other people.

2) Before the war ended, orders went out to <u>destroy</u> the camps — but there <u>wasn't</u> time.

3) After the war, people around the world found it <u>hard to believe</u> that this inhuman, cold-blooded extermination had taken place, and that <u>so many</u> soldiers were involved. It has been argued that they might have gone along with the Nazi leadership for various reasons:

- The Nazi guards felt they had to 'do their duty' and <u>obey orders</u>. They might have <u>feared</u> their leaders, or just felt that obeying orders was the <u>right thing</u> to do.

- Jews may not have been <u>regarded</u> as <u>fully human</u> — so killing them <u>didn't matter</u> to guards.

> **Comment and Analysis**
>
> The world only discovered the horror of the death camps as the Allies advanced in <u>1945</u>. Some historians claim there's evidence leaders like Churchill were <u>told</u> about the camps — but <u>didn't believe</u> the facts.

EXAM TIP

Historians continue to disagree about why the Holocaust took place

There is still a lot of disagreement about why the Holocaust happened, so it's important not to write down opinions as if they're facts. Remember to use evidence to support all of the points you make.

Exam-Style Questions

Q1 Describe two ways that Germany changed its economy to prepare for the outbreak of war in 1939.   [4 marks]

Q2 'Life in Nazi occupied countries was universally brutal and harsh.'

Explain how far you agree with this statement.   [18 marks]

Q3 What were the most important consequences of the Second World War for Germany between 1939 and 1945: economic consequences or social consequences?

Explain your answer, referring to both sets of consequences.   [12 marks]

Revision Summary

Well, that's Germany all wrapped up — now have a crack at a revision summary to see how much stuck.
- Try these questions and <u>tick off each one</u> when you <u>get it right</u>.
- When you've done <u>all the questions</u> for a topic and are <u>completely happy</u> with it, tick off the topic.

Germany and the Growth of Democracy, 1890-1929 (p.132-141) ☑

1) Describe how the government of the German Empire was structured under Kaiser Wilhelm.
2) Why did the Kaiser face difficulties ruling Germany between 1890 and 1914?
3) Describe the events of the German Revolution in 1918.
4) Name the three separate bodies of the Weimar government and describe what each one did.
5) Give five terms from the Treaty of Versailles and explain why they were unpopular in Germany.
6) Give two examples of unrest that occurred under the Weimar Republic between 1919 and 1922.
7) What was the Munich Putsch? Why did it fail?
8) How did Gustav Stresemann try to build better international relationships?
9) How did life improve for the working classes and women under the Weimar Republic?

Hitler's Rise to Power, 1929-1934 (p.145-148) ☑

10) What was the Great Depression?
11) Describe the trends in federal election results in Germany between 1928 and 1932.
12) Give three examples of social groups that were particularly drawn to the Nazis and explain why.
13) Describe how Hitler rose to the position of Chancellor.
14) What was the Enabling Act? When was it introduced?
15) What happened on the 'Night of the Long Knives'?

The Experiences of Germans Under the Nazis, 1933-1939 (p.151-158) ☑

16) Describe three powers the Nazis had that suggested Germany had become a police state by 1934.
17) What were the aims of Nazi propaganda?
18) What was the Reich Church?
19) Name two members of the Church who opposed the Nazis.
20) What expectations did the Nazi Party have of women?
21) Give three ways that the Nazi regime affected the lives of German workers between 1933 and 1939.
22) How was education in Germany affected while the Nazis were in power?
23) What were the Nuremberg Laws? Why were they important?
24) Describe the events of Kristallnacht.

The Second World War, 1939-1945 (p.164-169) ☑

25) What changes were made to the Nazi economy after the outbreak of World War Two?
26) What is 'total war'? How did it affect German civilians?
27) Who was Claus von Stauffenberg? What did he do to oppose Nazi rule?
28) Describe three different ways that people in Europe reacted to Nazi occupation.
29) What is a ghetto? Describe the role of ghettos in the Holocaust.
30) What was the role of Einsatzgruppen?
31) Name four groups of people who were targeted for execution in the Nazi death camps.

The Grand Alliance

The Grand Alliance was made up of the 'big three' allies from World War Two — Britain, the USA and the USSR. They were united by their desire to defeat Nazi Germany, but as the war ended, tensions emerged.

The 'Big Three' discussed Europe's Future at Tehran and Yalta

1) In 1943, the Grand Alliance held a conference in Tehran. The talks focused mainly on plans to defeat the Nazis. But the allies also started to discuss what would happen to Europe and Germany after the war.

2) Britain and the USA were politically very different from the USSR and there were tensions between the three allies. These were put aside during the war as they fought a common enemy (Germany).

3) The British Prime Minister Winston Churchill and US President Franklin D. Roosevelt agreed the USSR could claim a 'sphere of influence' in Eastern Europe after the war was over. Eastern European countries would be subject to Soviet policies and ideas.

> The USSR (Union of Soviet Socialist Republics) was also known as the Soviet Union.

4) The Grand Alliance made more decisions about the future of Europe at the Yalta Conference in February 1945:

- Free elections would be held in previously occupied countries in Eastern Europe.
- The United Nations (UN) would replace the failed League of Nations.

Comment and Analysis

The allies had different interpretations of a 'free' election. To the USA and Britain, it meant lots of political parties competing for votes. But Stalin (the leader of the USSR) believed only communist parties should run in elections as they were the only parties that truly represented the people.

Potsdam revealed the First Cracks in the Grand Alliance

1) After Germany surrendered in May 1945, the allied leaders met again at Potsdam over July and August.

2) They wanted to work on the finer details of their plans for Germany and Europe. Some important agreements were made at Potsdam:

- The new boundaries of Poland were agreed.
- The 'big three' plus France would divide Germany and Berlin between them.
- Nazi leaders would be tried for war crimes at Nuremberg.

3) Some things remained undecided. For example, Germany would be divided into four zones (one each for Britain, France, the USA and the USSR) — but the allies didn't decide if, or when, the zones could rejoin and form a country again.

> Britain also had a new leader — Clement Attlee replaced Churchill mid-conference.

4) Tensions were high. Roosevelt had died and Harry Truman had succeeded him as US President — Truman was more suspicious of the USSR and less willing to compromise.

5) Britain and the US were also alarmed by Stalin's actions in Poland — he had installed a government consisting of only pro-communist members. Britain and the US felt this went against the Yalta agreement.

The USA and the USSR had very Different Ideologies

The tension between the USA and the USSR was partly caused by their very different beliefs — the USSR was communist, while the USA was capitalist. Both countries also feared the other's intentions.

1) Communism meant state control of industry and agriculture. The USA, by contrast, valued private enterprise — the 'American Dream' was that anyone could work their way to the top.

2) The USSR only allowed one political party — the Communist Party. The USA valued political freedom.

3) Communism aimed at world revolution, and so it was seen by Americans as a danger to their democracy. However, the communists also feared worldwide American influence.

REVISION TASK

'East' and 'West' had different perspectives

Summarise how tension developed in the Grand Alliance between 1943 and August 1945. Include how the allies' relationships altered and why their attitudes changed.

The Two Superpowers

The USSR and the USA emerged from the Second World War as the two biggest powers in the world. But they were very suspicious of one another, and began to interpret each other's actions as threats.

The USA kept their Atom Bomb a Secret

1) Japan was on Germany's side in the war, and continued to fight after Germany surrendered in May 1945. In August 1945, the USA dropped two atom bombs on Japan — destroying the cities of Hiroshima and Nagasaki.

2) The atom bombs meant that military help from the USSR wasn't needed to defeat Japan. President Truman also refused to allow the USSR to take part in the US occupation of Japan.

3) The USA had kept the exact nature of the atom bomb a secret from the USSR at Potsdam in July 1945 (although Stalin's spies had passed on many details).

The atom bomb caused devastation in Hiroshima.

4) These nuclear weapons boosted the status of the USA. For four years it was the world's only nuclear power. Stalin saw the development of the atom bomb as an attempt to intimidate the USSR, and was angry that the USA had managed to surpass Soviet technology.

5) The atom bombs increased the rivalry between the USA and the USSR. The USSR sped up the development of its own atomic bomb, starting an arms race between the two countries (see p.176).

The USSR became Influential in Eastern Europe

1) At the end of the Second World War, the Red Army (the USSR's army) occupied Eastern Europe. These countries would pass into the USSR's sphere of influence after the war.

2) Between 1945 and 1948, Stalin installed pro-Soviet 'puppet' governments in Poland, Hungary, Romania, Bulgaria and Czechoslovakia.

- For a while it seemed that Czechoslovakia might remain democratic. But when the Communist Party seemed likely to lose ground in the next election, it seized power in February 1948.

- The exception to Soviet domination was Yugoslavia, which had freed itself from the Germans without the Red Army. Yugoslavia was communist but more open to the West. Its leader, Tito, argued with Stalin over political interference. Stalin cut off aid but didn't invade.

An 'Iron Curtain' Between East and West

- Increasing tensions between the USA and the USSR became known as the 'Cold War'. There was no direct fighting — both sides were afraid of another war, especially after 1949, when the USSR had its own nuclear weapons.

- Countries in Western Europe tended to support the USA. Most countries in Eastern Europe were dominated by the USSR. In a famous speech in 1946, Winston Churchill warned there was an 'Iron Curtain' dividing Europe.

Comment and Analysis

Churchill's 'Iron Curtain' speech demonstrates the breakdown of the Grand Alliance — Britain and the USA now viewed the USSR as a threat, not an ally.

Countries under the influence of the USSR became known as its 'satellite states' (in pink).

EXAM TIP

Tensions were growing between the two superpowers

In the exam, try to explain people's actions by considering the way they would have looked at a situation. Here, each country is acting for reasons that made sense to the people in charge.

Mutual Suspicion

The <u>Cold War</u> was a period of international tension — with each side <u>suspicious</u> of the other.

The 'Long' and 'Novikov' telegrams were detailed Reports

1) By 1946, tensions between the superpowers were <u>high</u>. Each country issued <u>secret telegrams</u> about the other. The 1946 telegrams were detailed reports describing the <u>motivations</u> and <u>intentions</u> of the other country.

The Long Telegram (February)

- Issued to <u>President Truman</u> about the USSR.
- It said that Stalin had given a speech in favour of the <u>destruction</u> of capitalism.
- It warned of the USSR trying to <u>weaken</u> and <u>divide</u> Western powers, while building the strength of its own military.

The Novikov Telegram (September)

- Issued to <u>Stalin</u> about the USA.
- The report claimed that the USA was pursuing <u>world supremacy</u>.
- It warned that the USA was trying to <u>limit the influence</u> of the USSR in Europe.

2) Neither country seemed to know for certain what the other was thinking. The reports <u>panicked</u> the Russian and American governments and <u>accelerated</u> the Cold War — the findings seemed to confirm their <u>worst fears</u>.

Truman Acted to Contain the Communist Threat

President Truman was extremely <u>worried</u> about the spread of communism to <u>Western Europe</u>. Many countries were undergoing <u>economic hardships</u>, which he thought might make communism look more <u>appealing</u>. The USA decided to <u>intervene</u> in Europe to try and <u>contain</u> the spread of communism.

The Truman Doctrine (Announced March 1947)

The USA pledged to <u>support</u> any nation threatened by a <u>communist takeover</u>. This support could be diplomatic, military or financial. For example, the USA gave $400 million of <u>aid</u> to <u>Turkey</u> and <u>Greece</u> to <u>stop</u> communism spreading.

The Marshall Plan (Announced June 1947)

This promised $17 billion of <u>aid</u> to European countries to help <u>rebuild</u> their <u>economies</u> — the areas of Germany under Western occupation benefited massively. Stalin, however, ordered all of his <u>satellite states</u> to <u>reject the plan</u>. He believed the USA was using <u>economic incentives</u> to lure Eastern European states away from the USSR.

The USSR Reacted by creating the Cominform

Stalin felt threatened by the Truman Doctrine, and reacted by <u>strengthening</u> and <u>uniting</u> his allies.

1) **The Cominform** (Communist Information Bureau) was set up in 1947. The organisation <u>brought together</u> all European communist parties and placed them <u>under the control</u> of the USSR.

2) **The Comecon** (the Council for Mutual Economic Assistance) was established in 1949. It countered the Marshall Plan by <u>nationalising</u> industries, <u>collectivising</u> agriculture and offering <u>economic aid</u>.

Comment and Analysis

Marshall Plan aid ensured that a lot of Western Europe became <u>allied</u> with the USA. Stalin's retaliation — his creation of the Cominform and, later, the Comecon — <u>strengthened</u> his alliances in Eastern Europe.

Stalin hoped this would <u>encourage</u> economic development in Eastern Europe and discourage trade with the <u>West</u>. It also <u>appeased</u> the countries that had been ordered to refuse Marshall aid.

 REVISION TASK

Each side viewed the other's actions with deep suspicion

In your own words, summarise what the USA and the USSR believed about each other after the Long and Novikov Telegrams were sent, and how this might have affected their actions.

The Berlin Crisis

Tension over the division of Germany had been building since the Potsdam Conference, and finally spilled over in the Berlin crisis in 1948. It resulted in an even larger rift between the two great powers.

In 1948 the USSR and the West Clashed over Berlin

1) Immediately after the war, there were four zones of occupied Germany, and four zones in Berlin. In 1947, the USA and Britain agreed to combine their zones to form 'Bizonia'. The next year, the French agreed to add their zone.

2) The new western zone had a single government, and in June 1948 introduced a new currency to help economic recovery.

3) This alarmed the USSR. Stalin did not want a unified western zone on his doorstep. West Berlin's strong capitalist economy embarrassed the USSR, and made communism look weak.

4) As a result, Stalin decided to blockade Berlin to try to force the West to withdraw from West Berlin. In June 1948, he ordered that all road, rail and canal links between West Berlin and the outside world should be cut off.

In East Germany (controlled by USSR)

Berlin was in East Germany. The French, British and US sectors formed West Berlin, while the Soviet sector was called East Berlin.

The Western Powers Wouldn't Give Up West Berlin...

- The West decided to bypass the blockade and fly in supplies. This became known as the Berlin Airlift, and lasted for 318 days.
- By 1949, 8000 tons of supplies were being flown in each day.
- Tegel airport was built in West Berlin to accommodate the large volume of flights. It meant supplies could be delivered in even greater numbers.

Stalin wanted to force the West to withdraw from Berlin altogether. The Western powers believed that if this happened, the Soviet Union would be tempted to invade West Germany.

The end of the Berlin blockade increased tensions as Stalin hadn't lifted the blockade willingly. The allies appeared strong, and had discredited and humiliated Stalin.

... so Stalin was Forced to End the Blockade

- When it became clear that the West was determined not to withdraw from Berlin, Stalin had to lift the blockade. It was also clear that Germany would remain divided.
- In 1949, two separate states were formed — West Germany (Federal Republic of Germany) and communist East Germany (German Democratic Republic).

The Two Powers formed Military Alliances

1) Stalin's blockade during the Berlin crisis showed how unprepared the West would be if there was a conflict with the USSR.

2) As a consequence, the Western Powers decided to form a military alliance. In 1949, NATO (the North Atlantic Treaty Organisation) was created.

3) All members of NATO agreed to respond together if any member of the alliance was attacked.

The USSR saw the formation of NATO as a real threat.

- In 1955, the USSR established the Warsaw Pact to rival NATO. All the USSR's satellite states (except Yugoslavia) became members.
- Its main aims were to improve the defensive capability of Eastern Europe and strengthen relations.
- There were now two power blocs in Europe — NATO and the Warsaw Pact.

Members of the Warsaw Pact formed the so-called 'Eastern Bloc'.

REVISION TASK

The Berlin Crisis embarrassed Stalin

Look at the events that took place between 1945 and the founding of NATO in 1949. Write a summary explaining which you think was most important in worsening relations between the two superpowers.

The Arms Race

In the Cold War, the USA and the USSR tried to gain an advantage by forming <u>military alliances</u> and developing ever more <u>powerful weapons</u>. The aim was to 'look strong' to <u>deter</u> the other from attacking.

The **USA** and the **USSR** began an **Arms Race**

1) During the Cold War, the USA and the USSR worked to develop the most powerful weapons they could — there was an <u>arms race</u>.

2) Neither side really wanted to <u>use</u> these weapons, but <u>both</u> felt the other <u>couldn't</u> be allowed to gain an <u>advantage</u>. The fear was that if either gained a <u>significant</u> military advantage, that country might be tempted to trigger a war to take advantage of it.

3) Instead, a <u>stand-off</u> developed where both countries <u>didn't dare</u> act against the other, but didn't dare get '<u>left behind</u>', either.

4) This <u>competition</u> sometimes spilled over into other areas. For example, when the USSR launched the first satellite into space, the USA quickly developed one of its own. This '<u>space race</u>' led to the USSR sending the <u>first</u> man into space in 1961, and to the USA sending astronauts to the <u>Moon</u> in 1969.

Both countries developed **Nuclear Stockpiles**

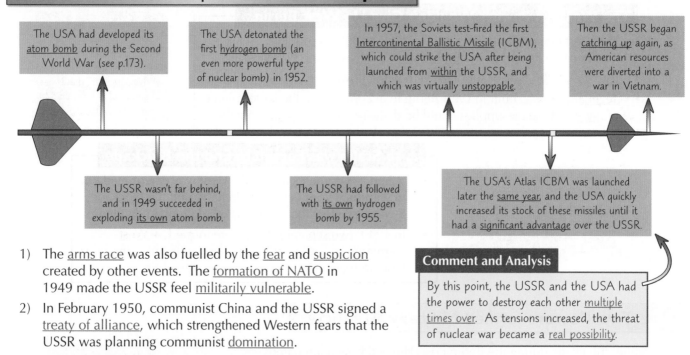

The USA had developed its <u>atom bomb</u> during the Second World War (see p.173).

The USA detonated the first <u>hydrogen bomb</u> (an even more powerful type of nuclear bomb) in 1952.

In 1957, the Soviets test-fired the first <u>Intercontinental Ballistic Missile</u> (ICBM), which could strike the USA after being launched from <u>within</u> the USSR, and which was virtually <u>unstoppable</u>.

Then the USSR began <u>catching up</u> again, as American resources were diverted into a war in Vietnam.

The USSR wasn't far behind, and in 1949 succeeded in exploding <u>its own</u> atom bomb.

The USSR had followed with <u>its own</u> hydrogen bomb by 1955.

The USA's Atlas ICBM was launched later the <u>same year</u>, and the USA quickly increased its stock of these missiles until it had a <u>significant advantage</u> over the USSR.

1) The <u>arms race</u> was also fuelled by the <u>fear</u> and <u>suspicion</u> created by other events. The <u>formation of NATO</u> in 1949 made the USSR feel <u>militarily vulnerable</u>.

2) In February 1950, communist China and the USSR signed a <u>treaty of alliance</u>, which strengthened Western fears that the USSR was planning communist <u>domination</u>.

Comment and Analysis

By this point, the USSR and the USA had the power to destroy each other <u>multiple times over</u>. As tensions increased, the threat of nuclear war became a <u>real possibility</u>.

Khrushchev raised hopes of **'Peaceful Co-existence'**

In 1953, Stalin <u>died</u> and another member of the Communist Party, <u>Nikita Khrushchev</u>, took power.

Comment and Analysis

Because Khrushchev continued to develop weapons, the West still felt <u>threatened</u> and the arms race <u>didn't</u> slow down.

1) Khrushchev said he wanted '<u>peaceful co-existence</u>' with the West. His words brought hope that there would be a '<u>thaw</u>' in the Cold War.

2) But Khrushchev remained <u>very competitive</u> with the USA.

3) He wanted communism to spread, but thought the best way to achieve this was to clearly demonstrate its <u>superiority</u> — not defeat the West in a war.

The rivalry between the USA and the USSR kept on going

When answering an exam question, always remember to give evidence to back up your points.

Divisions in Eastern Europe

Not all of the USSR's satellite states had <u>willingly</u> accepted communism, and the USSR soon faced unrest.

Unrest began to Stir in the Eastern Bloc

1) When Khrushchev came to power, he made a speech <u>criticising</u> Stalin's policies and brought in measures to '<u>de-Stalinise</u>' the USSR. These included the <u>abolition</u> of the <u>death penalty</u> and the <u>freeing</u> of <u>political prisoners</u> jailed under Stalin's regime.

> Communism created a lot of <u>economic hardship</u> — poor living conditions increased <u>anti-Soviet</u> sentiment.

2) Some satellite states hoped that their countries would also become 'de-Stalinised'. Khrushchev abolished the <u>Cominform</u> (see p.174), meaning that states in Eastern Europe would have more <u>political</u> and <u>economic freedom</u> from the USSR.

> Khrushchev wanted the Eastern Bloc to remain <u>communist</u> — he just <u>didn't agree</u> with Stalin's approach to communism. He thought that giving satellite states more <u>economic independence</u> would <u>stabilise</u> their communist regimes, but his plan <u>backfired</u>.

3) These moves allowed <u>tensions</u> in the <u>satellite states</u> to rise to the surface. Not all states had <u>chosen</u> communism, and saw the changes as a chance to <u>loosen</u> ties with the USSR.

4) In 1956, there was an <u>uprising</u> in Poland. The USSR threatened to intervene, but eventually allowed the new government to follow their <u>own version</u> of communism. This <u>encouraged</u> other states to consider revolt.

The USSR used the Hungarian Uprising to send a Message

1) After the Second World War, the USSR helped put <u>Mátyás Rákosi</u>, a brutal Stalinist, in charge of Hungary. His <u>authoritarian</u> regime became increasingly unpopular. In October 1956, the people of Budapest <u>protested</u> against the government of Rákosi.

2) Khrushchev <u>allowed</u> the liberal <u>Imre Nagy</u> to take over from Rákosi as Hungarian Prime Minister. Nagy hoped that Hungary could be a <u>neutral state</u>.

- In November 1956, Nagy announced that Hungary would <u>withdraw</u> from the Warsaw Pact and hold free elections — <u>ending communism</u> there.

- If Hungary was allowed to <u>turn away</u> from communism, other satellite states might do the same. The USSR felt it had to respond with <u>force</u> and make an <u>example</u> of Nagy.

- Khrushchev, who had only held power for <u>two years</u>, wanted to use the crisis to <u>assert</u> his <u>authority</u>.

- Soviet tanks <u>invaded</u> Hungary in November 1956. Thousands of Hungarians were <u>killed</u> or <u>wounded</u>. Nagy was <u>arrested</u> and <u>hanged</u>. János Kádár became Prime Minister and ensured <u>loyalty</u> to the USSR.

The Crisis Strengthened the USSR and Discredited the West

- Khrushchev's brutal response to Hungary demonstrated to satellite states that disloyalty <u>wouldn't</u> be tolerated. It also showed the Western powers that the USSR was <u>still in control</u>.

> The Western powers' reputation as upholders of democracy was <u>discredited</u>. Their <u>inaction</u> sent a clear message to Eastern Europe that they <u>wouldn't</u> receive Western help to move away from the USSR. The UN was shown to be <u>weak</u>.

- It was a <u>turning point</u> for Khrushchev — his actions <u>reasserted his authority</u> over the satellite states and destroyed any <u>illusions</u> in the West that his leadership signified a '<u>thaw</u>' in the Cold War.

- There was a <u>lack of intervention</u> from Western countries. They <u>condemned</u> the USSR's actions, but thought that helping Hungary would risk a <u>nuclear war</u>.

- The UN asked the USSR to <u>withdraw</u> from Hungary, but Kádár refused to take part in discussions. The situation remained <u>unresolved</u>.

The USSR kept a tight hold on its satellite states

REVISION TASK

Using information on this page and your own knowledge, write a list of ways in which Khrushchev was different to Stalin and another list of ways in which he was similar.

Worked Exam-Style Question

This sample answer will give you an idea of how to write an answer that explains the importance of something. Look at how each paragraph builds on the argument that's been introduced in the opening paragraph.

Q1 Analyse the significance of the creation of NATO (1949) for the progression of the Cold War. [8 marks]

This addresses the question in the <u>first sentence</u>.

<u>The creation of NATO in 1949 after the Berlin Crisis played a significant role in strengthening the divide between East and West</u> and worsening the severity of the Cold War.

The formation of NATO made the Western powers seem more threatening to the USSR, since there was now an agreement in place that would help them to act together if the USSR attacked a member state. <u>As a result, the USSR felt more intimidated by the Western powers, so it created its own military alliance with its satellite states (except Yugoslavia) through the Warsaw Pact in 1955.</u> This was significant for the progression of the Cold War, because it <u>worsened the relationship between the USA and the USSR, as both countries increasingly interpreted each other's actions as threatening</u>.

This makes it clear that <u>one development led to another</u>.

This explains how this <u>consequence</u> of the creation of NATO <u>strengthened the divide</u> between the East and West.

<u>The creation of NATO also resulted in the formation of two distinct sides in the Cold War.</u> The Western powers were united through NATO, while <u>the Warsaw Pact united the USSR and its satellite states, creating the Eastern bloc</u>. This increased the scale of the Cold War, as there were now two rival groups of powers that were bound by military alliances to act against one another if either side attacked the other. This created a more formal military division between the East and West and increased the risk of active conflict between the two sides.

Use <u>relevant knowledge</u> to back up your points.

This introduces <u>another reason</u> why NATO was <u>significant</u> for the progression of the Cold War.

<u>Another significant consequence of the creation of NATO was that it contributed to the arms race, which heightened the intensity of the Cold War.</u> Because the military alliance of the Western powers through NATO made the USSR feel more vulnerable, it invested more in trying to beat the USA in the arms race. As the arms race escalated, the USA and USSR became increasingly heavily armed. <u>This made the Cold War more dangerous by further increasing the chances that it would develop into an active conflict</u>.

This explains <u>why</u> this <u>consequence</u> was <u>significant</u>.

This introduces <u>another key factor</u> that's <u>relevant</u> to the issue in the question.

This gives a <u>clear answer</u> to the question.

Overall, <u>the creation of NATO was significant to the progression of the Cold War, because it formalised the division between the East and West</u>. It also increased the fear and tension that divided the USA and the USSR, resulting in the acceleration of the arms race, <u>which further divided the East and West and increased the risk of active conflict</u>.

This <u>sums up</u> why NATO was <u>significant</u> for the progression of the Cold War.

Exam-Style Questions

Q1
> Give two consequences of the Truman Doctrine (1947) and explain them. [8 marks]

Q2
> Examine:
>
> a) the significance of the Berlin Crisis (1948-49) for the progression of the Cold War. [8 marks]
>
> b) the significance of the arms race for the relationship between the USSR and the USA. [8 marks]

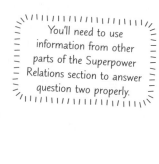

You'll need to use information from other parts of the Superpower Relations section to answer question two properly.

Q3
> Give an account examining the events that led to the Hungarian Uprising in 1956.
>
> You could mention the Cominform and 'de-Stalinisation' in your answer. [8 marks]

The Berlin Question

The 1950s saw more communication between the two superpowers, but underlying tensions remained.

There were some Steps to Improve East-West Relations...

President Eisenhower succeeded President Truman in January 1953, while Khrushchev came to power in September. This provided an opportunity to create a fresh start — there were several encouraging steps towards defusing tensions between the two powers:

- The USA and the USSR met in Geneva in 1955 and agreed to communicate more openly.
- In 1955, the USSR officially recognised the Federal Republic of Germany (West Germany) as a state.
- Khrushchev also freed some prisoners and reduced censorship in the USSR.

...but Berlin remained a Source of Tension

1) After the Berlin crisis in 1948 (see p.175), West Berlin was a unified zone and continued to develop economically, benefiting from a new currency and American (Marshall Plan) aid.

2) The situation in East Berlin was very different — the USSR had drained it of resources and its economy was slow to develop. Many people wanted to leave and go to the more prosperous West Berlin instead.

> By 1961, at least 3 million East Germans had emigrated from East Berlin to West Berlin.

3) The situation was hugely embarrassing for Khrushchev, as it suggested that people preferred life under capitalism to communism.

4) It also threatened East Germany's economy, as many of those who left were skilled workers in search of a better life.

5) The refugee crisis in Berlin led Khrushchev to issue his 'Berlin Ultimatum' in 1958. He demanded that US, British and French troops leave West Berlin within six months. West Berlin would become a free city.

6) Eisenhower refused the ultimatum. Khrushchev took no further action, but the Berlin issue wasn't solved.

Soviet Attitudes Towards Berlin

- The USSR felt threatened by the economic success in West Berlin.
- East Berlin had become dependent on trade links with West Berlin.
- The USSR worried the West was trying to use its strong economy to interfere in Eastern Europe.

Western Attitudes Towards Berlin

- After the Berlin Airlift, West Berlin became a symbol of democracy — it had to be supported or the West would lose credibility.
- People fleeing from East Berlin suited the West — it was good propaganda because it made communism look weak.

Khrushchev and Eisenhower held a Summit in 1959

1) In 1959, Khrushchev became the first communist leader to visit the USA. The meeting symbolised a new spirit of co-operation and communication between the two powers.

2) At the meeting they discussed Berlin. Eisenhower still didn't agree to withdraw from West Berlin, but did agree to discuss the matter more deeply.

3) The leaders decided to meet in Paris the following year. Although no firm decisions had been made, the arrangement of another summit promised to continue the optimistic dialogue they had started.

Both superpowers refused to compromise on Berlin

You need to show you understand how events are connected. Here you could show how the superpowers' attitudes towards Berlin were shaped by the Airlift or West Berlin's economic success.

The Berlin Wall

In 1961, around 2000 Germans crossed over from East to West Berlin every day. When it became clear that the situation wasn't going to be solved diplomatically, Khrushchev constructed the Berlin Wall.

Talks about Berlin **Broke Down**...

President Eisenhower and Khrushchev had agreed to discuss the Berlin question at the Paris Summit in 1960. Days before the summit was due to take place, the USSR shot down a U2 American spy plane over Soviet territory.

1) Eisenhower denied that it was a spy plane, but the USSR then produced the pilot (alive) and the plane's wreckage as evidence. When the USA refused to apologise, Khrushchev walked out of the Paris Summit.

2) The U2 incident hindered further negotiations about Berlin. Both countries met again at Vienna in June 1961 — by this time, John F. Kennedy had replaced Eisenhower as US President.

3) Kennedy vowed to take a tougher approach towards communism. He refused to compromise over Berlin, and no resolution was reached.

> **Comment and Analysis**
>
> After the Vienna Summit, the USSR believed that problems in Berlin wouldn't be resolved by negotiation. This sparked the creation of the Berlin Wall.

...so the **Berlin Wall** was **Put Up**

1) Khrushchev felt he had to act to stem the flow of refugees out of East Berlin. On 13th August 1961, a 27-mile barrier was built across the city of Berlin overnight, separating East from West.

2) It was fortified with barbed wire and machine gun posts, and was later strengthened and made into a more permanent barrier. Military checkpoints policed any movements into or out of East Berlin.

3) Before the wall, East Berliners had entered West Berlin freely. After the wall, they could no longer go to work in West Berlin and were instantly separated from friends and relatives.

4) Citizens from East and West Berlin were rarely allowed through the military checkpoints and anyone who tried to escape East Berlin was shot.

A photo of the newly-built Berlin Wall.

The **Berlin Wall** helped **Stabilise** the situation in **Europe**

After the Berlin Wall was put up, Cold War tensions over Berlin stabilised. The West condemned Khrushchev, but was actually relieved:

> 'It's not a very nice solution, but a wall is a hell of a lot better than a war.' — President Kennedy, 1961.

- Immediately after the Berlin Wall appeared, Soviet and Western troops were positioned either side of the wall, but then both powers agreed to back down.
- The USA condemned the building of the wall, but took no further military action.
- Kennedy was actually relieved — he'd been preparing for a confrontation of some sort.

1) The wall succeeded in stopping mass emigration to West Berlin. It also gave East Germany the opportunity to rebuild its economy, and strengthen itself as a communist state.

2) In the West, the Berlin Wall became a symbol of oppression and the failure of communism. In the USSR, it was seen as a sign of strength.

3) President Kennedy visited West Berlin in 1963 and gave a famous speech stating his solidarity with West Berlin and its people. He declared 'Ich bin ein Berliner' (I am a Berliner).

REVISION TASK

The wall confirmed the divide between East and West Berlin

Write a summary of the events that led to the construction of the Berlin Wall in 1961. Then make a list of all of the consequences of the wall's construction.

The Cuban Missile Crisis

As tension was increasing over Berlin, the USA also began to have problems closer to home. <u>Cuba</u> had long been the USA's economic <u>ally</u>, but revolution brought the <u>communist threat</u> to the USA's doorstep.

The **Cuban Revolution** in 1959 **Worried** the USA

1) Since 1952, Cuba had been <u>ruled</u> by Batista, a ruthless military <u>dictator</u>, who allowed American businessmen and the Mafia to make <u>huge profits</u> in a country where <u>most people</u> lived in <u>poverty</u>.

2) In 1956, a rebel called <u>Fidel Castro</u> began a <u>guerrilla war</u>. By 1959, he had enough support to take Cuba's capital, Havana, and <u>successfully</u> overthrew the government.

> In a '<u>guerrilla war</u>', small military units use tactics like <u>raids</u> to fight a larger opponent.

3) This revolution <u>worried</u> the USA. The USA had a long <u>economic history</u> with Cuba. It owned <u>half</u> of Cuba's land and held most of the <u>shares</u> in all <u>Cuban industries</u>.

4) The USA felt it had a <u>right</u> to be <u>involved</u> in Cuba's affairs. But Cubans had grown to <u>resent</u> American influence in their country — they didn't feel like an <u>independent</u> state.

> The USA had <u>occupied</u> Cuba from 1898 to 1902. When Cuba became <u>independent</u>, the two countries maintained <u>close economic ties</u>.

The USA **Accidentally** pushed Castro **Closer** to the **USSR**

1) When Castro seized power in 1959, he <u>nationalised US companies</u> and <u>increased taxes</u> on goods <u>imported</u> from <u>America</u>. This angered the USA.

> 'Nationalisation' means taking a <u>privately owned industry</u> and placing it under <u>public ownership</u>.

2) Eisenhower was concerned that Castro's drive towards <u>public ownership</u> showed that he was <u>moving towards communism</u>.

3) He threatened to <u>stop importing</u> Cuban sugar. Sugar was Cuba's <u>main</u> source of wealth, and the USA was sure that Castro would <u>back down</u>.

4) Instead, Castro signed a <u>trade agreement</u> with the <u>USSR</u> — the USSR promised to buy all sugar exports. All remaining American <u>property</u> in Cuba was <u>confiscated</u>.

5) In January 1961, the USA <u>severed</u> all <u>diplomatic relations</u> with Cuba — the new US President John Kennedy no longer <u>recognised</u> Castro's government.

Comment and Analysis

Khrushchev wanted to <u>help</u> Castro, who was <u>sympathetic</u> towards communism. He also saw an opportunity to <u>gain influence</u> near US soil.

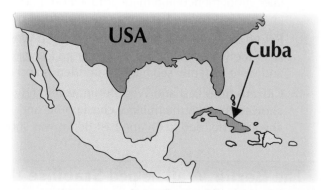

By 1961, Cuba had consolidated its ties with the USSR. As Cuba was only 100 miles from the USA, the communist threat had come dangerously close.

Rebels backed by the USA **Invaded Cuba** at the **Bay of Pigs**

Kennedy couldn't let a <u>communist state</u> emerge <u>next to</u> America — he <u>intervened</u>.

- In 1961, Kennedy authorised an <u>invasion</u> of Cuba by anti-Castro rebels.
- In April 1961, the rebels landed in the <u>Bay of Pigs</u>, but they were easily <u>defeated</u> and the USA didn't help — it was a bit of a <u>fiasco</u>.
- The USA was <u>humiliated</u>, and had pushed Cuba <u>even closer</u> to the USSR.

The Cuban Missile Crisis

Khrushchev agreed to help Castro and began to build nuclear missile sites in Cuba.

Tensions continued to Grow

1) The Bay of Pigs Invasion (see p.182) led Castro to decide that Cuba needed Soviet military assistance to defend itself. This sparked one of the biggest crises of the Cold War — the Cuban Missile Crisis.

2) In December 1961, Castro publicly announced that he was a communist, confirming US fears.

Khrushchev planned to put Nuclear Missiles in Cuba

1) In September 1961, Cuba asked the USSR for weapons to defend itself against further American intervention. By July 1962, Khrushchev had decided to put nuclear missiles in Cuba.

2) Although Khrushchev already had missiles that could reach the USA, missiles in Cuba would allow him to launch a nuclear attack on all of central and eastern USA with very little warning.

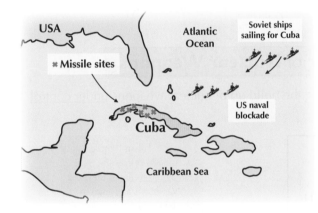

3) In October 1962, American U2 spy planes spotted that nuclear missile bases were being built in Cuba.

4) President Kennedy demanded that Khrushchev dismantle the missile bases and ordered a naval blockade of Cuba. All Soviet ships were to be stopped and searched to prevent missiles being transported to the island.

5) As tensions grew, US bombers were put in the air carrying nuclear bombs and the USA prepared to invade Cuba. The world was on the brink of nuclear war.

Khrushchev and Kennedy made a Deal to Avoid War

- On 27th October 1962, Khrushchev made a deal to dismantle the missile bases in Cuba and ordered his ships to turn around.
- In exchange the USA lifted the blockade, promised to not invade Cuba — and secretly agreed to remove their missiles from Turkey.

Comment and Analysis

The USA had placed missiles in Turkey right next to the USSR in April 1962. In Khrushchev's eyes, putting missiles in Cuba was a reasonable response.

The Cuban Missile Crisis brought the world very close to nuclear war

Write a list of main factors you believe helped lead to the Cuban Missile Crisis.
Write a short paragraph explaining which factor you believe was most important.

Superpower Relations and the Cold War, 1941-1991

The Cuban Missile Crisis

Although the Cuban Missile Crisis almost caused a <u>nuclear war</u> between the superpowers, it also brought about measures that would allow for a <u>limited peace</u> between the two rivals, including <u>controls</u> on nuclear stockpiles.

The crisis **Significantly Altered** the **Course** of the **Cold War**

1) The Cuban Missile Crisis was <u>important</u> because it forced everybody to face up to how quickly a tense situation could become an absolute catastrophe.

2) In the short term, efforts were made to <u>defuse tensions</u> and <u>improve communication</u> between the powers.

- In 1963, a telephone '<u>hotline</u>' was established between <u>Washington</u> and <u>Moscow</u>. This enabled the two superpowers to <u>talk directly</u> and more <u>quickly</u> in the event of a crisis.

- All nuclear missiles were <u>removed</u> from <u>Cuba</u>, and then from <u>Turkey</u> by April 1963.

- <u>Kennedy</u> emerged from the crisis as a <u>hero</u> who had <u>stood up</u> against the threat of communism.

- <u>Khrushchev</u>, however, was <u>discredited</u> — he'd forced the USA to <u>remove their missiles</u> from Turkey, but had agreed to keep the deal a <u>secret</u>. In the eyes of the public he'd <u>failed</u> and he <u>resigned</u> in 1964.

Steps were taken to **Control** the **Number** of **Nuclear Weapons**

In the long term, the crisis prompted <u>new measures</u> to bring the build up of nuclear weapons <u>under control</u>.

The Limited Test Ban Treaty

- Signed by <u>both powers</u> in 1963.
- It stated that all future <u>tests</u> of nuclear weapons had to be carried out <u>underground</u> to avoid polluting the air with <u>nuclear radiation</u>.

> The Cuban Missile Crisis was one of the most <u>dangerous events</u> in the Cold War, but it also marked the beginning of a period of '<u>détente</u>' (see p.188).

The Outer Space Treaty

- Drawn up in 1967.
- It <u>forbade</u> countries (including the USSR and the USA) from placing <u>weapons of mass destruction</u> in <u>space</u>.

The Nuclear Non-Proliferation Treaty

- Came into force in 1970.
- Both superpowers agreed <u>not to supply</u> nuclear weapons or related technology to countries that <u>didn't</u> already have nuclear arms.
- The treaty also encouraged nuclear <u>disarmament</u>, but it allowed countries to use nuclear technology for <u>peaceful</u> purposes (e.g. energy).

A lot of good came out of the Cuban Missile Crisis

Make sure you learn the name of each treaty, its date and how it controlled the number of nuclear weapons. The treaties show the impact of the Cuban Missile Crisis on the course of the Cold War.

The Prague Spring

In 1968, discontent within the Soviet Eastern Bloc stirred again. Czechoslovakia wanted more freedom from Moscow, and decided to move away from Soviet influence in a rebellion known as 'the Prague Spring'.

There was Opposition to Soviet Control in Czechoslovakia

1) Tension had been building in Czechoslovakia. It had become a communist state in 1948 and its policies were heavily influenced by the USSR.

> Soviet policies such as collectivisation and centralisation slowed economic progress in Czechoslovakia.

2) It was a member of the Warsaw Pact, which discouraged trade with countries outside the Eastern Bloc and promoted Soviet-style communism.

3) There was growing discontent about the extent of external control over Czechoslovakian affairs. In 1956, students and writers protested at the lack of free speech and free movement in the country.

Dubcek wanted to Move Away from Soviet policies

1) In January 1968, Alexander Dubcek became the leader of the Communist Party in Czechoslovakia. Dubcek wanted Czechoslovakia to follow its own version of communism.

2) In April 1968, he introduced a series of reforms that went against Soviet-style communism.

- Travel to the West was made available for all.
- The border with West Germany was re-opened.
- All industry became decentralised.
- Trade unions and workers were given more power.
- Freedom of speech and opposition parties were allowed.

> Decentralisation meant that companies were no longer controlled by Communist party officials — workers and local authorities were given more power.

3) Many of the reforms were aimed at improving the performance of Czechoslovakia's economy — partly by developing closer relations with the West.

4) This worried the USSR — it didn't want any Western involvement in its Eastern Bloc.

5) Even though some reforms moved away from Soviet policy, Dubcek was still a communist. He promised that Czechoslovakia would stay in the Warsaw Pact and remain a loyal ally to Moscow.

6) For four months, Dubcek's new policies were tolerated by the USSR, and Czechoslovakia enjoyed relative freedom. This period is known as the 'Prague Spring'.

The USSR was Under Pressure to Intervene

1) The USSR grew increasingly concerned about Dubcek's reforms. Dubcek promised he was still loyal to Moscow, but his new policies meant that the USSR had less control over Czechoslovakia.

2) The leader of the USSR, Leonid Brezhnev, was worried that Dubcek's reforms could lead to a rejection of communism in the Eastern Bloc and in the USSR itself. If Czechoslovakia pulled away, other satellite states might follow.

3) Events in August 1968 triggered a Soviet response:

- President Tito of Yugoslavia visited Prague. Yugoslavia had refused to sign the Warsaw Pact and had never accepted the USSR's version of communism. The trip was an ominous sign to Brezhnev that Czechoslovakia was no longer loyal to the USSR.
- The USSR received a letter from communists in Czechoslovakia, asking for help.

EXAM TIP

Dubcek wanted to reform Czechoslovakia peacefully

In the exam, always read the question carefully and work out what it wants you to do. It's very easy to just describe what happened — but often you need to analyse events, too.

The Prague Spring

In August 1968, the USSR decided to intervene militarily. Czechoslovakia returned to Soviet-style communism.

The USSR Invaded Czechoslovakia in August 1968

1) On 21st August 1968 500,000 Soviet troops invaded Czechoslovakia.

2) The Czechoslovakians responded with non-violent demonstrations — people took to the streets with anti-invasion banners, and in January 1969 a student burned himself alive in the street in protest.

> Czechoslovakia was keen to avoid the violence that erupted in the 1956 Hungarian Uprising (see p.177).

3) In April 1969, Dubcek was forcibly removed from office, and replaced with Gustav Husak. Husak was loyal to Soviet-style communism, and would ensure that Czechoslovakia remained close with the USSR.

Countries Criticised the USSR, but Didn't Act

There was an international outcry at the Soviet intervention in Czechoslovakia, but no action was taken.

Warsaw Pact forces enter Prague in August 1968.

- The UN denounced the invasion and proposed a draft resolution requesting the withdrawal of Soviet troops from Czechoslovakia. This was vetoed (rejected) by the USSR.

- Many countries condemned the Soviet action but didn't intervene. They were wary of interfering within the USSR's sphere of influence.

- Communist parties in the West criticised Brezhnev's reaction and sought to distance themselves from Soviet influence.

> The lack of reaction from the UN and the West made the Western powers appear weak.

Comment and Analysis

Countries were wary of taking action against the USSR. The Prague Spring occurred at a time when the Cold War had thawed slightly. Nobody wanted to re-ignite tensions between the two superpowers.

The Prague Spring Strengthened the USSR

1) The USSR succeeded in returning Czechoslovakia to Soviet-style communism.

2) Brezhnev used the Prague Spring as an opportunity to establish his authority in the Eastern Bloc. He showed he was prepared to invade a friendly satellite state in order not to weaken the anti-Western alliance. He also proved to the USA that he was a strong and determined leader.

Brezhnev Doctrine

- After the invasion, Brezhnev announced that in future the USSR would intervene in any country where communism was under threat.

- The Brezhnev Doctrine was important because it strengthened the USSR's control over its satellite states.

- It also sent a message to the Eastern Bloc that giving up communism wasn't an option — the USSR would respond with force.

3) Soviet-American relations continued to be strained. Despite recent moves towards reducing the nuclear threat (see p.184), both countries still distrusted one another.

4) The incident reminded both superpowers that the Cold War wasn't over. Brezhnev had proved he was still willing to risk conflict to uphold communism in the Eastern Bloc.

REVISION TASK

The Brezhnev Doctrine set the tone for the next twenty years
Make a timeline of the main crises that occurred in the Cold War between 1958 and 1970.

Exam-Style Questions

Q1

Give an account examining the events of 1958-1961 that led to the construction of the Berlin Wall.

You could mention the 'Berlin Ultimatum' and the U2 incident in your answer.   [8 marks]

Q2

Examine:

a) the significance of the Cuban Missile Crisis (1961) for the progression of the Cold War.   [8 marks]

b) the significance of the construction of the Berlin Wall (1961) for the relationship between the USSR and the USA.   [8 marks]

Q3

Give two consequences of the USSR's invasion of Czechoslovakia in 1968 and explain them.   [8 marks]

Détente — Easing of Tensions

In the 1970s there was a period of 'détente' — an easing in tension between the two superpowers.

The policy of Détente was Practical

1) The 1960s were marked by crises, including some of the most tense moments in the Cold War (p.180-186). Both the USA and the USSR wanted to avoid other near misses.

2) Boosting military power hadn't succeeded in reducing tensions. Both countries recognised that a new strategy was needed.

3) Both countries were also keen to reduce their military spending — the arms race was extremely expensive and led to falling standards of living.

> **Comment and Analysis**
>
> The USSR was especially worried about falling living standards in the Eastern Bloc. In 1970, there were riots in Poland in response to high living costs.

The Superpowers agreed to Reduce Arms and Co-operate

The two superpowers developed closer relations under détente. In 1975, Soviet and American spacecraft docked together in space. However, the most significant progress was achieved through diplomacy.

The First Strategic Arms Limitation Treaty (SALT 1)

1) SALT 1 was a treaty signed in 1972 by the USA and the USSR. It limited the number of ABMs (anti-ballistic missiles) each country could have and placed a temporary limit on the numbers of ICBMs (Intercontinental Ballistic Missiles) on both sides.

2) ABMs were designed to intercept incoming missiles and had the potential to upset the delicate 'nuclear balance' between the USSR and the USA.

3) By limiting the number of ABMs each country could have, SALT 1 reduced the likelihood of one country holding an advantage over the other. In the short term, the treaty was a success because it slowed down the arms race.

> If one side could use ABMs to destroy the other side's missiles then the threat of retaliation would be gone. The side with ABMs could launch a first strike and then just destroy the missiles that were fired back towards it.

The Helsinki Agreement

1) The Helsinki Agreement in 1975 was a pact between the USA, the USSR, Canada and most of Europe. All countries agreed to recognise existing European borders and to uphold human rights.

2) Both superpowers accepted the division of Germany and the USSR's influence over Eastern Europe.

3) The West viewed the USSR's agreement to uphold human rights as great progress, but the USSR didn't stick to its word. It didn't grant freedom of speech or freedom of movement to its citizens. This undermined the Helsinki agreement and made the USA distrust the USSR.

The Second Strategic Arms Limitation Treaty (SALT 2)

1) The SALT 2 Treaty was signed in 1979. The treaty banned the USA and the USSR from launching new missile programmes and limited the number of MIRVs (Multiple Independently targetable Reentry Vehicles) each country could have.

2) However the treaty was never ratified (approved) by the US Senate, so it didn't come into effect. See p.190 for more information.

> MIRVs are weapons which can carry several missiles at once and deploy them to different targets.

The superpowers took important steps towards limiting their nuclear arms during détente, but both countries continued to hold vast stockpiles of weapons.

The USA and the USSR began to work together in the 1970s

REVISION TASK List the reasons why each power wanted to pursue détente. Underneath each one, explain whether détente proved successful in achieving that aim. Use information from the rest of this section to help.

The Soviet Invasion of Afghanistan

The Soviet War in Afghanistan was a <u>turning point</u> for détente in the 1970s —
it demolished the <u>trust</u> that had been so carefully built up between the USA and the USSR.

The **USSR** got bogged down in a **War** in **Afghanistan**

1) In 1978, a <u>civil war</u> broke out in Afghanistan. Rebels were protesting at <u>new radical reforms</u> brought in by the <u>Afghan communist government</u>, which had <u>close ties</u> to the Soviet Union.

2) The Afghan government requested <u>help</u> from the <u>USSR</u>, which <u>invaded</u> Afghanistan in December 1979.

Comment and Analysis

The USSR used the <u>Brezhnev Doctrine</u> (see p.186) to justify the invasion. It was also concerned by the idea of an <u>anti-Soviet</u> government in Afghanistan, as the countries shared a <u>border</u>.

3) This decision turned out to be a <u>disaster</u> — the USSR found itself in a seemingly <u>unwinnable</u> conflict.

4) It had to fight in difficult <u>mountainous terrain</u> against determined opposition, who were supplied with <u>weapons</u> by the <u>USA</u>.

5) Around <u>1 million Afghan</u> civilians were killed and over <u>6 million</u> became <u>refugees</u>.

The **War** was **Disastrous** for the USSR

1) <u>15,000</u> Soviet troops were killed and the government spent huge amounts of money, but the USSR <u>couldn't win</u>.

2) The Soviet-Afghan War led to a <u>loss</u> of public support in the USSR for the communist regime. The Soviet people were <u>angry</u> at falling living standards, which had <u>deteriorated</u> as a direct result of <u>high spending</u> in Afghanistan.

3) It didn't work out too well for Brezhnev <u>internationally</u>, either:

Comment and Analysis

When <u>Mikhail Gorbachev</u> came to power in 1985, he admitted that the USSR <u>couldn't afford</u> to keep fighting. In <u>1988</u>, he began <u>withdrawing</u> Soviet troops from Afghanistan (see p.82).

- The war was an <u>embarrassment</u> for Brezhnev and <u>undermined</u> the USSR's strong military reputation, which was essential for keeping its satellite states under <u>control</u>.

- In January 1980, the UN <u>condemned</u> the invasion. It proposed a resolution demanding Soviet withdrawal, but the resolution was <u>vetoed</u> (rejected) by the USSR.

- In <u>1980</u>, the USA and over 50 other countries (including Canada and West Germany) <u>boycotted</u> the Moscow Olympic Games, in <u>protest</u> at the Soviet-Afghan War.

The Afghan war harmed the USSR's reputation at home and abroad

If you're asked about the importance of an event, think about its knock-on effects, e.g. the Soviet invasion of Afghanistan contributed to the end of détente and harmed Brezhnev's popularity.

The Second Cold War

Cold War tensions were <u>resurrected</u> during the 1980s, in a period now known as the 'Second Cold War'.

The **Superpowers** began to **Move Away** from **Détente**

The war in Afghanistan caused <u>tension</u> between the USSR and the USA to <u>resurface</u>. The situation was as <u>dangerous</u> as ever.

1) Soviet intervention in Afghanistan was <u>interpreted</u> by the USA as an act of <u>communist expansionism</u>.

2) In 1979, US President Jimmy Carter was so alarmed he stopped the <u>SALT 2 Treaty</u> (see p.188) being debated by the US Senate, meaning it could never come into effect. Instead he called for an <u>increase</u> in the <u>defence budget</u>.

3) The USA was also worried that the USSR was trying to <u>gain influence</u> in the <u>Persian Gulf</u>, close to the Afghan border. The oil-rich area had formed close economic ties with the West, and Carter thought Soviet influence in Afghanistan <u>threatened US interests</u> there.

4) Carter warned that the USA would <u>use force</u> to prevent the USSR from <u>gaining control</u> of the Gulf region. This warning became known as the <u>Carter Doctrine</u>.

The <u>Carter Doctrine</u> was the <u>first threat</u> of <u>aggression</u> between the superpowers since détente.

Reagan **Boosted** American **Defences**

After the Soviet invasion of Afghanistan, the policy of <u>détente</u> was badly damaged. It was in even more danger when US President Carter was <u>succeeded</u> by President <u>Ronald Reagan</u> in January 1981.

1) Ronald Reagan was a hardline <u>anti-communist</u>. His speeches were often full of anti-Soviet rhetoric and he called the USSR an '<u>evil empire</u>'. This increased hostility between the two superpowers.

2) Reagan <u>didn't believe</u> in the policy of détente. He was willing to <u>negotiate</u> with the USSR, but only from a position of <u>strength</u>.

3) This meant he wanted to <u>increase American defences</u>. American intelligence gathered in 1976 also suggested that the USA had <u>underestimated</u> the USSR's nuclear strength, and the USA felt it had to <u>catch up</u>.

Reagan Started the Biggest Arms Build-up in American History

- In the 1980s the USA spent <u>$550 billion a year</u> on conventional and nuclear weapons. This worried the USSR — it couldn't afford to <u>match</u> Reagan's spending.

- Reagan also <u>re-authorised</u> some weapons programmes that had been <u>abandoned</u> during détente. The USA began to develop the <u>neutron bomb</u>, which was designed to cause <u>maximum</u> loss of life and minimum damage to property.

The Cold War regained momentum in the early 1980s

The leaders of the USSR and the USA had to commit to détente if it was going to be a success. Reagan's decision to reject détente and strengthen the country increased tension.

The Second Cold War

Relations between the superpowers <u>worsened</u> when Reagan announced his <u>Strategic Defence Initiative</u> (<u>SDI</u>).

The USA **Launched** the **Strategic Defence Initiative**

There were <u>anti-nuclear demonstrations</u> as old fears resurfaced. This demonstration took place in Vienna in 1983. The banner reads '<u>create peace without weapons</u>'.

1) In March 1983, Reagan announced the development of the Strategic Defence Initiative, nicknamed '<u>Star Wars</u>'.
2) The program would develop weapons that would be <u>deployed</u> in <u>space</u> and that could destroy nuclear missiles <u>after</u> they had been launched.
3) It would be the <u>ultimate defence system</u> — even nuclear missiles already heading towards the USA could be stopped.
4) If successful, the SDI would <u>shift the balance</u> of the Cold War in the USA's <u>favour</u>.
5) By 1983, détente was truly <u>over</u>.

Comment and Analysis

The SDI is a typical example of the <u>differing perspectives</u> that kept the Cold War going. For the USA, the SDI was a means of <u>defence</u>. But the USSR viewed it as an act of <u>aggression</u> — the USA would theoretically be able to attack the USSR <u>without</u> fear of retaliation.

Reagan's attitude **Changed** after **1985**

When <u>Mikhail Gorbachev</u> became leader of the USSR in March 1985, Reagan <u>reassessed his attitude</u> towards the USSR. Gorbachev's leadership brought about a <u>thaw</u> in Cold War tensions, and <u>the return</u> of détente.

1) Gorbachev proposed <u>radical reforms</u> and was far <u>more open</u> towards the West than previous Soviet leaders. Reagan recognised that the USSR was being steered in a <u>new direction</u>.
2) The USA realised that this change could be good. Although initiatives like the SDI weren't scrapped, Reagan thought <u>negotiation</u> was now the best way to protect American interests.
3) Importantly, the two leaders <u>got on well</u>, creating a <u>better relationship</u> between the superpowers.

The **Cold War** created a **Crisis** in the **USSR**

By the 1980s, Soviet citizens were becoming increasingly <u>discontent</u>:

1) The <u>arms race</u> with the USA and the war in Afghanistan were hugely <u>expensive</u> and the Soviet economy just couldn't <u>support</u> this level of spending.

2) Soviet goods were <u>poor quality</u> and Soviet <u>farming</u> was <u>inefficient</u> — there <u>wasn't</u> <u>enough food</u> and millions of tonnes of grain had to be <u>imported</u> from the USA.

3) The communist government was becoming more <u>corrupt</u> and was unable to give the Soviet people the <u>same high living standards</u> as people had in the West.

REVISION TASK

Détente made a comeback when Gorbachev came to power in 1985

Write a list of reasons why Cold War tensions declined after Gorbachev became leader of the USSR.

Gorbachev's 'New Thinking'

Mikhail Gorbachev came to power in the USSR and radically changed Soviet policies. This was one of the biggest turning points in the Cold War — it laid the foundations for the collapse of the USSR.

Gorbachev introduced Radical Reforms

1) In 1985, Mikhail Gorbachev became General Secretary of the Communist Party. He was more open to the West than previous leaders and he admitted that the Soviet system had problems.

2) He introduced two major policies — 'perestroika' and 'glasnost'. These policies were part of what is known as Gorbachev's 'New Thinking'. Changes to foreign policy were part of it too.

Perestroika means 'Restructuring'

- Gorbachev wanted to make the Soviet economy more efficient.
- He moved away from the centralisation of industry — the government no longer told businesses exactly what they had to produce.
- Gorbachev also allowed private business ownership and allowed Soviet businesses to trade with the Western powers.

> Gorbachev didn't want to end communism — he wanted to modernise it. He hoped that reform would revive the USSR's struggling economy, which was falling further behind the USA's.

Glasnost means 'Openness'

- Gorbachev gave the Soviet people new rights.
- Thousands of political prisoners were released.
- Free speech was allowed and censorship was relaxed.
- In 1989, Gorbachev created the USSR's first elected parliament — Communist Party officials were chosen by the public for the first time.

Gorbachev changed Foreign Policy

1) Gorbachev improved relations with the West. He met with US President Reagan several times, for example at the Geneva Summit in 1985. Gorbachev's open attitude softened Reagan's hard approach.

2) In 1987, a disarmament treaty was signed — the INF Treaty (Intermediate-Range Nuclear Forces Treaty). The USA and the USSR agreed to remove medium-range nuclear missiles from Europe within three years.

3) The first missiles were dismantled in 1988. The INF Treaty was a milestone in American-Soviet relations — both countries actively reduced weapons for the first time.

4) Gorbachev reduced the scale of the USSR's commitments abroad. In 1988, he announced that all Soviet troops would withdraw from Afghanistan.

5) In 1988, he also announced the immediate reduction of the USSR's weapons stockpile and the number of troops in the Soviet armed forces.

> Gorbachev's decrease in military spending and his decision to withdraw from Afghanistan greatly defused tensions between the superpowers.

6) In the same year, Gorbachev decided to abandon the Brezhnev Doctrine (see p.186). He told the United Nations that Eastern Europe now had a choice — the USSR wasn't going to control it any longer.

'New Thinking' Energised Opposition

- Gorbachev's new policies encouraged reformist movements in Eastern Europe (see p.193).
- Gorbachev's 'New Thinking' also caused splits in the Soviet Communist Party because some members thought his reforms weren't radical enough, and others worried they were too radical. This made it more difficult to control Eastern European countries from Moscow.

Gorbachev wanted to improve communism

Draw a table with three columns labelled 'perestroika', 'glasnost' and 'foreign policy'. Put each of Gorbachev's 'New Thinking' policies into the table under the correct heading.

Eastern Europe Pulls Away

Gorbachev's 'New Thinking' was intended to <u>modernise</u> communism, but actually sparked its <u>decline</u>.

The satellite states **No Longer Feared** the USSR

Gorbachev's decision to abandon the <u>Brezhnev Doctrine</u> led to the USSR <u>losing control</u> of its satellite states.

- Gorbachev stated the USSR would <u>no longer use force</u> to uphold communism in its satellite states. In 1988, he announced the <u>withdrawal</u> of Soviet troops, tanks and aircraft from <u>Eastern Europe</u>.
- It was <u>fear</u> of Soviet military intervention that had kept opposition movements <u>under control</u> within the USSR's satellite states. Without it, they had a chance to <u>act</u>.

The Berlin Wall **Fell** in **November 1989**

1) In May 1989, communist Hungary <u>opened its border</u> with non-communist Austria. This let East Germans <u>travel</u> through Hungary to Austria, and then into West Germany.

2) Between August and September 1989, thousands <u>left</u> East Germany for West Germany. The East German government was <u>unable to control</u> the situation, and received <u>no help</u> from the USSR.

3) In October 1989, there were <u>mass protests</u> against the <u>communist regime</u>. The East German government finally agreed to <u>open</u> the border between East and West Berlin in November 1989. <u>Free elections</u> were promised and the wall was <u>torn down</u>.

4) The fall of the Berlin Wall showed that the relationship between East and West was <u>transforming</u>, and that the USSR was <u>losing its grip</u> over communist territory.

As news of the decision to open the wall spread, <u>Berliners gathered</u> at the wall. Here, <u>East German officials</u> wait for orders.

Communist governments in **Eastern Europe** started to **Collapse**

1) <u>Free elections</u> were also held in <u>Poland</u> in June 1989. In 1990, a new <u>non-communist</u> government came to power. The USSR <u>didn't intervene</u>.

2) In December 1989, communist governments <u>collapsed</u> in <u>Czechoslovakia</u>, <u>Bulgaria</u> and <u>Romania</u>. Hungary's Communist Party suffered a large <u>defeat</u> in <u>free elections</u> in March 1990.

3) In <u>October 1990</u>, communist East Germany and democratic West Germany <u>rejoined</u> to form a single state again. For many people this was a <u>powerful symbol</u> that the communist experiment was <u>over</u>.

Comment and Analysis

The <u>reunification</u> of Germany and the <u>decline</u> of communism in the USSR's satellite states symbolised a <u>new thaw</u> in the Cold War. Europe was no longer <u>ideologically divided</u> between East and West.

The **Republics** of the USSR **Wanted Independence**

As the USSR <u>lost its grip</u> on its satellite states, it was undergoing a <u>national crisis</u>.

1) In early 1990, some important regions in the Soviet Union demanded <u>independence</u>, especially the <u>Baltic republics</u> — Latvia, Lithuania, and Estonia.

2) They were encouraged by the <u>recent success</u> of revolutions across <u>Eastern Europe</u> and by Gorbachev's policy of '<u>glasnost</u>' (openness), which gave <u>greater power</u> to individuals and encouraged <u>constructive criticism</u> of Soviet policy.

3) Gorbachev <u>didn't want</u> to lose the Republics. He granted them <u>more power</u> — but <u>it wasn't enough</u>. The leaders of the Soviet republics no longer <u>listened</u> to Gorbachev, and he <u>lacked the authority</u> to make them comply with Soviet wishes.

The USSR was made up of <u>15 republics</u>. Each republic had its <u>own parliament</u>, but was <u>centrally controlled</u> by Moscow.

The USSR was losing its grip on Eastern Europe by the late 1980s

Look back at the information on Gorbachev's 'New Thinking' and the effect it had on Eastern Europe. Use this information to make a timeline of events between 1985 and 1990.

The Collapse of the Soviet Union

Despite the fall of communist regimes in Eastern Europe, the Cold War wasn't over until the USSR collapsed.

More Republics decided to become Independent

1) Lithuania declared itself independent in March 1990. Soviet troops were sent to Vilnius, the capital of Lithuania, in January 1991, and several civilians were killed in the violence that followed. But this only strengthened the independence movement.

2) In April 1991, Georgia declared its independence, followed by the Ukraine's declaration in August.

Comment and Analysis

As Gorbachev's authority weakened, independence movements gained in strength. He found that military intervention no longer deterred protests, it escalated them.

There was a Political Crisis in the USSR

1) By 1990, Gorbachev faced opposition from within his own party and the public. The Communist Party was divided — some members wanted more drastic reform and others wanted a return to former Soviet policies.

2) The public were unhappy because Gorbachev's reforms hadn't lived up to their high expectations.

Economic Reforms hadn't Worked...

- The USSR's economy hadn't improved, and in 1990 a quarter of its population was living below the poverty line.
- Economic corruption was still rife.
- Inflation was high and basic goods were in short supply.
- The cost of the arms race and the war in Afghanistan hindered the reforms.

... and the Communists Attempted a Coup

- More traditional Soviet communists were worried that the Communist Party was so divided it was going to split up. They thought Gorbachev's reforms had gone too far and plotted a coup against the government in August 1991.
- They arrested Gorbachev, tried to force him to resign, and sent tanks onto the streets of Moscow to deter protesters.
- The coup didn't go to plan — it was condemned by Boris Yeltsin, a Soviet politician who opposed Gorbachev and wanted the USSR to adopt capitalism.
- Yeltsin went onto the streets to rally opposition against the coup. There were mass protests in major cities, showing that Soviets had clearly rejected communism. The coup failed.

The Soviet Union Collapsed

1) On Christmas Day 1991, Gorbachev resigned.

2) The USSR was dissolved on the 26th December.

3) The republics that made up the Soviet Union became independent states. These included Latvia, Lithuania, Estonia and Belarus.

4) The biggest of the republics was Russia. Yeltsin was elected leader and adopted capitalism.

Comment and Analysis

As more and more countries declared their independence from the USSR, they also declared their intentions to pull out of the Warsaw Pact (p.175). This made it weaker and it eventually ended in July 1991.

The dissolution of the USSR marked the end of the Cold War

If you're asked to write an account of an event like the collapse of the Soviet Union, it's a good idea to outline key moments or developments that caused the event and explain how they're linked together.

Superpower Relations and the Cold War, 1941-1991

Worked Exam-Style Question

This sample answer will give you an idea of how to write an analytical narrative account. Look at the way it's structured and how the links between different events are explained.

Q1

Give an account that analyses the key events between 1985 and 1989 that led to the fall of the Berlin Wall.   [8 marks]

In 1985, Mikhail Gorbachev became General Secretary of the Communist Party and fundamentally changed Soviet policy. He created <u>closer ties</u> with US President Reagan, e.g. <u>at the Geneva Summit in 1985</u>, and <u>began withdrawing Soviet troops from Afghanistan in 1988</u>. This helped to reduce tensions between East and West, and brought hope that relations could improve further.

This <u>evidence backs up</u> the point.

In 1988, Gorbachev abandoned the Brezhnev Doctrine, which had promised that the USSR would intervene in any country where communist regimes were threatened. <u>This meant that countries in Eastern Europe no longer had to fear Soviet aggression</u> if they chose to turn away from communism.

This analyses the <u>impact</u> of an event by explaining how it <u>affected other countries' attitudes</u>.

This makes it clear that <u>one event led to another</u>.

<u>As a result</u>, Hungary felt it could open its border with Austria in May 1989 without fear of military consequences. This caused chaos for the East German government, as thousands of East Germans crossed the border to travel to West Germany. Public opposition to the government grew — in October 1989 there were anti-communist protests in East Germany. <u>As the USSR was now unwilling to give support to struggling communist regimes</u>, the government was forced to give in to public pressure, and opened the Berlin Wall in November 1989.

It's important that you make <u>connections between different events</u>.

Exam-Style Questions

Q1

Give two consequences of the Soviet invasion of Afghanistan (1979) and explain them.   [8 marks]

Q2

Examine:

a) the significance of Reagan's attitude between 1981 and 1985 for the progression of the Cold War.   [8 marks]

b) the significance of the fall of the Berlin Wall (1989) for Soviet relations with Eastern Europe.   [8 marks]

Q3

Give an account that analyses the main events between 1988 and 1991 that led to the collapse of the Soviet Union.

You could mention the political crisis in the USSR and the Soviet Republics in your answer.   [8 marks]

Revision Summary

That pretty much sums up the Cold War — now all you have to do is check it's all sunk in.

- Try these questions and <u>tick off each one</u> when you <u>get it right</u>.
- When you've done <u>all the questions</u> for a topic and are <u>completely happy</u> with it, tick off the topic.

The Origins of the Cold War, 1941-1958 (p.172-177) ☑

1) What was the Grand Alliance?
2) Describe the different ideologies followed by the USA and the USSR.
3) Why was the USSR in a position of influence over Eastern Europe after the Second World War?
4) What did Churchill mean when he said an 'Iron Curtain' divided Europe?
5) Why were the Long and Novikov Telegrams important?
6) What was the Truman Doctrine?
7) What was the Cominform? What did it do?
8) Describe the events of the Berlin Airlift.
9) Give two consequences of the 1948-49 Berlin Crisis.
10) What is meant by an 'arms race'?
11) What did Khrushchev mean by 'peaceful co-existence'?
12) Give two consequences of the Hungarian Uprising.

Cold War Crises, 1958-1970 (p.180-186) ☑

13) Why was Berlin a source of tension between the superpowers?
14) Describe Khrushchev's 'Berlin Ultimatum' of 1958.
15) How did the Paris and Vienna Summits affect the USSR's attitude towards Berlin?
16) Give two consequences of the establishment of the Berlin Wall.
17) Describe the main events of the Cuban Missile Crisis. How did it alter the course of the Cold War?
18) Why did the USSR end the Prague Spring?
19) How did other countries react to the Soviet invasion of Czechoslovakia?
20) What was the Brezhnev Doctrine?

The End of the Cold War, 1970-1991 (p.188-194) ☑

21) What does 'détente' mean?
22) Name three treaties signed by the superpowers in the 1970s.
23) How did the Soviet invasion of Afghanistan change relations between the USA and the USSR?
24) What was US President Reagan's attitude towards détente?
25) What was the SDI?
26) When did Mikhail Gorbachev become leader in the USSR?
27) What were 'perestroika' and 'glasnost'?
28) How did Gorbachev change Soviet foreign policy?
29) Why did opposition to communism rise in Eastern Europe after 1988?
30) Why was there a political crisis in the USSR by 1990?
31) Describe the events that led to the collapse of the Soviet Union from 1990-91.

Exam Skills

Exam Skills

These pages cover the main skills you'll need to tackle some of the most common types of exam question.

Learn the **Facts** about the **Periods** you've studied

You'll be asked to describe or outline some features of the period you've studied to test your knowledge of the facts. Make sure your points are clear and accurate.

Give two aspects of education in Elizabethan England, 1558-88. [4 marks]

For the Thematic Study, you might have to compare two aspects of your period — this means describing how a key feature of your period developed by explaining similarities or differences over time.

Give one way that beliefs about the spread of disease in the fourteenth century were similar to those in the seventeenth century. Explain your answer. [4 marks]

You'll be asked to **Analyse Features, Events** and **Developments**

1) Some questions will ask you to explain the causes of something, or the reasons why it happened. Consider what triggered certain developments and why the changes were fast or slow to happen.

2) You could be asked about why a change or event was important or significant — think about how the development influenced attitudes and later events, and link the event or development to wider issues.

3) If you're asked to write about the consequences of a change or event, think about its impact and what changed as a result of the development.

Explain how important the formation of NATO (1949) was to relations between the Soviet Union and the USA. [8 marks]

4) Use detailed and relevant information to support your points. Including specific dates, names and statistics shows you have a good knowledge and understanding of the period.

5) You could also be asked to write an account or a summary of developments in your period. Explain what happened and analyse it by using concepts such as cause, consequence and change (see p.2).

It's important that you make connections between different ideas when you're writing a narrative account or summary. This makes it clear that one event led to another and shows why things developed the way they did.

You need to know how **Analyse** a **Statement** or **Interpretation**

1) Some questions will give you a statement or interpretation and ask you how far you agree with it.

2) Decide your opinion before you start writing and state it clearly at the beginning and end of your answer.

3) Even if you agree with the statement in the question, you still need to analyse some counter-arguments — this shows you've considered all of the evidence and looked at different sides of the argument.

'Commercial rivalry was the most important reason for the outbreak of war with Spain in 1585.' Do you agree with this statement? Explain your answer. [16 marks]

- For example, if you're answering a question like this one, it's a good idea to consider other reasons why war broke out with Spain.
- You could talk about other long-term causes of tension (e.g. Elizabeth's religious settlement) or short-term factors (e.g. Elizabeth's decision to sign the Treaty of Nonsuch).
- You need to say whether the other factors you've mentioned were more or less important than the reason in the question.

Exam Skills

All these exam questions can seem tricky at first, but you'll get the hang of them if you put these skills into action.

Some Questions might ask you to Decide which Factor is More Important

1) You could also be asked to look at how or why something changed in the period you've studied.

2) You'll be given two factors to discuss, and will have argue in favour of one of them.

3) Talk about both factors and explain how they're linked.

4) You don't need to bring in other factors for this question type, but you should still use your own knowledge to support your argument.

> What was the most important reason why Hitler became Chancellor in 1933: Hitler's popularity or economic problems?
>
> Explain your answer, referring to both reasons. [12 marks]

You'll be asked to Analyse and Compare historical Interpretations

1) You'll be asked to compare interpretations and explain why two interpretations are different. Here are some tips on how to approach these questions:

- When you're working with interpretations, you need to figure out what the author is trying to say — look at what information they give, what their tone is and if they emphasise anything in particular.

- If the interpretation is visual, think about what's happening in the picture and what emotions are shown. Use your own knowledge to decide whether any important details have been missed out.

> If you're comparing two interpretations, make sure you analyse both of the interpretations. Use evidence from the interpretations to explain what they show.

2) If you're asked to decide how convincing an interpretation is or explain how far you agree with it, then you need to consider the event or issue that it is discussing and decide whether you think it describes it accurately.

3) Explain your decision using your own knowledge and refer to the interpretation.

There'll be some questions about Sources too

1) Some source questions will ask you to evaluate what a visual or written source is saying.

2) Other source questions will ask you to analyse sources and say how useful they are.

- When working with sources, it's not just a case of describing what you see or read. You need to analyse the source and use it to draw conclusions about the period you've studied.

- When you're analysing the usefulness of a source, always look at what it's saying and where it's from. Use details from the source to back up your points.

- Use the source and your own knowledge to decide if the source is reliable and if the content is relevant.

> Using your own knowledge shows that you have a good level of understanding.

Exam Skills

Here are some tips on how to tackle questions in the exam. In some papers, the examiner will also be marking you partly on your spelling, punctuation and grammar (SPaG) — SPaG is worth nearly 5% of your overall mark.

Remember these **Four Tips** for **Answering Questions**

Don't Spend Too Long on Short Questions

The more marks a question is worth, the longer your answer should be. Don't get carried away writing loads for a question that's only worth a few marks — leave time for the higher mark questions.

Use a Clear Writing Style

1) Essay answers should start with a brief introduction and end with a conclusion. Remember to start a new paragraph for each new point you want to discuss.

2) Try to use clear handwriting — and pay attention to spelling, grammar and punctuation (see p.201).

Plan your Essay Answers, but Not the Others

1) You don't need to plan answers to the shorter questions in the exam. That will waste time.

2) For longer essay questions, it's very important to make a quick plan before you start writing.

3) Think about the key words in the question. Scribble a quick plan of your main points — cross through this neatly at the end, so it's obvious it shouldn't be marked.

Stay Focused on the Question

1) Directly answer the question and back up your points with relevant facts. Don't just write everything you know about the topic.

2) Be relevant and accurate — e.g. if you're writing about the rise of the Nazi Party, don't include stories about a London camel called George who moved rubble during the Blitz.

3) It might help to try to write the first sentence of every paragraph in a way that addresses the question, e.g. 'Another way that better living conditions led to improved public health is...'

Remember to **Check** your **Spellings**

1) You should leave about five minutes at the end of the exam to check your work.

2) Check as many questions as you can, but make sure you read over the questions which award SPaG marks especially carefully. (Marks are shown very clearly at the end of each question.)

3) 5 minutes isn't long, so there won't be time to check everything thoroughly. Look for the most obvious spelling mistakes...

If you're not confident with any of these things, learn them now.

| where / wear / were | your / you're | silent letters, e.g. know, science, could |

| names of historical figures or places, e.g. Roanoke, Khrushchev, Scutari | there / their / they're | to / too / two | of / off |

| effect / affect | double letters, e.g. aggression, success | don't confuse 'past' with 'passed' | though / thought / through / thorough |

Spell **Technical Words** correctly

There are a lot of technical words in history. You need to be able to spell them correctly. Learn these examples to start you off. The underlined letters are the tricky bits to watch out for.

| alliance | argument | biased | controversial | consequences | defence | democracy |

| fascism | foreign | government | interpretation | parliament | source | successful |

Exam Skills

Here are some tips on how to use <u>punctuation</u> and <u>grammar</u> correctly in your answers — there are a few common mistakes to avoid. Learn this stuff now so you can bag those all important <u>SPaG marks</u> in the exam.

You need to **Punctuate Properly**...

1) Always use a <u>capital letter</u> at the start of a <u>sentence</u>.
Use capital letters for <u>names</u> of <u>particular people</u>, <u>places</u> and <u>things</u>. For example:

All <u>sentences</u> start with capital letters. → *In 1985, Gorbachev was made General Secretary of the Communist Party.*
The name of a <u>person</u>.   A <u>title</u>.   The name of an <u>organisation</u>.

2) <u>Full stops</u> go at the end of <u>sentences</u>, e.g. 'General Custer was killed in June 1876<u>.</u>'
<u>Question marks</u> go at the end of <u>questions</u>, e.g. 'How successful was the Nazi propaganda<u>?</u>'

3) Use <u>commas</u> when you use <u>more than one adjective</u> to describe something, or to separate items in a <u>list</u>:

Elizabeth I was <u>intelligent</u>, <u>confident</u> and <u>powerful</u>.

4) <u>Commas</u> can also <u>join two points</u> into one sentence with a joining word (such as '<u>and</u>', '<u>or</u>', '<u>so</u>' or '<u>but</u>'):

The work of Galen was central to medieval medical teachings, <u>so</u> doctors found it difficult to disagree with him.

5) <u>Commas</u> can also be used to separate <u>extra information</u> in a sentence:

The Civil Rights Act, <u>which was enacted in 1870</u>, was opposed by President Andrew Johnson.

...and use **Grammar Correctly**

1) <u>Don't change tenses</u> in your writing by mistake:

The mountain men <u>explored</u> the West first — they <u>hunted</u> animals for their skins.

<u>Both</u> verbs are in the <u>past tense</u> — which is correct. Writing '<u>hunt</u>' instead of '<u>hunted</u>' would be wrong.

2) Write your longer answers in <u>paragraphs</u>.
- A paragraph is a <u>group of sentences</u> which talk about the <u>same thing</u> or <u>follow on</u> from each other.
- You need to start a <u>new paragraph</u> when you start making a <u>new point</u>.

You show a <u>new paragraph</u> by starting a <u>new line</u> and leaving a <u>gap</u> (an <u>indent</u>) before you start writing:

From 1933, Hitler started a programme of public works, such as the building of huge new motorways. This gave jobs to thousands of people.
Even though there was increased employment, the Nazis altered the statistics so that things looked better than they were. Wages were also poor.

3) Make sure you avoid these <u>common mistakes</u>:

- Remember — '<u>it's</u>' (with an apostrophe) is short for '<u>it is</u>' or '<u>it has</u>'. '<u>Its</u>' (without an apostrophe) means '<u>belonging to it</u>'.
- It's always '<u>should have</u>', not 'should of' (and also 'could have' and 'would have' too).
- If you know that you <u>often</u> confuse two words, like 'it's' and 'its', <u>watch out</u> for them when you're checking your work in the exam.

That's that, then — all that's left to do now is to sit the exams...
Good SPaG is a great way to get marks in the exam, but you'll still need excellent knowledge of your topics to get top marks. Make sure you know all of the facts and can use them to support your answers.

In this section are some <u>practice exam papers</u> to test how well-prepared you are for your GCSE History exams.

- There are <u>five</u> exam papers in the section:

- You only need to do the papers for the exams you're sitting. Check with your teacher if you're not sure.

- Before you start each paper, read through all the <u>instructions</u>, <u>information</u> and <u>advice</u> on the front.

- You'll need some paper to write your answers on.

- When you've finished, have a look at the answers starting on page 216 — they'll give you some ideas of the kind of things you should have included in your answers.

- <u>Don't</u> try to do more than one of the papers in one sitting.

CGP   Practice Exam Paper
GCSE History

General Certificate of Secondary Education

GCSE
History

Health and Medicine in Britain, c.1000-present

Time allowed: 55 minutes

Centre name		
Centre number		
Candidate number		

Surname
Other names
Candidate signature

Instructions to candidates
- Answer **all** the questions.
- Write your answers in **black** ink or ball-point pen.
- Write your name and other details in the boxes above.
- Cross out any rough work that you do not want to be marked.

Information for candidates
- The marks available are given in brackets at the end of each question.
- There are 39 marks available for this exam paper.

Advice for candidates
- Read each question carefully before you begin your answer.
- If you have time at the end, use it to check your answers.

---

1 a) Give one way that monasteries were healthier places to live than towns in the Middle Ages.

(1 mark)

  b) Name one public health reform introduced between 1750 and 1900.

(1 mark)

  c) Give one example of how the government has tried to tackle unhealthy lifestyles between 1900 and the present day.

(1 mark)

2 Explain the similarities between the Black Death in the Middle Ages and the Great Plague in the 17th century.

(8 marks)

3 Why did the government's approach to public health change significantly in the 19th and 20th centuries?

You could talk about Chadwick's Report (1842) and the Beveridge Report (1942) in your answer.

(12 marks)

4 'The role of individuals has been the most important factor in the development of health and medicine in Britain.'

Explain how far you agree with this statement.

(16 marks)

CGP Practice Exam Paper
GCSE History

General Certificate of Secondary Education

GCSE
History

Surname	
Other names	
Candidate signature	

Centre name					
Centre number					
Candidate number					

America, 1789-1900

Time allowed: 1 hour 5 minutes

Instructions to candidates
- Answer **all** the questions.
- Write your answers in **black** ink or ball-point pen.
- Write your name and other details in the boxes above.
- Cross out any rough work that you do not want to be marked.

Information for candidates
- The marks available are given in brackets at the end of each question.
- There are 46 marks available for this exam paper.

Advice for candidates
- Read each question carefully before you begin your answer.
- If you have time at the end, use it to check your answers.

1 **a)** Give one example of a government policy directed at Native Americans that was introduced between c.1830 and c.1861.

(1 mark)

b) Name one of the four main cattle trails.

(1 mark)

c) Name one technique developed between c.1877 and c.1900 that helped settlers to farm more easily on the Great Plains.

(1 mark)

2 Write a summary explaining how law and order developed in the West between c.1877 and c.1900.

You could mention the Johnson County War (1892) and Bill Tilghman in your answer.

(9 marks)

3 Examine:

a) the significance of 'Manifest Destiny' for westward expansion.

(8 marks)

b) the significance of the Homestead Act (1862) for the development of the Great Plains.

(8 marks)

4 'Cattle ranching on the Great Plains was the main cause of the Indian Wars in the 1860s.'

Explain how far you agree with this statement.

(18 marks)

CGP Practice Exam Paper
GCSE History

General Certificate of Secondary Education

GCSE
History

Surname	
Other names	
Candidate signature	

Centre name					
Centre number					
Candidate number					

The Elizabethans, 1558-1603

Time allowed: 55 minutes

Instructions to candidates
- Answer **all** the questions.
- Write your answers in **black** ink or ball-point pen.
- Write your name and other details in the boxes above.
- Cross out any rough work that you do not want to be marked.

Information for candidates
- The marks available are given in brackets at the end of each question.
- There are 40 marks available for this exam paper.

Advice for candidates
- Read each question carefully before you begin your answer.
- If you have time at the end, use it to check your answers.

Interpretation 1 — an illustration showing Queen Elizabeth I
in Parliament. Two of her advisors, William Cecil and Francis
Walsingham, are shown standing on either side of her throne.

1 a) Look at Interpretation 1. Explain one way that the illustrator shows that the
power of Elizabeth I was central to Parliament's power.

(3 marks)

b) If you had to investigate another aspect of Interpretation 1, what would it be?

Explain how your choice would help historians understand more about Elizabethan government.

(5 marks)

2 Do you find this interpretation of the relationship between Elizabeth I and her Parliament
convincing?

Use the interpretation and your knowledge of the period to explain your answer.

(8 marks)

3 Give an account of the ways in which people responded to poverty during Elizabeth I's reign.

(8 marks)

4 'The success of Elizabeth I's religious settlement was never in any serious danger.'

Explain how far you agree with this statement.
You could mention Puritan opposition and Catholic plots in your answer.

(16 marks)

General Certificate of Secondary Education

GCSE
History

Surname	
Other names	
Candidate signature	

Centre name					
Centre number					
Candidate number					

Germany, 1890-1945

Time allowed: 1 hour 25 minutes

Instructions to candidates
* Answer **all** the questions.
* Write your answers in **black** ink or ball-point pen.
* Write your name and other details in the boxes above.
* Cross out any rough work that you do not want to be marked.

Information for candidates
* The marks available are given in brackets at the end of each question.
* There are 62 marks available for this exam paper.

Advice for candidates
* Read each question carefully before you begin your answer.
* If you have time at the end, use it to check your answers.

Source A — a Nazi propaganda poster from 1938.
The caption reads 'One people, one empire, one leader!'

1   Infer two things from Source A about how Hitler was portrayed in Nazi propaganda in the 1930s.

Explain each inference that you make.

(4 marks)

Source B — a cartoon from a Nazi Party newspaper, published in March 1929. The title of the cartoon is 'Fatherland!'. The family in the top half are leaving Germany because of economic conditions. The shops in the bottom half all have Jewish names.

I believed the National Socialists when they promised to do away with unemployment and with it the poverty of six million people. I believed them when they said they would reunite the German nation, which had split into more than forty political parties, and overcome the consequences of the dictated peace of Versailles.

Source C — an extract from the memoirs of Melita Maschmann, a German woman who was a teenager when Hitler came to power. The memoirs were published in Germany in 1963.

2 Explain how useful Sources B and C are for an investigation into the reasons why Germans supported the Nazi Party.

Use both sources, as well as your own knowledge, in your answer.

(8 marks)

As soon as the Nazi regime came into power, it revamped the educational structure from top to bottom, and with very little resistance... We five- and six-year-olds received an almost daily dose of nationalistic instruction, which we swallowed as naturally as our morning milk. It was repeated endlessly that Adolf Hitler had restored Germany's dignity and pride and freed us from the shackles of Versailles... Even in working democracies, children are too immature to question... what they are taught by their educators.

Interpretation 1 — an extract from a book by Alfons Heck, a boy who grew up under the Nazi regime. It was published in 1985.

Towards the end of the 1930s, some young people began to question the Nazi regime. Many teenagers rejected the values taught in the Hitler Youth and formed their own youth groups instead. One such group, the Edelweiss Pirates, had many local chapters across Germany; its members actively opposed the Nazis, sometimes coming into conflict with Hitler Youth members. This rebellion came with a price — in 1944, leading members of the Cologne branch of the Edelweiss Pirates were executed by the Nazis to send a message to other independent-minded young people. Despite this brutality, teenagers still signed up to oppose the Nazis through these groups.

Interpretation 2 — an extract from a history textbook aimed at secondary school pupils. It was written in 2016.

3   How is the view presented in Interpretation 1 different to that presented in Interpretation 2 about young people's attitudes to the Nazi regime?

(4 marks)

4   Explain why the author of Interpretation 1 might have a different view to the author of Interpretation 2 about young people's attitudes to the Nazi regime.

(4 marks)

5   Explain how far you agree with Interpretation 1 about young people's attitudes to the Nazi regime.

   Support your answer with reference to both interpretations and your own knowledge.

(16 marks)

6 Explain how the lives of Christians were affected by Nazi religious policies.

(8 marks)

7 'The Nazis controlled every aspect of life in Germany between 1933 and 1939.'

How far do you agree with this statement? Give reasons for your answer.

(18 marks)

General Certificate of Secondary Education

GCSE
History

Surname
Other names
Candidate signature

Centre name					
Centre number					
Candidate number					

Superpower Relations and the Cold War, 1941-1991

Time allowed: 45 minutes

Instructions to candidates
- Answer **all** the questions.
- Write your answers in **black** ink or ball-point pen.
- Write your name and other details in the boxes above.
- Cross out any rough work that you do not want to be marked.

Information for candidates
- The marks available are given in brackets at the end of each question.
- There are 32 marks available for this exam paper.

Advice for candidates
- Read each question carefully before you begin your answer.
- If you have time at the end, use it to check your answers.

1 Give two consequences of USSR's decision to intervene in the Hungarian Uprising (1956) and explain them.

(8 marks)

2 Give an account that analyses the main events of the Prague Spring (1968).

You could mention opposition to Soviet control and Dubcek's reforms in your answer.

(8 marks)

3 Examine:

a) the significance of the Bay of Pigs incident for the relationship between Cuba and the USA.

(8 marks)

b) the significance of the policy of détente in the 1970s for the relationship between the USA and the USSR.

(8 marks)

Answers

Use these pages to grade your answers to the <u>exam-style questions</u> in this book. For each question, we've covered some <u>key points</u> that your answer could include. Our answers are just <u>examples</u> though — answers very different to ours could also get top marks. Just remember, you can only gain marks for things that are <u>relevant</u> to the question.

Most exam questions in history are <u>level marked</u>. This means the examiner puts your answer into one of several <u>levels</u>. Then they award <u>marks</u> based on how well your answer matches the description for that level.

To reach a higher level, you'll need to give a '<u>more sophisticated</u>' answer. Exactly what 'sophisticated' means will depend on the type of question, but, generally speaking, a more sophisticated answer could include <u>more detail</u>, <u>more background knowledge</u> or make a <u>more complex judgement</u>.

Here's how to use levels to mark your answers:

1) Start by choosing which <u>level</u> your answer falls into — there are <u>level descriptions</u> at the start of each answer.

- Pick the level description that your answer matches <u>most closely</u>. If different parts of your answer match different level descriptions, then pick the level description that <u>best matches</u> your answer as a whole.

- A good way to do this is to start at 'Level 1' and <u>go up to the next level</u> each time your answer meets <u>all</u> of the conditions of a level. For example, if your answer meets all of the conditions for 'Level 3', but it has a few bits that match the description for 'Level 4', then choose 'Level 3'.

2) Now you need to chose a <u>mark</u> — look at the <u>range of marks</u> that are available <u>within the level</u> you've chosen.

- If your answer <u>completely matches</u> the level description, or parts of it match the <u>level above</u>, then give yourself a <u>high mark</u> within the range of the level.

- If your answer mostly matches the level description, but some parts of it <u>only just match</u>, then give yourself a mark in the <u>middle</u> of the range.

- Award yourself a <u>lower mark</u> within the range if your answer only just meets the conditions for that level or if parts of your answer only match the <u>level below</u>.

<u>Health and Medicine in Britain, c.1000-present</u>

<u>Page 11 — c.1000-c.1500: Medicine in Medieval Britain</u>

1 This question is level marked. How to grade your answer:

Level 1 1-3 marks	The answer shows some knowledge and understanding of the period. It provides a simple explanation of medieval beliefs about the causes of disease. There has been some attempt to organise ideas in a logical way.
Level 2 4-6 marks	The answer shows good knowledge and understanding of the period. It provides some analysis of the topic and shows links between some ideas. Most ideas are ordered logically.
Level 3 7-9 marks	The answer shows excellent knowledge and understanding of the period. It provides a detailed analysis of the topic and explains how different ideas are linked. All ideas are ordered logically.

Here are some points your answer may include:

- Some people believed disease was a punishment from God, so they thought people could be cured if they repented of their sins. This belief about the causes of disease was widely promoted by the Catholic Church, and so it changed little in the medieval period.

- Throughout the Middle Ages, some people believed disease had supernatural causes. They believed that disease was caused by evil beings like demons or witches. As a result, some members of the Catholic Church performed exorcisms as a form of treatment.

- The Theory of the Four Humours, created by Hippocrates and developed by Galen, was very popular in the Middle Ages. This theory led people to believe that disease was caused by an imbalance in the humours. The work of Hippocrates and Galen was promoted by the Church in the Middle Ages, so it

was difficult for people to question it. As a result, their ideas about the cause of disease weren't really challenged until the Renaissance period.

- Some people believed that disease was caused by breathing in bad air or 'miasma'. The miasma theory remained popular throughout the Middle Ages and beyond — it was only really challenged when Pasteur published his Germ Theory in 1861.

- There were some changes in beliefs about the causes of disease. For example, astrology was a new belief which was brought to Britain from the Islamic world between 1100 and 1300. Astrologers believed that the movements of the planets could cause disease.

- In the Middle Ages, people's beliefs about the causes of disease were mostly incorrect. As a consequence, their methods of treatment and prevention were often ineffective, and could be harmful. For example, bloodletting was a popular treatment because it fitted in with the Four Humours Theory, but it wasn't effective and could even be fatal if too much blood was taken.

2 This question is level marked. How to grade your answer:

Level 1 1-2 marks	Limited knowledge and understanding of the period is shown. The answer gives a simple explanation of why responses to the Black Death had a limited effect. Ideas are generally unconnected and don't follow a logical order.
Level 2 3-5 marks	Some relevant knowledge and understanding of the period is shown. The answer contains a basic analysis of why responses to the Black Death had a limited effect. An attempt has been made to organise ideas in a logical way.
Level 3 6-8 marks	A good level of knowledge and understanding of the period is shown. The answer explores multiple responses and analyses why they had a limited effect. It identifies some relevant connections between different points, and ideas are organised logically.

Level 4
9-10 marks   Knowledge and understanding of the period is precise and detailed. The answer considers a range of responses and analyses why they had a limited effect. All ideas are organised logically and connections between different points are identified to create a developed analysis of the topic.

Here are some points your answer may include:
- People didn't know that the Black Death was spread through the air or by fleas from rats. This meant they were unable to prevent the disease from spreading.
- People's beliefs about the cause of the Black Death were mistaken. They thought it was a punishment from God, or blamed it on miasma or an imbalance in the humours. This led to ineffective or harmful treatments, such as prayer, fasting or bloodletting.
- Local government tried to prevent the spread of the disease, but their attempts were mostly ineffective because they were based on mistaken beliefs about the causes of the disease. For example, Winchester built new cemeteries outside the town because the townspeople thought you could catch the disease from being close to the bodies of dead victims.
- Most people in towns lived in overcrowded and dirty conditions that allowed the disease to spread easily. For example, houses in towns were often overcrowded and crammed together, which made it easier for the airborne form of the plague to spread. This meant that any attempt to prevent the spread of the disease was limited by the environment that people were living in.
- There were very few places where people could receive care or treatment if they had the disease. Public hospitals were scarce, and had limited resources because they cared for the elderly as well as the sick. As a result, those who fell ill often stayed at home, exposing their families to the disease.

3   This question is level marked. How to grade your answer:
Level 1
1-4 marks   The answer shows limited knowledge and understanding of the period. It gives a simple explanation of one or more factors relating to progress in medicine in Britain during the medieval period. Ideas aren't organised with an overall argument in mind. There is no clear conclusion.
Level 2
5-8 marks   The answer shows some appropriate knowledge and understanding of the period. There is some analysis of how different factors relate to the topic. Ideas are organised with an overall argument in mind, but the conclusion isn't well supported by the answer.
Level 3
9-12 marks   The answer shows a good level of knowledge and understanding of the period, which is relevant to the question. It analyses how several different factors relate to the topic. Most ideas are organised to develop a clear argument and a well-supported conclusion.
Level 4
13-16 marks The answer shows an excellent level of relevant knowledge and understanding of the period. It analyses in detail how a range of factors relate to the topic. All ideas are well organised to develop a clear argument and a well-supported conclusion.

Here are some points your answer may include:
- There was little progress in ideas about the causes of disease. Most ideas were based on supernatural beliefs or the ideas of ancient doctors like Galen. The Church encouraged people to believe disease was a punishment from God and promoted Galen's ideas. This inhibited progress by making it difficult for people to question these ideas.

- There were some new ideas about the causes of disease in this period. For example, astrology was introduced from the Islamic world between 1100 and 1300. However, astrology was incorrect about the causes of disease, so its arrival didn't lead to any progress in medicine in Britain.
- There was a lack of progress in treatment. Medieval treatments were based on supernatural beliefs or the ideas of ancient doctors. People believed prayer could stop an illness. Bloodletting and purging were aimed at balancing the humours, but often caused more deaths than they prevented. The Church promoted these ineffective treatments because they fit with their preferred beliefs about the causes of disease. As a result, few people questioned these treatments and they continued to be used for hundreds of years. This also meant that few new treatments were developed.
- There was little improvement in access to care for ordinary people. Throughout the period, there were few trained doctors, and they were very expensive. Instead, most people depended on unqualified apothecaries, wise women or barber-surgeons for treatment, a situation which continued into the Renaissance period.
- There was some limited progress in surgery. Hugh of Lucca and his son Theodoric discovered that bandages soaked in wine could stop wounds becoming infected. John of Arderne created a recipe for a new anaesthetic, but it was risky to use as it could prove fatal.
- Some new discoveries were made in Islamic medicine which were then brought to Britain. Albucasis wrote books on how to remove bladder stones and perform dental surgery. Avenzoar described the parasite that causes scabies.

Page 19 — c.1500-c.1700: The Medical Renaissance in Britain

1   This question is level marked. How to grade your answer:
Level 1
1-2 marks   Limited knowledge and understanding of the period is shown. The answer gives a simple explanation of the importance of Harvey's work for the development of medicine. Ideas are generally unconnected and don't follow a logical order.
Level 2
3-4 marks   Some relevant knowledge and understanding of the period is shown. The answer attempts to analyse at least one point about the importance of Harvey's work. An attempt has been made to organise ideas logically.
Level 3
5-6 marks   A good level of knowledge and understanding of the period is shown. The answer explores two or more points about the importance of Harvey's work and analyses them in more detail. Ideas are organised logically.
Level 4
7-8 marks   Knowledge and understanding of the period is precise and detailed. The answer explores two or more points about the importance of Harvey's work and thoroughly analyses each one. Ideas are organised logically and connections between different points are identified to create a deeper analysis of importance.

Here are some points your answer may include:
- Harvey's work improved doctors' understanding of the human body, because he showed that blood circulates around the body, rather than being continually formed and consumed. This gave doctors a new understanding of how the body works, which was essential for the development of new treatments like blood transfusions and complex surgery.
- Harvey was important in questioning the ideas of Galen. His work showed that doctors should base their ideas on observation and not just on the books of ancient doctors. This led to developments in medicine.

218

- Harvey's work confirmed Vesalius' views about the importance of dissection. Increasing use of dissection improved doctors' understanding of the human body and led to important developments in medicine.
- It took a long time for Harvey's work to make an impact. For example, bloodletting continued as a treatment in the Renaissance period even though Harvey had shown that it was based on a mistaken belief. It wasn't until the 19th and 20th centuries that doctors began to carry out the complex surgery and blood transfusions made possible by Harvey's work.

2   This question is level marked. How to grade your answer:

Level 1 1-3 marks	Limited knowledge and understanding of the period is shown. The answer gives a simple explanation of changing ideas about the human body. Ideas are generally unconnected and don't follow a logical order.
Level 2 4-6 marks	Some relevant knowledge and understanding of the period is shown. The answer contains a basic analysis of reasons why ideas about the human body changed. An attempt has been made to organise ideas in a logical way.
Level 3 7-9 marks	A good level of knowledge and understanding of the period is shown. The answer explores multiple reasons why ideas changed. It identifies some relevant connections between different points, and ideas are organised logically.
Level 4 10-12 marks	**Answers can't be awarded Level 4 if they only discuss the information suggested in the question.** Knowledge and understanding of the period is precise and detailed. The answer considers a range of reasons why ideas changed and analyses each one. All ideas are organised logically and connections between different points are identified to create a developed analysis of the topic.

Here are some points your answer may include:

- Vesalius improved people's knowledge and understanding of the human body. He drew accurate diagrams of the human body and was the first to show that there were no holes in the septum of the heart.
- Harvey's work advanced knowledge of circulation. People originally thought that there were two types of blood, which were created and consumed. Harvey showed that there was only one type of blood, which circulated around the body.
- Dissections became a key part of medical training, allowing doctors to see inside the body for the first time. The work of Vesalius and Harvey showed the importance of dissection to developing new ideas about the human body.
- The printing press allowed individuals who made important discoveries about the human body to share them with others. For example, Vesalius published books of diagrams of the human body, such as 'The Fabric of the Human Body' (1543). The printing press allowed such books to be read by a larger audience.
- The Royal Society helped to spread new scientific theories, including new ideas about the human body. Its journal, 'Philosophical Transactions' allowed more people to read about these new ideas.
- Doctors began to challenge Galen for the first time, and this allowed new ideas about the human body to develop. In the Renaissance period, ancient texts were rediscovered which encouraged observation. This encouraged doctors to examine the human body for themselves rather than relying on Galen. Vesalius and Harvey showed that Galen was wrong about how the human body worked, which encouraged others to question

and challenge Galen. The declining influence of the Catholic Church, which had promoted Galen's ideas, also made it easier for doctors to challenge Galen.

3   This question is level marked. How to grade your answer:

Level 1 1-4 marks	The answer shows limited knowledge and understanding of the period. It gives a simple explanation of one or more factors relating to changing beliefs about medicine. Ideas aren't organised with an overall argument in mind. There is no clear conclusion.
Level 2 5-8 marks	The answer shows some appropriate knowledge and understanding of the period. There is some analysis of how different factors relate to the topic. Ideas are organised with an overall argument in mind, but the conclusion isn't well supported by the answer.
Level 3 9-12 marks	The answer shows a good level of knowledge and understanding of the period, which is relevant to the question. It analyses how several different factors relate to the topic. Most ideas are organised to develop a clear argument that supports the conclusion.
Level 4 13-16 marks	The answer shows an excellent level of relevant knowledge and understanding of the period. It analyses in detail how a range of factors relate to the topic. All ideas are well organised to develop a clear argument and a well-supported conclusion.

Here are some points your answer may include:

- Vesalius and Harvey changed people's beliefs about the human body. Vesalius drew accurate diagrams of the human body, while Harvey showed that blood circulates around the body.
- Ancient books discovered in the Renaissance period showed the value of observation and dissection. This encouraged doctors to learn by examining the body rather than relying on the theories of ancient doctors. This transformed doctors' beliefs about medicine.
- The rise of Protestant Christianity in Europe reduced the influence of the Catholic Church over medical teaching. This allowed doctors to challenge medical beliefs that had been promoted by the Catholic Church, such as Galen's teachings and supernatural beliefs about the causes of disease.
- Thomas Sydenham improved doctors' medical knowledge and altered their understanding of disease by introducing a new method of classifying diseases. This changed doctors' ideas about how they should treat their patients. Instead of focusing on prognosis, Sydenham encouraged doctors to examine patients' symptoms.
- The printing press allowed new ideas to spread quickly. Doctors and university students could learn about new ideas from printed books.
- The Royal Society encouraged people to question existing medical ideas. Its journal helped to spread new beliefs about medicine.
- Many people couldn't read, so new ideas didn't reach them. As a result, Galen's ideas about the causes and treatment of disease remained popular. Bloodletting was a common treatment during the Renaissance, even though Harvey had shown that it was based on a mistaken belief.
- Religious beliefs and the miasma theory remained popular in the Renaissance period. During the Great Plague, people used prayer, amulets and herbs (to purify the air) to prevent the disease. This shows that, despite the new discoveries in the Renaissance period, many people did not alter their beliefs about medicine.

Page 31 — c.1700-c.1900: Medicine in 18th and 19th Century Britain

1 This question is level marked. How to grade your answer:

Level 1 1-2 marks	The answer identifies some relevant features of the source and makes a simple statement about its usefulness.
Level 2 3-4 marks	The answer gives a simple analysis of the source's usefulness. The analysis is supported by basic knowledge and understanding of the topic.
Level 3 5-6 marks	The answer gives a more detailed analysis of the source's usefulness. The analysis is supported by good knowledge and understanding of the topic.
Level 4 7-8 marks	The answer gives a detailed analysis of the content of the source and its provenance. The analysis is supported by excellent knowledge and understanding of the topic. The answer reaches a well-supported judgement about the usefulness of the source.

Here are some points your answer may include:

- Source B is useful for understanding some of the reasons for poor public health in the 19th century. Chadwick argues that overcrowding and dirty living conditions contribute to public health problems. These conditions were caused by the rapid growth of towns as a result of the industrial revolution.
- Source B gives a useful insight into people's understanding of the link between public health problems and the spread of disease in the 19th century. Chadwick claims that disease is caused by 'atmospheric impurities', which suggests he believed in the miasma theory. At the time Chadwick was writing, miasma was believed to cause most diseases. It was only in the 1850s, when Snow published his study of the 1854 cholera epidemic, that people began to gain a more accurate understanding of how poor public health caused the spread of disease.
- Source B is useful for understanding Chadwick's ideas about how to improve public health among the poor. Chadwick suggests that removing waste from living areas and the improvement of water and drainage systems would be the best ways to improve living conditions. These ideas were eventually put into practice under the 1875 Public Health Act and the Artisans' Dwellings Act. These laws aimed to improve water and sewerage systems and to clear slum housing.

2 This question is level marked. How to grade your answer:

Level 1 1-4 marks	The answer shows limited knowledge and understanding of 19th century Britain. It gives a simple explanation of one or more factors relating to the improvement of people's health. Ideas aren't organised with an overall argument in mind. There is no clear conclusion.
Level 2 5-8 marks	The answer shows some appropriate knowledge and understanding of the period. There is some analysis of how different factors relate to the topic. Ideas are organised with an overall argument in mind, but the conclusion isn't well supported by the answer.
Level 3 9-12 marks	The answer shows a good level of knowledge and understanding of the period, which is relevant to the question. It analyses how several different factors relate to the topic. Most ideas are organised to develop a clear argument that supports the conclusion.
Level 4 13-16 marks	The answer shows an excellent level of relevant knowledge and understanding of the period. It analyses in detail how a range of factors relate to the topic. All ideas are well organised to develop a clear argument and a well-supported conclusion.

Here are some points your answer may include:

- The Germ Theory was an important breakthrough because it was the first time germs had been shown to cause disease. Before the Germ Theory, many people believed that disease was caused by miasma. This meant people did not know how to effectively prevent dangerous diseases like cholera.
- The Germ Theory allowed some diseases to be prevented through vaccination. Pasteur and his team successfully created vaccines for chicken cholera, anthrax and rabies.
- The Germ Theory showed that hygiene was important in preventing infection. This led to important improvements in surgery, such as Joseph Lister's use of antiseptic carbolic acid on instruments and bandages, and the development of aseptic surgery.
- The Germ Theory showed there was a link between poor living conditions and disease. This supported the findings of Edwin Chadwick and put pressure on the government to pass the 1875 Public Health Act.
- While the Germ Theory helped Pasteur to develop new vaccines, it was a long time before its full impact on the treatment of disease was felt. The first magic bullet was only developed in 1909. Penicillin, the first antibiotic, wasn't discovered until 1928.
- Many improvements to people's health in the 19th century took place before the discovery of the Germ Theory. Jenner's smallpox vaccine led to a big fall in the number of smallpox cases, even though people didn't know how it worked. Nightingale's improvements in hospital sanitation helped prevent deaths, even though she didn't know that germs caused disease.
- The Germ Theory did not explain all diseases. In the 20th century, scientists discovered that viruses, genetics and lifestyle factors can also cause disease.

Page 45 — c.1900-present: Medicine in Modern Britain

1 This question is level marked. How to grade your answer:

Level 1 1-2 marks	The answer gives a simple description of one difference between hospitals in the 20th century and the Middle Ages. Some knowledge and understanding of the periods is shown.
Level 2 3-4 marks	The answer explains one difference between hospitals in the two periods. Detailed knowledge and understanding is used to support the explanation.

Here are some points your answer may include:

- The purpose of hospitals in the 20th century was different to the purpose of hospitals in the Middle Ages. In the 20th century, the main purpose of hospitals was to treat disease and injury. In the Middle Ages, the main purpose of hospitals was to provide shelter and care for the sick or elderly.
- The range of technology and treatments available to patients in 20th century hospitals was greater than those offered by hospitals in the Middle Ages. Hospitals in the 20th century offered advanced technology like robot-assisted surgery, and treatments like penicillin. Hospitals in the Middle Ages had good water and sewerage systems, but lacked the technology and treatments available to 20th century hospitals.
- Since 1948, most hospitals have been run by the National Health Service, which is supported by the government. In the Middle Ages, most hospitals were set up and run by the Catholic Church.

220

2   This question is level marked. How to grade your answer:

Level 1 1-2 marks	Limited knowledge and understanding of the 20th century is shown. The answer gives a simple explanation of the importance of the First and Second World Wars for the development of health and medicine. Ideas are generally unconnected and don't follow a logical order.
Level 2 3-4 marks	Some relevant knowledge and understanding of the period is shown. The answer attempts to analyse at least one point about the importance of the wars. An attempt has been made to organise ideas logically.
Level 3 5-6 marks	A good level of knowledge and understanding of the period is shown. The answer explores two or more points about the importance of the wars and analyses them in more detail. Ideas are organised logically.
Level 4 7-8 marks	Knowledge and understanding of the period is precise and detailed. The answer explores two or more points about the importance of the wars and thoroughly analyses each one. Ideas are organised logically and connections between different points are identified to create a deeper analysis of importance.

Here are some points your answer may include:

- The huge number of serious injuries in the First World War forced doctors to find solutions to the problem of blood loss. In 1914, doctors found that sodium citrate stopped stored blood clotting. The first blood depot was set up in 1917, in order to provide blood for soldiers injured in the Battle of Cambrai.
- The large number of injuries in the First World War also led to improvements in diagnosis. In 1914, Marie Curie set up mobile X-ray units, allowing X-ray equipment to be transported. The war also increased the number of radiologists.
- The First World War was important in improving plastic surgery. Harold Gillies set up a plastic surgery unit for the British Army during the war. He used the unit to develop the use of pedicle tubes to complete skin grafts. Gillies' work was continued during the Second World War by Archibald McIndoe.
- The Second World War was important in the development of penicillin. Penicillin was discovered in 1928 and purified in 1938-40, but mass-production could not begin due to lack of funding. The US government began funding the mass-production of penicillin in 1941 when the US entered the war.
- Both wars led to improvements in living conditions, although the Second World War had a greater impact. Lloyd George promised 'homes fit for heroes' for soldiers returning from the First World War, but the reality failed to live up to his promise. Between 1945 and 1951, 800,000 new homes were built to replace houses destroyed by bombing in the Second World War.
- The Second World War was important in improving public health. The Beveridge Report, published in 1942, aimed to reward people with a better public health system once the war was over. Beveridge's proposals were so popular with the wartime public that the 1945 Labour government was elected on its promise to implement Beveridge's proposals. This led to the founding of the welfare state, including the 1946 National Insurance Act and the National Health Service in 1948.
- On the whole, the First World War and the Second World War impacted health and medicine in different ways. The First World War mainly caused changes in surgery, while the Second World War largely led to improvements in public health.

3   This question is level marked. How to grade your answer:

Level 1 1-4 marks	The answer shows limited knowledge and understanding of relevant periods. It gives a simple explanation of one or more factors relating to the improvement of people's health. Ideas aren't organised with an overall argument in mind. There is no clear conclusion.
Level 2 5-8 marks	The answer shows some knowledge and understanding of relevant periods. There is some analysis of how different factors relate to the topic. Ideas are organised with an overall argument in mind, but the conclusion isn't well supported by the answer.
Level 3 9-12 marks	The answer shows a good level of knowledge and understanding of relevant periods, which is focused on the topic. It analyses how the factor in the question and other factors relate to the topic. Most ideas are organised to develop a clear argument that supports the conclusion.
Level 4 13-16 marks	The answer shows an excellent level of knowledge and understanding of relevant periods. It analyses in detail how the factor in the question and a range of other factors relate to the topic. All ideas are well organised to develop a clear argument and a well-supported conclusion.

Here are some points your answer may include:

- In the 19th century, the government played the most important role in improving public health. The 1875 Public Health Act was the first compulsory government intervention in public health and was effective in improving towns' water and sewerage systems. The government also supported major projects to improve public health like Bazalgette's sewer system and the clearance of Birmingham's slums.
- In the 19th and 20th centuries, the government played an important role in preventing disease. In 1802, Parliament supported Jenner's smallpox vaccine with a £10,000 grant, and in 1853 the government made the vaccination compulsory for infants. In the early 20th century, the Liberal government introduced reforms to improve health by tackling poverty. The government also funded campaigns in the 20th century to prevent diseases caused by obesity, smoking and excessive alcohol consumption.
- In the 20th century, the government played the most important role in improving public health, as it significantly improved access to medical treatment. In 1948, the government established the National Health Service, which has improved people's health by offering a range of medical services free of charge. Furthermore, government action since the Second World War has led to the clearance of slum housing and the improvement of living conditions.
- Other factors were more important in improving public health before the 19th century, as the government believed in a very laissez-faire approach towards public health before this time. This did not begin to change until the government granted funding to Jenner's smallpox vaccination clinic in the early 19th century.
- During the medieval period, the Church was more important than the government in improving people's health, as it was monasteries that ran most hospitals and tried to provide care for the poor, sick and elderly.
- In the Renaissance period, the advancement of medical knowledge played a more important role than the government. For example, Sydenham's work on the symptoms of diseases helped doctors to diagnose certain diseases more easily.
- The development of technology like the printing press was also more significant, as it allowed new medical ideas to be spread more easily. This helped to disprove old ideas about medicine. For example, the printing press allowed many

people to read Vesalius' ideas about dissection and anatomy.

- In many cases, government action to improve people's health only came about because of advances in science and technology. For example, from 1861, the growing acceptance of Pasteur's Germ Theory meant that the link between poor living conditions and poor health became more obvious. This provided the scientific proof required to persuade the government to pass the 1875 Public Health Act.
- War has been an important factor in causing the government to act. Destruction during the Second World War caused the government to build 800,000 new homes and improve housing standards.

America, 1789-1900

Page 51 — America's Expansion, 1789-c.1830

1   This question is level marked. How to grade your answer:

Level 1 1-2 marks	The answer shows appropriate knowledge of the period by identifying at least one issue that made migration difficult.
Level 2 3-4 marks	The answer shows appropriate knowledge and understanding of the period by identifying two relevant issues and explaining how each one made migration difficult.

Here are some points your answer may include:

- Settlers moving from the East to the West had to cross the Great Plains. The weather there varies hugely, with droughts in the summer and heavy snow in winter, so settlers might have faced difficult conditions like lack of water and severe cold.
- The Rocky Mountains lie between the Great Plains and the west coast. The Rockies are a major mountain range, and their slopes were heavily wooded, so they would have been difficult to cross.
- There are areas of desert in the Plateaux region at the centre of the Rocky Mountains, which would have posed a problem for travellers because of limited water supplies.

2   This question is level marked. How to grade your answer:

Level 1 1-3 marks	The answer shows some knowledge and understanding of America between 1793 and c.1830. It provides a simple explanation of some reasons for the expansion of US territory. There has been some attempt to organise ideas in a logical way.
Level 2 4-6 marks	The answer shows good knowledge and understanding of the period. It provides some analysis of the key reasons for expansion, and some connections are made between reasons. Most ideas are organised logically.
Level 3 7-9 marks	The answer shows excellent knowledge and understanding of the period. It analyses several key reasons and the links between them in detail. Ideas are ordered logically.

Here are some points your answer may include:

- The Louisiana Purchase of 1803 secured a huge area of land for the US, which had belonged to the French. This expanded US territory northwards and westwards.
- The US expanded by occupying land by force. For example, the US secured West Florida, which they claimed was part of the Louisiana Purchase, by occupying the area when its inhabitants rebelled against Spanish rule. This led to the Adams-Onis Treaty with Spain, which granted Florida to the US.
- Before the US declared war on Britain in 1812, the British had helped Native Americans resist US expansion. When the war ended in 1815, the British stopped supporting the Native Americans. As a result, the Native Americans were no longer able to effectively resist US expansion.

- Tecumseh, a Shawnee war chief who had resisted US expansion, died in 1813 during the war with Britain. His death meant there was no one to unite the Native American tribes against US expansion. This enabled the US to make around 200 treaties with Native American tribes, which secured more territory for the US.
- New transport links, like the National Road from the east coast to Illinois and the Eerie canal from New York to the Great Lakes, improved access to the Northwest Territory and encouraged expansion.

3   This question is level marked. How to grade your answer:

Level 1 1-2 marks	Limited knowledge and understanding of America between 1793 and c.1830 is shown. The answer gives one or more simple explanations of why slavery expanded in the South. Ideas are generally unconnected and don't follow a logical order.
Level 2 3-5 marks	Some relevant knowledge and understanding of the period is shown. The answer contains a basic analysis of why slavery expanded. An attempt has been made to organise ideas in a logical way.
Level 3 6-8 marks	A good level of knowledge and understanding of the period is shown. The answer explores multiple reasons for the expansion of slavery and analyses the effects of some of them. It identifies some relevant connections between different points, and ideas are organised logically.
Level 4 9-10 marks	Knowledge and understanding of the period is precise and detailed. The answer considers a range of reasons for the expansion of slavery and analyses the effects of each one. All ideas are organised logically. Connections between different points are identified to create a developed analysis of the topic.

Here are some points your answer may include:

- The growth of the Atlantic slave trade meant that indentured servants, who had farmed labour intensive crops like tobacco, cotton and sugar on plantations in the South from the 17th century, were replaced by slaves.
- The industrial revolution in Britain in the early 19th century increased demand for cotton, enabling US planters to export more cotton to Britain. As a result, cotton plantations grew and used more slave labour.
- The invention of the cotton gin in 1793 meant cotton could be harvested much more quickly because the machine removed the cotton fibre from the seeds mechanically. This allowed cotton farmers to expand their cotton production, so they enlarged the labour force and increased the use of slavery.
- Cotton became the South's most important crop and the South's economy came to rely on cotton exports. As a result, the South became dependent on slave labour to farm cotton. Many southerners saw slavery as part of their way of life, which meant that slave trading and slave labour continued to exist in the South, despite the end of the Atlantic slave trade in 1808.

Page 61 — The West, c.1830-c.1861

1   This question is level marked. How to grade your answer:

Level 1 1-2 marks	The answer shows appropriate knowledge of the period by identifying at least one difference between the lifestyles of the Plains Indians and white settlers.
Level 2 3-4 marks	The answer shows appropriate knowledge and understanding of the period by identifying two relevant differences and explaining each one.

Here are some points your answer may include:

- Native Americans believed that land belonged to everyone and that it couldn't be bought and sold. This contrasted with

the views of the white settlers who wished to claim land as their own private property.
- Many Native American tribes lived a nomadic lifestyle, as they followed the buffalo herds that were their main source of food and livelihood. This contrasted with the lifestyles of white settlers, who built permanent houses and farmed the land to survive.
- Native American tribes were organised into bands and each band had a chief and a council of elders, while white settlers were under the authority of a more centralised system of government.

2   This question is level marked. How to grade your answer:

Level 1 1-3 marks	The answer shows limited knowledge and understanding of the period. It explains one or both factors in a general way.
Level 2 4-6 marks	The answer shows some appropriate knowledge and understanding of the period. It gives a simple analysis of one or both factors, using knowledge of the period to justify its points.
Level 3 7-9 marks	The answer shows a good level of appropriate knowledge and understanding of the period. It analyses both factors in more detail, using knowledge of the period to justify its points.
Level 4 10-12 marks	The answer shows detailed and precise knowledge and understanding of the period. It analyses both factors in detail, using knowledge of the period to justify its points. It makes connections between the factors and comes to a clear conclusion about which one was more important.

Here are some points your answer may include:
- The recession of 1837 created economic and social problems in the East. This encouraged people to leave the East, since they could no longer rely on finding work and earning good wages.
- High levels of immigration from Europe led to overcrowding in the East. This caused problems, as there was a lack of land to farm. Since there were huge amounts of fertile land available in the West, more people were drawn to the West when conditions in the East worsened.
- Overcrowding caused diseases like cholera and yellow fever to spread in the East, and made migrating to the West more attractive.
- The availability of fertile land in the West was an important cause of westward expansion, as many people moved to the West to create their own homesteads.
- The government encouraged migration by creating opportunities for settlers to buy land in the West. For example, the Distributive Preemption Act of 1841 meant that settlers could buy 160 acres of land at a low price if they'd lived there for 14 months.
- Huge numbers of people were drawn to California by the opportunity to find gold. Migration to the West in the 1840s was gradual, until the discovery of gold in California in 1848 created expectations that people could make a fortune in the West.
- The Mormons migrated to the West because they faced persecution for their beliefs and practices, such as polygamy. They were driven from their homes in the East, so they wanted to find somewhere they could live freely. The West was attractive, as they were able to build their own community away from those who had persecuted them in the East.
- Problems in the East and new opportunities in the West were closely linked — it is unlikely that people would have moved away from the relative safety of the East, despite its economic issues, unless the West offered the chance of a better life.

3   This question is level marked. How to grade your answer:

Level 1 1-2 marks	The answer shows some knowledge and understanding of America between 1830 and 1850. It provides a simple explanation of some factors that affected the relationship between the Plains Indians and the white settlers. There has been some attempt to organise ideas in a logical way.
Level 2 3-5 marks	The answer shows good knowledge and understanding of the period. It provides some analysis of the key factors and some connections are made between them. Most ideas are organised logically.
Level 3 6-8 marks	**Answers can't be awarded Level 3 if they only discuss the information suggested in the question.** The answer shows excellent knowledge and understanding of the period. It analyses several key factors and the links between them in detail. Ideas are ordered logically.

Here are some points your answer may include:
- The creation of the Permanent Indian Frontier as part of the 1830 Indian Removal Act caused conflict, because some Native American tribes resisted being moved onto the Plains. However, this policy eventually reduced tensions between settlers and Native Americans, because it separated the two groups and gave each their own territory.
- From the Great Migration of 1843 onwards, there was an increase in the number of people travelling across the Great Plains to the West, which meant that there was more contact between the Plains Indians and white settlers. Even so, the relationship between the settlers and the Native Americans was still mostly peaceful. Some Native Americans acted as guides for white settlers and traded with them.
- The development of the California and Oregon trails and the California Gold Rush significantly increased the number of settlers crossing the Plains in the late 1840s. This negatively affected the relationship between Native Americans and settlers, because the settlers disrupted the buffalo herds that the Native Americans relied on.
- As a result, the Native Americans became more hostile towards the settlers and sometimes attacked their wagons. The settlers became increasingly afraid of the Native Americans and distrusted them.

4   Use the levels below to mark questions 4a and 4b separately. How to grade your answers:

Level 1 1-2 marks	Limited knowledge and understanding of the period is shown. The answer gives a simple explanation of the significance of the topic. Ideas are generally unconnected and don't follow a logical order.
Level 2 3-4 marks	Some relevant knowledge and understanding of the period is shown. The answer attempts to analyse at least one point about the significance of the topic. An attempt has been made to organise ideas logically.
Level 3 5-6 marks	A good level of knowledge and understanding of the period is shown. The answer explores two or more points about the significance of the topic and analyses them in more detail. Ideas are organised logically.
Level 4 7-8 marks	Knowledge and understanding of the period is precise and detailed. The answer explores two or more points about the significance of the topic and thoroughly analyses each one. Ideas are organised logically and connections between different points are identified to create a deeper analysis of significance.

Here are some points your answer for 4a may include:

- The Gold Rush increased America's population by encouraging international immigration. For example, people came from China, Mexico and South America to look for gold.
- The Gold Rush increased US settlement in California, because more people moved West, believing that they could make a fortune and have a better life.
- Mining resulted in the development of California. The non-Native American population rose and mining towns expanded significantly. The large numbers of people settling in California meant that better links were needed between the East and the West, which resulted in improved mail and transport links.
- Gold mining generated wealth, which helped the US economy to grow and gave it an important role in world trade.

Here are some points your answer for 4b may include:

- The Fort Laramie Treaty damaged the relationship between the government and the Native Americans, because it broke the government's promise, made in the Indian Removal Act of 1830, that the Native Americans could have the Great Plains.
- The Fort Laramie Treaty marked the start of the government's policy of moving Native Americans onto reservations. The reservation system failed the Native Americans and eventually caused their relationship with the government to break down, which helped to cause the Indian Wars.
- The government failed to respect the Fort Laramie Treaty. In the 1850s and 1860s, it made new treaties that took more land from the Native Americans, going against the Fort Laramie Treaty. This angered the Native Americans and made it harder for them to trust the government.
- Many Native Americans also broke the Fort Laramie Treaty, either because they didn't know it existed or because they disagreed with its terms. This made it difficult for the Native Americans and the government to trust one another, as both sides had shown that they were willing to break their promises.

Page 70 — Civil War and Reconstruction, c.1861-c.1877

1   This question is level marked. How to grade your answer:

Level 1 1-4 marks	The answer shows limited knowledge and understanding of the period. It gives a simple explanation of one or more factors relating to the outbreak of the American Civil War. Ideas aren't organised with an overall argument in mind. There is no clear conclusion.
Level 2 5-9 marks	The answer shows some appropriate knowledge and understanding of the period. There is some analysis of how different factors relate to the outbreak of the Civil War. Ideas are organised with an overall argument in mind, but the conclusion isn't well supported by the answer.
Level 3 10-14 marks	The answer shows a good level of knowledge and understanding of the period, which is relevant to the question. It analyses how several different factors contributed to the outbreak of the Civil War. Most ideas are organised to develop a clear argument that supports the conclusion.
Level 4 15-18 marks	The answer shows an excellent level of relevant knowledge and understanding of the period. It analyses in detail how a range of factors contributed to the outbreak of the Civil War. All ideas are well organised to develop a clear argument and a well-supported conclusion.

Here are some points your answer may include:

- Lincoln's election showed that the northern states had enough power to elect a president that the South did not support, since he won the election despite failing to secure a single vote in ten southern states. This increased southern fears that the North's superior political power (due to its high population) would allow it to abolish slavery by passing a law. This led to further division between the North and the South.
- Lincoln's personal views on slavery were unacceptable to many in the South. They felt that their right to practise slavery would be threatened by Lincoln if he became president, so his election caused seven states to secede. Secession meant that civil war became more likely, as it caused further division between North and South.
- While Lincoln's election triggered secession, which made war more likely, this did not make civil war inevitable. Lincoln had always said that he would not interfere in southern slavery, despite his personal views. He also made it clear that he would not attack the South unless it attacked the North first. If the South had not attacked Fort Sumter, it is possible that war would not have broken out.
- Slavery was a more important cause of civil war, as it was the root cause of tensions between North and South. As the US expanded, the South wanted new territories to become slave states, but the North didn't want slavery to spread. The South saw slavery as crucial to their way of life and feared that the North wanted to abolish it. Lincoln's election increased these fears and made the South feel that they had to protect their rights by seceding. However, these fears had been developing for a long time before Lincoln was elected.
- In the past, agreements like the Missouri Compromise had settled tension between the North and the South over slavery in new territories. When this compromise failed due to the Kansas-Nebraska Act of 1854, there was no longer an official, peaceful way to settle tension over slavery. This made civil war more likely.
- The actions of northern abolitionists like Harriet Beecher Stowe greatly increased southern fears that the North would try to abolish slavery in the South. This tension had been growing for decades before Lincoln's election. However, the Republican Party, which Lincoln represented, was dedicated to stopping the spread of slavery, so Lincoln's election made southerners even more fearful.

2   Use the levels below to mark each consequence separately. One consequence can get a maximum of 4 marks. How to grade your answer:

Level 1 1-2 marks	Some general knowledge and understanding of the period is shown. The answer gives one consequence of the American Civil War and attempts a simple explanation.
Level 2 3-4 marks	Detailed knowledge and understanding of the period is shown. The answer gives one consequence of the war and explains it using knowledge of the period.

Here are some points your answer may include:

- The Civil War caused hardship in the South. Union blockades of Confederate ports prevented the South from importing food, southerners were cut off from northern markets and lots of southern farmland was destroyed by the fighting.
- The war caused inflation in the North and the South, but things were more serious in the South, because food shortages and Davis' decision to print too many paper notes made the inflation problem worse.
- The North's economy benefited from the Civil War. Its agricultural and industrial production boomed, since the Union army created a demand for food and weapons. This boosted employment, which led to increased prosperity for northerners.

- The war caused social tension in the North, since many freed slaves performed jobs that had been left behind by soldiers who were fighting in the South. Some were angry that freed slaves were taking 'white jobs', and this increased racism and violence against black Americans.
- Slavery was formally abolished after the war. Lincoln's Emancipation Proclamation of 1863 freed all slaves in Confederate states, while the Union victory secured the freedom of those in the border states.

3 This question is level marked. How to grade your answer:

Level 1	The answer shows some knowledge and
1-3 marks	understanding of the period. It provides a simple explanation of some stages of Reconstruction. There has been some attempt to organise events in a logical way.
Level 2	The answer shows good knowledge and
4-6 marks	understanding of the period. It provides some analysis of the stages of Reconstruction. Most events are organised logically and some connections are made between them.
Level 3	The answer shows excellent knowledge and
7-9 marks	understanding of the period. It provides a detailed analysis of the key stages of Reconstruction. Events are ordered logically and strong connections are made between them.

Here are some points your answer may include:

- Andrew Johnson's Presidential Reconstruction, which started in 1865, was quite lenient. He pardoned white southerners, returned property to its original owners instead of redistributing it, allowed the southern elite to regain power and let southern states pass Black Codes, which limited the freedom of African Americans. Johnson also vetoed the Civil Rights Act, which would have given citizenship to all who were born in the US, except Native Americans.
- Radical Republicans weren't happy with Johnson's Presidential Reconstruction. They believed his version of Reconstruction was too lenient — they wanted racial equality and greater punishment of Confederate leaders. As a result, radical and moderate Republicans created an alliance to overturn Johnson's veto of the Civil Rights Act and ensured that the Act became law.
- Radical Republicans took control of Reconstruction in 1867. During Radical Reconstruction, the South was put under military control and laws were passed to protect African Americans, such as the 15th Amendment and the Enforcement Acts.
- Reconstruction lost political support in the North from 1873. Events such as economic depression in the North in 1874 meant that northerners lost interest in the South.
- The power of the 14th Amendment to protect black people's civil rights was weakened by Supreme Court decisions. This meant that many violent crimes against African Americans in the South went unpunished.
- Republicans lost support in the North as a result of the depression, and scandals under President Grant. As a result, the Democrats won control of the lower house of Congress in 1874 for the first time since the Civil War. In 1876, Hayes (a Republican) was elected President — he ended federal military involvement in the South and allowed the Democrats to control the South. This marked the end of Reconstruction.

Pages 80-81 — Development of the Plains, c.1861-c.1877

1 This question is level marked. How to grade your answer:

Level 1	The answer gives one or more differences
1-2 marks	between the interpretations. Differences are based on some analysis of content from the interpretations.
Level 2	The answer gives differences between the
3-4 marks	interpretations. A detailed analysis of content from the interpretations is given to explain differences.

Here are some points your answer may include:

- Interpretation 1 says that settlers are justified in moving Native Americans off their land because the settlers are superior. In Interpretation 2, the Ponca chief argues the opposite and says that the President has no right to take the land from him because he has farmed it and has kept all his promises to the President.
- Interpretation 1 suggests that the government's policy of relocating Native Americans is necessary because Native American culture is incompatible with that of the settlers — he argues that 'civilisation and barbarism... cannot coexist'. Interpretation 2, on the other hand, highlights the fact that the Ponca have adopted certain elements of settler culture, such as planting crops.
- Interpretation 1 does not see the relocation policy as immoral or negative, despite recognising that the land was 'wrested' from the Native Americans. Interpretation 2 expresses sorrow and a sense of betrayal over the relocation policy.
- Interpretation 1 emphasises the benefits of relocation for Christian settlers, while Interpretation 2 focuses on the cruelty and injustice of relocation.

2 This question is level marked. How to grade your answer:

Level 1	The answer gives appropriate reasons why the
1-2 marks	interpretations are different. The reasons are based on a simple analysis of the interpretations' provenance.
Level 2	The answer gives appropriate reasons why the
3-4 marks	interpretations are different. The reasons are well supported by knowledge of the period and a detailed analysis of the interpretations' provenance.

Here are some points your answer may include:

- Interpretation 1 was written by the Commissioner of Indian Affairs, who works for the US government and supports its policy. Interpretation 2 is from an interview with the Chief of the Ponca Tribe. He has a negative view of the policy because his tribe was relocated to a smaller area, despite co-operating with the government.
- The author of Interpretation 1 expresses the government view that Native Americans are inferior and settlers would put their land to better use. As a Native American himself, the Chief of the Ponca in Interpretation 2 does not agree that settlers are superior and does not believe they have a right to take his land.
- Interpretation 1 is written by someone who has no direct experience of relocation, therefore it is more detached and sees relocation as a positive thing. Interpretation 2 takes a negative view of relocation as a result of the Ponca chief's personal experiences.

3   This question is level marked. How to grade your answer:

Level 1 1-2 marks	The answer shows support for one or both interpretations. It is based on a simple analysis of the interpretations and basic knowledge of the topic.
Level 2 3-4 marks	The answer evaluates the credibility of one interpretation. It is supported by a more detailed analysis of the interpretations and some relevant knowledge of the topic.
Level 3 5-6 marks	The answer evaluates the credibility of both interpretations and gives a judgment about which one is more convincing. Is is supported by a detailed analysis of the interpretations and a good level of relevant knowledge of the topic.
Level 4 7-8 marks	The answer evaluates the credibility of both interpretations and comes to a clear judgement about which one is more convincing. It is supported by a strong analysis of the interpretations and a wide range of relevant knowledge of the topic.

Here are some points your answer may include:
*   Interpretation 1 recognises the scale of the relocation policy, since it points out that a large portion of US territory was taken from the Native Americans. This is convincing, since the Native American tribes lost the majority of their land as a result of the relocation policy.
*   Interpretation 1 is convincing about the reasons for the relocation policy. It shows that the government thought settlers were superior, and that they had more right to the land than the Native Americans. This attitude was a key reason why the government kept relocating Native Americans and giving their land to white settlers.
*   Interpretation 1 convincingly represents 'Manifest Destiny' — the idea that white settlers were destined to occupy all of North America — since it describes the settlers as 'enlightened and Christian people' taking land that is rightfully theirs. The idea of 'Manifest Destiny' was a key factor that drove the government's relocation policy.
*   Interpretation 2 convincingly reflects the fact that relocation was about the needs of settlers, and not the needs of Native Americans. For example, it focuses on how the Ponca were forced to relocate several times, despite the fact that they had farmed the land and stayed within the bounds laid down by government treaties.
*   Interpretation 2 convincingly shows that the government was willing to break its promises to Native Americans, even when tribes had complied with government demands. For example, the government broke the 1868 Fort Laramie Treaty when gold was discovered in the Black Hills of Dakota in 1874.
*   Although Interpretation 1 argues that relocation was a good policy, it does recognise that Native American tribes were often relocated by force. However, Interpretation 2 gives a more convincing representation of the impact of relocation on Native Americans, as it gives an emotional account of the betrayals that the Ponca suffered. Interpretation 1 does not fully consider the impact of the relocation policy on the lives of Native Americans.

4   Use the levels below to mark each consequence separately.
One consequence can get a maximum of 4 marks.
How to grade your answer:

Level 1 1-2 marks	Some general knowledge and understanding of the period is shown. The answer gives one consequence of the growth of cattle trails and attempts a simple explanation.
Level 2 3-4 marks	Detailed knowledge and understanding of the period is shown. The answer gives one consequence of the growth of cattle trails and explains it using knowledge of the period.

Here are some points your answer may include:
*   The cattle trails allowed ranchers to drive their cattle to markets in the North when beef became very popular there in the 1850s. The trails linked the supply of cattle to demand, which made it very profitable and led to the 'Beef Bonanza'.
*   The cattle trails made some ranchers very successful and they became powerful cattle barons as their herds grew into the thousands. For example, John Iliff had 35,000 cattle in Wyoming and Colorado. He made lots of money supplying beef to railroad construction gangs and the Sioux reservation.
*   Cow towns developed as a result of the cattle trails, since ranchers like Joseph McCoy, who built the cow town of Abilene, needed somewhere to drive their cows that was away from homesteaders' lands.
*   The cattle trails caused conflict between homesteaders and ranchers, since cattle often destroyed ranchers' crops and brought diseases that killed their animals.

5   Use the levels below to mark questions 5a and 5b separately.
How to grade your answers:

Level 1 1-2 marks	Limited knowledge and understanding of the period is shown. The answer gives a simple explanation of the significance of the topic. Ideas are generally unconnected and don't follow a logical order.
Level 2 3-4 marks	Some relevant knowledge and understanding of the period is shown. The answer attempts to analyse at least one point about the significance of the topic. An attempt has been made to organise ideas logically.
Level 3 5-6 marks	A good level of knowledge and understanding of the period is shown. The answer explores two or more points about the significance of the topic and analyses them in more detail. Ideas are organised logically.
Level 4 7-8 marks	Knowledge and understanding of the period is precise and detailed. The answer explores two or more points about the significance of the topic and thoroughly analyses each one. Ideas are organised logically and connections between different points are identified to create a deeper analysis of significance.

Here are some points your answer for 5a may include:
*   The introduction of windpumps made water more readily available, which made it easier to farm and survive on the Plains.
*   The invention of an iron plough called the 'sodbuster' by James Oliver in 1868 made ploughing machines available to more people. This product was a cheaper alternative to John Deere's steel plough, so more settlers could afford to buy it and farm their land more easily.
*   Settlers learned which crops were best suited to the land they were farming. For example, Turkey Red Wheat, which grew well on the Plains, was brought over from Russia in around 1874, while settlers in Kansas and Nebraska realised that wheat and corn grew well on their land. This increased the amount of crops they were able to produce, so more food was available.
*   The Timber Culture Act of 1873 gave settlers who had already been granted fertile land by the government an extra 160 acres if they planted a quarter of their land with timber. The Act was designed to increase the amount of timber available on the Plains, which meant that settlers didn't have to build their houses out of unhygienic sod. It also increased the amount of fuel available, which improved conditions for settlers on the Plains.
*   From 1874, homesteaders began to use barbed wire to create cheap fences around their land. This protected their crops from cattle, but made cattle driving harder, as it stopped

cattlemen from accessing water sources. This contributed towards growing conflict between ranchers and homesteaders over land on the Plains.

Here are some points your answer for 5b may include:

- The Indian Wars were a series a conflicts between the government and Native American tribes who had been forced onto reservations and were struggling to survive. These conflicts showed the government that their aggressive policies weren't working, and persuaded them to adopt more peaceful policies towards Native Americans.
- In 1867, the Indian Peace Commission negotiated the Medicine Lodge Treaty to try and bring the Indian Wars to an end. It moved southern Plains Indians away from settlers onto smaller reservations. This policy of separation was more peaceful than building forts on Native American land to protect settlers, but it still had a negative impact on the lives of Native Americans.
- In response to the Indian Wars, President Grant introduced his 'Peace Policy' in 1868. This made assimilation a key part of the government's policy towards Native Americans. However, the Peace Policy didn't completely stop violence against Native Americans, as the government still used military action against those who refused to assimilate.
- The policies of separation and assimilation introduced in response to the Indian Wars failed because the Native Americans did not want to give up their way of life and President Grant did not stop settlers from encroaching on Indian land. This shows that the Indian Wars didn't fully change government policy, since the government still broke its promises to Native Americans.

Page 91 — Conflict and Conquest, c.1877-c.1900

1   This question is level marked. How to grade your answer:

Level 1 1-3 marks	The answer shows limited knowledge and understanding of the period. It explains one or both reasons in a general way.
Level 2 4-6 marks	The answer shows some appropriate knowledge and understanding of the period. It gives a simple analysis of one or both reasons, using knowledge of the period to justify its points.
Level 3 7-9 marks	The answer shows a good level of appropriate knowledge and understanding of the period. It analyses both reasons in more detail, using knowledge of the period to justify its points.
Level 4 10-12 marks	The answer shows detailed and precise knowledge and understanding of the period. It analyses both reasons in detail, using knowledge of the period to justify its points. It establishes connections between the reasons and comes to a clear conclusion over which one was more important.

Here are some points your answer may include:

- The government's relocation policy, which moved Native Americans onto smaller and smaller reservations, was more damaging to the Native American way of life than any other factor, as the infertility of the reservations made many Native Americans reliant on government aid for their survival. The government used this power to force Native Americans to assimilate and abandon their way of life.
- The Dawes Act (1887) broke up reservations into small allotments and assigned them to Native Americans, who were encouraged to give up their way of life and farm instead. This was particularly damaging to the Native American way of life because tribal communities were broken up, and men lost the status and honour that they got from hunting and warfare.
- The government sent Native American children to Indian schools, which required them to dress like white Americans

and banned them from speaking tribal languages. This made it harder to pass Native American culture on to the next generation.

- Increasing settlement disrupted the Native Americans' way of life. The development of the railroads brought thousands of settlers to the Plains and led to the growth of large settler communities. Native Americans were increasingly driven onto smaller reservations to make way for these growing communities.
- White settlers had a negative impact on the buffalo, which were vital to the survival of the Native Americans — there were 13 million buffalo on the Plains in 1865, but they were almost extinct by 1900. The destruction of the buffalo forced Native Americans to accept life on the reservations, because it made them more dependent on the government for food and survival.
- While many settlers took Native American land, it was government policies like the Desert Land Act of 1877 and their willingness to break their treaties that allowed settlers to take over Native American land. This loss of land forced more Native Americans onto reservations, which damaged their way of life.

2   This question is level marked. How to grade your answer:

Level 1 1-2 marks	Some knowledge and understanding of the period is shown. The answer describes one or more changes to the lives of African Americans, but does not explain them.
Level 2 3-4 marks	Appropriate knowledge and understanding of the period is shown. The answer describes some valid changes. It explains the reasons for one of the changes, using knowledge of the topic to justify its explanation.
Level 3 5-6 marks	A good level of knowledge and understanding of the period is shown. The answer explains the reasons for two or more changes, using detailed knowledge of the topic to justify its explanations.
Level 4 7-8 marks	Excellent knowledge and understanding of the period is shown. The answer considers more complex patterns of change and explains the reasons for all identified changes, using detailed knowledge to justify its explanations.

Here are some points your answer may include:

- When Reconstruction ended, African Americans lost many of the rights they had gained after the Civil War because laws protecting them were overturned. For example, the 1875 Civil Rights Act, which prevented discrimination against black Americans in public places, was declared unconstitutional, allowing segregation to be introduced. The Supreme Court strengthened segregation by ruling in the 1896 Plessy v. Ferguson case that railway coaches could be segregated in Louisiana.
- As early as 1876, many African Americans lost the protection of the Enforcement Acts when the Supreme Court ruled that only states could prosecute people under the Acts. This resulted in many violent crimes like lynchings going unpunished.
- The end of Reconstruction resulted in economic hardship among African Americans, since many were restricted to low paid jobs or sharecropping. Legal restrictions and violent intimidation forced many to work in unskilled professions where there was little chance of escaping poverty.
- Segregated education was brought in after Reconstruction ended. African American schools were poorly funded, preventing African Americans from accessing the same quality of education that white Americans received.
- The end of Reconstruction affected the political influence of African Americans, as voting restrictions like poll taxes and literacy tests were introduced to deliberately restrict the

number of African Americans who were eligible to vote. Since those who couldn't vote couldn't stand for office, African Americans were also forced out of political positions.

3 This question is level marked. How to grade your answer:

Level 1 1-2 marks	Limited knowledge and understanding of America between c.1870 and c.1900 is shown. The answer gives one or more simple explanations of why America's economy grew. Ideas are generally unconnected and don't follow a logical order.
Level 2 3-5 marks	Some relevant knowledge and understanding of the period is shown. The answer gives a basic analysis of why the economy grew. An attempt has been made to organise ideas in a logical way.
Level 3 6-8 marks	A good level of knowledge and understanding of the period is shown. The answer explores multiple reasons for the economic growth and analyses some of them. It identifies some relevant connections between different points, and ideas are organised logically.
Level 4 9-10 marks	Knowledge and understanding of the period is precise and detailed. The answer considers a range of reasons for the economic growth and analyses each one. All ideas are organised logically. Connections between different points are identified to create a developed analysis of the topic.

Here are some points your answer may include:
- America's economy changed from an agricultural to an industrial economy during the period known as the Second Industrial Revolution. As a result, successful steel and oil industries developed.
- New technologies like electricity and new types of machinery led to the development of mass production, which increased the efficiency of factories and led to economic growth.
- Increasing industrialisation caused big businesses and corporations to grow and take over the economy, forcing out smaller businesses. Rich corporation owners like John Rockefeller, who founded the Standard Oil Company, used their growing wealth to develop new techniques and methods of production, which further accelerated economic growth.
- Industrialisation created more jobs. This led to high levels of immigration from Europe and mass migration from rural areas to cities like New York and Chicago. The development of cities contributed to economic growth as new suburbs, skyscrapers and transport networks were built to cater for the growing population.

The Elizabethans, 1558-1603

Page 102 — Elizabeth's Court and Parliament

1 Each aspect is marked separately and you can have a maximum of two marks per aspect. How to grade your answer:
- 1 mark for describing one credible aspect of Elizabeth's character.
- 2 marks for describing one credible aspect and using your own knowledge to support it.

Here are some points your answer may include:
- Elizabeth was intelligent and well educated, which helped her to become a powerful and successful leader, despite a lack of training.
- Elizabeth was very cautious, so she only trusted a small number of advisors who became her 'favourites'.
- Elizabeth could be indecisive, as she considered all of the possible consequences of her decisions very carefully.
- Elizabeth was determined, which helped her to hold on to her authority when others thought that she should allow her male counsellors or a potential husband to rule instead.

2 This question is level marked. How to grade your answer:

Level 1 1-4 marks	The answer shows limited knowledge and understanding of Elizabethan England. It gives a simple explanation of one or more factors relating to the challenges Elizabeth faced when she became queen. Ideas aren't organised with an overall argument in mind. There is no clear conclusion.
Level 2 5-8 marks	The answer shows some appropriate knowledge and understanding of the period. There is some analysis of how different factors relate to the topic. Ideas are organised with an overall argument in mind, but the conclusion isn't well supported by the answer.
Level 3 9-12 marks	The answer shows a good level of knowledge and understanding of the period, which is relevant to the question. It analyses how several different factors relate to the topic. Most ideas are organised to develop a clear argument that supports the conclusion.
Level 4 13-16 marks	**Answers can't be awarded Level 4 if they only discuss the information suggested in the question.** The answer shows an excellent level of relevant knowledge and understanding of the period. It analyses in detail how a range of factors relate to the topic. All ideas are well organised to develop a clear argument and a well-supported conclusion.

Here are some points your answer may include:
- The Privy Council and Parliament repeatedly asked Elizabeth to name an heir or marry, as there was a risk of civil war breaking out if she died without a legitimate heir. This put pressure on Elizabeth to make a statement about the succession.
- Finding a suitable husband so she could secure the succession was a challenge, since Elizabeth would alienate certain groups if she chose the wrong man. Suitors like King Eric of Sweden or King Philip II of Spain would have given another European country too much influence in England. Marriage to an English noble would have offended those nobles who weren't chosen.
- The succession was a challenging issue because Elizabeth would have faced threats to her authority regardless of what she did. Naming a legitimate claimant, like Mary, Queen of Scots, as her heir might have encouraged plots against Elizabeth's rule, while failing to name an heir caused ongoing uncertainty about the succession.
- Parliament and the Privy Council tried to put pressure on Elizabeth to settle the succession, but Parliament needed Elizabeth's permission to discuss it. Elizabeth refused to discuss the matter or to name a successor, which allowed her to focus on more important issues.
- Some people didn't want Elizabeth to rule. Some Protestants questioned her legitimacy as a result of Henry VIII's declaration that she was illegitimate after the execution of her mother, Anne Boleyn. While Henry later retracted this declaration, there was still doubt over her legitimacy. Elizabeth also faced opposition from those who believed a female monarch should not have power and should just be a figurehead.
- England's economy was weak and the Crown was in debt when Elizabeth took the throne. This was a bigger challenge for Elizabeth than the succession, as she had to reduce the debt without angering her supporters and the nobility by raising taxes.
- Religious divisions in England threatened Elizabeth's rule. England was in religious turmoil, as the monarchs who had come before Elizabeth had repeatedly changed the national

religion. Elizabeth's religious settlement of 1559 aimed to stabilise the situation, but she faced threats from those who didn't approve of the settlement, such as Puritans and devout Catholics.
- Elizabeth faced threats from France and Scotland at the start of her reign. While she worked quickly to end the war with France, Mary, Queen of Scots' marriage to the heir to the French throne in 1558 meant that Elizabeth faced the possibility of a French invasion from Scotland.

3   This question is level marked. How to grade your answer:

Level 1 1-2 marks	Limited knowledge and understanding of Elizabethan England is shown. The answer gives one or more simple explanations of why patronage was important. Ideas are generally unconnected and don't follow a logical order.
Level 2 3-4 marks	Some relevant knowledge and understanding of the period is shown. The answer gives a basic analysis of how patronage affected Elizabeth's rule. An attempt has been made to organise ideas in a logical way.
Level 3 5-6 marks	A good level of knowledge and understanding of the period is shown. The answer explores multiple effects of patronage and analyses how they affected Elizabeth's rule. It identifies some relevant connections between different points, and ideas are organised logically.
Level 4 7-8 marks	Knowledge and understanding of the period is precise and detailed. The answer considers a range of effects of patronage and analyses how each one affected Elizabeth's rule. All ideas are organised logically. Connections between different points are identified to create a developed analysis of the topic.

Here are some points your answer may include:
- Elizabeth gave lands and official positions to nobles and other Elizabethans. This meant that they often relied on her for their status or income, so they were more likely to be loyal. This was very useful to Elizabeth, since she faced lots of threats from inside and outside the country.
- Elizabeth's decision to spread her patronage widely helped to make England more politically stable. Since lots of families benefited from her patronage, there was less chance of a rebellion developing against Elizabeth.
- The power of the older noble families was weakened by Elizabeth's decision to give her patronage to lots of different individuals. Elizabeth effectively created a new elite that relied on her for their position, so they were more likely to be loyal to her. The nobility lost some of their power as a result of the growth of this new elite, so it was harder for them to challenge Elizabeth.
- Effective use of patronage stopped Elizabeth's courtiers from opposing her government. This was shown by the fact that there was conflict at court in the 1590s when Elizabeth stopped using patronage so effectively.

4   This question is level marked. How to grade your answer:

Level 1 1-2 marks	The answer shows some knowledge and understanding of Elizabethan England. It provides a simple explanation of the challenges Elizabeth faced. There has been some attempt to organise ideas in a logical way.
Level 2 3-5 marks	The answer shows good knowledge and understanding of the period. It provides some analysis of the topic and shows links between some ideas. Most ideas are ordered logically.

Level 3 6-8 marks	The answer shows excellent knowledge and understanding of the period. It provides a detailed analysis of the topic and explains how different ideas are linked. All ideas are ordered logically.

Here are some points your answer may include:
- In the 1590s, the make-up of Elizabeth's Privy Council changed due to the deaths of some of her key advisors, like Francis Walsingham. These advisors had ensured that Elizabeth's government ran smoothly, so her government became less effective without them. This weakened Elizabeth's authority.
- The Earl of Essex's rise led to the development of two rival groups at court. One centred on Essex and the other on William Cecil and his son Robert. Instead of distributing patronage evenly as she did at the start of her reign, Elizabeth allowed the Cecils to become too powerful, which caused resentment and tension between the two groups.
- Elizabeth's inability to defuse the tension damaged her authority as it made her look weak and showed that she was unable to control the competing groups at court.
- In 1599, Elizabeth sent Essex to put down Tyrone's Rebellion in Ireland, but he failed and left Ireland without Elizabeth's permission. Elizabeth arrested Essex and later removed his main source of income.
- In response, Essex rebelled against Elizabeth and challenged her authority. Essex's rebellion aimed to replace Elizabeth's closest advisors like Robert Cecil, who had gained too much power. Although Essex's rebellion failed, it affected Elizabeth's authority, as it showed that she was not in control of her most powerful courtiers.
- The rebellion was encouraged by nobles who felt marginalised by Elizabeth. This highlighted the fact that Elizabeth's failure to use patronage effectively had weakened her authority.
- Although Elizabeth's authority at court became weaker in the last fifteen years of her reign, her authority in the country as a whole remained strong. This was shown by the lack of popular support for Essex's rebellion.

Pages 114-115 — Life in Elizabethan Times

1a How to grade your answer:
- 1 mark for identifying one way the artist shows the popularity of the theatre.
- 2 marks for explaining how the identified feature shows the popularity of the theatre.
- 3 marks for giving a more detailed explanation of how the identified feature shows the popularity of the theatre.

Here are some points your answer may include:
- The theatre has a large audience, which suggests that theatre shows were very popular. The more expensive seats in the stalls are just as full as the area for the poorer groundlings, which shows that the theatre was popular among both the rich and the poor.
- The theatre is depicted as a permanent wooden structure with a stage and seating designed specifically for the viewing of plays. This demonstrates the fact that by the 1570s the theatre had become popular enough to move from temporary venues (e.g. inn courtyards and village squares) to permanent, purpose-built buildings.

1b This question is level marked. How to grade your answer:

Level 1	1-2 marks	The answer shows knowledge of the Elizabethan period. It attempts to explain how further investigation of an aspect of the interpretation would help historians to understand more about Elizabethan theatre. It shows limited understanding of a historical concept (e.g. continuity, change, cause, consequence).
Level 2	3-4 marks	The answer shows appropriate knowledge and understanding of the Elizabethan period. It explains how further investigation of an aspect of the interpretation would help historians to understand more about Elizabethan theatre. It shows some understanding of a historical concept (e.g. continuity, change, cause, consequence).
Level 3	5 marks	The answer shows appropriate knowledge and understanding of the Elizabethan period. It fully explains how investigation of an aspect of the interpretation would help historians to understand more about Elizabethan theatre. It shows strong understanding of a historical concept (e.g. continuity, change, cause, consequence).

Here are some points your answer may include:

- Further research into the ways in which the design of the theatre separated the poor (e.g. the groundlings) from the wealthier patrons in the galleries would help historians to understand more about the social and cultural consequences of the growing divide between rich and poor in Elizabethan England.
- Investigating the location of theatres such as the Globe in Interpretation 1 might help historians to understand how the attitudes of certain groups, like the Puritans and the London authorities, affected the development of the theatre in the Elizabethan period.
- Studying the ways Elizabeth and other members of the elite supported the theatre could help historians to understand the role of patronage in the growing popularity and importance of the theatre.

2 This question is level marked. How to grade your answer:

Level 1	1-2 marks	The answer shows some understanding of the interpretation. It gives a basic statement about how convincing the interpretation is about Elizabethan theatre. The analysis is based on content from the interpretation.
Level 2	3-4 marks	The answer shows good understanding of one aspect of the interpretation. It gives a simple evaluation of how convincing the interpretation is. The evaluation is based on the interpretation and knowledge of the period.
Level 3	5-6 marks	The answer shows good understanding of more than one aspect of the interpretation. It gives a developed evaluation of how convincing the interpretation is. The evaluation is based on the interpretation and good knowledge of the period.
Level 4	7-8 marks	The answer shows good understanding of many different aspects of the interpretation. It gives a complex evaluation and an overall judgement of how convincing the interpretation is. The evaluation and overall judgement are based on the interpretation and good knowledge of the period.

Here are some points your answer may include:

- The image depicts both well-dressed, wealthy patrons in the seating area at the bottom of the image and a crowd of poorer groundlings next to the stage. This reflects the fact that groups of varying social status attended the theatre at the same time.
- The image accurately reflects the design of Elizabethan theatres, as it shows common features such as a raised stage pushing into the audience on the ground, and an open-air design.
- The image shows the theatre as a permanent structure, which is convincing because it reflects the fact that permanent theatres were built in England from the 1570s onwards.
- A less convincing element is the way that the groundlings and those in the lowest seated area at the bottom of the image are shown, since one or two of the groundlings are sitting on the wall that divides the richer, seated audience members from the poorer groundlings. This is unconvincing, since the theatre was designed to maintain and emphasise the social division between these two classes; it is therefore unlikely that the richer members of the audience would have allowed this kind of mixing.
- The interpretation is quite one-sided, as it gives a very idealised representation of the theatre. The audience members are shown as calm and well-behaved, and they are facing the stage in an orderly way. This does not reflect the negative reputation of the theatre and its audience members among groups like the Puritans and the London authorities, who saw the theatre as a source of disorder and immorality.

3 This question is level marked. How to grade your answer:

Level 1	1-3 marks	Limited knowledge and understanding of the Elizabethan period is shown. The answer gives a simple explanation of the problem of poverty in Elizabethan England. Ideas are generally unconnected and don't follow a logical order.
Level 2	4-6 marks	Some relevant knowledge and understanding of the period is shown. The answer gives a basic analysis of reasons why poverty was a growing problem. An attempt has been made to organise ideas in a logical way.
Level 3	7-9 marks	A good level of knowledge and understanding of the period is shown. The answer explores multiple reasons for the growth of the problem of poverty. It identifies some relevant connections between different points, and ideas are organised logically.
Level 4	10-12 marks	**Answers can't be awarded Level 4 if they only discuss the information suggested in the question.** Knowledge and understanding of the period is precise and detailed. The answer considers a range of reasons why the problem of poverty grew and analyses each one. All ideas are organised logically and connections between different points are identified to create a developed analysis of the topic.

Here are some points your answer may include:

- The population increased massively during Elizabeth's reign. This caused food prices to increase because food production didn't keep up with the demands of the growing population. This in turn led to food shortages, which resulted in malnourishment and starvation.
- Population growth caused the standard of living to fall, because prices for food and other goods rose faster than wages. As a result, many workers could no longer afford the essentials and were pushed into poverty.
- Population growth meant that more people had to compete for land. This caused rents to rise, making land harder to afford and putting more financial pressure on those who were already struggling.

- New farming techniques like enclosure reduced the number of farmers who were needed to farm the land, which resulted in many farmers being evicted. This led to unemployment and homelessness among the poorer members of society, many of whom became vagabonds.
- Many landowners stopped growing wheat and started to farm sheep instead, since wool exports were more profitable than grain farming. This added to the problem of poverty, as it made food shortages worse by reducing the amount of grain available to buy in England.
- Poor harvests in the 1590s made poverty even more extreme, as food shortages intensified and prices rose even higher.
- Traditionally, monasteries had provided support for the poor. However, Henry VIII had closed down England's monasteries, so there was little support for those in need.

4 This question is level marked. How to grade your answer:

Level 1 1-2 marks	The answer shows some knowledge and understanding of Elizabethan England. It provides a simple explanation of how living standards changed during Elizabeth's reign. There has been some attempt to organise ideas in a logical way.
Level 2 3-5 marks	The answer shows good knowledge and understanding of the period. It provides some analysis of the topic and shows links between some ideas. Most ideas are ordered logically.
Level 3 6-8 marks	The answer shows excellent knowledge and understanding of the period. It provides a detailed analysis of the topic and explains how different ideas are linked. All ideas are ordered logically.

Here are some points your answer may include:
- Rapid population growth meant that wages struggled to keep up with rising food prices and rents. As a result, living standards among the poor decreased, as there was more malnutrition, starvation and homelessness.
- The incomes of landowners rose. New farming methods like enclosure made farming more efficient and profitable, and landowners benefited from increasing rents and food prices. This helped to improve the living standards of the gentry and the nobility, as they used their increasing wealth to build more comfortable homes. For example, many could now afford large glass windows, which made their homes lighter, and large fireplaces, which heated their homes more efficiently.
- The growth of national and international trade increased the incomes of merchants. As a result, many could improve their living standards by buying land and joining the gentry.
- Thanks to rising incomes and increasing access to grammar schools, more professionals and members of the gentry could afford to give their male children an education. However, this development only affected the minority as most children had to work to help their families survive.

5 This question is level marked. How to grade your answer:

Level 1 1-4 marks	The answer shows limited knowledge and understanding of Elizabethan England. It gives a simple explanation of one or more factors relating to Drake's career. Ideas aren't organised with an overall argument in mind. There is no clear conclusion.
Level 2 5-8 marks	The answer shows some appropriate knowledge and understanding of the period. There is some analysis of how different factors relate to the topic. Ideas are organised with an overall argument in mind, but the conclusion isn't well supported by the answer.
Level 3 9-12 marks	The answer shows a good level of knowledge and understanding of the period, which is relevant to the question. It analyses how several different factors relate to the topic. Most ideas are organised to develop a clear argument that supports the conclusion.
Level 4 13-16 marks	The answer shows an excellent level of relevant knowledge and understanding of the period. It analyses in detail how a range of factors relate to the topic. All ideas are well organised to develop a clear argument and a well-supported conclusion.

Here are some points your answer may include:
- Drake was only the second man to ever successfully sail around the world. The significance of this achievement is shown by the fact that Drake was knighted by Elizabeth when he returned home.
- During his circumnavigation, Drake overcame the dangers of sailing in Elizabethan times and avoided the Spanish fleet. This was a significant achievement — other sailors, like John Hawkins, suffered the loss of their fleet when faced with these threats.
- Drake returned from his circumnavigation with lots of Spanish treasure. This was one of the main reasons why Elizabethans went on sailing expeditions, so it was a significant achievement.
- Drake overcame problems with navigation that all Elizabethan sailors faced. For example, he successfully navigated areas of the world that European sailors had never explored, which meant that he had no maps or charts to guide him. This was a major achievement.
- Drake was also involved in other important expeditions, such as the raid on the Spanish port of Cadiz in 1587, which successfully stalled the preparation of the Spanish Armada. His role in defeating the Spanish Armada in 1588 also contributed to his image as a successful sailor.
- The failure of sailors like Raleigh made Drake's success seem more significant. Raleigh's attempt to organise the colonisation of Roanoke would have been considered a major success if the Spanish fleet hadn't delayed the colony's supply ships.
- James Lancaster sailed around the Cape of Good Hope to India in 1591. After this, lasting trading links were set up with Asia when the East India Company was established in 1600.
- Drake and Raleigh were both favourites of the Queen, but Raleigh lost her favour in 1592. This might have had an impact on how their achievements were perceived and celebrated in Elizabethan England.

Page 130 — Troubles at Home and Abroad

1 Each aspect is marked separately and you can have a maximum of two marks per aspect. How to grade your answer:
- 1 mark for describing one credible aspect of Puritan opposition to Elizabeth I's religious settlement.
- 2 marks for describing one credible aspect of Puritan opposition to Elizabeth I's religious settlement and using your own knowledge to back it up.

Here are some points your answer may include:
- The Puritans didn't think the religious settlement went far enough, because they wanted to remove all elements of Catholicism from the English Church.
- The Puritans directly opposed the religious settlement during the Vestment Controversy of the 1560s. Puritan priests refused to wear the surplice, which Elizabeth had made compulsory in the Royal Injunctions of 1559.

- The Puritans introduced the Prophesyings in the 1570s, to teach priests how to preach. Elizabeth thought this would encourage more Puritan opposition to the religious settlement.
- In the 1580s, some Puritans threatened to break away from the English Church when they realised that further reform would not happen. Elizabeth saw these separatists as a major threat to the religious settlement and arrested some of their leaders.

2   This question is level marked. How to grade your answer:

Level 1 1-2 marks	Limited knowledge and understanding of Elizabethan England is shown. The answer gives a simple explanation of one or more ways in which Mary's presence in England affected Elizabeth's rule. Ideas are generally unconnected and don't follow a logical order.
Level 2 3-4 marks	Some relevant knowledge and understanding of the period is shown. The answer gives a basic analysis of how Mary's presence in England affected Elizabeth's rule. An attempt has been made to organise ideas in a logical way.
Level 3 5-6 marks	A good level of knowledge and understanding of the period is shown. The answer explores multiple consequences of Mary's presence and analyses how they affected Elizabeth's rule. It identifies some relevant connections between different points, and ideas are organised logically.
Level 4 7-8 marks	Knowledge and understanding of the period is precise and detailed. The answer considers a range of consequences and analyses how each one affected Elizabeth's rule. All ideas are organised logically. Connections between different points are identified to create a developed analysis of the topic.

Here are some points your answer may include:
- Mary's presence in England posed a threat to Elizabeth's rule since Mary was a Catholic who had a legitimate claim to the English throne. This made her a rallying point for Catholic opposition to Elizabeth.
- As a result, Mary was implicated in many Catholic plots to depose Elizabeth, such as the Ridolfi Plot (1571) and the Babington Plot (1586). These plots negatively affected Elizabeth's authority and the stability of her rule.
- Mary's presence forced Elizabeth to deal with Mary's alleged role in the murder of Darnley and, later, her involvement in the Catholic plots. This was problematic because Elizabeth did not want to execute Mary, as she saw her as a legitimate monarch. This caused tension between Elizabeth and her Parliament and Privy Council as they wanted Elizabeth to execute Mary to reduce the Catholic threat.
- Mary's presence encouraged Spanish involvement in the Catholic plots, which increased the tension between England and Spain. The execution of Mary in 1587 made Philip more determined to invade England. This posed a direct threat to Elizabeth's rule.
- As a result of the Catholic plots fuelled by Mary's presence, Elizabeth's reign became less tolerant of Catholics. Elizabeth introduced anti-Catholic laws in 1581 and 1585 which increased the persecution of Catholics.

3   This question is level marked. How to grade your answer:

Level 1 1-2 marks	The answer shows some knowledge and understanding of Elizabethan England. It provides a simple explanation of how the actions of missionary priests affected Elizabethan England. There has been some attempt to organise ideas in a logical way.
Level 2 3-5 marks	The answer shows good knowledge and understanding of the period. It provides some analysis of the topic and shows links between some ideas. Most ideas are ordered logically.
Level 3 6-8 marks	The answer shows excellent knowledge and understanding of the period. It provides a detailed analysis of the topic and explains how different ideas are linked. All ideas are ordered logically.

Here are some points your answer may include:
- From 1568, missionary priests trained at colleges in Europe like the one at Douai. From 1574, they returned to England and secretly ministered to English Catholics. This strengthened Catholicism in England.
- As a result, Elizabeth's attitude towards recusancy changed. Before the missionary priests arrived, she had tolerated recusancy in the hope that Catholicism would fade away on its own. However, the arrival of the missionary priests made this less likely and heightened the threat that Catholicism posed to the religious settlement.
- The missionary priests were also seen as a direct threat to Elizabeth herself because they supported the Catholic plots against her.
- As a result, persecution of Catholics increased. Two anti-Catholic Acts were passed in 1581 and 1585, which brought in harsher penalties for those Catholics who went against the religious settlement. For example, those who said Catholic Mass could be imprisoned or fined, while converting to Catholicism or encouraging others to do so became punishable by death.

4   This question is level marked. How to grade your answer:

Level 1 1-4 marks	The answer shows limited knowledge and understanding of Elizabethan England. It gives a simple explanation of one or more factors relating to the defeat of the Spanish Armada. Ideas aren't organised with an overall argument in mind. There is no clear conclusion.
Level 2 5-8 marks	The answer shows some appropriate knowledge and understanding of the period. There is some analysis of how different factors relate to the topic. Ideas are organised with an overall argument in mind, but the conclusion isn't well supported by the answer.
Level 3 9-12 marks	The answer shows a good level of knowledge and understanding of the period, which is relevant to the question. It analyses how several different factors relate to the topic. Most ideas are organised to develop a clear argument that supports the conclusion.
Level 4 13-16 marks	**Answers can't be awarded Level 4 if they only discuss the information suggested in the question.** The answer shows an excellent level of relevant knowledge and understanding of the period. It analyses in detail how a range of factors relate to the topic. All ideas are well organised to develop a clear argument and a well-supported conclusion.

Here are some points your answer may include:
- Poor weather prevented the Armada from returning to Calais after it was attacked by English fireships, and gave the English the chance to advance. This stroke of luck gave the English a big advantage as they were able to attack the Armada when it was vulnerable.
- The English were lucky that the leader of the Armada, the Duke of Medina Sidonia, had little military or naval experience. His decision to sail back to Spain by going around Scotland and Ireland resulted in the destruction of more than half of the fleet due to bad weather and the death of many men from starvation and disease.
- Francis Drake's attack on Cadiz in 1587 contributed significantly towards the defeat of the Armada. The attack

temporarily damaged the Armada and delayed it by over a year, which gave England more time to prepare. This raid was successful because it was well planned and executed, not because of luck.

- Drake's raid weakened the Armada that eventually set sail in 1588. The capture of planks of seasoned wood during the raid forced the Spanish to use inferior, unseasoned wood to build their supply barrels. As a result, the Armada suffered from a poor supply of food and water which weakened Spanish morale.
- The English tactic of sending fireships to attack the Armada at Calais played a key role in the defeat of the Armada, as it forced the Spanish to flee their defensive position at Calais.
- The Armada was seriously weakened by the tactics of Dutch ships, which blockaded the Duke of Parma and prevented him from meeting up with the Armada at Dunkirk.

Germany, 1890-1945

Page 144 — Germany and the Growth of Democracy, 1890-1929

1 This question is level marked. How to grade your answer:

| Level 1 | The answer shows limited knowledge and |
| 1-3 marks | understanding of the period. It explains one or both reasons in a general way. |

| Level 2 | The answer shows some appropriate knowledge |
| 4-6 marks | and understanding of the period. It gives a simple analysis of one or both reasons, using knowledge of the period to justify its points. |

| Level 3 | The answer shows a good level of appropriate |
| 7-9 marks | knowledge and understanding of the period. It analyses both reasons in more detail, using knowledge of the period to justify its points. |

| Level 4 | The answer shows detailed and precise |
| 10-12 marks | knowledge and understanding of the period. It analyses both reasons in detail, using knowledge of the period to justify its points. It makes connections between the reasons and comes to a clear conclusion about which reason was more important. |

Here are some points your answer may include:

- The industrialisation of Germany's economy created lots of jobs in new and developing industries, like the steel and iron industries, which gave the working classes more economic power and reduced the economic power of the upper class. This caused the working classes to become more aware of their identity and demand better representation in politics, which increased the popularity of socialism.
- The rapid industrialisation of Germany's economy meant that the population of Germany's cities and towns increased rapidly. As a result, working and living conditions for industrial workers were often poor. This fuelled the growth of socialism because the working classes supported parties like the Social Democratic Party, who promised to deal with these social problems.
- The government did little to address social issues like poor working and living conditions. This increased support for socialist groups and parties because these groups did offer to relieve suffering.
- The First World War made the social problems caused by rapid industrialisation worse — many in the working classes were close to starvation by the end of the war. This made the government unpopular and increased the appeal of socialist parties, shown by the fact that socialist parties called for the abdication of the Kaiser during mass protests against the government in November 1918.

- While social problems played a more important role in increasing the popularity of socialism, it was the industrialisation of Germany that created the conditions that gave the working classes enough economic power to demand social change.

2 This question is level marked. How to grade your answer:

| Level 1 | Limited knowledge and understanding of |
| 1-3 marks | Germany in the 1920s is shown. The answer gives a simple explanation of the economic recovery. Ideas are generally unconnected and don't follow a logical order. |

| Level 2 | Some relevant knowledge and understanding |
| 4-6 marks | of the period is shown. The answer gives a basic analysis of some reasons for the economic recovery. An attempt has been made to organise ideas in a logical way. |

| Level 3 | A good level of knowledge and understanding |
| 7-9 marks | of the period is shown. The answer explores multiple reasons for the economic recovery. It identifies some relevant connections between different points, and ideas are organised logically. |

| Level 4 | **Answers can't be awarded Level 4 if they** |
| 10-12 marks | **only discuss the information suggested in the question.** Knowledge and understanding of the period is precise and detailed. The answer considers a range of reasons for the economic recovery and analyses each one. All ideas are organised logically and connections between different points are identified to create a developed analysis of the topic. |

Here are some points your answer may include:

- Stresemann took steps to fix the economy when he became Chancellor in August 1923. For example, his decision to end the strike in the Ruhr meant that the government no longer had to compensate striking workers.
- Stresemann's introduction of the Rentenmark in November 1923 helped the economy by replacing the failed German Mark and stabilising Germany's currency.
- Stresemann created a political coalition between moderate, pro-democracy socialist parties in the Reichstag to make it easier to pass legislation. This co-operation meant that decisions about the economy were no longer hindered by political differences.
- Stresemann made an effort to improve Germany's relationships with other countries when he was appointed Foreign Minister in November 1923. This approach led to agreements that addressed the problem of German war reparations. For example, the Dawes Plan (1924) made the repayment terms for Germany's reparations more realistic. The Young Plan (1929) reduced the reparations. This relieved pressure on the German economy.
- The Dawes Plan played a big role in helping the German economy to recover, since the USA lent money to Germany so that it could pay reparations to Britain and France. This gave Germans a chance to rebuild their economy as they were no longer struggling as much with reparations payments. The importance of the Dawes Plan is shown by the fact that the German economy collapsed again once the USA was no longer able to lend Germany money following the Wall Street Crash in 1929.
- The government's house building programme, which resulted in more than 2 million homes being built between 1924 and 1931, provided employment opportunities for Germans. This strengthened the economy as more Germans had a wage and could afford to spend money.

3   This question is level marked. How to grade your answer:

Level 1 1-2 marks	Some knowledge and understanding of the Weimar Republic is shown. The answer describes one or more changes to the lives of Germans, but does not explain them.
Level 2 3-4 marks	Appropriate knowledge and understanding of the period is shown. The answer describes some valid changes. It explains the reasons for one of the changes, using knowledge of the topic to justify its explanation.
Level 3 5-6 marks	A good level of knowledge and understanding of the period is shown. The answer explains the reasons for two or more changes, using detailed knowledge of the topic to justify its explanations.
Level 4 7-8 marks	Excellent knowledge and understanding of the period is shown. The answer considers more complex patterns of change and explains the reasons for all identified changes, using detailed knowledge to justify its explanations.

Here are some points your answer may include:

- The reparations laid down in the Treaty of Versailles placed a lot of pressure on the German economy, which made it very weak. As a result, many Germans suffered extreme poverty, starvation and illness under the Weimar Republic.
- Germany's economic problems got worse in 1923 when there was a hyperinflation crisis. German money became almost worthless and there were serious food and goods shortages. This made starvation and poverty in Germany even more critical.
- The lives of German people improved between 1923 and 1929, as Stresemann became Foreign Minister and worked with other European countries and the USA to restore Germany's economy using agreements like the Dawes Plan. The government also introduced reforms to protect the unemployed, increase wages and build housing. This period was known as the 'Golden Years', as living conditions improved for many ordinary people.
- The middle classes suffered under the Weimar Republic. Their bank savings were made worthless by the hyperinflation crisis, and they were unable to access the benefits that were introduced by the government to help the working classes during the 'Golden Years'.
- More people had access to political power and influence as the voting age was lowered to 20 and women were given voting rights for the first time. Proportional representation ensured that even the smallest political parties had access to the Reichstag, which meant that more people in Germany felt they were fairly represented.
- Women gained more freedom and autonomy than they'd had before the Weimar Republic. For example, 112 women were elected to the Reichstag between 1919 and 1932. More young women were employed and divorce became easier.

Page 150 — Hitler's Rise to Power, 1929-1934

1   This question is level marked. How to grade your answer:

Level 1 1-3 marks	Limited knowledge and understanding of the period is shown. The answer gives a simple explanation of why Hitler's personality attracted support. Ideas are generally unconnected and don't follow a logical order.
Level 2 4-6 marks	Some relevant knowledge and understanding of the period is shown. The answer gives a basic analysis of some reasons why Hitler's personality attracted support. An attempt has been made to organise ideas in a logical way.
Level 3 7-9 marks	A good level of knowledge and understanding of the period is shown. The answer explores multiple reasons why Hitler's personality attracted support. It identifies some relevant connections between different points, and ideas are organised logically.
Level 4 10-12 marks	**Answers can't be awarded Level 4 if they only discuss the information suggested in the question.** Knowledge and understanding of the period is precise and detailed. The answer considers a range of reasons why Hitler's personality attracted support and analyses each one. All ideas are organised logically and connections between different points are identified to create a developed analysis of the topic.

Here are some points your answer may include:

- Many Germans blamed the Weimar leaders for signing the Armistice Agreement and the Treaty of Versailles, as they believed these politicians had agreed to surrender when Germany still had a chance of winning the war. Hitler's image as a patriotic saviour and his promises to make Germany great again provided a contrast to this negative image of the Weimar leaders.
- Many Germans thought that the Weimar leaders performed weakly when it came to international affairs. They had given in to the demands of the Allies by signing the Treaty of Versailles, and they were unable to prevent Belgium and France from occupying the Ruhr in 1923. Hitler, on the other hand, had shown himself to be decisive and strong in his leadership of the Nazi Party, which made him more appealing to Germans than the Weimar leaders.
- The Weimar Republic's system of proportional representation meant that there were many small parties in the Reichstag. This made it difficult for parliament to make decisions. People lost faith in democracy and wanted a strong leader who would take control. Hitler's full control over the SA and his party made him look strong, so he seemed capable of solving Germany's problems.
- Hitler's passion, energy and strong public speaking abilities made the Nazis stand out against the other extremist parties that were becoming increasingly popular after the Wall Street Crash. Hitler's speeches gave German people hope that things could get better.

2   This question is level marked. How to grade your answer:

Level 1 1-3 marks	The answer shows limited knowledge and understanding of the period. It explains one or both reasons in a general way.
Level 2 4-6 marks	The answer shows some appropriate knowledge and understanding of the period. It gives a simple analysis of one or both reasons, using knowledge of the period to justify its points.
Level 3 7-9 marks	The answer shows a good level of appropriate knowledge and understanding of the period. It analyses both reasons in more detail, using knowledge of the period to justify its points.
Level 4 10-12 marks	The answer shows detailed and precise knowledge and understanding of the period. It analyses both reasons in detail, using knowledge of the period to justify its points. It makes connections between the reasons and comes to a clear conclusion about which reason was more important.

Here are some points your answer may include:

- The Weimar Republic's system of proportional representation made it difficult for parliament to make decisions. The Nazi Party used the 1932 election to paint Hitler as a hero who was standing up to the weak Weimar government. His personality and strong leadership appealed to those who wanted more decisive government.

- The Weimar Republic's inability to solve the mass unemployment caused by the Great Depression in the early 1930s meant that it lost the support of many in the working class, who had been strong supporters in the past. Instead, the German people were willing to consider any political party that promised to address the social and economic issues that the country faced, and so the Nazis seemed increasingly appealing.

- The Weimar Republic's failure to deal with Germany's economic and social issues in the early 1930s meant that the SPD lost support. Instead, more people started to support left-wing parties like the KPD, as well as right-wing parties like the Nazis. These parties became more popular because they offered solutions to the issues facing Germany, unlike the Weimar government. Therefore, the weakness of the Weimar Republic created a political situation where the Nazi Party could grow.

- While the weakness of the Weimar Republic created opportunities for other parties to grow, the Nazi party grew faster than the KPD, which suggests that its policies and leadership may have been more appealing to the German public than those of other extremist parties.

- The Nazis promised that they would make Germany great again, which appealed to young people who felt that they had no future after the events of the Great Depression. However, if the Weimar Republic had been stronger, this Nazi promise might not have been so successful at drawing people in.

- The Nazi Party's promise to create economic prosperity appealed to businessmen who'd suffered as a result of the Depression. This policy was very appealing when contrasted with the failure of the Weimar Republic to restore the economy.

- Some people supported the Nazis because of their anti-Semitic and anti-communist policies. These policies attracted those who shared the Nazis' anti-Semitic views and blamed Jews and communists for the issues facing Germany in the early 1930s.

3   This question is level marked. How to grade your answer:

Level 1 1-4 marks	The answer shows limited knowledge and understanding of the period. It gives a simple explanation of one or more turning points in Hitler's consolidation of power between 1933 and 1934. Ideas aren't organised with an overall argument in mind. There is no clear conclusion.
Level 2 5-9 marks	The answer shows some appropriate knowledge and understanding of the period. There is some analysis of different turning points in Hitler's consolidation of power. Ideas are organised with an overall argument in mind, but the conclusion isn't well supported by the answer.
Level 3 10-14 marks	The answer shows a good level of knowledge and understanding of the period, which is relevant to the question. It analyses several different turning points in Hitler's consolidation of power. Most ideas are organised to develop a clear argument that supports the conclusion.
Level 4 15-18 marks	The answer shows an excellent level of relevant knowledge and understanding of the period. It analyses in detail a range of turning points in Hitler's consolidation of power. All ideas are well organised to develop a clear argument about which turning point was the most important. There is a well-supported conclusion.

Here are some points your answer may include:

- The fire in the Reichstag in 1933 gave Hitler the opportunity to whip up people's fears about the threat of a communist revolution. As a result, Hitler was granted emergency powers to deal with the supposed communist threat. This was an important turning point, because it was the first step towards Hitler's dictatorship — it showed Hitler that he could manipulate the German government and people in order to take extra powers with little opposition.

- Hitler's appointment to the Chancellorship in January 1933 was an important turning point, because it was this appointment that made it possible for Hitler to gain extra powers and grant himself more and more control. If he had not been made Chancellor, it is less likely that he would have been able to take the steps that led to the creation of the dictatorship as other politicians could have exercised more control over him.

- The introduction of the Enabling Act in March 1933, which allowed Hitler to govern for four years without the input of the Reichstag, was a key turning point, as it limited the ability of parliament to stop Hitler from gaining too much power. For example, the Reichstag was unable to stop Hitler from banning trade unions in May 1933.

- Hitler's decision to ban all political parties except the Nazis in July 1933 was a key moment. Germany became a one-party state with the Nazi Party in control.

- Another key turning point was the Night of the Long Knives in June 1934, as this removed all threats to Hitler from within the SA and the Nazi Party. However, the fact that Hitler went unpunished for these organised murders, and was able to declare them legal, shows that he already had considerable power over Germany at this point.

- The death of Hindenburg in August 1934 created the opportunity for Hitler to make himself the Führer and fully consolidate his power. While this was the start of the dictatorship, Hitler had already consolidated his power to the point where he was able to declare himself the Führer without any opposition. Therefore, Hindenburg's death was less of a turning point and more of a final step in Hitler's bid for total power.

Page 163 — The Experiences of Germans Under the Nazis, 1933-1939

1   This question is level marked. How to grade your answer:

Level 1 1-3 marks	Limited knowledge and understanding of Nazi Germany is shown. The answer gives a simple explanation of why Nazi propaganda was effective. Ideas are generally unconnected and don't follow a logical order.
Level 2 4-6 marks	Some relevant knowledge and understanding of the period is shown. The answer gives a basic analysis of some reasons for the effectiveness of Nazi propaganda. An attempt has been made to organise ideas in a logical way.

Level 3
7-9 marks
A good level of knowledge and understanding of the period is shown. The answer explores multiple reasons for the effectiveness of Nazi propaganda. It identifies some relevant connections between different points, and ideas are organised logically.

Level 4
10-12 marks
Answers can't be awarded Level 4 if they only discuss the information suggested in the question. Knowledge and understanding of the period is precise and detailed. The answer considers a range of reasons for the effectiveness of Nazi propaganda and analyses each one. All ideas are organised logically and connections between different points are identified to create a developed analysis of the topic.

Here are some points your answer may include:

*   The Nazis used a wide range of methods to spread their propaganda, including the media, posters, films, art and spectacular events and displays. This meant that people were exposed to propaganda in all areas of their lives.
*   The Nazis' control over the media was very strong. By 1939, 70% of German households had a radio. Since the Nazis controlled radio broadcasts, many Germans were exposed to Nazi propaganda through the radio. The Nazis also had increasing control of German newspapers. This ensured that most Germans only heard and read Nazi points of view, as the Nazis were able to censor the media and control what was said.
*   Goebbels' 'propaganda machine' repeated simple ideas to try and unite Germans against others and make them view the Nazis as the party that could make Germany great again. A key tactic was to encourage Germans to hate those countries which had signed the Treaty of Versailles by claiming that they had stolen German territory and treated Germany unfairly after the war.
*   Nazi propaganda was very effective when it built on existing ideas. For example, the Nazis used lots of anti-communist and anti-Semitic themes in their propaganda. These prejudices already existed in Germany before the Nazis rose to power, so Nazi propaganda relating to Jewish people and communists appealed to many people.
*   Nazi propaganda encouraged a return to traditional values and culture. Many people had disapproved of cultural changes during the Weimar Republic and thought the Weimar government was too liberal, so they were receptive to the Nazis' message that Germany should return to its traditional roots.

2   This question is level marked. How to grade your answer:
Level 1
1-2 marks
Some knowledge and understanding of Nazi Germany is shown. The answer describes one or more changes to the lives of Jewish people, but does not explain them.

Level 2
3-4 marks
Appropriate knowledge and understanding of the period is shown. The answer describes some valid changes. It explains the reasons for one of the changes, using knowledge of the topic to justify its explanation.

Level 3
5-6 marks
A good level of knowledge and understanding of the period is shown. The answer explains the reasons for two or more changes, using detailed knowledge of the topic to justify its explanations.

Level 4
7-8 marks
Excellent knowledge and understanding of the period is shown. The answer considers more complex patterns of change and explains the reasons for all identified changes, using detailed knowledge to justify its explanations.

Here are some points your answer may include:

*   The Nazis believed that Jews were 'inferior' and blamed them for many of Germany's problems. This meant that anti-Semitism was now allowed and encouraged by the state, leaving Jewish people vulnerable to persecution and prejudice.
*   The Nazis' racial policies made it increasingly difficult for Jews to earn a living. Jews were banned from working in an increasing number of professions during the 1930s. The SA also organised a boycott of Jewish shops in 1933. Later, Jews were banned from working altogether and were forced to sell their businesses. This placed Jewish people in an increasingly difficult financial position.
*   In 1933, the SA-organised boycott of Jewish shops led to violent attacks on Jews. However, this violence was unpopular with the German people. As a result, the Nazi regime changed its tactics and attacked the Jewish population using legal persecution.
*   The Nuremburg Laws, introduced in 1935, stripped Jewish people of many legal rights. Jews and non-Jews were no longer able to marry or have sexual relationships, and Jews were stripped of their German citizenship. This separated Jews from the rest of society and made them more vulnerable to persecution.
*   By 1938, restrictions had been introduced to stop Jewish people from going to public places like theatres. Jewish children were banned from going to German schools.
*   The Nazis' racial policies were designed to isolate Jews. The Nazis encouraged non-Jews to break off their friendships with Jews to further isolate them.
*   By the late 1930s, the Nazis felt able to use violence against Jewish people again. In November 1938, the Nazis organised violent attacks on Jewish shops and synagogues across Germany. After this event, known as Kristallnacht, thousands of Jews were arrested and sent to concentration camps. Kristallnacht laid the foundations for increasingly brutal acts of violence against Jews.

3   This answer is level marked. How to grade your answer:
Level 1
1-4 marks
The answer shows limited knowledge and understanding of Nazi Germany. It gives a simple explanation of one or more factors relating to the threat posed by German opposition. Ideas aren't organised with an overall argument in mind. There is no clear conclusion.

Level 2
5-9 marks
The answer shows some appropriate knowledge and understanding of the period. There is some analysis of different factors relating to the topic. Ideas are organised with an overall argument in mind, but the conclusion isn't well supported by the answer.

Level 3
10-14 marks
The answer shows a good level of knowledge and understanding of the period, which is relevant to the question. It analyses several different factors relating to the topic. Most ideas are organised to develop a clear argument that supports the conclusion.

Level 4
15-18 marks The answer shows an excellent level of relevant knowledge and understanding of the period. It analyses in detail a range of factors relating to the topic. All ideas are organised to develop a clear argument and a well-supported conclusion.

Here are some points your answer may include:

- The Nazis didn't face any serious opposition from the political left, since they had banned parties like the KPD and the SPD. This weakened the left's ability to oppose the Nazis directly, and forced them to resort to underground resistance, like organising industrial strikes.
- This underground opposition was relatively weak, since the parties were divided and did not co-operate with one another. The strong hold that the Nazis had over Germany meant that the weak and divided opposition from the left didn't pose a significant threat.
- The Gestapo infiltrated the networks formed by the political left and arrested their members. The effectiveness of the Gestapo reduced the threat posed by the political left.
- The Confessing Church offered an alternative religious viewpoint to the Nazi-sponsored Reich Church. However, the Nazis dealt very harshly with any direct opposition from its members. For example, one of its founders, Martin Niemöller, spent years in concentration camps for objecting to Nazi persecution.
- Opposition from the Catholic bishop Clemens August von Galen forced the Nazis to keep its killing of disabled people secret, but it did not stop the murders.
- Youth movements like the Edelweiss Pirates and the Swing Kids only offered low-level resistance to the Nazis. Although these young people questioned Nazi ideology and actively went against Nazi values, in the 1930s they were mostly ignored. This suggests that the Nazis didn't see them as a threat.
- Most resistance between 1933 and 1939 was relatively low level and did not pose a significant threat to the regime as a whole. However, the Gestapo was kept busy by the actions of anti-Nazi groups, which suggests that suppressing even low-level resistance was seen as a priority for Hitler and the Nazis.

Page 170 — The Second World War, 1939-1945

1 This question is level marked. How to grade your answer:

Level 1
1-2 marks The answer shows appropriate knowledge of the period by identifying at least one way that Germany changed its economy.

Level 2
3-4 marks The answer shows appropriate knowledge and understanding of the period by identifying two relevant changes and explaining each one.

Here are some points your answer may include:

- Germany changed its economy by introducing the Four-Year Plan in 1936, which focused on building up Germany's war industries (like the chemical and weapons industries) and increasing Germany's agricultural output.
- Many workers were retrained for jobs in the chemical and weapons industries, which helped to build up these industries to be ready for the outbreak of war.
- Hermann Göring worked to make Germany self-sufficient by increasing Germany's production of essential goods so that Germany wouldn't be reliant on imports from other countries during the war.

2 This question is level marked. How to grade your answer:

Level 1
1-4 marks The answer shows limited knowledge and understanding of the period. It gives a simple explanation of life in one or more Nazi occupied countries. Ideas aren't organised with an overall argument in mind. There is no clear conclusion.

Level 2
5-9 marks The answer shows some appropriate knowledge and understanding of the period. There is some comparison of life in different Nazi occupied countries. Ideas are organised with an overall argument in mind, but the conclusion isn't well supported by the answer.

Level 3
10-14 marks The answer shows a good level of knowledge and understanding of the period, which is relevant to the question. It compares several different aspects of life in different Nazi occupied countries. Most ideas are organised to develop a clear argument that supports the conclusion.

Level 4
15-18 marks The answer shows an excellent level of relevant knowledge and understanding of the period. It compares in detail a range of aspects of life in different Nazi occupied countries. All ideas are well organised to develop a clear argument and a well-supported conclusion.

Here are some points your answer may include:

- Nazi occupation was universally brutal and harsh for Jewish people across Europe. The Nazis' hatred of Jews meant that they were subjected to extreme violence and were forced to live in terrible conditions in ghettos. They also faced terrible conditions in concentration camps and around 6 million were eventually killed.
- The Nazis believed that people in western Europe were part of the Aryan race, whereas those in eastern Europe were seen as biologically inferior. As a result, people in occupied countries in western Europe were treated less harshly than those in eastern Europe.
- The Nazis wanted to use the resources of countries in western Europe, so people in these countries faced extreme shortages of agricultural and industrial goods.
- Citizens of western countries were forced to work for the Nazis, but their working conditions were generally reasonable. Working conditions were much harsher for people from eastern Europe. For example, 2 million non-Jewish Poles were subjected to slave labour and experienced terrible conditions.
- The Nazis responded harshly to resistance wherever it was found. People from western Europe could be arrested, detained or sent to concentration camps for any act of resistance.
- Eastern countries had a much harsher experience than western countries. The Nazis intended to use the territories they'd occupied in the east to create Lebensraum for the German people, and so they tried to 'cleanse' these areas of their non-Aryan populations.
- Polish people experienced great brutality. The Nazis allowed and encouraged the killing of all Poles — both Hitler and Himmler openly called for the murder of Polish men, women and children. This was part of their wider policy to kill all those in the east who were considered unsuitable for 'Germanisation'.
- In the east, the Nazis built death camps to systematically murder those who were seen as undesirable. Mainly Jewish people were killed, but other groups were targeted as well, for example Slavs (e.g. Russians and Poles), Romani, black people, homosexuals, disabled people and communists.
- During the invasion of the Soviet Union in 1941, Einsatzgruppen were ordered to follow the German army and kill all Jews and other 'enemies' of the Nazi state. This systematic and merciless killing contrasts with the less brutal treatment of 'Aryan' populations in western Europe.

3   This question is level marked. How to grade your answer:

Level 1	The answer shows limited knowledge and
1-3 marks	understanding of the period. It explains one or both sets of consequences in a general way.
Level 2	The answer shows some appropriate knowledge
4-6 marks	and understanding of the period. It gives a simple analysis of one or both sets of consequences, using knowledge of the period to justify its points.
Level 3	The answer shows a good level of appropriate
7-9 marks	knowledge and understanding of the period. It analyses both sets of consequences in more detail, using knowledge of the period to justify its points.
Level 4	The answer shows detailed and precise
10-12 marks	knowledge and understanding of the period. It analyses both sets of consequences in detail, using knowledge of the period to justify its points. It establishes connections between the sets of consequences and comes to a clear conclusion about which set of consequences was more important.

Here are some points your answer may include:

- The outbreak of war in 1939 had significant consequences for Germany's economy. Hitler accelerated his Four-Year Plan, which had been introduced in 1936 to prepare Germany's economy for war. As a result, Germany's weapons and chemical industries were expanded. Agricultural output was also increased in an attempt to make Germany self-sufficient.
- From 1942, Germany began to prepare for total war, which had a major impact on the economy. Albert Speer was put in charge of the economy and he made sure that it was completely focused on the war effort. Speer increased weapons production and improved economic efficiency. Industries that weren't important to the war effort stopped production, while non-essential businesses were closed.
- The economic consequences of the war had a big impact on German society because the German workforce was retrained to support the war economy. In 1939, a quarter of the workforce was involved in war-related industries. Two years later, three-quarters of the workforce was part of the war economy. This social consequence was directly linked to the economic consequences of the outbreak of war.
- Another social consequence of the economic changes brought by the war was that more women and children had to work — during the war, many men were conscripted but Germany still wanted to maintain high industrial output. This social change contrasted with the Nazis' earlier commitment to encouraging women to stay in the home and discouraging them from working.
- The economic consequences of the war also affected living standards for German workers. Wages were lower than they had been before the Nazis took control and working hours were increased.
- During the war, the German government introduced rationing of food and many other goods. The social consequences of rationing were limited at first — it actually improved the diet of some Germans. However, by 1942, the rations available to Germans were becoming increasingly poor. For example, many people were forced to live on vegetables, potatoes and bread.
- From 1942, American and British forces began to bomb German cities very heavily. This had severe social consequences. About half a million German civilians were killed and many more were made homeless. A large number of refugees also came into Germany from other German territories that had been bombed. These people received very little support and suffered poor living conditions and hardship.

- The social consequences became more significant later in the war. After major defeats in 1942, Germany began to prepare for total war. This meant that even more women had to work or join the army (though not on the front line) and those men who were not in the army had to join the Volkssturm, a part-time defence force.
- Many of the social consequences of World War Two were linked to Hitler's economic policies and his desire to massively increase war production. While the social consequences of the war were significant, they were largely caused by economic changes.

Superpower Relations and the Cold War, 1941-1991

Page 179 — The Origins of the Cold War, 1941-1958

1   Use the levels below to mark each consequence separately. One consequence can get a maximum of 4 marks.
How to grade your answer:

Level 1	Some general knowledge and understanding
1-2 marks	of the period is shown. The answer gives one consequence of the Truman Doctrine and attempts a simple explanation.
Level 2	Detailed knowledge and understanding of
3-4 marks	the period is shown. The answer gives one consequence of the Truman Doctrine and explains it using knowledge of the period.

Here are some points your answer may include:

- The Truman Doctrine was an open declaration of support for any country that might face a communist takeover. This increased tension between the USSR and the USA, since the USSR wanted communism to expand and the USA had made it very clear that they would act to stop that from happening.
- As part of the Truman Doctrine, the USA gave $400 million of aid to Turkey and Greece to try and stop communism spreading across Europe. Truman believed that easing economic hardship would make communism less appealing.
- The Truman Doctrine laid the foundation for the Marshall Plan, which offered $17 billion to European countries that had struggling economies. This caused the USSR to develop the Comecon and offer its own aid and economic incentives to support Eastern European countries, which resulted in an economic divide between the East and the West.
- Stalin felt more threatened by the USA after the Truman Doctrine, so he reacted by strengthening his alliance with the Soviet satellite states. For example, he introduced the Cominform in 1947 to bring all communist parties under the control of the USSR.

2   Use the levels below to mark questions 2a and 2b separately.
How to grade your answers:

Level 1	Limited knowledge and understanding of the
1-2 marks	period is shown. The answer gives a simple explanation of the significance of the topic. Ideas are generally unconnected and don't follow a logical order.
Level 2	Some relevant knowledge and understanding
3-4 marks	of the period is shown. The answer attempts to analyse at least one point about the significance of the topic. An attempt has been made to organise ideas logically.
Level 3	A good level of knowledge and understanding
5-6 marks	of the period is shown. The answer explores two or more points about the significance of the topic and analyses them in more detail. Ideas are organised logically.

Level 4
7-8 marks

Knowledge and understanding of the period is precise and detailed. The answer explores two or more points about the significance of the topic and thoroughly analyses each one. Ideas are organised logically and connections between different points are identified to create a deeper analysis of significance.

Here are some points your answer for 2a may include:

- The Berlin Crisis increased the tension between the USA and the USSR because Stalin's decision to blockade West Berlin represented an escalation towards more forceful opposition to the USA. The Berlin Airlift showed that the USA would not back down easily in the face of such force.
- The Berlin Crisis showed the West that they were not ready to fight the USSR if war actually broke out, which led to the creation of NATO, a military alliance of the Western powers. This in turn provoked the formation of the USSR's Warsaw Pact with the states in the Eastern bloc. These developments escalated the Cold War by creating two distinct sides that were formally divided — treaties bound each side to take military action if the other attacked.
- The Berlin Crisis resulted in the formal division of Germany into West Germany, controlled by the USA and its allies, and East Germany, controlled by the communist USSR. This increased tensions in the Cold War by highlighting the division between the USA and the USSR and between the capitalist and communist areas of Europe.
- The division of Berlin caused capitalist West Berlin to develop a stronger economy than communist East Berlin. This made communism look weaker than capitalism, which damaged the position of the USSR and resulted in people trying to leave East Berlin to live in West Berlin. This migration was a source of tension between the USSR and the USA, and eventually led to Khrushchev's 'Berlin Ultimatum' in 1958.
- The division of Berlin following the Berlin Crisis caused political conflict because the USSR felt that the economic strength of West Berlin posed a threat to East Berlin and the USSR's influence in Eastern Europe. This caused conflict between Khrushchev and Eisenhower in the late 1950s and Khrushchev and Kennedy in the early 1960s.

Here are some points your answer for 2b may include:

- During the arms race, the USSR and the USA spent lots of money trying to develop new or more powerful weaponry and build up the largest stockpile of nuclear missiles. For example, in 1957, the USSR and the USA developed ICBMs, which had a very long range. As a result, each side posed a very real threat to the existence of the other if a war actually broke out. This created an atmosphere of tension and fear that dominated relations between the USSR and the USA until both sides began to limit weapons production in the 1970s.
- When Khrushchev came to power in 1953, his decision to continue developing nuclear weaponry meant that his policy of dealing with the West more peacefully did not thaw the tension between the USA and the USSR as much as it might have done if he had abandoned the arms race.
- The arms race created tense situations that worsened relations between the USSR and the USA. For example, the events that led up to the Cuban Missile Crisis and the crisis itself were considered to be very threatening as both sides were aware that the weapons involved could cause devastation if used.
- In the 1980s, Reagan's decision to increase defence spending on arms following the Soviet invasion of Afghanistan reignited the arms race and reversed many of the steps that were taken towards disarmament during the 1970s, when a policy of détente was being followed. This worsened relations between the USSR and the USA again.

3 This question is level marked. How to grade your answer:

Level 1
1-2 marks

The answer shows some knowledge and understanding of the period. It provides a simple explanation of some events that led to the Hungarian Uprising. There has been some attempt to organise events in a logical way.

Level 2
3-5 marks

The answer shows good knowledge and understanding of the period. It provides some analysis of the key events that led to the Uprising. Most events are organised logically. Some connections are made between events to show how they led to the Uprising.

Level 3
6-8 marks

Answers can't be awarded Level 3 if they only discuss the information suggested in the question. The answer shows excellent knowledge and understanding of the period. It provides a detailed analysis of the key events that led to the Uprising and events are ordered logically. Strong connections are made between events to show how they combined to cause the Uprising.

Here are some points your answer may include:

- Khrushchev wanted to de-Stalinise the USSR, so he reversed some of Stalin's more restrictive policies. For example, he freed political prisoners who had been imprisoned by Stalin and abolished the death penalty.
- As part of his attempts at de-Stalinisation, Khrushchev also abolished the Cominform, which had placed all communist parties under the control of the USSR in 1947. This meant that the satellite states in the Eastern bloc gained some independence from the USSR.
- This allowed tensions to rise in satellite states that had not willingly surrendered to the USSR and the communist regime, as they saw Khrushchev's de-Stalinisation as an opportunity to loosen their ties with the USSR.
- The USSR allowed Poland to follow its own version of communism after the uprising there in 1956. This gave other satellite states hope that they would be able to escape the influence of the USSR, which encouraged them to revolt.
- In response to popular protests in Hungary against the Stalinist leader Mátyás Rákosi, Khrushchev installed Imre Nagy. Nagy was a liberal and hoped that Hungary would become a neutral state.
- Khrushchev's plan to give Hungary more freedom backfired as Nagy responded to the loosening of control by trying to get rid of communism altogether. He announced that Hungary was withdrawing from the Warsaw Pact and holding free elections. The USSR feared that other countries could do the same if Hungary's uprising was not dealt with swiftly. As a result, it responded with force to make an example of Nagy and Hungary, and to stop other countries from trying to throw off communism.

Page 187 — Cold War Crises, 1958-1970

1 This question is level marked. How to grade your answer:

Level 1
1-2 marks

The answer shows some knowledge and understanding of the period. It provides a simple explanation of some events that led to the construction of the Berlin Wall. There has been some attempt to organise events in a logical way.

Level 2
3-5 marks

The answer shows good knowledge and understanding of the period. It provides some analysis of the key events that led to the construction of the Berlin Wall. Most events are organised logically. Some connections are made between events to show how they led to the building of the Berlin Wall.

Level 3
6-8 marks **Answers can't be awarded Level 3 if they only discuss the information suggested in the question.** The answer shows excellent knowledge and understanding of the period. It provides a detailed analysis of the key events that led to the construction of the Berlin Wall and events are ordered logically. Strong connections are made between events to show how they combined to cause the building of the Berlin Wall.

Here are some points your answer may include:

- There was a refugee crisis in Berlin since many people were leaving communist East Berlin and moving to capitalist West Berlin, where the economy was stronger. This weakened East Berlin's economy even further and caused embarrassment for Khrushchev, as it suggested that capitalism was more successful than communism.
- In 1958, Khrushchev announced his 'Berlin Ultimatum'. He wanted the Allies to leave West Berlin in the next six months and make it a free city. However, President Eisenhower rejected his demands and the issue remained unresolved.
- In 1959, Eisenhower and Khrushchev met at a summit in the USA where they discussed Berlin. Although they didn't reach an agreement, the discussion showed a new potential for co-operation between the two nations since it was the first time a communist leader had visited the USA.
- Another summit was scheduled to be held in Paris in 1960. However, just before the summit was about to start, the Soviet Union shot down a U2 American spy plane that was flying in the USSR's territory. The USA claimed it wasn't a spy plane, but the USSR proved it was by showing them the pilot (who had survived) and the plane. The USA refused to apologise for this incident, which became known as the U2 incident. As a result, Khrushchev walked away from the Paris summit.
- There was another summit in Vienna in 1961. President Kennedy had taken over in the USA and he had promised to stand his ground over the Berlin question. Once again, no resolution was reached. This made the USSR believe that negotiation and co-operation wouldn't produce a solution, so Khrushchev decided to construct the Berlin Wall to stop the flow of refugees from East Berlin to West Berlin.

2 Use the levels below to mark questions 2a and 2b separately.
How to grade your answer:

Level 1
1-2 marks   Limited knowledge and understanding of the period is shown. The answer gives a simple explanation of the significance of the topic. Ideas are generally unconnected and don't follow a logical order.

Level 2
3-4 marks   Some relevant knowledge and understanding of the period is shown. The answer attempts to analyse at least one point about the significance of the topic. An attempt has been made to organise ideas logically.

Level 3
5-6 marks   A good level of knowledge and understanding of the period is shown. The answer explores two or more points about the significance of the topic and analyses them in more detail. Ideas are organised logically.

Level 4
7-8 marks   Knowledge and understanding of the period is precise and detailed. The answer explores two or more points about the significance of the topic and thoroughly analyses each one. Ideas are organised logically and connections between different points are identified to create a deeper analysis of significance.

Here are some points your answer for 2a may include:

- The severity of the Cuban Missile Crisis led to some important changes which aimed to defuse the tensions of the Cold War. For example, a 'hotline' was set up between Washington and Moscow. This was intended to improve communications between the two nations in the event of a crisis, so that situations like the Cuban Missile Crisis would not escalate so seriously in future.
- Nuclear missiles were taken out of Cuba and Turkey by April 1963, which was a big step towards reducing tension after the Missile Crisis was averted. This also demonstrated that negotiation between the USA and the USSR could be successful, even when the military situation had escalated to a serious level.
- The crisis caused embarrassment for Khrushchev as his successful negotiations to remove the USA's nuclear weapons from Turkey were performed in secret. He was seen to have failed during the crisis and resigned in 1964. His replacement, Brezhnev, adopted a more aggressive approach towards maintaining communism which contributed to the strained relations between the USSR and the USA in the 1960s.
- The crisis led to several treaties being signed in order to keep the number of nuclear weapons under control. The Limited Test Ban Treaty was signed in 1963 and both countries agreed that testing of nuclear weapons would occur underground in future to ensure the air wouldn't be polluted with nuclear radiation. The Outer Space Treaty, in which countries agreed not to put weapons of mass destruction in space, was created in 1967. These treaties were significant as they showed that both sides were willing to make agreements to avert active conflict.
- The Cuban Missile Crisis also prompted the start of the policy of détente that was pursued in the 1970s. Both sides wanted to avoid tense situations like the Cuban Missile Crisis happening again, so they worked together to ease the tension between them.

Here are some points your answer for 2b may include:

- The Berlin Wall temporarily resolved the Berlin question, as it ended the refugee crisis by preventing people leaving East Berlin for more prosperous West Berlin. This had been a source of tension between the USA and the USSR.
- The Berlin Wall gave East Berlin a chance to strengthen its economy, as it stopped skilled workers from leaving and gave East Berlin time to build up its industries. This made Khrushchev feel less threatened by the strength of West Berlin's economy, which reduced tension between the USA and the USSR.
- In 1961, tensions over Berlin were high after the U2 incident and the failure of negotiations at the Vienna summit. The Berlin Wall helped to defuse these tensions. When the wall was first built, both sides stationed troops on their side, but they both agreed to back down. The USA condemned the wall, but it did not act against it. President Kennedy had been expecting a confrontation and was quite relieved that the wall had offered a peaceful solution.
- The construction of the Berlin Wall showed that the USA and the USSR struggled to negotiate effectively. Their relationship was so weak in 1961 that neither side trusted the other enough to reach a negotiated solution.
- The wall was viewed differently in the East and the West. The West saw the wall as a symbol of the failure of communism, while the East saw it as a symbol of strength. Therefore, while the wall offered a temporary solution to the Berlin question, it also highlighted the differences between the two sides in the Cold War.

3   Use the levels below to mark each consequence separately.
    One consequence can get a maximum of 4 marks.
    How to grade your answer:

    Level 1   Some general knowledge and understanding
    1-2 marks   of the period is shown. The answer gives
                   one consequence of the Soviet invasion
                   of Czechoslovakia and attempts a simple
                   explanation.
    Level 2   Detailed knowledge and understanding
    3-4 marks   of the period is shown. The answer gives
                   one consequence of the Soviet invasion of
                   Czechoslovakia and explains it using knowledge
                   of the period.

    Here are some points your answer may include:

    • The USSR's invasion of Czechoslovakia in 1968 resulted
      in mass protests. These protests were non-violent since
      Czechoslovakia wanted to avoid conflict like that which
      occurred during the Hungarian Uprising in 1956.
    • The invasion resulted in the removal of Dubcek and his
      replacement with Gustav Husak. Husak was loyal to the
      USSR's version of communism and would restore the USSR's
      influence over Czechoslovakia.
    • The UN criticised the USSR, and requested that the USSR
      remove its troops from Czechoslovakia, which it refused
      to do. This made the West look weak, as it was unable to
      exercise authority over the USSR.
    • Other countries were critical of the USSR, but because they
      didn't want to get involved in the Soviet Union's sphere of
      influence or put a strain on relations, they didn't act any
      further. The Cold War had thawed slightly following the
      Cuban Missile Crisis, so other countries didn't want to risk
      reigniting the Cold War. This also made the West look
      weak as it was unable to effectively respond to the USSR's
      aggression.
    • The invasion of Czechoslovakia allowed the USSR to tighten
      its grip on its satellite states. It showed other countries in the
      Eastern bloc that the USSR would not allow them to deviate
      too far from communism.
    • The invasion led to Brezhnev unveiling his doctrine, which
      said that the USSR would step in to restore communism
      if it was under threat in a country. This was an aggressive
      warning that the USSR would not allow Eastern Europe
      to abandon communism and that it would act if the USA
      interfered in its satellite states.

Page 196 — The End of the Cold War, 1970-1991

1   Use the levels below to mark each consequence separately.
    One consequence can get a maximum of 4 marks.
    How to grade your answer:

    Level 1   Some general knowledge and understanding
    1-2 marks   of the period is shown. The answer gives
                   one consequence of the Soviet invasion of
                   Afghanistan and attempts a simple explanation.
    Level 2   Detailed knowledge and understanding
    3-4 marks   of the period is shown. The answer gives
                   one consequence of the Soviet invasion of
                   Afghanistan and explains it using knowledge of
                   the period.

    Here are some points your answer may include:

    • The Soviet invasion of Afghanistan destroyed the trust
      that had been built up between the USA and the USSR as
      a result of détente. This caused tension with the USA to
      reignite, as they believed that the USSR was trying to expand
      communism.
    • The invasion led to a marked shift away from détente, shown
      by President Carter's decision to raise the USA's defence
      budget, and his declaration in the Carter Doctrine that the

USA would use force to prevent the USSR from gaining
control in the Gulf and threatening the USA's interests there.
    • The war had a negative impact on the USSR. There were
      15,000 Soviet casualties and it was very expensive to fund,
      but the USSR couldn't beat the Afghan rebels. This failure
      damaged the USSR's military reputation, which it needed to
      maintain in order to keep control of its satellite states.
    • Funding the war had a negative impact on standards of living
      in the Soviet Union, which caused many in the USSR to
      withdraw support for the communist regime.
    • The invasion damaged the USSR's reputation in the world
      and there was widespread condemnation of its actions. For
      example, the USA and more than 50 other countries refused
      to attend the Moscow Olympic Games in 1980 in protest
      against the war.

2   Use the levels below to mark questions 2a and 2b separately.
    How to grade your answer:

    Level 1   Limited knowledge and understanding of the
    1-2 marks   period is shown. The answer gives a simple
                   explanation of the significance of the topic.
                   Ideas are generally unconnected and don't follow
                   a logical order.
    Level 2   Some relevant knowledge and understanding
    3-4 marks   of the period is shown. The answer attempts to
                   analyse at least one point about the significance
                   of the topic. An attempt has been made to
                   organise ideas logically.
    Level 3   A good level of knowledge and understanding
    5-6 marks   of the period is shown. The answer explores
                   two or more points about the significance of the
                   topic and analyses them in more detail. Ideas are
                   organised logically.
    Level 4   Knowledge and understanding of the period is
    7-8 marks   precise and detailed. The answer explores two
                   or more points about the significance of the
                   topic and thoroughly analyses each one. Ideas
                   are organised logically and connections between
                   different points are identified to create a deeper
                   analysis of significance.

    Here are some points your answer for 2a may include:

    • In the early 1980s, Reagan's anti-communist rhetoric and
      hardline attitude towards the USSR increased hostility and
      tension between the USSR and the USA.
    • Reagan's aggressive position made it more difficult to return
      to the policy of détente, which had been damaged by the
      Soviet invasion of Afghanistan. Reagan didn't believe détente
      was effective and preferred to negotiate with the USSR from a
      position of strength.
    • Reagan's attitude reignited the arms race. He spent massive
      amounts of money on defence, including attempts to develop
      a neutron bomb. These actions caused concern for the USSR,
      because it couldn't afford to match the USA's $550 billion
      annual weapons budget, especially because of the financial
      burden of action in Afghanistan. As a result, the USSR was at
      a military disadvantage.
    • From 1983, Reagan's attempt to develop the SDI increased
      Cold War tensions even further, because of the different
      perspectives of the East and the West. The SDI was seen as
      an act of defence by the USA, but the USSR interpreted it as
      an act of aggression since it would give the USA an advantage
      if nuclear weapons were ever deployed.
    • Reagan changed his attitude towards the USSR in 1985 when
      Mikhail Gorbachev became the leader of the USSR. This was
      a result of Gorbachev's attempts to reform the USSR and be
      more open with the West. Reagan's response to Gorbachev
      helped to improve relations between the two superpowers.
      It paved the way for a less aggressive relationship between
      them.

Here are some points your answer for 2b may include:
- The fall of the Berlin Wall in 1989 showed that the USSR was losing its power over its satellite states in Eastern Europe since it couldn't stop free elections from taking place in Germany. The USSR had to bow to popular pressure and allow Germany to be reunified.
- The USSR's acceptance of the fall of the Berlin Wall demonstrated that it would not use force to prevent people from abandoning Soviet communism and influence. This meant that Eastern countries became hopeful that they might be released from USSR control and be allowed to choose their own forms of government.
- The fall of the Berlin Wall resulted in communist governments collapsing or being replaced in several Eastern European countries, including Poland, Czechoslovakia, Bulgaria and Romania, since the USSR could no longer force them to accept communism.
- The fall of the Berlin Wall triggered demands for independence from several Soviet Republics, like Latvia, Lithuania and Estonia. The USSR lacked the authority to stop these Republics from securing their independence. As a result, several countries declared their intentions to pull out of the Warsaw Pact, leading to its collapse in July 1991. A few months later, in December 1991, the USSR was dissolved.

3 This answer is level marked. How to grade your answer:

Level 1 1-2 marks	The answer shows some knowledge and understanding of the period. It provides a simple explanation of some key events that led to the collapse of the Soviet Union. There has been some attempt to organise events in a logical way.
Level 2 3-5 marks	The answer shows good knowledge and understanding of the period. It provides some analysis of the key events that led to the collapse of the Soviet Union. Most events are organised logically. Some connections are made between events to show how they led to the collapse of the USSR.
Level 3 6-8 marks	**Answers can't be awarded Level 3 if they only discuss the information suggested in the question.** The answer shows excellent knowledge and understanding of the period. It provides a detailed analysis of the key events that led to the collapse of the Soviet Union and events are ordered logically. Strong connections are made between events to show how they combined to cause the collapse of the USSR.

Here are some points your answer may include:
- Gorbachev's decision to abandon the Brezhnev Doctrine as part of his attempts to reform the USSR in the late 1980s meant that countries in the Eastern bloc were released from USSR control and given a choice over whether they wanted to be communist countries.
- Gorbachev removed Soviet troops from Eastern Europe in 1988. This removed the threat of military action, which had kept many anti-communist opposition groups in line. As a result, these groups were now free to act.
- The USSR did not intervene when Hungary opened its border with Austria, allowing people to travel from East Germany to West Germany. This led to the fall of the Berlin Wall in 1989, which showed that the USSR was losing control over its satellite states.
- The USSR didn't interfere when Poland held free elections in 1989, which led to a non-communist government taking power there in 1990. The reunification of Germany in 1990 was also seen as a sign that the communist experiment was over.
- Many Soviet satellite states, like Latvia, Lithuania and Estonia, demanded independence. The USSR lost control over the Soviet Republics, as they no longer had to listen to Gorbachev and could make their own decisions.
- Lithuania declared itself independent in 1990, which led to Soviet troops being sent into Lithuania's capital in 1991. This violence strengthened the movement for independence, and Georgia and Ukraine both declared independence in 1991.
- There was an attempted coup against the USSR's government in 1991 as some Soviet communists feared that Gorbachev's reforms had gone too far and they wanted to remove him from power. The coup failed because the politician Boris Yeltsin, who supported capitalism, rallied opposition in the streets. These mass protests showed that the Soviets rejected communism.
- Gorbachev responded to this rejection of communism by resigning on Christmas Day 1991. The USSR was dissolved the next day and the republics that had been part of it became independent.

Practice Papers

Page 203 — Health and Medicine in Britain, c.1000-present Practice Paper

1a 1 mark for any answer that is historically accurate. Here are some possible answers:
- In monasteries, water systems were properly separated from sewerage systems, but in towns they were not.
- Monasteries usually had a supply of clean water, either from rivers or man-made water courses, but towns often did not.
- Monasteries separated living areas, kitchens, latrines and places of work. In towns there was no separation, with businesses and houses coexisting.

1b 1 mark for any answer that is historically accurate. Here are some possible answers:
- 1848 Public Health Act
- Smallpox vaccination made compulsory for infants in 1853
- 1875 Public Health Act
- 1875 Artisans' Dwellings Act

1c 1 mark for any answer that is historically accurate. Here are some possible answers:
- To prevent lung cancer, cigarette advertisements were banned from television in 1965.
- In 1971, the government forced cigarette companies to put a health warning on cigarette packets, in order to prevent lung cancer.
- The 2004 Drinkaware campaign aimed to reduce disease caused by excessive alcohol consumption.
- To prevent lung cancer, smoking was banned in public places in England and Wales in 2007.
- The 2009 Change4Life campaign promoted healthy diets and active lifestyles in an effort to reduce obesity.

2 This question is level marked. How to grade your answer:

Level 1 1-2 marks	The answer shows some appropriate knowledge and understanding of the Middle Ages and the 17th century. It identifies one or more similarities between the Black Death and the Great Plague.
Level 2 3-4 marks	The answer shows a good level of appropriate knowledge and understanding of the periods. This is used to give a simple explanation of at least one similarity.
Level 3 5-6 marks	The answer shows a very good level of appropriate knowledge and understanding of the periods. This is used to give a more detailed explanation of two or more similarities.
Level 4 7-8 marks	The answer shows an excellent level of appropriate knowledge and understanding. This is used to analyse two or more similarities in detail.

242

Here are some points your answer may include:
- Both the Black Death and the Great Plague killed a lot of people. Some historians think at least a third of the British population died as a result of the Black Death. The Great Plague is believed to have killed around 100,000 people in London alone.
- People did not know what caused either the Black Death or the Great Plague. Both epidemics were believed by many to be caused by miasma or were seen as a punishment from God. In both periods, people prayed and tried to purify the air in an attempt to prevent the disease.
- Superstition influenced attempts to prevent both the Black Death and the Great Plague. People tried to prevent the Black Death by carrying charms or using magic potions containing arsenic. Similarly, during the Great Plague people wore lucky charms and amulets, and made remedies using dried toad to prevent the disease. In both periods, these measures based on superstition were ineffective at preventing the disease.
- During both the Black Death and the Great Plague, local government attempts at prevention were limited and ultimately ineffective. During the Black Death, Winchester built cemeteries for plague victims away from houses, while Gloucester's attempt to avoid the Black Death by shutting itself off from the outside world didn't stop the disease from spreading. Similar techniques were used during the Great Plague — local councils quarantined plague victims and placed dead victims' bodies in mass graves away from houses.
- There was no national government response to either the Black Death or the Great Plague. King Edward III closed Parliament in January 1349 as a result of the Black Death, but did nothing to prevent the disease elsewhere in the country. Likewise, there was no national government response to the Great Plague.

3 This question is level marked. How to grade your answer:

Level 1 1-3 marks	Limited knowledge and understanding of the 19th and 20th centuries is shown. The answer gives a simple explanation of why the government's approach to public health changed. Ideas are generally unconnected and don't follow a logical order.
Level 2 4-6 marks	Some relevant knowledge and understanding of the period is shown. The answer gives a basic analysis of reasons why the government's approach to public health changed. An attempt has been made to organise ideas in a logical way.
Level 3 7-9 marks	A good level of knowledge and understanding of the period is shown. The answer explores multiple reasons for change. It identifies some relevant connections between different points, and ideas are organised logically.
Level 4 10-12 marks	**Answers can't be awarded Level 4 if they only discuss the information suggested in the question.** Knowledge and understanding of the period is precise and detailed. The answer considers a range of reasons for change and analyses each one. All ideas are organised logically and connections between different points are identified to create a developed analysis of the topic.

Here are some points your answer may include:
- Early in the 19th century, people believed in a laissez-faire style of government — they thought that the government shouldn't get involved in people's lives. As a result, the government rarely took action on public health. This began to change from the mid-19th century, as the government started to intervene more and more in public health.
- This change in the government's approach to public health was partly a result of the findings of reports into living conditions. Edwin Chadwick's 1842 report demonstrated a link between poor living conditions and poor health. This eventually led the government to introduce the 1848 Public Health Act. Investigations into urban poverty by Booth (1889) and Rowntree (1901) also helped to highlight the link between poverty and poor health. This led the Liberal government to introduce social reforms between 1906 and 1911 to improve health by reducing poverty.
- Scientific investigation in the 19th century showed there was a link between poor living conditions and disease. Snow's investigation into the 1854 cholera epidemic showed there was a link between dirty water and cholera. In 1861, Pasteur's Germ Theory proved that poor living conditions could cause disease.
- Political change led to greater government intervention in public health. The 1867 Reform Act, which gave more industrial workers the vote, was important in the breakdown of laissez-faire. After 1867, the government had to listen to these workers' concerns about health.
- By the mid-20th century, there was support for even more direct government intervention in public health. Beveridge's report argued that the government had a duty of care to all citizens. This led to the establishment of the National Health Service in 1948. Further government intervention followed, including a campaign to promote the polio vaccine in 1956 and a ban on cigarette advertisements on television in 1965 in order to tackle lung cancer.
- War also affected the government's approach to public health by making the government realise that poorer people required better healthcare. When the Boer War broke out in 1899, 40% of volunteers were physically unfit for military service. This made the Liberal government take notice of poverty-related illnesses and pass reforms to combat them. During the Second World War, many children from poorer households were evacuated from towns to live with wealthier families in the countryside. This increased the awareness among wealthier families of the health problems the poor faced.
- Improved communications made it easier for the government to intervene in public health. Newspapers, radio and television helped the government to make people aware of vaccination programmes and lifestyle campaigns.

4 This question is level marked. How to grade your answer:

Level 1 1-4 marks	The answer shows limited knowledge and understanding of relevant periods. It gives a simple explanation of one or more factors relating to the development of health and medicine. Ideas aren't organised in with an overall argument in mind. There is no clear conclusion.
Level 2 5-8 marks	The answer shows some knowledge and understanding of relevant periods. There is some analysis of how different factors relate to the topic. Ideas are organised with an overall argument in mind, but the conclusion isn't well supported by the answer.
Level 3 9-12 marks	The answer shows a good level of knowledge and understanding of relevant periods, which is focused on the topic. It analyses how the factor in the question and other factors relate to the topic. Most ideas are organised to develop a clear argument that supports the conclusion.
Level 4 13-16 marks	The answer shows an excellent level of knowledge and understanding of relevant periods. It analyses in detail how the factor in the question and a range of other factors relate to the topic. All ideas are well organised to develop a clear argument and a well-supported conclusion.

Here are some points your answer may include:

- In the Renaissance period, individuals like Vesalius and Harvey made important discoveries about human anatomy that advanced medical knowledge. However, the impact of these ideas on health and medicine relied on improvements in communication. Without developments like the invention of the printing press, it is unlikely that individuals like Vesalius would have been able to spread their ideas as widely as they did.
- In the Renaissance period, changing attitudes helped create the conditions for individuals' discoveries. For example, the decline of the Catholic Church's influence made it easier for individuals like Harvey and Vesalius to question Galen's teachings on the human body.
- The work of individuals was a very important factor in the development of health and medicine in the 18th and 19th centuries. In the late 18th century, Jenner developed the smallpox vaccine. In the 19th century, Pasteur and Koch made important discoveries about the causes and prevention of disease. The work of Simpson and Lister helped to make surgery safer in the 19th century. These individuals all helped to advance the development of health and medicine in Britain.
- In the 19th and 20th centuries, individuals were important in highlighting public health problems and campaigning for change. Nightingale campaigned for better hospital care. Chadwick, Booth and Rowntree played a role in the development of public health provision. Beveridge and Bevan were important in the founding of the NHS. However, it was the government's willingness to act on the concerns of these individuals that led to significant developments in health and medicine.
- Government funding was also an important factor in the development of health and medicine in the 19th and 20th centuries. In the early 19th century, the government paid a total of £30,000 to fund Jenner's vaccination clinic. In 1948, the government responded to Beveridge's proposals by funding the foundation of the NHS, which has since had a major impact on health and medicine.
- Technology was an important factor in the development of health and medicine in the 1900s as it played a significant role in improving diagnosis and treatment. For example, X-ray machines and CT scanners have both helped to improve diagnosis of lung cancer.
- Technology also helped many individuals make their discoveries. Harvey's discoveries about the heart were inspired by a new water pump. Pasteur's Germ Theory was aided by more powerful microscopes which allowed him to see germs more clearly.

Page 205 — America, 1789-1900 Practice Paper

1a 1 mark for any answer that is historically accurate.
Here are some possible answers:
- 1830 Indian Removal Act
- The Permanent Indian Frontier
- 1851 Indian Appropriations Act
- 1851 Fort Laramie Treaty

1b 1 mark for any answer that is historically accurate.
Here are some possible answers:
- Goodnight-Loving Trail
- Western Trail
- Chisholm Trail
- Shawnee Trail

1c 1 mark for any answer that is historically accurate.
Here are some possible answers:
- dry farming
- use of machinery (e.g. reapers, binders, harvesters)
- bonanza farming

2 This question is level marked. How to grade your answer:

Level 1 1-3 marks	The answer shows some knowledge and understanding of the period. It provides a simple explanation of the development of law and order in the West. There has been some attempt to organise ideas in a logical way.
Level 2 4-6 marks	The answer shows good knowledge and understanding of the period. It provides some analysis of the topic. Most ideas are organised logically and some connections are made between them.
Level 3 7-9 marks	**Answers can't be awarded Level 3 if they only discuss the information suggested in the question.** The answer shows excellent knowledge and understanding of the period. It provides a detailed analysis of the topic. Ideas are organised logically and strong connections are made between them.

Here are some points your answer may include:

- As the development of the West advanced, big companies, cattle barons and railroad companies gained more power than smaller ranchers, homesteaders and prospectors. This imbalance of power sparked violence, and made it difficult to enforce law and order.
- Groups often took law and order into their own hands. For example, after a cattle baron called John Tunstall was murdered in the Lincoln County War (1878), a gang of outlaws called the Regulators took revenge on his killers.
- In Wyoming, tension between cattle barons and homesteaders over the use of land escalated into conflict in the Johnson County War (1892). The government eventually had to send in the army to rescue vigilantes fighting on behalf of the cattle barons.
- As a result of the Johnson County War, the cattle barons and vigilantes lost their power in Wyoming. This led to an improvement in law and order, as there was less conflict between the cattle barons and homesteaders.
- Some lawmen made the problem of law and order in the West worse by taking sides. The lawman Wyatt Earp, who was on the side of the corporations and big businesses, ended up killing three men who had been accused of cattle rustling and other crimes at the OK Corall in 1881. This added to the violence in the West.
- Other lawmen were more effective at enforcing law and order. For example, Bill Tilghman gained a reputation for being honest and he did not resort to violence as quickly as other lawmen did. From 1892, he was Deputy US Marshal in Oklahoma and he played a major role in stopping outlaws in that area.
- The development of larger communities in the West contributed to an improvement in law and order. The increasing numbers of homesteaders demanded better law and order, and the growth of towns created a more civilised atmosphere.
- The expansion of the railroads and improving communications made it easier to enforce law and order in the West, as news of trouble spread more rapidly and law enforcement officials could reach affected areas more easily.

- The development of more territories into states meant that more areas in the West were directly responsible for maintaining law and order. They were less reliant on the federal government for justice, and could call on law enforcement officials closer to home.

3 Use the levels below to mark questions 3a and 3b separately. How to grade your answers:

Level 1 1-2 marks	Limited knowledge and understanding of the period is shown. The answer gives a simple explanation of the significance of the topic. Ideas are generally unconnected and don't follow a logical order.
Level 2 3-4 marks	Some relevant knowledge and understanding of the period is shown. The answer attempts to analyse at least one point about the significance of the topic. An attempt has been made to organise ideas logically.
Level 3 5-6 marks	A good level of knowledge and understanding of the period is shown. The answer explores two or more points about the significance of the topic and analyses them in more detail. Ideas are organised logically.
Level 4 7-8 marks	Knowledge and understanding of the period is precise and detailed. The answer explores two or more points about the significance of the topic and thoroughly analyses each one. Ideas are organised logically and connections between different points are identified to create a deeper analysis of significance.

Here are some points your answer for 3a may include:

- The idea of 'Manifest Destiny' changed attitudes towards the West, making it seem like an increasingly desirable destination for white settlers. This contrasted with the earlier view that the West was an uninhabitable 'Great American Desert'. As a result, more people migrated to the West, advancing westward expansion.
- 'Manifest Destiny' led many to idealise life in the West, which encouraged more people to migrate. For example, the idea of 'Manifest Destiny' was exploited by railroad companies like the Union Pacific Railroad, which used idealised descriptions of Nebraska to encourage people to migrate there in 1870.
- The growth of the idea of 'Manifest Destiny' contributed to the government's policy of relocating Native Americans, since it caused the government to believe that 'civilised' white settlers had a duty to settle land that was occupied by Native Americans. This policy caused conflict with the Native Americans and eventually contributed to the destruction of their way of life.

Here are some points your answer for 3b may include:

- The Homestead Act opened up land in the West to people who could not afford to move west before this. It made land free to anyone who promised to farm for 5 years. Therefore, more women, former slaves and immigrants began to migrate, increasing settlement across the Plains.
- The Act strengthened communities on the Plains, as it resulted in more settlers migrating and taking up farming. The clause that required settlers to farm for five years discouraged speculators who only wanted land in the West as an investment. Therefore, more people who owned land in the West actually moved there and formed communities.
- The Homestead Act encouraged more families to move to the Plains, instead of just single men looking for work (e.g. as miners). This made communities in the West more civilised, and more churches and schools were built to cater for families.

- The Act led to more Native Americans being moved onto reservations to free up lands for homesteaders. This led to more conflict on the Plains, as many Native Americans resisted relocation.

4 This question is level marked. How to grade your answer:

Level 1 1-4 marks	The answer shows limited knowledge and understanding of the period. It gives a simple explanation of one or more factors relating to the outbreak of the Indian Wars. Ideas aren't organised with an overall argument in mind. There is no clear conclusion.
Level 2 5-9 marks	The answer shows some appropriate knowledge and understanding of the period. There is some analysis of how different factors contributed to the outbreak of the wars. Ideas are organised with an overall argument in mind, but the conclusion isn't well supported by the answer.
Level 3 10-14 marks	The answer shows a good level of knowledge and understanding of the period, which is relevant to the question. It analyses how the factor in the question and other factors contributed to the outbreak of the wars. Most ideas are organised to develop a clear argument that supports the conclusion.
Level 4 15-18 marks	The answer shows an excellent level of relevant knowledge and understanding of the period. It analyses in detail how the factor in the question and a range of other factors contributed to the outbreak of the wars. All ideas are well organised to develop a clear argument and a well-supported conclusion.

Here are some points your answer may include:

- The development of the cattle trails caused clashes between Native Americans and ranchers, as ranchers built ranches on Indian territories, while their cowboys often drove cattle through Native American lands.
- Cattle ranching often disrupted buffalo herds, which were vital to the survival of the Native Americans. Since the threat of starvation played a major role in triggering conflicts like the Cheyenne Uprising during the Indian Wars, cattle ranching was indirectly responsible for some of the Indian Wars.
- A more important cause of the Indian Wars was the government's policy of relocating Native Americans to reservations. Both Little Crow's War (1862) and the Cheyenne Uprising (1864) were directly linked to the fact that Native Americans were struggling to survive on their reservations. If these tribes had not been facing starvation, it is less likely that conflict would have broken out.
- The discovery of gold in Montana in 1862 was also an important cause of the Indian Wars because it prompted the government to break its treaties with the Native Americans so that prospectors could take advantage of the discovery. The government's willingness to break its promises added to the tension on the Plains and made conflict more likely.
- Red Cloud's War (1866-68) was directly linked to the discovery of gold in Montana. It was a response to the attempts of white settlers to create the Bozeman trail, which linked the gold fields of Montana and the Oregon trail by passing through Sioux hunting grounds.
- Railroad companies broke government treaties by building on Native American land. This angered the Native Americans and contributed to the tensions that led to the Indian Wars.
- Railroad companies also sold land around the railroad to settlers and encouraged buffalo hunting. These activities

caused tension and further deprived Native Americans of their livelihood, which was a key reason why tribes like the Cheyenne went to war.

Pages 207-208 — Elizabethans, 1558-1603
Practice Paper

1a How to grade your answer:
- 1 mark for identifying one way the artist shows that the power of Elizabeth I was central to Parliament's power.
- 2 marks for explaining how the identified feature shows the nature of Elizabeth's power.
- 3 marks for giving a more detailed explanation of the how the identified feature shows the nature of Elizabeth's power.

Here are some points your answer may include:
- The artist has emphasised Elizabeth's superiority by making her the focus of the image. She is in a very prominent position in the room and is elevated above most of the other people in the image. This suggests that Elizabeth's power is central to the proceedings of Parliament.
- Elizabeth's royal status is highlighted in the image. She is seated on a grand throne and there is a coat of arms above her head. This demonstrates Elizabeth's central position in Parliament by highlighting the fact that her royal status authorises and legitimises many of its discussions.

1b This question is level marked. How to grade your answer:

Level 1 1-2 marks	The answer shows knowledge of the Elizabethan period. It attempts to explain how further investigation of an aspect of the interpretation would help historians to understand more about Elizabethan government. It shows limited understanding of a historical concept (e.g. continuity, change, cause, consequence).
Level 2 3-4 marks	The answer shows appropriate knowledge and understanding of the Elizabethan period. It explains how further investigation of an aspect of the interpretation would help historians to understand more about Elizabethan government. It shows some understanding of a historical concept (e.g. continuity, change, cause, consequence).
Level 3 5 marks	The answer shows appropriate knowledge and understanding of the Elizabethan period. It fully explains how investigation of an aspect of the interpretation would help historians to understand more about Elizabethan government. It shows strong understanding of a historical concept (e.g. continuity, change, cause, consequence).

Here are some points your answer may include:
- Investigating the roles of Cecil and Walsingham, who are standing on either side of Elizabeth, might help historians to better understand how the role of Elizabeth's advisors and 'favourites' changed over the course of her reign.
- Further research into the roles of the various groups who are represented in this image, such as MPs and members of the Privy Council, might help historians to understand how the extent of Parliament's influence over government policy changed during Elizabeth's reign.
- Investigating the speeches that Elizabeth gave to Parliament during her reign would help historians to explore Elizabeth's relationship with Parliament. This would help historians to understand the extent to which Elizabeth's control over Parliament changed or stayed the same over the course of her reign.

2 This question is level marked. How to grade your answer:

Level 1 1-2 marks	The answer shows some understanding of the interpretation. It gives a basic statement of how convincing the interpretation is. The analysis is based on content from the interpretation.
Level 2 3-4 marks	The answer shows good understanding of one aspect of the interpretation. It gives a simple evaluation of how convincing the interpretation is. The evaluation is based on the interpretation and knowledge of the period.
Level 3 5-6 marks	The answer shows good understanding of more than one aspect of the interpretation. It gives a developed evaluation of how convincing the interpretation is. The evaluation is based on the interpretation and good knowledge of the period.
Level 4 7-8 marks	The answer shows good understanding of more than one aspect of the interpretation. It gives a complex evaluation and an overall judgement about how convincing the interpretation is. The evaluation and overall judgement are based on the interpretation and good knowledge of the period.

Here are some points your answer may include:
- The image is a convincing representation of Elizabeth's authority in her relationship with Parliament. She is depicted as a powerful monarch who dominates the room. This accurately reflects Elizabeth's power over the discussions that took place in Parliament, since Parliament needed her permission to discuss important topics like foreign policy and the succession.
- The image is convincing, because Elizabeth's advisors are very prominent. William Cecil and Francis Walsingham, key members of Elizabeth's Privy Council, are shown standing on either side of Elizabeth's throne. Like Elizabeth, they are overlooking most of the other people in the image, which highlights their importance. This is convincing as a representation of the balance of power between Elizabeth, her advisors and Parliament, since the Privy Council played a much more important role than Parliament in government.
- A less convincing element of the image is that it depicts Elizabeth in Parliament as if she normally presided over its workings in person and played a key role in its proceedings. In fact, Elizabeth only called Parliament 13 times during her whole 44-year reign, so it didn't have many opportunities to contribute towards the government of England. As a result, the image does not reflect the limited extent to which Elizabeth and Parliament interacted during her reign.
- Elizabeth has the most prominent position in the image, which suggests that Parliament could not operate without her presence. This is slightly unconvincing because, while Parliament needed Elizabeth's authority to discuss the most important issues, it could discuss certain economic and social policies without her input.
- While Elizabeth had a lot of power over Parliament, she also relied on Parliament for permission to raise taxes. This image focuses on Elizabeth's power over Parliament, so it does not reflect the limits of her power.

3 This question is level marked. How to grade your answer:

Level 1 1-2 marks	The answer shows some knowledge and understanding of Elizabethan England. It provides a simple explanation of the ways in which people responded to poverty. There has been some attempt to organise ideas in a logical way.

Level 2
3-5 marks
The answer shows good knowledge and understanding of the period. It provides some analysis of Elizabethan responses to poverty. Most ideas are ordered logically. Some connections are made between ideas.

Level 3
6-8 marks
The answer shows excellent knowledge and understanding of the period. It analyses a range of responses over the period and the links between them in detail. All ideas are ordered logically.

Here are some points your answer may include:

- Changes in agriculture and increasing rents caused many people to be evicted, which contributed to increasing poverty in rural areas. Many of those who had been evicted responded by migrating to towns and cities to find work. These migrant workers were seen as vagabonds and many people were afraid that they might turn to crime or violence to survive.
- People's attitudes towards poverty changed — they increasingly realised that poverty had become too serious to be solved by charitable donations and the efforts of individuals. This changed responses to poverty, because more people started to believe that the government should intervene and address the problem of poverty.
- As a result, the government responded to poverty by introducing more formal ways of supporting the 'deserving poor' and the 'helpless poor'. For example, the government introduced a Poor Law in the 1560s, which raised money for the poor through a tax called the 'poor rate'.
- When poverty reached crisis levels in the 1590s, the government responded by introducing two further Poor Laws in 1597 and 1601. They made the 'poor rate' compulsory across England and introduced local officials to collect the tax.
- High levels of poverty led to increased crime rates and food riots. The government responded by introducing harsher punishments for the 'undeserving poor', such as whipping, as part of the Poor Laws. This response was prompted by the belief that vagabonds and other members of the 'undeserving poor' posed a threat to social stability.

4 This question is level marked. How to grade your answer:

Level 1
1-4 marks
The answer shows limited knowledge and understanding of Elizabethan England. It gives a simple explanation of one or more factors that threatened the success of Elizabeth's religious settlement. Ideas aren't organised with an overall argument in mind. There is no clear conclusion.

Level 2
5-8 marks
The answer shows some appropriate knowledge and understanding of the period. There is some analysis of how different factors relate to the topic. Ideas are organised with an overall argument in mind, but the conclusion isn't well supported by the answer.

Level 3
9-12 marks
The answer shows a good level of knowledge and understanding of the period, which is relevant to the question. It analyses how several different factors relate to the topic. Most ideas are organised to develop a clear argument that supports the conclusion.

Level 4
13-16 marks
Answers can't be awarded Level 4 if they only discuss the information suggested in the question. The answer shows an excellent level of relevant knowledge and understanding of the period. It analyses in detail how a range of factors relate to the topic. All ideas are well organised to develop a clear argument and a well-supported conclusion.

Here are some points your answer may include:

- Elizabeth's policy of pursuing the 'middle way', which aimed to make concessions for both Catholics and Protestants, satisfied the majority of the population. It was only the most devout Catholics and Puritans who actively opposed the religious settlement.
- As a result, most of the Catholic nobility and the ordinary people supported Elizabeth during the Northern Rebellion in 1569. They chose loyalty to Elizabeth over their religion, even when given a chance to replace her with a Catholic monarch.
- There was little public support for Catholic plots like the Ridolfi Plot and the Babington Plot. These plots were also ineffective as Walsingham and his spies ensured they were uncovered before they could be carried out.
- Elizabeth successfully dealt with Puritan opposition to the religious settlement. During the Vestment Controversy of the 1560s, Elizabeth ordered the Archbishop of Canterbury to enforce the Royal Injunctions, which many Puritan priests had challenged. Elizabeth used her authority to arrest or remove Puritan priests who continued to oppose her.
- The Puritan threat in the 1580s was weak. The Puritan separatists who wanted to break away from the Church of England following Whitgift's campaign against the Prophesyings did not receive the backing of any powerful figures and could not convince more moderate Puritans to join them.
- The Catholic missionary priests who secretly ministered to English Catholics from 1574 strengthened Catholicism in England. This endangered the religious settlement, because it became less likely that devout Catholics would fully accept it. The introduction of anti-Catholic laws in 1581 and 1585 shows how seriously this threat was taken.
- Mary, Queen of Scots, had a strong claim to the throne and was supported by powerful Catholic countries, especially Spain. This meant that she posed a serious threat to Elizabeth and her religious settlement, despite the lack of popular support for the Catholic plots to put Mary on the throne.
- King Philip II of Spain's opposition to the religious settlement was a serious threat. As well as his support for Catholic plots, the outbreak of war with Spain in 1585 meant there was a real threat of a Spanish invasion. This was only prevented by the defeat of the Spanish Armada in 1588. If Philip's invasion had been successful, it's likely that he would have attempted to overturn the religious settlement and make England Catholic again.

Pages 210-213 — Germany, 1890-1945
Practice Paper

1 Each inference is marked separately and you can have a maximum of two marks per inference. How to grade your answer:
- 1 mark for giving one credible inference.
- 2 marks for giving one credible inference and using content from the source to back it up.

Here are some points your answer may include:

- Hitler was portrayed as a strong leader. He is shown standing in a powerful pose and is looking towards the horizon with a determined expression on his face.
- Hitler was presented as a leader who was capable of returning Germany to greatness. The tagline 'One people, one empire, one leader!' emphasises that Hitler is working towards regaining the German empire for the German people.
- Hitler was portrayed as having great personal power over Germany and within the Nazi Party. He is at the centre of the image and there is nothing else on the poster apart from the tagline, which further emphasises Hitler's position as the Führer.

2 This question is level marked. How to grade your answer:

Level 1	The answer gives a simple analysis of the
1-2 marks	sources to come to a basic judgement about their
	usefulness. It shows a basic understanding of the
	sources and displays some relevant knowledge of
	the topic.
Level 2	The answer analyses the sources in more detail
3-5 marks	to make judgements about their usefulness. It
	shows a good understanding of the sources
	and uses relevant knowledge to support its
	judgements.
Level 3	The answer evaluates the sources to make
6-8 marks	judgements about their usefulness. It shows a
	detailed understanding of the sources and uses
	relevant knowledge to analyse their content and
	provenance, and to support its judgements.

Here are some points your answer may include:

- Source B is useful because it is a contemporary Nazi cartoon from 1929, so it shows the sorts of messages the Nazis used to try and influence the opinions of the German people and gain their support.
- Source B is useful because it shows that the Nazis used anti-Semitic messages to try and gain support. The cartoon presents a negative image of Jewish people and blames them for Germany's economic problems.
- Source B is useful as it shows that the Nazis used patriotic themes win support. For example, the term 'Fatherland' is written above the German family. The cartoon suggests that the 'Fatherland' is being threatened by Jewish people — they are shown to prosper while an Aryan family suffers.
- The usefulness of Source B is limited because it doesn't show whether the messages in the cartoon actually persuaded people to support the Nazis.
- Source B is from 1929, so it isn't useful for studying why people carried on supporting the Nazis in the 1930s and 1940s.
- Source C is useful because it is from the perspective of someone who experienced life in Nazi Germany. It is likely to be reliable because it was published in 1963 when the author no longer had to fear the Nazis and could be honest about her attitude towards them.
- Source C shows that people were taken in by Nazi propaganda. The author states several times that she believed the Nazis' promises and felt hope at the prospect of Germany being reunited. This is a useful demonstration of how effective Nazi patriotic propaganda actually was, as it shows that people were eager to believe that the Nazis could make Germany great again.
- Source C is useful because it shows that the economic and political weaknesses of the Weimar Republic were an important reason why people supported the Nazis.
- Source C is useful as it suggests that the terms of the Treaty of Versailles and their impact on Germany led some people to support the Nazis.
- Source C only focuses on how the author felt about the Nazis' promises, so it is not useful for discovering how she felt about the policies that they actually enacted.

3 This question is level marked. How to grade your answer:

Level 1	The answer gives credible differences, which are
1-2 marks	based on some analysis of content from one or
	both interpretations.
Level 2	The answer gives credible differences, which are
3-4 marks	based on a detailed analysis of content from both
	interpretations.

Here are some points your answer may include:

- Interpretation 1 focuses on the attitudes of very young people who were exposed to the teachings of the Nazi regime at school, whereas Interpretation 2 discusses the reactions of teenagers who were exposed to the Nazi regime through groups like the Hitler Youth.
- Interpretation 1 suggests that many children accepted the Nazi regime because they were unable to recognise the ways that it controlled them. In contrast, Interpretation 2 looks at how some young people rebelled against the Nazis' attempts to control them by forming organisations like the Edelweiss Pirates.
- Interpretation 1 explains how the Nazis used education to shape the attitudes of young people, while Interpretation 2 demonstrates that the Nazis used fear and intimidation to force young people to support their regime. For example, Interpretation 2 draws attention to the execution of the leaders of the Cologne Edelweiss Pirates in 1944, while Interpretation 1 shows that young children were instructed in Nazi ideology in a more subtle way that was as natural as being given their 'morning milk'.
- Interpretation 1 suggests that young people are not always mature enough to question what they are being taught. Interpretation 2, on the other hand, describes how young people began to question the Nazis in the late 1930s and fought back against Nazi teachings by opposing official groups like the Hitler Youth and forming their own youth groups.

4 This question is level marked. How to grade your answer:

Level 1	The answer gives a basic explanation of reasons
1-2 marks	why the interpretations are different. This is
	based on a simple analysis of the interpretations
	or on knowledge of the topic.
Level 2	The answer gives a detailed explanation of
3-4 marks	reasons why the interpretations are different.
	This is well supported by a detailed analysis of
	the interpretations and knowledge of the topic.

Here are some points your answer may include:

- The author of Interpretation 1 personally experienced the Nazi regime's educational propaganda as a very young child, which could explain why he focuses on the Nazi regime's impact on schoolchildren. The author of Interpretation 2 did not experience Nazi propaganda first-hand, therefore their account has a broader focus.
- The author of Interpretation 1 is discussing the experiences of children who were exposed to Nazi propaganda from a young very age, which could explain why he feels that it was difficult for children to question the Nazis. The author of Interpretation 2 focuses more on teenagers who were not necessarily subjected to the same Nazi teachings when they were very young and had a greater capacity to question the Nazis. This could explain why the author discusses more rebellious attitudes to the Nazis among young people.
- The interpretations are discussing reactions to two different stages of the Nazi regime. This helps explain why they talk about different levels of resistance to the Nazis. Interpretation 1 focuses on the early years of the regime when the Nazis had yet to reveal the full extent of their brutality. Interpretation 2, however, looks at how attitudes developed as the Nazis became increasingly extreme from the late 1930s.

5 This question is level marked. How to grade your answer:

Level 1	The answer either supports or disagrees with the
1-4 marks	interpretation. This is based on a simple analysis
	of one interpretation and basic knowledge of the
	topic.
Level 2	The answer shows support or disagreement by
5-8 marks	evaluating the interpretation. The evaluation
	draws on analysis of both interpretations and
	some relevant knowledge of the topic. An overall
	judgement is made, but it isn't well supported by
	the answer.

Level 3	The answer shows support or disagreement
9-12 marks	by evaluating the interpretation in detail. The evaluation draws on a detailed analysis of both interpretations, which considers their different viewpoints and shows a good level of relevant knowledge. An overall judgement is made that is partly supported by the answer.
Level 4	The answer considers both sides of the argument.
13-16 marks	It draws on an accurate and detailed analysis of both interpretations, which considers their different viewpoints and shows an excellent level of relevant knowledge. An overall judgement is made that is well supported by the answer.

Here are some points your answer may include:

- Interpretation 1 talks about teachers having to teach children nationalistic values on an almost daily basis. Since most teachers joined the Nazi Teachers Association and were trained in Nazi teaching methods, Interpretation 1 probably gives a fairly accurate representation of the school environment.
- Interpretation 1 suggests that children accepted the messages of Nazi propaganda — it says that they were encouraged to hate the Treaty of Versailles and were told that Hitler had restored Germany's dignity. This seems like an accurate reflection of the Nazi Party's interference in education, since subjects were rewritten to follow Nazi ideas. It is probably also correct that many children accepted this nationalistic instruction, as they were also exposed to other forms of Nazi propaganda outside school that were repeating the same messages.
- Interpretation 1 suggests that children were encouraged to see Hitler as a saviour. This is quite realistic, since making children support Hitler was a key aim of the Nazis' educational regime. Children were expected to say 'Heil Hitler' throughout the school day, while older children had to attend Hitler Youth in their spare time.
- Interpretation 1 suggests that children passively accepted what they were taught. This is not entirely true, since children were expected to report their teachers if they didn't stick to Nazi teachings. This shows that the Nazis made children take a more active role in making sure that Nazi ideas were upheld than Interpretation 1 suggests.
- Interpretation 1 doesn't show that young people held different attitudes towards the Nazis depending on their age and experiences. While some children accepted the ideas that the Nazis taught in school, others were in a better position to reject Nazi teachings. For example, Interpretation 2 shows that some teenagers came into conflict with members of the Hitler Youth and resisted the Nazis by joining groups like the Edelweiss Pirates.
- Interpretation 1 implies that it was very difficult for children to question their authority figures. However, the idea that young people were helpless to resist is not completely accurate. They continued to join groups like the Edelweiss Pirates, the Swing Kids and the White Rose Group, even after members of these groups had been executed. As Interpretation 2 points out, this shows that some young people knew the risks of opposing the Nazi regime and chose to do it anyway.

6   This question is level marked. How to grade your answer:

Level 1	Some knowledge and understanding of Nazi
1-2 marks	Germany is shown. The answer describes one or more changes to the lives of Christians, but does not explain them.

Level 2	Appropriate knowledge and understanding of
3-4 marks	the period is shown. The answer describes some valid changes. It explains the reasons for one of the changes, using knowledge of the topic to justify its explanation.
Level 3	A good level of knowledge and understanding
5-6 marks	of the period is shown. The answer explains the reasons for two or more changes, using detailed knowledge of the topic to justify its explanations.
Level 4	Excellent knowledge and understanding of the
7-8 marks	period is shown. The answer considers more complex patterns of change and explains the reasons for all identified changes, using detailed knowledge to justify its explanations.

Here are some points your answer may include:

- Under the Concordat, the Nazis promised not to interfere with the Catholic Church in Germany as long as it stayed out of German politics. However, despite this agreement, the Nazis were able to reduce the role of the Catholic Church in education. They removed crucifixes from schools in 1936, and Catholic education was completely destroyed by 1939.
- The Nazis started to arrest Catholic priests in 1935 and put them on trial, while Catholic newspapers were suppressed and the Catholic Youth Group was disbanded. These actions weakened the influence of the Catholic Church on the lives of German Catholics.
- Many Christians were afraid to speak out against Nazi religious policies, especially when threatened with concentration camps. Even when the Pope condemned Hitler's interference in the Catholic Church in Germany, many Catholics believed that the only way to protect their religion was to avoid angering the Nazi Party.
- While German Catholics were persecuted, the German Catholic Church itself was not destroyed. For example, the Nazis did not execute Clemens August von Galen when he used his sermons to preach against them. This suggests that German Catholics did not lose all of their power under the Nazis.
- Before the Nazis came to power, there were several different Protestant Churches in Germany. In 1936, the Nazis forced them to unite and form the Reich Church, which was controlled by the Nazis. Non-Aryan ministers were suspended and only Nazis were allowed to give sermons. This gave the Nazis more control over Protestants and the messages that they were exposed to.
- The Reich Church was Nazified and Protestants were subjected to Nazi propaganda. For example, the crucifix was replaced with the swastika, and the Bible was replaced with Hitler's 'Mein Kampf'.
- Some members of the Confessing Church, a Protestant group that opposed the Reich Church, were sent to concentration camps or executed for speaking out against Nazi religious policies. For example, Martin Niemöller was sent to a concentration camp for protesting against the persecution of Church members in his sermons, while Dietrich Bonhoeffer was executed for resisting the Nazis.

7   This question is level marked. How to grade your answer:

Level 1	The answer shows limited knowledge and
1-4 marks	understanding of Nazi Germany. It gives a simple explanation of how the Nazis controlled life in Germany. Ideas aren't organised with an overall argument in mind. There is no clear conclusion.

Level 2 5-9 marks	The answer shows some appropriate knowledge and understanding of the period. There is some analysis of how extensive some elements of Nazi control were. Ideas are organised with an overall argument in mind, but the conclusion isn't well supported by the answer.
Level 3 10-14 marks	The answer shows a good level of knowledge and understanding of the period, which is relevant to the question. It explores several elements of Nazi control and analyses how extensive they were. Most ideas are organised to develop a clear argument that supports the conclusion.
Level 4 15-18 marks	The answer shows an excellent level of relevant knowledge and understanding of the period. It analyses in detail a range of elements of Nazi control and analyses how extensive Nazi control was as a whole. All ideas are well organised to develop a clear argument and a well-supported conclusion.

Here are some points your answer may include:

- The Nazis introduced laws that allowed them to carry out surveillance on the German people. The Enabling Act of 1933 gave them the power to read people's communications and search their homes. Under the leadership of Reinhard Heydrich, the Sicherheitsdienst aimed to bring all Germans under constant supervision.
- The Law for the Reconstruction of the Reich (1934) meant that the Nazis had complete control over local government, as well as being the only national political party — the Nazis had banned all other political parties in 1933. This gave them complete political power across Germany at every level.
- The Nazis imposed their ideology on the German justice system. They forced judges to make decisions based on Nazi ideas and policies, and introduced special courts in 1933 that removed people's rights to question or appeal against evidence given against them. From 1934, political crimes were tried in the People's Court — defendants were almost always declared guilty.
- Germany became a police state where the SS and the Gestapo exercised significant power. Local wardens were also appointed and encouraged to report disloyalty. This meant that many ordinary Germans were too fearful to criticise the Nazis, since they risked being arrested and sent to concentration camps.
- The Nazis had almost complete control over the media, art and culture. This enabled them to spread propaganda, and meant that their ideas were rarely challenged in public.
- The Labour Front replaced Trade Unions and brought all workers under Nazi control. They could no longer go on strike.
- The Nazis had control over the religious lives of Protestants, since all Protestant Churches were consolidated into the 'Nazified' Reich Church. However, the Nazis' control over the Catholic Church was less complete. While its power to intervene in German politics was suppressed by the Concordat, and Catholic education was destroyed, the Catholic Church itself remained active.
- Schools and youth movements were used to control young people. It was compulsory to join the Hitler Youth from 1936 and Hitler schools were used to train high achieving boys to become Nazi leaders. The Nazis also created the Nazi Teachers' Association to ensure that teachers instilled Nazi ideology in their pupils.
- The Nazis did not have total control over young people. The existence of rebellious groups like the Edelweiss Pirates and the Swing Kids shows that the Nazis' educational policies weren't fully effective at gaining control. Also, attendance at the Hitler Youth actually fell in late 1930s, which suggests that not all parents and their children were under the control of the Nazis.

Page 215 — Superpower Relations and the Cold War, 1941-1991 Practice Paper

1 Use the levels below to mark each consequence separately. One consequence can get a maximum of 4 marks. How to grade your answer:

Level 1 1-2 marks	Some general knowledge and understanding of the period is shown. The answer gives one consequence of Soviet intervention in Hungary and attempts a simple explanation.
Level 2 3-4 marks	Detailed knowledge and understanding of the period is shown. The answer gives one consequence of Soviet intervention in Hungary and explains it using knowledge of the period.

Here are some points your answer may include:

- Thousands of Hungarians were killed or wounded as a direct result of the USSR's decision to send tanks and soldiers into Hungary to put down the Hungarian Uprising in 1956. This military intervention also led to the hanging of Nagy, the Hungarian leader who had gone against the USSR.
- The USSR's intervention in Hungary showed that, while Khrushchev was willing to give satellite states more independence than Stalin had, he would not allow them to reject communism. This strengthened the USSR's authority over its satellite states.
- Khrushchev's interference in Hungary showed the USA that his leadership would not lead to a 'thaw' in Cold War tensions as they hoped it might.
- The West's weak reaction to the USSR's decision to intervene in Hungary showed the satellite states that they wouldn't receive help if they tried to break away from the USSR. This discredited the idea that countries in the West were defenders of democracy.

2 This answer is level marked. How to grade your answer:

Level 1 1-2 marks	The answer shows some knowledge and understanding of the period. It provides a simple explanation of some events of the Prague Spring. There has been some attempt to organise events in a logical way.
Level 2 3-5 marks	The answer shows good knowledge and understanding of the period. It provides some analysis of the key events of the Prague Spring. Most events are organised logically. Some connections are made between events.
Level 3 6-8 marks	**Answers can't be awarded Level 3 if they only discuss the information suggested in the question.** The answer shows excellent knowledge and understanding of the period. It analyses several key events and the links between them in detail. Events are ordered logically.

Here are some points your answer may include:

- Tension had been building in Czechoslovakia since 1948, when it became a communist country under the control of the USSR. Soviet policies like collectivisation and centralisation negatively affected Czechoslovakia's economic development, which was a source of tension. Many were also unhappy with the level of Soviet control over Czechoslovakia's affairs.

- In January 1968, Alexander Dubcek became the leader of the Communist Party in Czechoslovakia. He introduced reforms that went against the Soviet version of communism. For example, he decentralised industry, which gave workers and unions more power and reduced the Communist party's control.
- The USSR tolerated Dubcek's reforms for a few months during the Prague Spring because Dubcek was a communist who had promised to remain loyal to Moscow. However, the reforms meant that the USSR had less control over Czechoslovakia, so Moscow viewed the country with increasing concern.
- President Tito of Yugoslavia visited Prague in 1968. This helped to provoke a Soviet response because Yugoslavia had never accepted the USSR's version of communism and was not a member of the Warsaw Pact. Tito's visit to Czechoslovakia suggested that Dubcek had abandoned his loyalty to the USSR.
- Communists in Czechoslovakia sent a letter to the USSR asking for help. As a result, the USSR invaded Czechoslovakia with 500,000 troops in August 1968. This signalled the end of the Prague Spring.

3   Use the levels below to mark questions 3a and 3b separately. How to grade your answer:

Level 1 1-2 marks	Limited knowledge and understanding of the period is shown. The answer gives a simple explanation of the significance of the topic. Ideas are generally unconnected and don't follow a logical order.
Level 2 3-4 marks	Some relevant knowledge and understanding of the period is shown. The answer attempts to analyse at least one point about the significance of the topic. An attempt has been made to organise ideas logically.
Level 3 5-6 marks	A good level of knowledge and understanding of the period is shown. The answer explores two or more points about the significance of the topic and analyses them in more detail. Ideas are organised logically.
Level 4 7-8 marks	Knowledge and understanding of the period is precise and detailed. The answer explores two or more points about the significance of the topic and thoroughly analyses each one. Ideas are organised logically and connections between different points are identified to create a deeper analysis of significance.

Here are some points your answer for 3a may include:
- During the Bay of Pigs incident in 1961, the USA launched a direct attack on Cuba. The USA wanted to stop Fidel Castro from turning Cuba into a communist state that would support the USSR. As a result, the relationship between the USA and Cuba was damaged.
- Cuba developed closer relations with the USSR after the Bay of Pigs incident. The USA's aggressive actions pushed Cuba away and made it feel that it needed Soviet military assistance to defend itself against the USA.
- Castro accepted Soviet military assistance and declared Cuba to be a communist state after the Bay of Pigs incident, which created a formal division between Cuba and the USA. Cuba asked the USSR to provide weapons to defend it against the USA, and by 1962 Khrushchev had decided to put nuclear missiles in Cuba.
- Cuba became a significant threat to the USA and the USA's position in the Cold War because of its alliance with the USSR. When work began on nuclear missile sites in Cuba, the USA prepared to invade Cuba, bringing the world to the brink of nuclear war.

Here are some points your answer for 3b may include:
- The policy of détente aimed to defuse tension between the USSR and the USA, and to help prevent situations like the Cuban Missile Crisis from escalating to a dangerous level.
- Détente reduced the conflict between the USA and the USSR and encouraged them to co-operate through diplomatic means, instead of pursuing military supremacy. It helped to defuse tension by creating the conditions for negotiation and making military action less likely.
- Several treaties were created as a result of détente. For example, the First Strategic Arms Limitations Treaty (SALT 1) limited the number of ABMs and ICBMs the USSR and the USA could have. Both countries signed the treaty in 1972. It helped to improve the relationship between the USA and the USSR by controlling the arms race.
- The Helsinki Agreement was signed in 1975 by the USA, Canada, the USSR and most European countries. It stated that the borders already established in Europe had to be accepted and human rights should be respected. This reduced tension between the USA and the USSR as each side had agreed not to interfere with each other's sphere of influence.
- There was still tension between the USA and the USSR during détente. The Soviet Union didn't follow through with the human rights conditions outlined in the Helsinki Agreement as it didn't allow freedom of speech or movement. This made it difficult for trust to develop between the USA and the USSR.
- Détente was a practical policy that aimed to control the arms race and prevent dangerous situations like the Cuban Missile Crisis happening again. However, it didn't do anything to resolve the underlying differences that had caused tension between the USA and the USSR to develop in the first place.

Index

Index